HITLER'S WAR

HITLER'S WAR

Edwin P. Hoyt

McGRAW-HILL BOOK COMPANY
New York   St. Louis   San Francisco
Toronto   Hamburg   Mexico

The map on page 363 is from Telford Taylor, *Munich: The Price of Peace,* Doubleday, Garden City, 1979.

The maps on pages 364 and 365 are from H. R. Trevor Roper (ed.), *Hitler's War Directives: 1939–1945,* Pan Books, London, 1964.

The map on page 366 is from David Kahn, *Hitler's Spies: German Military Intelligence in World War II,* Macmillan, New York, 1978.

ISBN 0-07-030622-2

1 2 3 4 5 6 7 8 9 DOC DOC 8 9 2 1 0 9 8

Library of Congress Cataloging-in-Publication Data

Hoyt, Edwin Palmer.
   Hitler's war.

     1. World War, 1939–1945. 2. World War, 1939–1945—
Germany. 3. Germany—History, Military—20th century.
4. Hitler, Adolf, 1889–1945. I. Title.
D743.H725 1988   940.53   87-26273
ISBN 0-07-030622-2

Designed by Eve Kirch

CONTENTS

PREFACE

Corporal Adolf Hitler of Kaiser Wilhelm's army was not a person of great importance. He was a creature of a Germany created by World War I, and his behavior was shaped by that war and its consequences. He had emerged from his native Austria with many prejudices, including a powerful prejudice against Jews. Again, he was a product of his times, for many Austrians and Germans were prejudiced against the Jews. The history of Europe is studded with tales of pogroms against the Jews. In Hitler's case the prejudice had become maniacal; it was a dominant force in his private and political personalities. Anti-Semitism was not a policy for Adolf Hitler; it was a religion. And in the Germany of the 1920s, stunned by defeat and the ravages of the Versailles treaty, it was not hard for a leader to convince millions that one element of the nation's society was responsible for most of the evils heaped upon it.

The fact is that Hitler's anti-Semitism was a self-inflicted obstacle to his political success. The Jews, like other Germans, were shocked by the discovery that the war had not been fought to a standstill, as they were led to believe in November 1918, but that Germany had, in fact, been defeated and was to be treated as a vanquished country. Had Hitler not embarked on his policy of disestablishing the Jews as Germans, and later of exterminating them in Europe, he could have counted on their loyalty. There is no reason to believe anything else.

They had served loyally under Bismarck. They had continued their loyalty to the German Empire under Kaiser Wilhelm II. The National Socialist Workers' Party, calling for government ownership of much of the productive machinery and for the breakup of great trusts, was not racist in the beginning. Hitler made it so.

But the fact was that by adopting the policy of anti-Semitism Hitler turned the world against himself and against Germany. He made it necessary for Germany to be prepared to fight the world, to conquer or be conquered.

And from that point, philosophically speaking, one excess led to another. That was hardly the position envisaged by the unhappy German people in the 1920s when the harsh terms of the Versailles treaty and the runaway inflation were making Germany ready for any political palliative that might be offered.

*   *   *

Anti-Semitism, then, can be placed at the top of the list of reasons for Hitler's ultimate failure and defeat, about which this book is concerned. The world might even have accepted his Pan-Germanism had the policy not been so blatantly racial. And anti-Semitism begot further racism. Hitler's treatment of the Poles and the people of Russia—Greater Russians, Ukrainians, and the rest—was an extension of his anti-Semitism.

A second error Hitler made was pursuing his delusion that a dictatorship with a population base of some 80 million people could conquer a dictatorship of some 200 million people. His entire Russian campaign was based on his deep prejudice against communism. At first, Hitler really believed that the people of the U.S.S.R. would welcome him as their savior from Stalinism. He had not read the story of the Napoleonic wars very carefully. His generals were shocked by the very idea of taking on a war on two major fronts. But by that time Hitler had so compounded his errors of judgment that he no longer believed anything the generals said. The odd thing about Hitler and the generals is that the latter allowed themselves to be cowed. Actually, Hitler's early victories—the march into the Rhineland, the rearmament program, the annexation of Austria, even the initial triumph over Czechoslovakia—were political victories. In this book I indicate that if the western Allies had stood up to Hitler at any time before and through

1938 he would have been forced into collapse. He did not have the military resources to defeat France and Britain, to say nothing of those countries assisted by the very loyal and very potent Czechoslovak army. But Hitler was shrewd first, in assessing the world weariness of the western democracies and later in taking every advantage of it. Until Poland, Hitler won victory after victory with virtually no shots fired.

After Poland, Hitler really believed he could bully the world into submission. He held up the war in the west while waiting for France and England to come around to acceptance of his conquests. But he reckoned completely wrong. Being a man without principle himself, he failed to recognize the existence of principle in other countries, particularly in Britain. By 1939, Hitler's social and racial policies had put him and Germany beyond the pale. The British, doped by years of unpreparedness, were slow to respond and rearm. That is the way it is with the western democracies, or at least that is the way it used to be. But, prepared or not, Britain responded finally to Hitler's bullying by going to war over Poland. Hitler failed to see the lesson here. It was not until after the failure of his 1940 effort to destroy Britain's air force that he began to understand that the war was real and that there would be no temporization by Britain. Hitler was not prepared to deal with the long-range problem. Had he been prepared, he would have made wise use of his single greatest weapon against Britain, the U-boat campaign to starve Britain out of the war. It very nearly succeeded in 1941, and it would have succeeded if Hitler had listened to Admiral Karl Dönitz even as late as 1940. But instead of starving Britain, Hitler starved the U-boat force, keeping it at minimal strength while he devoted his efforts to building up force for the disastrous second front against Russia.

Another of Hitler's major mistakes was his decision to declare war on the United States. It is true that he had plenty of provocation. For a year the Americans had been openly helping Britain militarily, convoying British vessels on part of their dangerous voyage across the Atlantic. There had been a number of military incidents involving American warships and German U-boats. But, in the great scale, these were hardly more than annoyances and could have been borne. When the war came to America, launched by the Japanese at Pearl Harbor and Manila, most Americans expected the response

to be against Japan. And it would have been, had not Hitler declared war on the United States. Had he refrained, President Franklin Roosevelt would not have been able to commit the growing
strength of American resources first against Germany. In the fall
and early winter of 1941, Congress was still in no mood to go to
war with anyone. The Japanese attack, of course, made the Pacific
war inevitable, but it did not make American involvement in the
European war inevitable. In this matter, Hitler showed an almost
total ignorance of the realities in America.

When the war in the east began to go sour, Hitler might have
stopped, and retreated, and turned his efforts once again toward
consolidating his gains in Europe and defeating the British in Africa. Stalin would have welcomed a peace and the respite it would
give him to rebuild the Soviet forces. The Russians were ever mindful of the threat on the east, where the Japanese maintained their
strongest army (the Kwantung Army). They also knew that General Tojo was one of the prime advocates of a preemptive strike on
Russia and that this policy was under consideration as late as the
spring of 1942 when the decision was made to attack Midway Island at all. It was not until the summer of 1942 that the prospect of
a Japanese invasion of the U.S.S.R. was laid aside.

But by that time Hitler was bogged down in the morass of his
own making. His offensives in Russia were ever more expensive
and unproductive. In Africa the Americans were preparing to join
the battle and thus tip the scales against the brilliant Field Marshal
Rommel. At sea the American commitment to saving Britain was
total; American merchant vessels were rushing off the ways, as were
warships and thousands of aircraft. Only then did Hitler begin to
realize that he had unleashed a Goliath when he declared war on
the United States.

After the summer of 1942 the inevitability of German defeat was
apparent to the world. But not to Germany's leaders. The prospect
of defeat was impossible for Hitler to consider, because there could
be no mercy by the Allies. The excesses of Germany had been too
great. So everything that happened from that point on was even more
excessive and more brutal. The murder of the Jews, of Poles, and
of Soviet citizens became more intense. The stage was set for such
brutalities as the Malmedy massacre during Hitler's last, abortive

winter offensive against the west. By that time, late 1944, Hitler had gone so far that nothing could be done save ensure his destruction. If that could have been accomplished, the war in Europe could have been brought to an end at least a year earlier than it was. As is noted in this book, the German generals tried, but in a desultory fashion, and they were offered no assistance and little sympathy by the western powers, although the westerners knew of their intentions. This failure was certainly one of western political intelligence. A truly determined campaign to assassinate Hitler, employing fully the resources of Britain's Special Operations Executive (dirty tricks) MI5 and the American Office of Strategic Services, could have saved millions of lives between 1942 and 1945. As the deterioration of the machinery of the Third Reich showed in the winter and spring of 1945, despite the ambitions of the lesser leaders, there was no one in Germany who could really succeed Hitler—not Hermann Göring, the official "heir," who had lost the confidence of Hitler and of the lesser leaders; not Heinrich Himmler, the leader of the SS and holder of half a dozen important posts, all of which he handled badly, who was hated by the generals and by most of the party officials; certainly not Dr. Josef Goebbels, the propaganda minister, who was never better than an inspired henchman; and not Martin Bormann, Hitler's secretary, whose importance in the scheme of things has been blown out of all proportion.

What I have tried to show in this book is the inevitability of Germany's defeat as early as 1942 and the trap into which Hitler had put Germany, from which there was no conceivable way out. The contrast with what happened in Italy in 1943 is quite striking. One tends to forget that in the 1930s Mussolini's Black Shirts were the mirror image—more, the 1920s prototypes—of Hitler's Brown Shirts, that Italian excesses in Libya and Ethiopia were enormous, that at one time the Italian Fascists were regarded on an equal plane with German Nazis as a menace to the world. All that really evaporated after 1943. Only Mussolini and a handful of his immediate followers ever felt the wrath of the victors. One reason is that Mussolini's excesses were overshadowed by Hitler's, but another reason must be that by quitting the war, the Italians saved themselves. The Germans had no such opportunity after the failure of the ill-planned and botched generals' plot against Hitler, a plot that should have come to fruition several years before it did.

If there is a lesson to be learned from this book it is that even in

wartime political objectivity and even compromise are enormously
important. The Allies hampered themselves in dealing with the Germans, as with the Japanese, by blind adherence to the policy of "unconditional surrender" when an amelioration of that policy even in
1942 might well have shortened the war. Here I have dealt only with
the war in the west. In the east, it was still another story....

INTRODUCTION
Design for Disaster

November 11, 1918. Great news! An armistice is signed between Germany and the Allied powers. The long European war has ended. This news overshadows another report: Wilhelm II, the emperor of Germany, has abdicated and gone into exile in Holland because he has been convinced that he can no longer command the loyalty of his Officer Corps. For all practical purposes that abdication ends the German Second Reich and also ends a ten-day period of confusion during which the Social Democrats have proclaimed a republic from a window of the Reichstag building. Waiting in the wings are the Bolsheviks, confident that soon enough the social democratic Weimar republic will fall. All that stands between the German people and a true republic, says Rosa Luxemburg, one of the leading Red revolutionaries, has been the Kaiser and the German army. Already, on November 9, the revolutionaries are demonstrating, hoping to cause the overthrow of the Weimar government just as the Bolsheviks in Russia broke the Kerensky social democratic government in 1917.

*   *   *

On the night of November 9, as Wilhelm II had been forced to announce his abdication, the deal between the new republic and the

1

army was concluded. That night the government's leaders received a telephone call from General Wilhelm Gröner, one of the three most important military officers of Germany, the man who had told Wilhelm that he had lost the support of his Officer Corps.

"Will the Government protect Germany from anarchy and restore order?" Gröner had asked.

"Yes," replied the civil rulers.

"Then the High Command will maintain discipline in the Army and bring it home peacefully," promised the first quartermaster-general.

"What do you expect from us?" asked Chancellor Friedrich Ebert.

"The High Command expects the Government to cooperate with the Officer Corps in the suppression of Bolshevism and in the maintenance of discipline in the Army. It also asks that the provisioning of the Army shall be ensured and all disturbance of transport and communications prevented. There will be no major change in the Army command," said General Gröner.

Thus in one telephone conversation the army leaders secured the backing of the civil government and the promise that the army would lack for nothing. Given the economic and political condition of Germany at that moment, and the foreseeable worsening of that climate month after succeeding month, it was a most remarkable promise, and one that ultimately would lead to the death of representative government in Germany.

As General Gröner talked with Chancellor Ebert, other German leaders were negotiating with French Marshal Ferdinand Foch at Compiègne for the conclusion of an armistice. It was called an armistice because the Germans, although exhausted, were in no mental condition to face the terrible truth: they had lost the war, and they ultimately would have to accept the Allies' condition of "unconditional surrender." But to have forced that semantic issue at that moment would have been to break the slender staff of authority that still remained with the army High Command. For the revolution in Germany had come from the army ranks itself when the men of a number of units rebelled against authority, set up a "soviet," elected their own officers, and declared that their units were now run by soldiers' councils. If that rebellion spread, then the Officer Corps army would be lost, and almost certainly the Bolsheviks would triumph.

Gröner's deal with the civil government cut the ground from under the soldiers' councils, and in a matter of hours the German General Staff was once more in firm command of the army.

The myth of a peace among equals was carefully maintained in Berlin during this delicate period. Although the generals and the government were under few illusions about the sort of peace they were going to have to accept, the dark truth was kept from the German people.

On December 11, a month after the conclusion of the armistice, returning German soldiers marched up the Unter den Linden with their flags flying and bands playing. At the Brandenburger Tor they were met and hailed by Chancellor Ebert: "I salute you, who return unvanquished from the field of battle."

Thus the chancellor absolved the generals of guilt for the war just lost and reinforced his promise to let the army run its own affairs. The matter was settled and the future sealed permanently a few days later. The soldiers' councils became restless. On December 16 the First Soviet Congress of Germany assembled in the Prussian Diet. The immediate aim was the dissolution of the German Officer Corps. When the congress's demands were not met by the government in Berlin, the "people's soldiers" marched on the Chancellery on December 23, 1918, and besieged the cabinet. Chancellor Ebert telephoned General Kurt von Schleicher at General Staff headquarters:

"The government is held prisoner. We need your support. You must act."

"I will give orders at once to General von Lequis to march from Potsdam to liberate you."

That promise was enough to cause the collapse of the soldiers' revolt. The army emerged supreme, and from 1918 it would remain the strongest, most unified element in German society. Little else of the traditional fabric of German society would survive so well the coming period of turmoil.

In 1919 the Germans had no collective sense of guilt about the war just past. They had been told that since they had eliminated the monarchy, submitted to the conditions of surrender, and established a democratic republic, they would be rewarded at the peace table with impartial justice. That meant President Woodrow Wilson's famous Fourteen Points. But when the negotiations opened at Versailles in the spring of 1919, the Germans soon learned that "the hour of collecting the accounts against these boors has come," as France's Premier Georges Clemenceau announced grimly.

The German people had been protected all these years from learning how detested they were in western Europe. Now they would learn. Among the conditions of peace the losers found most infuriating was the Allied insistence that Germany be disarmed and remain so. The Officer Corps was to be cut to 4000 men and the whole army to 100,000. Germany could have no military aircraft, tanks, or weapons of offense. The German General Staff was to be dissolved and never to be reconstituted. The German battle fleet was to be replaced by a coastal defense force, with no vessel to exceed 10,000 tons (the size of a light cruiser).

Wailed Konstantin Fehrenbach, president of the German National Assembly: "Our enemies have laid before us a treaty which surpasses by far the fears of our greatest pessimists."

All across Germany the Versailles treaty was debated, in government halls, in *bierstuben,* in churches. Uniformly, the German people detested the treaty they found unfair. The Allies, particularly the French, refused to budge.

A special session of the National Assembly was called in the great hall of the University of Berlin, and for five hours the important and the educated of Germany denounced the draft treaty. Fehrenbach finally closed the meeting with a warning to the Allies:

> The hardships of this treaty will create a generation in Germany in whom the will to break the chains of slavery will be implanted from their earliest childhood.

> The words were greeted with silence.
> The world had been warned.
> The world was not listening.

Summer 1923. Germany was in chaos. Political stability was impossible because of the economic destruction of Germany, begun by the four years of war, which sapped the country of its men and resources, and perpetuated by the peace, in which the Allies sought to reconstruct their own economies at the expense of the defeated enemy. It would be interesting to speculate on what might have happened had the British, French, and Italians been intelligent enough to show a generosity that encouraged the reconstruction of all countries. But they did not, and France was the major offender. Virtually all of Germany's capital resources were supposed to be dedicated to the payment of reparations to France and to Britain. Under the Treaty of Versailles, the French had taken over Alsace-Lorraine and the Saar, and they had occupied the Rhineland and other industrial centers. The German colonies were gone. Czechoslovakia had been created from territory the Germans and Austrians had long claimed. Another strip of land, "The Corridor," had been taken from Germany and given to the new state of Poland; Danzig had been declared a free state; and other territorial concessions had been made. These humiliations inflicted by the victorious Allies magnified the psychological and material effect of the economic blows that would come one after the other.

Wealthy Germans—and there were still many of them at the end of the war—detested the republic, largely because it was dominated by the Social Democrats. They also detested the Versailles treaty.

The German mark had been falling steadily in value since the end of the war. In 1921 there were 75 marks to the dollar; in 1922 there were 400 to the dollar. Under Allied pressure the Germans ceded Upper Silesia to Poland in 1922, thus sacrificing about 30 percent of their heavy-industry potential. The mark fell further. In the autumn of that year the French occupied the Ruhr industrial district because the Germans had defaulted on payment of reparations in timber. This degradation further split Germany, and it made the majority of people furious with the Allies. In early January 1923 the value of the mark fell to 7,000 to the dollar; it dropped to 18,000 to the dollar by the end of the month. By July 1923 it was down to 160,000 to the dollar—it took virtually a wheelbarrow full of banknotes to buy a loaf of bread. By August 1 there were a million marks to the dollar. After that even the postage stamp denominations could not keep pace with the plunge in value of the German currency, and post offices had special rubber "overprint" stamps that they changed nearly every day. (Ultimately it would cost 71 billion marks to mail a letter.) In November 1923 a dollar was worth 4 billion marks. The next step was into the trillion-mark class. The inflation wiped out the savings of every German who had money in marks.

Only the rich, who had their money in land, industry, and foreign investments, were safe. Consequently, by the end of 1923 the people of Germany had lost faith in their government, their society's structure, and the world around them. They were ready to consider any change and to lend an ear to any would-be leader who would promise them a good life.

Such a man existed. His name was Adolf Hitler.

Hitler was an Austrian by birth but a German by inclination. He had fought in the Great War and was twice decorated for bravery, winning the Iron Cross, First Class, which was practically unknown for an enlisted man. Hitler was a strange soldier: he never complained as did all the others in his unit, and he was not very popular. Occasionally he would launch into a tirade, almost always against the Jews and Communists, whom he blamed for all the troubles of the world, particularly those of Germany. His vitriolic attacks on the Jews half-frightened many of his fellow soldiers, whose trench world seemed already full enough of fear and conflict.

When the war ended, Adolf Hitler went back to Munich, a town he loved. He found the city and all Bavaria in ferment. The Wittelsbach king of Bavaria, Ludwig III, had abdicated, and a social democratic government had come to power, only to fall in April 1919 and be replaced by a Bavarian Soviet republic. That regime lasted a few weeks and then fell in its turn to another government dominated by the right wing. The real power behind this government was the German army. Many officers had chosen to move to Bavaria, and by March 1920 that part of Germany had become the center for all those who wanted to destroy the Versailles treaty and to establish an openly authoritarian regime whose purpose would be to put Germany back on the world political map as a leader of nations.

Hitler stayed on in the army. His job was with the Press and News Bureau of the political department of the army district command in Bavaria. This job gave him access to all political matters in which the army was interested, and this meant everything political, because the German army had emerged from the war as an intensely political organization, its leaders hoping to stamp out social democracy and bring into existence a state that would give the army a large share of independence.

And it was to this element that Hitler naturally turned for his support.

Soldier Adolf Hitler got on very well with the army officers, who shared his feelings about Jews and Communists. Soon he was given the job of educational officer of a Munich army regiment. His main task was to make speeches, and he chose to make most of his speeches against the Jews. He loved the work, needless to say, and he was very effective at it.

Toward the end of 1919 the generals had begun talking openly of staging a military coup and restoring the monarchy. The support for such action came from a great many elements of German society, stunned as the Germans were at the harsh terms of the Versailles treaty. So there was talk, in Munich and elsewhere, of a putsch—a coup to seize power. General Freiherr Walther von Lüttwitz did try to seize power, but his attempt failed. One of those supporting him was General Erich Ludendorff, the splendid line commander of infantry in World War I who had cost Germany so many of its young men. By then Ludendorff was fat, bemedaled on both sides of his chest, and bore a striking resemblance to a St. Bernard dog in photos from that time. His political intelligence was on about the same level as his appearance. So the 1920 military putsch failed miserably, not even supported at the end by Lüttwitz's own staff officers. But Ludendorff did not forget. The dream of a military government remained with him.

There was, however, another element in the army, and this element now stepped forward. As noted, under the terms of the Versailles treaty, the Germans were allowed an Officer Corps of only 4000. Colonel General Hans von Seeckt, new chief of staff of the army, set about removing all the deadwood from the army tree; he wanted officers who were young, adaptable, and yet thoroughly imbued with loyalty to the Officer Corps system which had kept the German army together for two generations. In other words, the army was to respond to the new political system, but always to ensure the survival of the army. Immediately the army set about to purge itself of "disloyal" elements. Under the Reichswehr law of March 6, 1919, and under the Versailles treaty, every German citizen was free to enlist in the service without regard to religion, social position, profession, or political opinion. In fact, by 1919 the army's attention to these four factors was complete. Jews and leftists were systematically excluded from the service. Recruits from urban ar-

eas (who might be expected to be liberal in outlook) were also dis-
couraged. Preference was given to the sons of noncommissioned
officers, who might be expected to have the "right" ideas.

In order to make their judgments, the army authorities needed
information about various political movements. In September 1919,
under orders from his army bosses in the political department, Adolf
Hitler began an investigation of the German Workers' Party, a small
right-wing movement. The generals distrusted workers' parties; they
tended to be Marxist in nature or at least ultraliberal. But not this
one. Hitler was impressed with its theme; he sensed that the party's
"anti-interest" campaign embodied the sort of rhetoric that would
appeal to a dispirited Germany. Hitler went to some meetings, but
he was not impressed by the party as such. He did meet Anton Drex-
ler, who had worked out the essentials of a new movement which
would appeal to the working class but which would be, unlike the
social democratic movement, strongly nationalistic. This idea appealed enormously to Hitler.

A few days later he was offered membership in the German
Workers' Party and he accepted. He immediately became a leader
of this tiny splinter movement, serving as the seventh member
of the party steering committee. At the meetings he met Ernst
Röhm and Dietrich Eckart, men who shared his burning hatred
for the German leaders who had "stabbed Germany in the back"
in 1918.

Hitler became the party's principal organizer. He mimeographed
invitations to party meetings. He put ads in the newspapers. He made
speeches and he conducted street corner meetings. By 1920 his organizational ability had shown itself so strongly that he was able to
stage a meeting of nearly 2000 people at Munich's Hofbrauhaus.
There, although he was really a sidebar speaker, his fervent oratory and electrical presence captured the imaginations of his listeners, and he spoke for nearly four hours. In this hall Hitler laid out
the twenty-five points of the program of the German Workers' Party,
points which he and a handful of his friends had drawn hastily a
few days earlier. This program became the agenda of the National
Socialist German Workers' Party (Nazi) when it succeeded the old
workers' party.

The most important planks of the party's platform—the ones that
would survive the next few years—are worth repeating, seeing that

they predated Hitler's political and military manifesto, *Mein Kampf,* by four years.

1. All Germans would be united in a Greater Germany. It would include all the ethnic ("racial") Germans who had been told they were now Poles, or Frenchmen, or Czechoslovaks, or Austrians.

2. All Jews were to be denied public office and excluded from employment in or ownership of the press. Ultimately they were to be denied citizenship. Any Jew who had entered Germany after August 2, 1914, was to be expelled from Greater Germany.

3. The Versailles treaty was to be renounced.

4. The state was to create and hold central power over all Germany.

Most of the other points represented concessions to the members of the party who truly sought to implement the ideology of national socialism: the death penalty for usury and profiteering, communalization of department stores, nationalization of industry, creation of a strong middle class, abolition of unearned income (from stocks, bonds, rents, etc.). These planks would fall one by one as Hitler sought the support of the wealthy of Germany.

* * *

In the summer and early fall of 1923 Germany was wracked with dissension. No one seemed to know how to deal with the industrial and monetary crisis, and the public, from the mass of workers to the army, was ready to rebel. Reichspresident Ebert had to call upon General von Seeckt for promises that the government would be upheld. And it was, although the cost to the central government was that von Seeckt became, as Reichswehr commander, the most powerful man in Germany. For the next six months the army governed Germany through the generals commanding the seven military districts. Their sway extended to prices, currency, and labor conditions.

In 1923 regional rebellions threatened the unity of Germany. In Saxony and Prussia the authority of the central government was challenged by groups of local people.

In Prussia, on the night of September 30, a number of officers and men occupied three fortresses, raised the old Imperial flag of red, black, and white, and declared a rebellion. Von Seeckt sent troops, the rebels were put down, and their leaders were tried for treason and given ten years' imprisonment.

In Saxony the Communists rebelled late in October 1923. Again von Seeckt acted, and the rebellion was broken up.

But the truly important rebellion was bubbling in Bavaria, in Munich.

The Reichswehr in Bavaria was looking for a political party to serve its needs. Adolf Hitler provided that party in his National Socialist Workers' Party.

By 1923 Hitler had taken over that party and was its principal leader. The army was very pleased with his announced policies: Greater Germany, abrogation of the Versailles treaty, *Lebensraum* (living and expansion room) for Germans, and establishment of a national army with compulsory military service. His anti-Semitism appealed to most army officers, but they did not pay much attention to it, or to some of the economic ideas in Hitler's twenty-five points. What they failed to understand was that Hitler regarded the twenty-five points as immutable policy, and if the German army was going to have universal military service, it was also going to live with anti-Semitism and the other issues.

In 1921 Hitler had chosen the new name for his party: *Nationalsozialistische Deutsche Arbeiterpartei* (NSDAP). The Nazi party was established. Hitler did not trust the army as much as the army trusted him, so he had also in 1921 formed the Storm Detachment of the party (*Sturmabteilung,* or SA), bullies trained in strong-arm tactics and street fighting, which Hitler envisioned as an eventual auxiliary to the army and the police, dependent on his wishes. Within a year the SA rose to a force of 6000 men. (In twelve years it would total 2.5 million.)

In these very early years many in the High Command expressed their admiration for Hitler's ability to produce an idea that would attract recruits to the cause of nationalism. They saw no dichotomy. Hitler did not disabuse them.

The occupation of the Ruhr by the French in January 1923 appeared to Hitler to be the signal for a general uprising which would allow him to take control of the German central government. He failed, however, to arouse the people. But in Bavaria the atmosphere was different. There, a number of paramilitary groups had sprung up, nearly all of them headed by former military officers. The acknowledged moral leader of these was General Ludendorff, now retired and living in Munich but still a hero of the German people.

Hitler saw in Ludendorff an instrument of power. During the spring and summer of 1923 he devoted himself to organizing various organizations into a single unit. General Otto von Lossow, chief of the Reichswehr in Munich, became the object of Hitler's almost undivided attention for weeks. Von Lossow thought Hitler a political fool who did not have the sense to recognize reality from dream; but he saw that Hitler had enormous ability as a propagandist, and he decided to use him as such. But...

In 1923 Hitler was chafing for action. The year before, Benito Mussolini had shown what could be done with effective politico-military action in these times of trial. He had marched on Rome with a handful of his black-shirted Fascisti partisans, and presto, he had become ruler of Italy. It was an example to stir Hitler's heart. With ever-increasing fervor Adolf Hitler stood up in meeting after meeting to lambaste the Jews and the "Jew-infested, Marxist-ridden regime" that was the Weimar republic. He called for a march on Berlin and the installation of a national dictatorship of the Nazi party.

By late September, under the titular leadership of General Ludendorff, Hitler had organized all the patriotic organizations into a *Kampfbund,* which was now preparing to challenge the leadership of the national and Bavarian governments.

On October 6, so insurrectionary had Hitler's diatribes become that General von Seeckt ordered the suppression of the Nazi party newspaper, the *Völkischer Beobachter*. It was just what Hitler wanted: confrontation.

General von Lossow, in Bavaria, refused to suppress the paper. He termed Hitler "one of our best patriots." Von Seeckt fired von Lossow from his army command, but the latter was reinstated by Gustav von Kahr, the Bavarian state commissioner.

Munich seethed with political steam. In the second week of November Hitler was prepared to launch a putsch to seize power. But the conspirators fell out among themselves: General von Lossow refused to go along, and so did other military men. On November 9, 1923, Hitler faced his hour of decision. He had expected the army in Bavaria to respond to his leadership. The army had rejected him. Hitler proposed now to abandon the putsch, but General Ludendorff rejected this idea. The die was cast, reasoned Ludendorff, and they must go on.

"We march," said Ludendorff.

"But general, if we march we will be fired upon by the troops."

"We march," said General Ludendorff again.

So that day the columns of patriotic organizations were formed up, about 4000 strong, and moved out before noon to march through the outskirts of Munich. They moved toward the broad Odeonsplatz. To get there, they had to pass through the narrow Residenzstrasse, so confining that only a column of fours could march through. All around the entrances to the Odeonsplatz the army and police had taken stations to prevent violence. The entry of the Residenzstrasse was guarded by a cordon of police. General Ludendorff saw the police, saw the rifles leveled at the marchers, and did not bat an eye. He continued to march forward.

The tension was palpable.

Out of the crowd of marchers jumped Ulrich Graf, Hitler's personal bodyguard. "Don't shoot," he shouted to the policemen. "It is his Excellency Ludendorff."

The police, commanded by Freiher von Goldin, did not waver. Their rifles were leveled and steady.

From the Nazi side someone fired a shot—several people said it was Adolf Hitler—and it was answered by a police volley. Several marchers fell, dead or wounded. Ludendorff stopped for a moment. Suddenly he realized that the magic of the Ludendorff name had gone. But he hesitated only for that moment; then he walked forward, alone, through the cordon of police into the Odeonsplatz, and into ignominy. No longer was the name "Ludendorff" a symbol of German martial glory. He had become a crabbed old man, and now he had been used in a reckless attempt to seize power through naked force. The attempt had failed. The Nazis and their *Kampfbund* were in confusion and they broke ranks. The November Munich putsch did not even overcome the Munich garrison, let alone seize power in Berlin.

1

PLANS OF A DEMAGOGUE

The failed putsch of November 9, 1923, very nearly ruined Adolf Hitler's reputation as a coming leader in the new Germany. The members of the *Kampfbund* were, at the very least, embarrassed by the disaster. Some of them were dead; some of them were nursing their bullet wounds. None of that made them very happy. The man responsible, many of them felt, was Adolf Hitler, the man who had called on them to march. General Ludendorff's stroll through the lines of rifles had brought him some small, temporary honor, but there was none for Hitler, who did not distinguish himself in any way (unless he had actually been the man who fired the first shot, and that was never proved).

Instead of bringing about the putsch, the march on the Munich Odeonsplatz had restored the authority of the Berlin central government when the police responded to the call to maintain law and order. In November Hitler's standing hit a new low with his own party and its outriders.

But by February 26, 1924, when the treason trial of the conspirators was opened in the People's Court at Munich, the national political climate had taken a turn for the better. With order restored, confidence returned to the German people. The fall of the mark had been stopped, and—miraculously, it seemed—the mark was now on the rise, under the administration of Hjalmar Schacht as com-

missioner of currency. The Americans were interceding to amelio-
rate some of the harsher provisions of the Versailles treaty and its
offshoots. With the prospect of good times, better tempers prevailed.
So when the trial of Hitler, General Ludendorff, and eight other conspirators opened, the atmosphere in the courtroom was more or less
neutral. If anything, it was pro-Hitler. Some of the judges and other
officials of the People's Court had been willing listeners to Hitler's
beer-hall harangues over the preceding two or three years. The government, of course, intended to prove that Hitler and Ludendorff
had conspired to overthrow the state.

This approach played directly into Hitler's hands. He intended to
prove that he had, indeed, made a serious effort on November 9 to
overthrow the Weimar republic. His purpose, he said, was to free Germany from the men of the republic who had allowed Germany to be
shackled by the Versailles treaty and to eliminate the tyranny of that
treaty.

Hitler had another motive in the manner of his defense. He and
the Reichswehr—the army—had fallen out because of General von
Seeckt's ironfisted discipline. Hitler wanted to reforge the old links.
It was essential to his future program that he do so, that he have a
friendly army at his side and not an unfriendly army at his back.

On March 27, 1924, Adolf Hitler made his final speech of defense to the court:

> When I learned that it was the "Green Police"* which had fired,
> I had the happy feeling that at least it was not the Reichswehr which
> had besmirched itself. The Reichswehr remains as untarnished as
> before. One day the hour will come when the Reichswehr will stand
> at our side, officers and men. The army which we have formed
> grows from day to day; from hour to hour it grows more rapidly.
> Even now I have the proud hope that one day the hour is coming
> when these untrained bands will become battalions, when the bat-
> talions will become regiments, and the regiments divisions; when
> the old cockade will be raised from the mire, when the old ban-
> ners will once again wave before us; and then reconciliation will
> come in that eternal last Court of Judgment—the Court of God—
> before which we are ready to take our stand.

---

*"Green Police" referred to the military force of the Bavarian Government. It was as if
the shooting had been done by the U.S. state militia (national guard) rather than regular
army troops.

If those words seem short on logic, even in translation they are long on rhetoric. The emotional appeal of the speech was so powerful that it gave goosebumps to sympathetic listeners and made them want to get up and shout. The courtroom's public galleries were filled with people who applauded and stamped their feet, despite many warnings, when Hitler spoke.

That Court of Honor will not ask us "Did you commit high treason or did you not?" That court will judge us, the Quartermaster-General [Ludendorff] of the old army, his officers and soldiers, who as Germans, desired only the good of their people and fatherland; who wanted to fight and to die. You may pronounce us guilty a thousand times over, the goddess who presides over the Eternal Court of History will with a smile tear into shreds the indictment of the Public Prosecutor and the judgment of this court, for she declares us guiltless.

Finally, everyone had had his say, and the judges had to decide. They might have dealt with Adolf Hitler as an Austrian citizen, which he still was. In that case, they could have sentenced him to a long term in prison, to be followed by deportation as an undesirable person. But they did no such thing.

Sentencing day was April 1. That morning to the court came all sorts of people to see the spectacle: ladies in expensive gowns, with rosettes of black, red, and white ribbons; gentlemen with boutonnieres, also of the monarchist colors. The accused came into court, and they were presented with bouquets of flowers. The judges gave the sentences.

To his disgust, General Ludendorff was acquitted entirely of wrongdoing. "I consider my acquittal a disgrace for the uniform and decorations that I wear," he growled.

Ernst Röhm, the Storm Troop leader, and Wilhelm Frick, the assistant to the Bavarian police minister and a staunch Nazi, were both convicted of conspiracy but released immediately. Adolf Hitler was given the lightest penalty the law allowed for one convicted of treason: five years detention in a fortress. It was also understood by all concerned that the full sentence would not be served.

After the sentencing, the defendants all went out into the courtyard to have their pictures taken. Seven of the defendants were wearing their respective uniforms, Ludendorff with his spiked helmet perched straight up on his head, leaning on his ceremonial sword, with his right hand in his pocket. Frick was wearing his morning suit, wing-collared white shirt, and formal day dress tie, with his sash of office across the breast. Hitler was wearing a business suit, soft hat, and rain-coat and was by far the least impressive figure in the photograph.

And then it was time for Hitler to go to Landsberg-on-the-Lech and enter the fortress prison there.

The prison term was almost a lark for Adolf Hitler. It gave him six months, for that was all he was going to serve, in which to pause and write the memoirs he wanted to use to show the world his vi-sion of what Germany was going to become under his suzerainty.

Rudolf Hess joined Hitler at the prison. Herr Hitler was a fa-vored prisoner: he had a private room and everything he needed. He began to dictate his memoirs to Hess, who wrote them down. *Vier und ein halb Jahren von Kampf gegen Lügen, Dummheit, und Feigheit* was the title.*

The book was a compendium of personal history and polemics. Hitler spoke of his birthplace, Braunau on the Inn River, "situated on the border between those two German states" (Germany and Austria). Immediately, in the second sentence of the book, he launched into a polemic:

> German-Austria must return to the Great German motherland, and not because of economic considerations of any sort.... Common blood belongs in a common Reich.

So there, on the opening page of his book, Adolf Hitler had fore-cast the amalgamation of Austria into the new German Empire. More-over, he had laid out for the world his greater plans for Europe:

> *Only when the boundaries of the Reich include even the last German...does there arise...the moral right to acquire foreign soil and territory.* (Italics added.)

---

*Four and a Half Years' Struggle Against Lies, Stupidity and Cowardice.

There for the Czechoslovaks and the Poles to see, as well as the Austrians, was the master plan of integrating all "racial" Germans into the great Reich that Hitler foresaw arising under his dictatorship. Oh, yes, dictatorship. For in the Munich putsch attempt he had made it quite clear to all concerned that he, Adolf Hitler, would become the dictator of Germany. General Ludendorff was shocked to learn that Hitler and not he, Ludendorff, was to occupy the top spot, but since the plan hadn't succeeded, it was of little importance—except to the Nazis and the people around them, who now knew which way their leader was going to travel.

Hitler told how he had become a student in Linz; how, when he was thirteen, his father had died suddenly; how his mother had agreed that he should become an artist if he wished; and how she had agreed that he was to go to the *Akademie* in Vienna. He spent two happy years at the *Realschule* in preparation. But then his mother died, and Hitler, suitcase in hand, headed for Vienna. He had hoped to enroll at the *Akademie* as an art student, but the authorities decided his paintings showed so little promise that they refused him admission.

His education had been a hodgepodge. He had no certificate from a secondary school. He had no certificate from the polytechnic school. Worse (something he did not confide in his book), he was virtually penniless, and for months in 1909 he lived in the Refuge for Men in Vienna-Brigittenau, where he subsisted on charity, "a bit of human flotsam who in addition kept pretty well to himself."

Legend has it that Hitler became a housepainter. Never. He was a derelict, a struggling artist with little talent, who earned as much money shoveling snow in the streets of Vienna as he did from his sketches and paintings. But he never painted a house. At this interval, too, Hitler had a number of Jewish friends who occasionally helped him out, or whom he met in the cafes to read the house newspapers and talk endlessly about the politics of the day.

Hitler began to hate the city of Vienna and the rich people who flocked there in these halcyon days of the Habsburg Empire: "The longer I observed the game, the more my aversion grew against the metropolis which so greedily sucked the people in only to destroy them."

In Vienna Hitler also had his first encounter with social democracy. He got a construction job—he never said what job, but it was obviously a building job—and for three days all went well. Then he

was asked to join the union. He refused. He said he did not understand the whole process. The union members put up with this attitude for a little while. Hitler then began studying. "I drank my bottle
of milk and ate my piece of bread somewhere on the side, cautiously
studying my surroundings."

He got hold of pamphlets, read them, and argued against the social
democratic conception of a class war between worker and capitalist.
Ultimately he was warned that he had the choice of leaving the job or
being thrown off the scaffold one day. He left the job, but he never
forgave the Social Democrats of the world. Destructive, he called them:
"In the course of a few decades under [social democracy's] skilled
hand, the means for protecting social and union rights had become the
instrument for the destruction of national economics."

Since many of the Social Democrats Hitler knew were Jews, Hitler transferred some of the vitriol from his soul to the Jews: "Meanwhile I learned to understand the connection between this doctrine
of destruction and the nature of a race, which hitherto had been
unknown to me." Specifically,

*Understanding Jewry alone is the key to the comprehension of the
inner, the real, intention of Social Democracy.* (Italics added.)

At home in Braunau and then in Linz, he had never been aware of
Jews. It was only when Hitler was about 14 years old that it occurred
to him that the Jews he knew were extremely political people. He did
not know that the Jews had been persecuted—not until he arrived in
Vienna, the center of Austrian Jewry, with a Jewish population of
200,000 among the 2 million inhabitants. Here he discovered that much
of the "liberal" press was edited by Jews. Then Hitler saw his first
Orthodox Jew, a man in a long black caftan, with a little black cap on
his head and long curls around his face. This was a Jew. Was he also
a German, an Austrian? Hitler began to debate that question with himself, and he came to the conclusion that no, the Jew was not also an
Austrian, a German. He was a Jew.

Where ever I went I saw Jews, and the more I saw of them, the
sharper I began to distinguish them from other people. The inner city especially and the districts north of the Danube canal

swarmed with a people which through its appearance alone had no resemblance to the German people.

Then he discovered the existence of Zionism—the movement dedicated to the return of the Jews to the land of Israel. From that moment on Hitler was convinced that the Jews were people apart, people with whom he wanted no contact. And he perceived to his own satisfaction that the world press was dominated by these Jews. The social democratic press was entirely dominated by Jews, he believed, but this was not true.

Hitler then began searching out Jewish intellectuals and arguing with them in cafes and on the streets. Often he found himself outmaneuvered in the debates with some of his opponents. "One did not know what to admire more, their glibness of tongue or their skill in lying....I gradually began to hate them."

Hitler now began to study Marxism. He concluded that Marxism, the basis of social democracy, was "a Jewish doctrine."

The Jewish doctrine of Marxism rejects the aristocratic principle in nature; instead of the eternal privilege of force and strength, it places the mass of numbers and its dead weight, thus denies the value of the individual in man....

If with the help of the Marxian creed, the Jew conquers the nations of this world, his crown will become the funeral wreath of humanity.

And so, he wrote, "from a feeble cosmopolite I had turned into a fanatical anti-Semite."

All this happened before 1912, the year Hitler left Vienna for Munich. He was then a young man of 24, his mind full of hatred and very little else.

He hated Jews.

He hated Marxism in all its forms.

He hated the Austro-Hungarian empire.

He regarded himself as a pure German.

His mission was to save the German "race."

New phrases began to creep into his vocabulary, new conceptions: "the international Jewish world finance," "International Jewry," and "the fight against Marxism."

*   *   *

When the Great War came in 1914, Adolf Hitler, as a foreigner, had to petition the king of Bavaria for permission to join a Bavarian army regiment. He did and was accepted. He was 25 and felt that he was now serving his adopted country and would have a new start in life.

He served well, as noted, and was decorated twice. He was also gassed and in 1918 was in the hospital for treatment of his lungs and eyes. He was discharged from the hospital, but chose to remain in the army after the war ended, and thus began his political career, also as noted.

During the war, as a soldier, Hitler had come "home" to Munich occasionally. When he did, he was appalled to discover that "the offices of the authorities were occupied by Jews. Almost every clerk a Jew and every Jew a clerk. I was amazed by this multitude of fighters of the Chosen People and could not help comparing them with the few representatives they had at the front."

(The fact was that Jewish citizens of Germany in 1914 numbered 550,000. Of the 100,000 of these who were in uniform, 80,000 saw duty at the front. There were 12,000 Jewish casualties. The ratio was the same as that for the rest of the population. Of the total army contingent, 35,000 Jews were decorated for bravery, 23,000 were promoted in rank, and 2000 received commissions in the field, although before the war the army had barred its officer ranks to Jews.)

"In the business world, things were even worse," said Hitler. "As early as the year 1916–17 almost the entire production was indeed under the control of the Jewry of high finance."

On and on the young demagogue talked in Landsberg prison, and the faithful Rudolf Hess took down every word. A long chapter of fifty-six pages was devoted entirely to the question of race, mainly elucidating Hitler's claim that the Aryan "race" must be preeminent and that mixing with other races must be forbidden.

For a racially pure people, conscious of its blood, can never be enslaved by the Jew. It will forever only be the master of bastards in this world.

The Jew must be controlled. The Jew must be put down. The Jew must be destroyed. These intentions were quite plain, even in Hitler's muddy prose.

The book ended with a chapter on the formation of the National Socialist German Workers' Party. And then the six months ended. Hitler was released from his fortress prison, and the book was nearly ready to be published.

Back in Munich, Max Amann, the manager of the Nazi party's publishing company, took one look at the book and snorted. He had hoped for a personal story of the manner in which Hitler, rising from obscure beginnings, had become a major political figure in Germany. Instead, he had a polemic so boring that he was not sure he could sell copies even to the Nazis.

Amann insisted that the unworkable title be changed. *Vier und ein halb Jahren von Kampf gegen Lügen, Dummheit, und Feigheit* became *Mein Kampf*—a distinct commercial improvement. At least a potential reader could hope to understand the notion of a book called "My Struggle." But when the work appeared, its story turned out to be one of very little struggle, though there was a great deal of polemic.

Rudolf Hess was not an editor, but two of Hitler's associates tried to help out. They cleaned up the bad grammar and removed some of the more specious arguments. All this work was done in a comfortable inn at Berchtesgaden, and finally the first volume of the book was published. Hitler then got down to work on the second.

The first volume of *Mein Kampf* was anything but a roaring success. In 1925 it sold 9000 copies, and by 1928 sales were down to 3000 copies a year. The main sales were to the party faithful.

The Nazi party and its newspaper, *Völkischer Beobachter*, had been banned in Bavaria following the abortive putsch. At the end of 1924, when Hitler left prison, his first move was to go to see the Bavarian authorities and secure the lifting of the bans. He promised good behavior. No more putsch attempts.

"The wild beast is checked," said Dr. Heinrich Held, the prime minister of Bavaria, proving himself to be one of the worst political seers in world history.

He ordered the lifting of the political ban, and the Nazis were back in business in 1925.

But not for long. Hitler had made one grave miscalculation. He did not take Dr. Held seriously when the doctor said that the Nazi leader must continue with his "reformation." Within a few days after Hitler had made his promise, he was back on the same old podiums making the same threats of violence against the Bavarian government and the Berlin government. Dr. Held was quick to act. He again banned Hitler from speaking in public. The other states of Germany soon followed. So Hitler was muzzled—Hitler the orator, whose oratory was his strongest suit. The ban, which turned out to be national in scope, would seriously hamper the Nazi party for the next two years.

By the end of 1925 the dues-paying membership of the Nazi party was only 27,000 people. Unable to speak, Hitler turned his abilities to organizing.

His first step was to divide the party into districts, as the country was divided. The organizational schema went down to the street cell and block level. Special party organizations for young men, young women, and married women were also created. There was an organization for virtually everyone: doctors, lawyers, civil servants, and the Nazi *Kulturbund* to bring in intellectuals. The members of Röhm's SA, or "Brown Shirts," were the bully boys, whose task was to break up opposing party meetings, protect Nazi party meetings, and beat up anyone who annoyed Hitler. By 1930 this goon squad had become a private army of more than a hundred thousand. Also, Hitler created the SS (*Schutzstaffel*), whose members wore black uniforms and swore a personal oath of loyalty to Adolf Hitler; not to the party, not to the state, but to the Führer. After several false starts in finding the appropriate leader for the SS, Hitler came upon him in the person of a chicken farmer from a village near Munich. His name was Heinrich Himmler. In 1929 Himmler took over the Hitler bodyguard of 200 men and immediately began building an empire of his own. By 1933 the SS numbered 3 million.

Another young empire builder to join the Nazis was a failed novelist and scriptwriter, Josef Goebbels, a clubfooted young man who saw a road to glory for himself. By late 1928 he had become party propaganda chief and by 1929 he was also Hitler's *Gauleiter* of Berlin, entrusted with the difficult task of cleaning up the act of the brown-shirted SA men there, who had given the Nazis a very bad name in the capital.

Aside from working on *Mein Kampf* and finishing up that book, Hitler did not do much in 1925 and 1926. He spent most of his time on the Obersalzberg above Berchtesgaden talking about the old times and the new, meeting with the faithful, fooling around with girls. (He was sorely tempted by girls, but he finally renounced the whole idea of romance and marriage in favor of his quest for power.) At this time he had an affair with his niece, Geli Rabaul, which caused some scandal within the party until the liaison broke of its own weight and Geli committed suicide.

But that was in the offing.

The next few years seemed to bear out Dr. Held's view: of the 31 million votes cast in the election of 1928, the Nazis polled only 810,000. That meant the Nazis won only a dozen of the 491 seats in the lower house of the Reichstag. The Social Democrats, with 153 seats, were the most powerful party in Germany.

The second volume of *Mein Kampf* came out without much fanfare. It elaborated on the theme of racial purity:

> We still have in our German national body great stocks of Nordic-Germanic people who remain unblended, in whom we may see the most valuable treasure for our future.

And the world was again warned of Hitler's plan:

> The German Reich, as a state, should include all Germans, not only with the task of collecting from the people the most valuable stocks of racially primal elements and preserving them but also to lead them, gradually and safely, to a dominating position.

The traditional anthem "Deutschland über Alles" was to acquire a "racial" connotation.

Even more than volume I, the second volume of *Mein Kampf* wandered errantly over political and socioeconomic topics. Hitler discussed syphilis at length and also the sterilization of whole populations:

> The prevention of the procreative faculty and possibility on the part of physically degenerated and mentally sick people, for only six hundred years, would not only free mankind of immeasurable misfortune, but would also contribute to a restoration that appears hardly believable today.

The wave of the future was revealed:

> In the folkish State the folkish view of life has finally to suc-
> ceed in bringing about the nobler era when men seek their care
> no longer in the better breeding of dogs, horses, and cats, but
> rather in the uplifting of mankind itself, an era in which the one
> knowingly and silently renounces, and the other gladly gives and
> sacrifices.

The renouncers, of course, were going to have to be the Jews
and the other "mongrel races." The "sacrificers" would be the pure
Germans, who would breed, and breed, and breed, without regard
for emotional involvement but with regard only for establishing and
perpetuating the purity of a Nazi-defined German race.

What Hitler wanted, he said in the chapter on the state, was to
mold the children of Germany into his new superrace. Oh, he knew
how to do it: get the blond young *Mädchen* and the young men, and
put them together in camps, everyone wearing as little clothing as
possible.

> The young man who during the summer walks about in long pipe-
> like trousers, covered up to the neck, loses merely through his
> clothes, a stimulus for his physical fitness. For ambition too,
> and we may as well say it, vanity also have to be applied. Not
> the vanity in beautiful clothes, which not everyone is able to
> buy, but the vanity in a beautiful, well-shaped body which ev-
> eryone can help in building up.
>   This is of use also for the future. The girl should become
> acquainted with her knight. If today physical beauty were not
> pushed completely into the background by our dandified fash-
> ionableness, the seduction of hundreds of thousands of girls by
> bowlegged Jewish bastards would never be possible. Also this
> is in the interest of the nation, that most beautiful bodies find
> one another and thus help in giving the nation new beauty.

This second volume was also more specific in some ways than
the first, partly because Hitler was addressing himself to the problems of government that he hoped to address once in power. He
attacked Marxism unmercifully. He outlined his methods of propaganda. He again predicted the amalgamation of Germany with Aus-

tria, while he damned federalism and urged the truly unified national state. Hitler laid out his milestones on the road to power, but few outside the Nazi party paid much attention.

The world economic crash that began in 1929 seemed made to order for Adolf Hitler. The base for the recovery of Germany, which was moving along steadily under revised reparations programs pushed by the Americans, was trade and loans from the international bankers of London and New York. Suddenly, with the collapse of the Wall Street stock markets, followed by the crash in London, the bottom dropped out of the loan and trade arrangements. Germany was hard hit very quickly. Industrial production fell by half between 1929 and 1932. Banks failed. Small businesses collapsed. Big businesses fired workers by the thousands. The American gesture of a moratorium on all war debt did not even slow the tide. The Great Depression was upon the world, and Germany was a major victim, for her institutions were too new and not strong enough to weather the storm. All Hitler's talk about the greed of international bankers suddenly began to become credible to harried Germans.

In the summer of 1930 Chancellor Heinrich Brüning, the social democratic leader, found that he was having so much trouble getting laws through the Reichstag that he asked President Paul von Hindenburg to dissolve the Parliament and order new elections.

Here was Hitler's chance. For years he had been advocating hard solutions to hard problems. Now, with the two-year suspension of his right to speak ended, he conducted a furious campaign of promises.

He would make Germany strong again.

He would refuse to pay more reparations.

He would repudiate the Versailles treaty.

He would stamp out corruption.

He would bring the bankers under control.

He would see that every German had a job and food on the table.

An unhappy Germany, disillusioned by the failures of the Social Democrats who had controlled the Reichstag for ten years, responded. When the election returns were in, Hitler's Nazi party, which had polled 810,000 votes in the previous election, now, in 1930, received 6,400,000. But Hitler's bitter enemies, the Communists, also polled a large number—more than 4,600,000 votes. These tallies were at the expense of the center parties. Suddenly Hitler's Nazis had become the second most powerful party in Germany, and the Communists were third. Germany's parliamentary system had been turned topsy-turvy and was threatened from both right and left.

Hitler had been wooing the army steadily for the preceding two years. He had assured the generals that his Brown Shirts and Black Shirts were not and never would be soldiers. They were party police, and when and if the Reichswehr allied itself with the Nazis, the army would have nothing to fear from these groups.

The army was not quick to respond. Several of the senior generals saw the Nazis as the greatest threat yet to Germany, a far greater threat than the Communists. But Hitler was already invading the army ranks. In 1930 three young lieutenants were arrested at Ulm and charged with spreading national socialist propaganda through the ranks.

Two of them were tried. The trial became a cause célèbre, and showed how disaffected much of the army had become. Hitler went to Leipzig for the proceedings; as a witness he made a major speech in which he assured army leaders that he would not challenge them. The speech created an international sensation, for in it Hitler promised that he would take power only through legal means. But then he said, ''I can assure you that when the National Socialist Movement is victorious in its fight, then there will come a National Socialist Court of Justice, then November 1918 will find its retribution, and then heads will roll.''

Much of the rest of the world understood what Hitler was saying, but non-Germans were in no position to do anything about this demagogue who, after all, still did not hold power. And whether they fully understood or not, a great many Germans were not interested in doing anything about him, except to flock to his banner. The Nazi party was growing very rapidly because of the general disaffection of the German people with their government. Hitler's oratory was persuasive, and the wants of the Germans even more so. Hitler offered them the hope they had nearly lost.

The Leipzig trial resulted in the conviction of the two Nazi army officers, partly because Hitler had thrown them to the wolves, disavowing their revolutionary attempts. But virtually nobody in Germany cared about that; the important matter was that Adolf Hitler had shown Germans a new direction.

Hitler's declaration that he had no intention of undermining the Reichswehr convinced many of the officers. Another result of the publicity was a spurt of enlistment into the Storm Troops. The young men of Germany wanted action, and Hitler promised them a "legal revolution." What could be wrong with joining the SA and helping to carry out that aim?

The army's top leadership finally began to see the handwriting on the wall. By the end of 1930 General Kurt von Schleicher, the army commander, was seeking contacts with the Nazi party. Ernst Röhm, shortly to be appointed chief of staff of the SA, was sent as emissary to von Schleicher on January 1, 1931, and the next day the army announced that for the first time in six years Nazi party members could be considered for army enlistment. Hitler promised that there would be no SA violence, but the SA in Berlin objected and became riotous. Hitler and Berlin *Gauleiter* Goebbels expelled several members of the SA from the party, thus reassuring the army once more. From the open enmity of three years earlier the army and the Nazi party grew steadily closer.

*   *   *

In the spring of 1932 the army used its enormous political influence to force the resignation of the civilian government of Chancellor Heinrich Brüning. It was replaced by an army-backed government, an administration under the leadership of a foppish nobleman, Franz von Papen. By midsummer other changes were in the wind, for Hitler, as head of what was now the largest party in Germany, had begun to insist that he should be made chancellor of the republic. Minister of Defense General von Schleicher, with the power of the army behind him, was the man who could assure Hitler the job. They began to meet privately. But von Schleicher wanted the post of chancellor for himself, and he managed to get it in December. Briefly the army then reached the high point of its power. Never before and never again would the German army actually be running the country. But by mid-January the army government had produced nothing that would capture public support, and the von Schleicher cabinet fell. The replacement was ready. On January 30, 1933, Adolf Hitler became chancellor of Germany.

A few hours later, by adroit political maneuvering, the new chancellor called for the dissolution of the Reichstag and for new elections. "Now it will be easy," wrote Josef Goebbels, Hitler's propaganda genius, "for we can call on all the resources of the State. Radio and press are at our disposal. We shall stage a masterpiece of propaganda. And this time, naturally, there is no lack of money."

"Naturally," said Goebbels. What he meant was that after the Nazis had polled 6 million votes in 1930, showing themselves to be a political faction with which to reckon, the big businessmen of Germany began sidling over to them and offering money. Hitler's principal assistants, Hermann Göring, the World War I flying ace, and Goebbels encouraged the money men, indicating that once the Nazis were in power they would put the workers down and let business owners and managers run their enterprises as they wished. On February 20 at Göring's palace (which Göring occupied as president of the Reichstag) the most important businessmen of Germany assembled to get the word from their new Führer. In the room were Krupp von Bohlen, the greatest magnate of all; Dr. Karl Bosch and Dr. Georg von Schnitzler of I. G. Farben, which was to the rest of industry what Krupp was to steel; and Albert Voegeler, the head of United Steel. Hitler and Göring promised the industrialists that the next election would be the last for ten years. Stability they wanted, and stability they would have under the Nazis. Then Dr. Hjalmar Schacht, Hitler's financial man, passed the hat among the guests. He collected 3 million marks in about ten minutes.

By this time Hitler had developed a strong antipathy toward the army leadership, which had stood against him on two important occasions: in 1923 during his abortive putsch and in 1932 when he had to contend with von Schleicher for the chancellorship. But that was a problem he had some leisure to ponder. Now that money was available, Hitler's immediate goal was to completely eliminate from political running the Nazis' major enemies, the Communists.

The first step was to bring Nazis into all positions of police power. Goebbels and Göring managed this, the latter through his authority as minister of the interior of Prussia, the state which made up two-thirds of Germany. On February 22, 1933, Göring established an auxiliary police force of 50,000 men, of whom 80 percent were taken from the SA and the SS.

Two days later Göring's police raided the Communist headquarters in Berlin. They got the goods: huge piles of propaganda posters that, the Nazis said, proved that the Reds were preparing a violent revolution in Germany. But they did not get their hands on the Communist leaders, for most of them had already gone underground or had left the country for Soviet Russia to escape what they saw coming.

What the Communists foresaw came on the night of February 27, 1933. Someone set fire to the Reichstag.

Immediately, as if they had had a portent, Hitler, Göring, and other Nazi leaders were on their way to the scene.

"This is the beginning of the Communist revolution!" Göring shouted. "We must not wait a minute.... Every Communist official must be shot;... every Communist deputy must this very night be strung up..."

The fact was, as was proved many years later, that the Nazis had set the Reichstag fire to provoke the incident that would allow them to act just days before the March 5 elections.

On the day following the fire, Hitler persuaded President von Hindenburg to suspend the sections of the German constitution that guaranteed civil liberties. Goebbels then played on the fears of the people: unless they voted for the Nazis, his propaganda machine trumpeted, the Communists would win the elections and Germany would be enslaved by the Soviet Union.

Four thousand Communist officials and thousands of Social Democrats were arrested in the next few hours. Truckloads of SA and SS toughs roared through the streets, stopping and rounding up innocents who were taken to barracks or empty warehouses and then tortured, beaten, or even held for ransom. Not only Communists were victimized. Jews, of course, were always prey for the bullies of the SA. The SA, it seemed, was above the law.

The Communist press and all independent newspapers were suppressed. Only the Nazis were free.

Göring did as he had promised. The state radio became a Nazi facility and the voice of Hitler rang throughout the land. The streets were alive with the red, white, and black swastika flags of the Nazis. Billboards were plastered with Nazi propaganda.

March 5 was the key day. The people went to the polls and spoke.

The Nazis took 17,300,000 votes, but that was only 44 percent of the total. They did not have a clear majority. But although the Communists still were able to secure nearly 5,000,000 votes, Franz von Papen's Nationalist party, which supported the Nazis, polled 3,200,000. This vote gave the Nationalists 52 seats in the Reichstag. These seats, added to the 288 seats of the Nazis, meant control. Hitler had a majority of 16 in the Reichstag.

Within three weeks Hitler had wrecked the German constitution. He secured passage of a measure that put the power of legislation into the hands of the Reich cabinet for a period of four years. It would take him only a fraction of that time to seize Germany by the throat.

Hitler was now, by law, dictator of Germany.

Within weeks, Hitler did what Bismarck had been afraid to do: he established the central authority of his government over all Germany, treading on the historic rights of the German states. By July 14—Bastille Day, the anniversary of the day France had liberated itself from an autocratic regime—Hitler had enslaved his adopted country. The Nazi party, said the new decree promulgated that day, was the only legal party in Germany.

The totalitarian state was in being.

But...the problems of governing Germany—making peace with the army, solving the country's economic problems, and rearming—all remained. And so did a putative rebellion among the Nazi masses, many of whom really expected a "revolution" that would carry out the announced social purposes of the National Socialist German Workers' Party. They did not know that Hitler had abandoned his avowed revolutionary principles once he achieved power and that he was ready to sell out many of the precepts of the party in order to fulfill those he considered the most important to his personal agenda.

Hitler's relationship with the army had not improved. In general, it had not been good since the 1923 putsch. In the years since, most of the senior officers had grown to distrust the Nazis. They particularly distrusted the SA and the SS, which they suspected of trying to become armies unto themselves. Something had to be done about that.

Hitler was already moving toward what would ultimately become one of his greatest errors: an attempt to link his power with that of the generals and, eventually, to dominate them completely.

In February he had begun assembling the top military and naval leaders at various generals' homes to address them on his vision of the future of the Third Reich and its armed forces.

He was cunning enough to repeat a theme he had used three years earlier:

It is impossible to build up an army and give it a sense of worth if the object of its existence is not the preparation for battle. Armies for the preparation of peace do not exist; they exist for triumphant exertion in war.

Hitler's plan was to keep the army on his side until his government became so well established that he could deal with the generals on his own terms. To do this, he was willing to do anything and say anything that would make them happy. In the end, of course, this tactic persuaded the generals of their own importance. As we shall see, it also turned out to be one of Hitler's most costly errors.

Word of Hitler's meetings with his generals leaked out of the country; but whether in disbelief or in fear, the Western Allies seemed paralyzed, even in 1933, when it had to have been obvious that the power of Hitler's new Germany was extremely limited.

On March 21, 1933, the "wedding" of army and Nazi government was solemnized when Hitler and President von Hindenburg, the old field marshal, met and shook hands over the tomb of Frederick the Great at Potsdam. Now began the unholy alliance in which the army and Nazi government conspired to secretly rearm Germany in violation of the terms of the Versailles treaty.

In May 1933, as the world waited to see which way Hitler would turn Germany, he delivered what came to be known as his "Peace Speech" before the Reichstag. Just the day before, President Franklin D. Roosevelt of the United States had made a call to the world for disarmament and for the immediate abandonment of offensive weapons.

Hitler began his speech by endorsing Roosevelt's proposals. Germany, he said, was ready to destroy all its offensive weapons if the armed nations would destroy theirs. As for war, "War is madness," said the German chancellor.

What a moderate speech! said the world.

The world at large did not notice the kicker: "Germany demands equality of treatment with all other nations in the matter of armaments," said Adolf Hitler. If Germany did not get this concession, it would withdraw from the League of Nations and the coming disarmament conference.

Equality of treatment? The Versailles treaty had been prepared to deal with that point to keep Germany disarmed forever. But the Allies wavered. It would take them eight years to bring their armaments down to Germany's level, they said.

That was all Hitler wanted. On October 14 he announced that an abused Germany was going to withdraw from the League and the Geneva disarmament conference. He dissolved parliament and called for a national plebescite to certify his withdrawal from the League of Nations. Secretly, the army was ordered to resist if the Allies tried to use force against Germany.

But Hitler need not have worried. The Allies were dispirited by the world economic depression, preoccupied with their domestic affairs, and unwilling to take strong action against anyone, including Germany.

The new elections were to be held on November 12, 1933. There would be a single slate of candidates, all Nazis. The issue of the plebescite was the "recovery of honor," which could be achieved only by withdrawing from the League, said the Nazis.

The German people agreed. Of the 96 percent of the electorate that voted, 95 percent voted for withdrawal from Geneva and 92 percent approved the Nazi Reichstag candidates. It could no longer be said that Hitler did not have the overwhelming support of the German people. He had just that.

In his drive to seize power, Hitler had relied heavily on the SA. Ernst Röhm, the Storm Troop leader, had risen high in the councils of the Nazi party to become a government vice-chancellor and member of the cabinet. Röhm now had a highly inflated ego, and he was quite capable of causing trouble because he really believed in the "revolution" that Hitler had promised. Letting him rise so high had been an error, one that Hitler now proposed to rectify.

Röhm overreached himself when he submitted to the cabinet the proposition that he be made minister of defense, in charge of managing a new army that would be made up of the SA, the SS, and the old army.

General Walther von Brauchitsch stated the views of the army: "Rearmament is too serious and difficult a business to permit the participation of peculators, drunkards and homosexuals.'' All these types were to be found in the SA and the SS. Röhm himself was an infamous homosexual.

The relations between the army and the SA deteriorated rapidly. Expediency convinced Hitler that he must quietly side with the army. He showed this attitude to his military chiefs on April 1, 1934, when he took a secret trip aboard the cruiser *Deutschland* with several high-ranking officers, including the commanders of the army and navy. On the way to the spring military maneuvers in East Prussia, he proposed to the officers that he become the successor to the ailing President von Hindenburg. In exchange for their support, he promised, he would tether the SA, and he again assured the officers that he would restore the might of the armed forces.

On May 16, the highest officers of the army met privately and endorsed Hitler as the successor to President von Hindenburg. So... Hitler had the army in his pocket. The generals would follow his bidding. The price was to be the sacrifice of the SA.

The struggle for power within the Nazi kingdom continued. Göring and Heinrich Himmler, head of the SS, conspired against Röhm, head of the SA. Göring made Himmler head of the Prussian Gestapo.

At the beginning of June 1934, Hitler and Röhm had a showdown meeting that lasted five hours. At the end Röhm professed his desire to put things right by stopping the fulminations of his SA for revolution. It was later reported that he left the meeting to plot to seize power from Hitler—or so Hitler said. It seems most unlikely. Röhm was Hitler's oldest friend among the Nazis, and he truly believed in Hitler. Ambitious as he was, he would have accepted discipline. But Hitler had gone too far; he had promised to appease the army. He now needed an excuse for what he was about to do.

The SA was told to go on leave for the month of July. No uniforms were to be worn. There would be no parades or military exercises. Röhm went to the town of Wiessee near Munich, and made an appointment with Hitler to meet there with the SA leaders on June 30.

Yes, said the Führer, he would be there without fail.

June moved along. Hitler was in trouble with the army because he had not honored his promise to destroy the SA. There were rumors that President von Hindenburg was about to turn over control of the country to the army. That would mean the end of the Nazis. So Hitler decided he must act.

He assembled Himmler's SS troops and Göring's own little army, the Landespolizeigruppe General Göring. Quietly they gathered in Berlin and other cities. Hitler made a brief tour of Essen and Westphalia, whiling away the time. On June 29 he was at Bad Godesburg on the Rhine, staying at an inn. That night he learned of a "putsch attempt" by Röhm and his SA men in Berlin and Munich. At two o'clock in the morning Hitler flew to Munich. As his plane was in the air, SA leader Röhm and his friends were asleep in their beds at the Hanslbauer Hotel in Wiessee on the Tegernsee.

At 4 a.m. on Saturday Hitler arrived in Munich and the action began. One of the first to go was Ernst Röhm, arrested in his hotel by Hitler and taken to a jail cell where a pistol was laid out for him. He refused to commit suicide, so two officers shot him dead. Hundreds of other SA leaders were shot down that night. So was General von Schleicher, whose major crimes had been to face Hitler down and to side with Röhm in the critical period of 1933. Killing von Schleicher was another of Hitler's mistakes, for von Schleicher was an old member of the Officer Corps clan, with whom the murder did not sit well. Many generals developed new reservations about Hitler.

When dawn came, the leaders of the SA were no more. Perhaps a hundred of them had been murdered in what came to be known as the "night of the long knives." Within a month, Heinrich Himmler's SS had supplanted the SA as the chief enforcement agency of the Nazi party.

The army had gotten rid of the SA, but the new threat was just as great.

On August 2, 1934, President von Hindenburg died at the age of 94. Hitler had planned well. He ordered a plebescite again, this time to approve the assumption of total power over the Third Reich by Adolf Hitler. Ninety-five percent of the people voted, and 38 million of them, 90 percent, voted for Adolf Hitler. The 4 million dissenters were in for trouble. The Führer would not forget. He had a pledge for the German people: "There will be no other revolution in Germany for the next one thousand years."

The "Thousand-Year Reich," that was his promise to Germany.

What did the Thousand-Year Reich mean to Germany?

First of all it meant the persecution of the Jews. One might say that this was one of Hitler's major mistakes. The showing of the Jews in Germany's past wars had always been excellent. There is no reason to believe that the Jews would have deserted Hitler or Germany had they not been persecuted. There is every reason to believe they would have accepted the trampling on general civil liberties as almost all other Germans did.

It is easy to say that Hitler's behavior was a dreadful strategic error, but that is too simple. By 1934 Hitler's entire philosophy was built around the creation of a master race in Germany and the ejection of all the "inferiors." Practically, it was impossible, of course. Year after year the most embarrassing situations cropped up: a general just promoted or otherwise honored would be found to have a Jewish grandmother, and either the fact had to be swept under the rug or the general sacrificed. Time and again records had to be altered to protect the faithful from the "sins" of their progenitors.

So one can hardly call Hitler's policy toward the Jews an error in the ordinary sense. It was a fundamental precept of his Thousand-Year Reich. But it was also one of the major flaws that would one day bring the whole structure tumbling down. The policy was revealed to the world through the Nuremberg laws of 1935. In July the Law of Revocation of Naturalization took the unprecedented step (in Germany) of depriving citizens (Jews) of their citizenship. In September a whole series of laws limited citizenship to people of Aryan stock. The Law for the Protection of German Blood and German Honor stated, "The purity of German blood is a prerequisite for the continued existence of the German people." This second law deprived all Jews in Germany of German citizenship. Hereafter they would become "subjects." Woe to the Jews.

"Jews Forbidden" signs went up all over Germany, and many hotels refused to give Jews lodging. The disease spread rapidly.

Oppression was practiced too against steadfast believers of the Christian faiths. Hitler soon discovered that opposition lay inside their church walls.

*　　　*　　　*

The symbol of Christian dissent was Pastor Martin Niemöller, a submarine officer in World War I, who had welcomed Hitler's coming to power, but who now began speaking out against Nazi excesses. He ended up in a concentration camp, where he stayed until the end of World War II.

A thousand other pastors were arrested in the next few years.

Church newspapers were closed down, as were ordinary newspapers. By 1936 Hitler had total control of the information media in Germany, and if there was dissent, it was no more than underground rattlings.

Then came the nazification of the German people. After March 1933 so many people flocked to join the movement that a new term was coined to describe them: the *Märzgefallen* (the "heroes of March"). But the old Nazis were in charge. Goebbels took over much of this work, as the Nazis seized control of music, art, literature, journalism, theaters—every aspect of German life. Films became instruments of propaganda and had no other purpose. The radio glorified nazism in song, story, and news reports. Books had to be acceptable to the party to be published. Education was made an instrument of the party. The universities bowed their heads to the new movement. The Hitler Youth movement took over the destiny of young men and young women and prepared them for breeding the new master race. By 1938 there were 7 million Hitler Youth members in uniform, which meant there were 4 million youths who had not joined. The independence of those 4 million infuriated the Nazis, and by 1939 all German youths were conscripted into the movement. Farms, businesses, industry, labor—all were turned to the purposes of the state, which was the party as well. Justice, of course, was Nazi justice, which was simply an extension of Hitler's brutalization of the people. The codes were the creations of the Nazi mind. There was no historical precedent, no system of balances. "Justice" existed to punish the enemies of the Nazi state and for no other reason. Hitler was the supreme executive, the supreme legislator, and the supreme judge of Germany.

Adolf Hitler had come a long way. By 1936 he was in total control of the destiny of the German people. And the vast majority of Germans, 95 percent at least, did not seem to mind a bit.

2

THE ROAD
TO WAR

In the summer of 1934 the German generals were elated. The hated
SA had been hobbled and Ernst Röhm, its driving leader, was dead.
So were most of the other leaders of the gang. On July 13 Hitler
had told the Reichstag that the army was the sole protector of Germany. Even the modus vivendi had been laid out: Hitler had said
that in matters of national security he would delegate his authority
to the minister of defense. The army would have free reign—as long
as the generals kept out of politics. The generals now could get down
to the serious business of rearming Germany. He, Hitler, would take
care of foreign policy and make sure that nothing happened to curb
them.

The generals took Hitler at his word and began work on their
part of the bargain. They reorganized the SA, and starting in July,
they began incorporating the physically and morally acceptable SA
men into the army. Admiral Erich Raeder and his staff were moving ahead with the secret construction of naval vessels, and Hermann
Göring was building military aircraft by the thousands, all in violation of the Versailles agreement.

In *Mein Kampf* Hitler had declared that one of his first priorities
after taking power would be the unification of Aryan German-
speaking peoples. All spring the Nazis of Austria, backed by those
of Germany and supplied with weapons and explosives, had been

37

conducting a campaign of terror, blowing up railroad stations and other public buildings and murdering supporters of Austrian Chancellor Engelbert Dollfuss. The violence was so pervasive that Mussolini protested that the Germans must leave Austria alone, the protest arising because Dollfuss was a Fascist, too, and Mussolini felt that Austria came within his sphere of influence.

Hitler had promised publicly that Austria would be secure from outside interference, so now he moved through the local Nazis to overthrow the Dollfuss government and try to install a puppet regime. On July 25 the local Nazis were ready to try a putsch. At noon 150 of them, dressed in Austrian army uniforms, broke into the Austrian Chancellery in Vienna and shot down Chancellor Dollfuss. He soon died of his wounds. Other Nazis seized the state radio station and announced that Dollfuss had "resigned." But the coup was bungled. Loyal Austrian forces quickly surrounded the Chancellery and forced the Nazis to surrender. If Hitler wanted Austria, he would now have to send in troops. But Hitler also had news that day that an angry Mussolini had mobilized four divisions at the Brenner Pass: if the Germans moved into Austria, they would have to fight the Italians too. Hitler backed down.

In that incident were messages for the world:

1. Adolf Hitler was trying to fulfill the program he had stated in *Mein Kampf*.

2. If others stood up to Hitler, he would back down.

Unfortunately, the sole other dictator in western Europe seemed to be the only person who understood Hitler and who could deal with him on his own terms.

The Führer learned from his overeagerness. He was not yet strong enough to face the world, but his army was making the strides that would solve that problem.

General Ludwig Beck, the army's chief of staff, ordered the ground forces increased from 100,000 to 300,000 by the end of the year. The following spring, Hitler had promised, he would decree universal military training, thus openly breaching the Versailles treaty. For the moment Hitler publicly talked only peace. He gave interviews to friendly foreign newspaper reporters, particularly those of the London *Daily Mail*, which was open in its admiration for him. He warned Goebbels that the German General Staff must never be mentioned in propaganda. It might easily give away what was really happening inside Germany, for under the Versailles treaty no German General Staff was permitted to exist. The fiction must be maintained for a while yet.

U-boats were being built, many of them in Dutch yards, ostensibly for the Spanish and other buyers. Not a word was said about U-boats for Germany, but in the Kiel and Hamburg shipyards strange hangars went up and no one was allowed inside the guarded entrances without a special pass. At Kiel and Wilhelmshaven work was being done on "improved 10,000-ton ships," warships of the size stipulated as the maximum in the Versailles treaty. But the ships were actually 25,000-ton pocket battleships as well as larger vessels. The *Scharnhorst* and the *Gneisenau* were being built just then.

Hermann Göring, who had kept German air skills going during the leanest years by sponsoring glider clubs, now extended that activity through the League for Air Sports. Germans began to take an unprecedented interest in air races. A young man named Willy Messerschmitt had some unique ideas about the design of racing planes.

In the Ruhr industrial district, the Krupp organization was making tanks and guns. The I. G. Farben firm was setting up production of synthetic gasoline and synthetic rubber. By mid-1934 a quarter of a million factories in Germany were assigned to production of war materials. By that time the violations of the Versailles treaty had become so obvious that even the most myopic foreign correspondents could not miss it.

Actually the British, in particular, had known for months that the Germans were rearming. Against the advice of Winston Churchill, the British government was prepared to accept the German rearmament if Germany would join in a general treaty guaranteeing peace in Europe.

As 1935 began, Hitler got back his first bit of the territory taken away from Germany at Versailles. In a plebiscite fomented by the Germans, the inhabitants of the Saar industrial basin voted 10 to 1 to rejoin their territory with Germany.

In the spring of 1935 the British made overtures to Hitler for talks to secure and extend the mutual defense alliance established at Locarno; they hoped to retain the working agreement between Britain, France, and Italy. The Treaty of Locarno, at least theoretically, guaranteed peace in the west, but not in the east.

Hitler did not want any more treaties because they would tie his hands in the east, and it was eastward that he really wanted to move. So he stalled. He sent up a trial balloon to see how strong the Allies were and how far he might go. Through a friendly English newspaperman, Ward Price of the London *Daily Mail*, he let it be known that Germany had broken the Versailles treaty by building a military air force. Then Hitler sat back and waited for the reaction.

As he had hoped, there was no reaction at all except from France, where it was confined to loud grumbling and snarling.

So...Hitler continued to press his luck.

On March 16, 1935, Hitler decreed the establishment of universal military service. The German army would be increased to twelve corps and thirty-six divisions, with a half million men.

What would England and France do?

They did nothing.

March 17: Heldengedenktag, Heroes Memorial Day. In 1935 the holiday was something special. In Berlin the generals gathered, the old army in its field gray and spiked helmets, the new army in its new field gray, the navy in black, the new Luftwaffe in powder blue. There was Hitler, beside Field Marshal August von Mackensen, the last of the old field marshals, the marshal in his spiked helmet and Hitler in his simple soldier's uniform (tailored model), wearing on his left breast the Iron Cross he had earned for his valor in World War I. There was, the correspondents reported, a general air of jubilation in the State Opera House that day. Hitler and the generals knew that they had won another round in the struggle with the Allies.

April 11: The British, French, and Italian foreign ministers met at Stresa to condemn Germany's violation of the Versailles treaty. Their countries, with America, were the old western Allies of World War I.

April 12: The council of the League of Nations condemned Germany.

All this was followed by the rattling of sabers and shuffling of papers. The Soviets signed a new defense treaty with France and another with Czechoslovakia.

May 21: Adolf Hitler decreed the Reich Defense law, a secret order that reorganized the armed forces and placed Dr. Hjalmar Schacht in charge of war production. The Reichswehr became the Wehrmacht that day. Hitler, as chancellor and Führer, was supreme commander of the Wehrmacht. General Werner von Blomberg, head of the army, became minister of war and commander in chief of all the armed forces. Navy, army, and Luftwaffe all had their own commanders in chief and general staffs.

All this was accomplished in the deepest secrecy. That same evening, without a qualm, the man who was preparing for war arose in the Reichstag to make what he called the most important speech on peace he had yet offered. He assured the world that he wanted nothing but peace. "War is senseless. War is a horror," he thundered.

He was specific in this three-hour speech. He offered thirteen proposals for peace: the essence of them all was mutual action, mutual disarmament, mutual security. He offered a German-British naval force ratio of 35 to 100—heavily in favor of the British, that is.

The world greeted the German dictator's words with joy. "Reasonable, straightforward, comprehensive," gushed the London *Times*. The British then made a private deal with the Germans to carry out the proposed ratio, without consulting the French or the Italians. Hitler had achieved a new triumph. He had split the old Allies.

Mussolini was furious. Further, he saw that Hitler was getting away with murder, so why not Italy? On October 3, 1935, Mussolini invaded Ethiopia. The League of Nations protested, and sanctions were ordered. But the sanctions accomplished virtually nothing, except to put an end to the alliance that bound Italy to France and England. Hitler had won another round without doing anything at all.

In the spring of 1935, as he talked peace, Hitler was preparing to occupy the demilitarized zone of the Rhineland, established by the Versailles treaty as a buffer between France and Germany.

October 15: The *Kriegsakademie* (War College), closed down in 1920, was rededicated by Adolf Hitler. The German military had regained its old training institute.

February 1936: The German government officially protested to France and Czechoslovakia their recently initiated treaties with the Soviet Union. These endangered the peace of Europe, claimed Hitler.

Czechoslovakia demurred. France ratified its treaty anyhow. Hitler fulminated. The generals and the admirals reminded him that the remilitarization program was proceeding more slowly than Hitler had expected. He did not have even half of the thirty-six divisions ordered. He must go slowly and not antagonize the French and the British.

March 1: Hitler made the decision. Germany would invade the Rhineland. The order had already gone out to General von Blomberg, and he passed it on to Admiral Raeder and General Göring. The plan was ready for Z day. Only the date had been missing. Now it was set: March 7.

March 7: Units of the German army entered the Rhineland for the first time since 1918. The German foreign minister handed the British, French, and Italian ambassadors notes which made nonsense of the Treaty of Locarno. At noon the German troops moved into Aachen, Trier, and Saarbrücken. Hitler rose in the Reichstag to make the announcement. He defied the world, but he also said Germany wanted nothing but peace.

Britain and France consulted. Neither government could bring itself to act. In Potsdam the German generals urged Hitler to pull back the troops before it was too late. He had made his defiance public. Now let him not court a war the German army was not capable of waging. Poland offered France help if France would move.

The next forty-eight hours were misery for the German chancellor. He had taken the great gamble. Now he must see how it would come out. Von Blomberg had warned him: if France and England marched, the Germans must retreat.

Later, when it did not make any difference, Hitler summed it all up in a boast that this was his greatest gamble:

> We had no army worth mentioning, at that time it would not even have had the fighting strength to maintain itself against the Poles. If the French had taken any action, we would have been easily defeated; our resistance would have been over in a few

days. And what air force we had then was ridiculous. A few Junkers 52s from Lufthansa, and not even enough bombs for them.

Hitler waited, confident at one moment and in despair the next. What would France and England do?

They did nothing.

The forty-eight hours passed. Hitler and his entourage went by special train to Munich. Everyone on board knew what was happening to the west, and the tension from the Führer's compartment radiated through the train. Then the train screeched to a stop at a station, and the stationmaster handed up a message. It was rushed to the Führer's compartment.

Hitler had once been congratulated by King Edward VIII for his stability. The king had indicated that he approved of a resurgent Germany. "At last," said Hitler after reading the message, "the King of England will not intervene. He is keeping his promise. That means it can go well."

Hitler knew that he had won the Rhineland—and much more. He had won two victories: one over the western Allies, who had demonstrated they would not fight, and one over the German generals, who had been too timid. His ego now soared to new heights, setting the stage for a major future error. No longer would Hitler have much confidence in the judgment of his generals. His intuition had proved right. He would rely on that in the future.

Until the Rhineland, Hitler had relied upon the German generals as his base of power. Now he saw that they had feet of clay. His contempt was complete; he no longer feared the army; he had amassed more real power of his own. He could see that the generals, whom he had feared for so long, were now psychologically incapable of resisting him and that there was no danger of a coup against him.

April 1: With a fine sense of irony, Hitler made von Blomberg the first Nazi field marshal and promoted Werner von Fritsch, chief of staff of the army, to colonel general. But while the uniforms were bedecked, the men were demeaned: from this point on, Hitler had little use for their counsel, and more and more they were excluded from his circle of advisers.

Within months the generals began to react. Nothing happened, but their resentment burned. They saw themselves losing power. They disliked Nazi foreign policy with all its adventurism. Hitler, they saw, was headed for war: ultimately the French and British would have to fight, no matter what the Führer believed. The policy in the east—alignment with Japan, which Hitler was seeking; rapprochement with Poland, which he had already courted—brought the threat of war with the Soviet Union. To the generals this meant another two-front war, and they shuddered to contemplate it.

Autumn 1936: The Führer's contempt for the army generals seeped down into the ranks of the Nazi party. Heinrich Himmler, the leader of the SS, saw his opportunity to climb toward greater power over the backs of the generals. He began a smear campaign against the leading officers. Von Fritsch and his friends, Himmler told Hitler, were planning to overthrow the Nazi regime and restore the kaiser to the throne. Himmler's deputy, Reinhardt Heydrich, a 32-year-old former naval officer who had been drummed out of the service after his involvement with a teenage girl, was quick to take up the cudgels. Heydrich hated the Officer Corps and the system that had wrecked his naval career over a matter of "honor." Under the new Hitler Youth program girls such as the one with whom he had dallied were being deflowered every day without complaint. Himmler had given him the power to do something about his resentment: Heydrich was now head of the *Sicherheitsdienst,* the secret security service of the SS, and head of the Gestapo. From these positions he could plot to humble old-school military officers like those who once had humbled him.

*   *   *

Actually, there were no plots against the party or Hitler within the army. General Beck and his associates might believe Hitler's foreign policy disastrous, but the successful march into the Rhineland had destroyed much of the military hierarchy's self-confidence. There would be no coup.

Hitler really did not pay much attention to the charges of disloyalty made against the army by Himmler and Heydrich. He was used to subordinates who tried to backstab one another to enhance their own positions. He could sense that the generals were not united in anything. His main concern about them was whether or not they would fight. He no longer worried about the prospect of their en-

gaging in politics; he had convincing indications that they were not—
and would not do so in the future.

In that summer of 1936 Hitler's mind was on other matters: mostly
on achieving for Germany a new respect.

The first step in this campaign to attain world prominence was
staged at the Olympic Games of 1936 in Berlin. In spite of one re-
vealing incident involving the American black runner Jesse Owens,
which emphasized Nazi racism, the Olympic Games of 1936 were a
triumph for Josef Goebbels's propaganda machine. Germany was
shown as flourishing, strong, and genial. The "Jews Not Welcome"
signs had been removed from shop windows, beer garden entrances, and theater box offices. The persecution of the Jews was halted
for the summer. Goebbels and Göring gave parties for visiting dignitaries; one night Goebbels had a thousand guests. The games were
a grand success, particularly with some Americans and Britishers
who began to believe—at least some of them—that Germany was
on the road to prosperity and happiness and that "that fellow Hitler
can't be so bad after all."

The summer of 1936 was also marked by the signing of a new agreement between Austria and Germany. The Germans affirmed the independence of Austria and promised not to interfere with Austrian
internal affairs. Even as the agreement was signed, Franz von Papen,
now German ambassador to Vienna, wrote Hitler, "National Socialism must and will overpower the new Austrian ideology."

Several secret codicils to the agreement opened the door for the
Nazis to infiltrate the Austrian government, particularly one para-
graph in which that government conceded the appointment of a specified number of National Opposition (Nazi) supporters to positions
of importance.

Throughout the summer Europe saw a frenzy of Fascist initia-
tives. Mussolini conquered Ethiopia, and the League of Nations stood
by dumbly and watched it happen. General Francisco Franco rebelled
against the Spanish republic, and civil war began. Within a week Hitler was supporting the Franco forces with guns and aircraft. So was
Mussolini. The lines were drawn in western Europe then: the totalitarian states against the democracies. Mussolini poured men as well
as money and equipment into Spain. But the rewards went to Hitler,
for by prolonging the Spanish Civil War, he kept France off balance

and made it impossible for the British to reach a rapprochement with Mussolini, which they would have liked to have done to safeguard their interests in the Mediterranean.

October 1936: Hitler was drawing Mussolini to him like a spider bringing in a fly from its web. The Rome-Berlin Axis was established by treaty, providing for a common stance by Italy and Germany against the other European countries.

November 1936: Germany and Japan signed an anti-Comintern treaty. The Japanese people were not very happy about it, but the Japanese army had achieved control of the political mechanism and, having swallowed Manchuria, was moving to control the rest of China. The treaty with the Germans would keep the Russians from interfering.

*   *   *

Autumn 1937: For months Europe had been quiet, with only the sound of guns from Spain punctuating the silence. Hitler was engaged in building up his forces. His architect, Albert Speer, was beginning to change the face of Berlin, creating the colossal edifices that Hitler wanted for his capital in order to surpass the grandeur of Paris and Rome. A great new avenue was to course across the city, with an enormous new meeting hall on the north side near the Reichstag. This huge avenue was to be broader and longer than the Champs-Elysées in Paris. In every way Berlin was to be fitted out with the masonry of a capital city befitting the magnificence of the Thousand-Year Reich.

Germans were being reeducated and indoctrinated in the precepts of nazism, and most of them did not mind at all. Hitler had brought back German self-respect; his enormous rearmament program had brought back prosperity. To the German people in the summer and fall of 1937 life seemed very sweet; all Europe listened when Berlin spoke, but Berlin spoke of peace and prosperity. The present was good and so were the prospects.

November 5: Five men appeared at the Reich Chancellery for a meeting with the Führer. They were:

Field Marshal von Blomberg, minister of war and commander in chief of the armed forces

Colonel General Baron von Fritsch, commander in chief of the army

Admiral Raeder, commander in chief of the navy

Colonel General Göring, commander in chief of the Luftwaffe

Baron von Neurath, foreign minister of the Reich

Hitler appeared at 4:15 in the afternoon and began to speak. He had been thinking over the condition and direction of Germany, and he now wished to make clear to these men the plan he had for the future:

> The aim of German policy is to make secure and to preserve the racial community and enlarge it. It is a question of space, *Lebensraum*. The German people have a right to a greater living space than other peoples. Germany's future is therefore wholly conditional upon the solving of the need for space.

Britain and France, Hitler warned, stood in Germany's way. They were "hate-inspired countries." Ultimately Germany would have to fight them, and to fight Russia. At the moment, however, he was sure that the British and French had already written off Czechoslovakia. So Hitler would annex that country as well as Austria.

For four hours Hitler talked. His subordinates could hardly believe what they were hearing. The Führer was telling them that Germany was definitely going to war; the only question that remained was the exact date and the order in which the Germans took on their enemies. When Hitler finished, the leaders of his military forces and diplomatic corps knew what was coming.

For anyone who cared to consider the problem, it had all been laid down in the pages of *Mein Kampf* in the 1920s. Only now Hitler was more specific. He told his underlings that they must be ready for war by 1938 and that it would most certainly come by 1943.

After the speech questions were asked by Field Marshal von Blomberg, by General von Fritsch, and by Baron von Neurath. It was apparent that they were appalled by the plan. Hitler did not like the type of questions they asked, and he did not forget who had asked them.

The meeting broke up and all the high-ranking officers went home. Hitler retired to ponder his next moves, among them the need to make changes in high places.

Himmler and Heydrich were waiting in the wings with their stories of the disloyalty of many in the army High Command. And though Hitler still did not believe them completely, their repetition began to tell.

Von Neurath, who had a weak heart, suffered several seizures in the next few days as he contemplated the enormity of the Führer's message. The foreign policy von Neurath had tried to pursue was aimed at preserving peace while giving the Germans maneuvering space; what Hitler demanded was outright confrontation with the expectation that it would lead to war.

Von Neurath was so upset that he sought out General Beck, the army chief of staff, and General von Fritsch, the army commander, and discussed with them methods by which Hitler might be persuaded to alter his policy. The meetings were duly noted by informers of the Gestapo and SS. General Beck prepared a written critique of Hitler's plans, showing how they were doomed to failure. But he showed it to no one. He and von Fritsch did agree that the latter would seek another meeting with Hitler to try to change the Führer's mind. Von Fritsch did see Hitler again, on November 9. He got nowhere, except for raising new suspicions about himself.

The Führer learned of the foreign minister's continuing opposition to his plan. Secluded at his house at Berchtesgaden, Hitler would not permit his foreign minister to call upon him. It was not until the middle of January 1938 that von Neurath managed another appointment.

Hitler had problems with others of his cabinet as well. Hjalmar Schacht, the official whose acumen was responsible for financing the Third Reich, had bluntly told Hitler that the plan—devised by the party's inner circle—to make Germany "self-sufficient" in four years was impossible to fulfill. So Hitler cooled toward Schacht and put Göring in charge of implementing the plan. Schacht, who still had important responsibilities in regard to the economy, found

Göring less than an economic genius, and he determined to give up his own position in despair. Schacht went to Berchtesgaden and handed in his resignation as economic czar of Germany. Hitler did not want to accept it, but Schacht insisted. There was no way he could bail the Nazis out of the economic mess they were creating, he said. Neither would recourse to printing more money help the situation; the German experience of 1922–1923 had proved that to both men. Hitler insisted that, for the sake of world opinion, the highly regarded Schacht stay in the cabinet, and the Führer made him minister without portfolio. He also retained Schacht as president of the Reichsbank, but Schacht's influence on Hitler was at an end because he had dared to argue. That, of course, was one of Hitler's fundamental and continuing errors in the management of Germany: as the years rolled along, he found it easier to work with toadies than with independent people. Little by little the toadies were taking over, and the independent minds were leaving the Nazi hierarchy. Some, indeed, were about to be pushed.

3

A NEW
WEHRMACHT

Three days before Christmas, 1937, Field Marshal Werner von Blomberg, chief of all Germany's armed forces, approached his Führer and asked if he might get married. Such was Hitler's power over his associates that the request did not seem in the slightest bit out of place. The occasion of the request was a bit outré: the funeral of General Erich Ludendorff, Hitler's associate in the ill-fated Munich "beer-hall putsch." But even that juxtaposition was in its way symbolic. Ludendorff was the last of the old, and Blomberg was the first of the new military leaders under the Nazi regime. Ludendorff would never have thought of asking Hitler for permission to marry. Von Blomberg would not have thought of marrying without that permission.

If Hitler did not show surprise at his field marshal's request, it was because he already knew all about it, the name of the girl, and the fact that Blomberg had interrupted his dalliance with the young lady at a resort hotel to come to this funeral. Himmler and Heydrich were continuing to keep close tabs on the German generals, reporting to Hitler any juicy little bits of scandal that they thought might ingratiate them with their Führer.

Von Blomberg reminded Hitler that his wife had died five years before. If his Führer would give his gracious consent, there was nothing to stop him from marrying again.

Hitler knew that the girl was Fräulein Erna Grühn. She worked for the Reich Egg Board. The fact that she was less than half von Blomberg's age was not very important. Why should not a general marry youth in the autumn of his life?

Hitler not only gave his consent, he agreed to act as a witness to the wedding, and he dragooned Hermann Göring, the chief of the Luftwaffe, to be another. The wedding was held on January 12 in the War Ministry, and the happy couple set off immediately to resume their interrupted idyll.

Toward the end of January Count von Helldorf, the chief of police of Berlin, called on General Wilhelm Keitel, von Blomberg's chief of staff, and questioned the morals of Field Marshal von Blomberg's new wife. Keitel, who said he had seen the lady only at the graveside during the funeral ceremonies for von Blomberg's mother a few days earlier, said he did not know what she looked like.

Keitel did not want to get into the matter. But Count von Helldorf persisted and finally pulled out of his pocket a change of address registration card with a photograph of a young woman named Erna Grühn on the card. The card reported her move from an apartment to von Blomberg's flat in the Ministry of War building on Tirpitzufer. It had been sent to the chief by the local police station.

Was this von Blomberg's wife?

General Keitel would not answer the question. But Count von Helldorf was insistent, and from his agitation Keitel could tell that something out of the ordinary was involved here.

So, as Keitel reported in his memoirs, he telephoned von Blomberg's office. The minister was not available. He had gone out to put his mother's affairs in order.

Von Helldorf listened to the conversation and saw Keitel's puzzlement. Finally he came out with the truth: Fräulein Erna Grühn was a common prostitute.

Keitel said he was distressed and offered to show the card to von Blomberg. The field marshal, he said, would undoubtedly dissolve the marriage if this were proved to be true. But Count von Helldorf would not let the card out of his hands. Keitel then referred him to Hermann Göring who, as a witness to the wedding, must know the young lady by sight. Keitel telephoned Göring's office, and von Helldorf immediately went over there.

That evening, von Helldorf telephoned Keitel. Göring had confirmed the identity. The bride of the field marshal was indeed none other than the prostitute Erna Grühn. It was, said the chief of police of Berlin, a catastrophe of the first order.

Hitler had gone to Munich to open an arts and crafts exhibition. On January 24 he came home early in the evening and found Göring waiting for him at the Chancellery. Göring seemed agitated. He asked to speak to Hitler privately, and the Führer took him into the study.

Göring could not contain himself. "Blomberg has married a whore. He tricked us into being witnesses."

Hitler opened the folder. It confirmed in detail all that he did not want to know. Photos showed the girl in various sexual poses with a man and a wax candle. The details of her life were there: she had moved in with a man at the age of 18, and soon she was posing for pornographic photographs. When they were sold in Berlin, the man had been arrested and so had Erna Grühn. She was released because it was apparent that she had been duped and had not profited from the transaction. After that, she had never been arrested, nor had any fingers of suspicion pointed her way.

Hitler erupted in fury. So this was how his generals repaid his confidence! He ordered Göring to tell von Blomberg about the lady's criminal past. If von Blomberg was prepared to have the marriage dissolved on the spot, Hitler would find a way to avoid a public scandal. Count von Helldorf had already been sworn to secrecy, and he had, in turn, told his police officials that not a word was to be said.

But that incident was enough for Hitler. He agreed with Göring that von Blomberg had inveigled them into giving their approval to the marriage and into standing up with him to put the seal on it.

"Is there nothing I can be spared?" asked the miserable Führer.

"Blomberg will have to resign," insisted Göring. Hitler said nothing. He accompanied Göring to the entrance hall and then withdrew to his private apartment. Göring's ambition to become defense minister was well known, and his satisfaction at von Blomberg's plight was apparent to many, including Hitler.

*

So the first real military management crisis truly had arisen. If von Blomberg was to go—and he had a real following among the senior military officers—who was to succeed him? Hitler would have to choose the new war minister and chief of the armed services either from the Officer Corps or from the ranks of the party faithful.

The principal army candidate was General Werner von Fritsch, chief of the land forces; those from the party were Göring and Himmler.

What of von Fritsch? He was a plumber of a general; he knew all the rules but he had little imagination. He still had not grasped the real possibilities of the armored division: speed, maneuverability, and enormous power; he underestimated the psychological shock value of massed armor, as well as its ability of appearing as a virtually impregnable defense.

Further, and this was a much more serious charge in the book of Hitler, a man who had been trumpeting so long the call for racial purity that he had become a sort of Nazi puritan in his approach to the personal lives of his subordinates, von Fritsch had breached the moral code, and worse, he threatened to embarrass the Führer. A new man must take over.

Himmler had a dossier on the general, one which consisted almost entirely of a statement by a known homosexual, a blackmailer, who claimed that von Fritsch was one of his clients. Himmler had tried to show this dossier to Hitler in 1936, but Hitler told him to destroy it. Himmler did nothing of the kind. Again in 1937 he pulled out the dossier and put it in front of Hitler. Once again Hitler refused to look at it. Now the SS leader mentioned it again, apparently reading the Führer's mind and knowing that von Fritsch, whatever his failings of military talent, still would be deemed far and away superior to himself in that regard.

Hitler was exasperated with the whole von Blomberg affair and the implications that the army was full of sex deviates. He decided to call in von Fritsch and put the whole problem to him. At 2:15 on the morning of January 25 Hitler summoned his military adjutant, Colonel Friedrich Hossbach, to come to the Chancellery and talk. Hossbach believed Hitler must be joking, and he didn't appear. So the Führer stayed awake all night in his great dark bed, brooding over the difficulties his generals were causing him.

After daybreak, Göring came bustling around, full of himself and obviously enjoying his role in the crisis. He said he had seen General Keitel and had told him to have a talk with von Blomberg. Keitel found that von Blomberg was as furious as Hitler. He felt he had been betrayed. Had Hitler and Göring stood behind him, there would have been no trouble, he said. The girl had only one unfortunate incident in her past. Although von Blomberg was talking like a rational man, appearances were more important than reality in the Third Reich.

Von Blomberg, who spoke with General Keitel that day, laid the blame for the whole problem on Göring's ambition to succeed him as minister of defense, and certainly there was much to that allegation. Later that day Hitler and von Blomberg met. Hitler put it squarely to his hitherto favorite general: Would he abandon the woman? No, said von Blomberg. She was his wife. She had committed an early indiscretion, but he loved her and he would not abandon her. Hitler then grimly told the field marshal that he would have to resign, and von Blomberg said calmly that he was ready for that.

The announcement was prepared. Field Marshal von Blomberg was resigning from his office as chief of defense for reasons of ill health. He and his wife were going to take a long journey.

Hitler still thought enough of von Blomberg and his popularity among the generals that he asked the sacked officer whom he believed should succeed him. That long trip mentioned in the press release had been Hitler's idea. "If war comes," Hitler said, "you will be again at my side." Meanwhile, said Hitler, the government granted von Blomberg a free trip around the world and the right to stay away from Germany for at least a year. So they parted amicably enough, and von Blomberg headed for Italy.

The von Blomberg crisis had its secondary fallout, which was the jettisoning of General von Fritsch. Hitler now was prepared to believe evil of almost anyone, and the von Fritsch scandal ate at him. But there was a silver lining, for he saw in this matter a chance to permanently cement his power over the generals.

Keitel and Göring now had a frank talk during the course of which Göring admitted that, as chief of the Luftwaffe, he did not like the idea of taking orders from other generals and that he wanted to give the orders from that point on. The savvy but relatively apolitical Keitel then endeared himself to the powerful Nazi by suggesting that Göring was indeed the frontrunner for the Defense Ministry job.

At five o'clock on the afternoon of January 26 (Hitler always was a late worker—sometimes his conferences went on until two or three o'clock in the morning) Keitel was summoned to the Reich Chancellery for a conference. Whom did Keitel suggest for the Defense Ministry? Hitler asked.

Keitel said he thought Göring ought to have the job, and he explained why: Göring did not want to take orders from the army.

That was too bad, said Hitler. No, Hermann was not the one for the job. He already had too many responsibilities: the Luftwaffe, the economic four-year plan, chief executive officer of Prussia, and a host of others. Besides, Göring, as the predestined successor to Hitler as Führer, needed some more political experience. The Defense Ministry was not the place for that.

Then Keitel suggested General von Fritsch. Hitler went to his desk and produced a Justice Ministry indictment of General von Fritsch for the penal offense of homosexuality. Hitler insisted he could no longer ignore the matter; the Defense Ministry was at issue—the whole case would have to be thoroughly investigated.

If von Fritsch were cleared, asked Hitler, then whom would Keitel suggest for von Fritsch's old job as army chief?

Von Brauchitsch, replied Keitel.

All right, said Hitler. He would talk to both men, and Keitel was to return the next day.

When Keitel returned to the *Reichskanzlerei* the following day, he found Hitler very agitated. The Führer said that he had seen von Fritsch and that his impression was not good when he had suddenly questioned him about the homosexual charge. Besides, Himmler and company had brought the blackmailer out of prison and stood him in a corner of the entry to the Chancellery when von Fritsch entered; the man had sworn that von Fritsch was the officer whom he had seen engaging in sexual relations with a lad in November 1933.

So Hitler had straightaway relieved von Fritsch as commander of the army, and for the time being confined him to his flat. He had also issued an announcement to the press that von Fritsch had resigned due to ill health.

Keitel said that the welfare of the armed forces required fast ac-

tion to fill the two new vacancies. Hitler said he was going to take
over the defense post himself, temporarily. That was a shock for
the army. Never before in modern German history had the armed
services reported to anyone except a military officer, and he to the
political leader. Hitler had changed the whole armed forces command mechanism with that one move.

Before Keitel could digest that information, Hitler said that Keitel was to remain as his chief of staff. If that did not work out, then
Keitel would be appointed chief of the army.

That night Keitel visited General von Fritsch. The general showed
Keitel his resignation, which he had just written out, and his demand
for trial by court-martial. Keitel agreed that this would be necessary if
von Fritsch's name was to be cleared.

Hitler did not like the idea at first, but suddenly agreed that it
was necessary. A court was appointed, with Göring as chief judge.
The others were the commanders in chief of the other armed services, with two professional judges to assist them on points of law.

In the following days Hitler consulted many people about the defense matter. General Beck was interviewed, and so was General
Gerd von Rundstedt, who would have been ideal in von Fritsch's
old post but was deemed too old. Admiral Raeder's advice was so-
licited too.

The one serious problem with von Brauchitsch was that he had
been very loud in his denunciation of national socialism and Nazi activities in the past. Hitler knew all that; Himmler had reported on the
matter. Now von Brauchitsch was called in to talk. Keitel warned him
that he had best be careful what he said, and von Brauchitsch was
careful. After the talks were over Hitler was convinced that the general shared all his views on military and social matters. On February
4, 1938, General von Brauchitsch was appointed commander in chief
of the army. General Keitel was appointed chief of Oberkommando
der Wehrmacht. This was the big change. Keitel was, in effect, supreme commander of the military forces under Adolf Hitler. In other
words, the Defense Ministry as such remained in Hitler's hands, and
would continue to do so, but Keitel became the officer with the greatest military *authority* in the land under the new system. As a sop for
the refusal to make Göring defense minister, Hitler made him a field

marshal, which meant Göring was now the highest *ranking* active duty officer in the Reich, although the power over the army still rested in Hitler's hands and, on strictly military matters, in the hands of Keitel.

At the time, General Keitel believed all that had happened was only a temporary change. After von Fritsch was acquitted, as he was certain the general must be, affairs would return to normal and the military caste would once again direct the nation's military activities as it had done since 1918.

Himmler and his associates now invested every effort to destroy General von Fritsch. The general employed a lawyer named Count Rüdiger von der Goltz, whose previous clients had included Goebbels. Himmler introduced a document to show that von der Goltz himself also had been a victim of the blackmailer. But the lawyer was able to prove that it was a case of mistaken identity. Otto Schmidt, the blackmailer, had made those false charges against a lawyer named Herbert Goltz, and that man was dead.

Himmler was hardly abashed. He kept trying. As the von Fritsch trial came up, von der Goltz proved that the "von Fritsch" referred to by blackmailer Schmidt was really a retired cavalry captain, Achim von Frisch. The names were even spelled differently! The lawyer produced the receipt from Schmidt for 2500 marks he'd been paid by von Frisch.

General Walther Heitz of the court took this alarming news to Hitler, and Hitler was at first determined to call off the von Fritsch trial. But Himmler intervened. The Fritsch and Frisch cases, he said, were quite different.

So the trial went on, beginning March 10, 1938.

Göring was the hero of the trial, oddly enough. In his cross-examination of the blackmailer, Schmidt, he proved that Schmidt could not have been telling the truth about von Fritsch, and Schmidt finally confessed that his whole testimony had been a tissue of lies. The lies had been assembled by the Gestapo, and on the eve of the trial the head of the Gestapo homosexual branch had threatened Schmidt with death if he did not stick to his sworn testimony. Himmler had put the Gestapo up to all of it.

That day the court erupted in furor, and it became apparent that there was no case at all against von Fritsch. He was honorably acquitted.

But what did acquittal mean to a military man who had been deprived of his command?

General von Brauchitsch sought an interview with Hitler to clear von Fritsch in every way. The Führer agreed that von Fritsch was innocent, but he postponed action. Von Fritsch fumed, and then he sat down and wrote a twelve-point indictment of the Gestapo and of Heinrich Himmler and concluded by challenging Himmler to a duel with pistols. The difficulty was that he could get no one to deliver the challenge. Göring refused. Keitel refused. Hitler would not hear of it.

Hitler still refused to act. What was needed was a public statement of support for von Fritsch. The army waited. The statement did not come. Hitler did not want to make a public statement, but Keitel reported that the generals were getting into an ugly mood. With all the military matters now coming to a head, Austria having been taken over and the Czechoslovakian crisis in process, Hitler decided something had to be done unless he wanted to face a mass resignation of senior officers of the army, which still would be very dangerous to him and the Nazi movement.

The generals were furious that Hitler had not announced publicly the verdict on von Fritsch and the implication of Himmler and Heydrich in the plot. Some of them even dared hope that the resulting scandal would topple Hitler.

Berlin was tense with the impending crisis. There was talk that the generals were preparing a rebellion against the Nazis. The French ambassador heard all sorts of rumors which he passed on to Paris, and thence they made their way to London.

Hitler knew the crisis could ruin him. He called a secret meeting of the generals at a remote Pomeranian airfield and there had read out to the officers the acquittal of General von Fritsch. Hitler then called on his generals for sympathy. He had told the people of Germany that von Fritsch had resigned because of ill health. What was he now to tell them? He could not tell the truth, could he?

Himmler had been busy covering his own indiscretions in this matter, throwing the blame on his subordinates, and Hitler believed him.

"The allegations against General von Fritsch were not malicious," the Führer said. "A minor official blundered." He had ordered the blackmailer to be shot. He appealed for the confidence of the army. The generals would simply have to follow his lead. Von Fritsch was the unfortunate victim of circumstance, and although the Führer sympathized with him mightily, there was nothing to be done.

So the von Fritsch affair ended there. That day many of the generals left the Pomeranian airfield believing that their Führer had indeed been faced with an impossible situation and that the army must go along. General von Fritsch saw it more clearly. He knew who the culprits were: Himmler and Heydrich in his case; Göring and Himmler in the case of von Blomberg.

Von Fritsch talked it all over with General Keitel. Either Hitler would have to make a decision one day to make sure that "people like Himmler and Heydrich get their deserts, or he will continue to cover for the misdeeds of these people, which case I fear for the future," he said.

The generals soon settled down. Von Fritsch retired and said very little to anyone except a few friends. Privately his view was that Hitler had taken over the army and every other aspect of German power. He had gotten rid of Foreign Minister von Neurath and replaced him with the malleable Joachim von Ribbentrop. "This man—Hitler—is Germany's destiny for good and for evil. If he now goes over the abyss—he will drag us all down with him. There is nothing we can do."

4

ANSCHLUSS OF AUSTRIA

Hitler's assumption of the position of war minister had forever shattered the power of the German army's officer class. From that time on the officials of the foreign office, too, would be totally subservient to him. The German army was now only one of the three supports of the Third Reich, equal to, but not superior to (as in the past), the Nazi party and the German government.

Hitler had really been very lucky in that winter of 1938. The crisis over von Fritsch's removal might have been far more serious except for a turn of events outside Germany—events which had kept the army from concentrating its resources on the von Fritsch affair. These were the political developments in Austria.

At a secret meeting in November 1937, when Hitler had revealed his plans for conquest to his generals and admirals, he had called for the annexation of Austria. Actually, however, nothing had been done by the German government to further this plan. That is not, however, to say that nothing was being done by Germans and by Austrians to bring about the fall of the Austrian government. The Nazi party of Austria, financed and supported by the Nazi party of Germany, was extremely active in subversion in its homeland and had been since 1934.

Indeed, Hitler's ambassador to Vienna, Franz von Papen, found the Austrian Nazi leader, Captain Josef Leopold, to be a painful thorn in his side. Leopold was continually blowing up bridges and frightening people, while von Papen was trying to work for the Austrian annexation through much higher authority. Making insidious efforts, too, was the pro-Nazi Viennese lawyer Arthur Seyss-Inquart, who had high hopes for a diplomatic course of action.

Early in January 1938 some disquieting rumors coursed through Vienna. One of the local Nazis had bragged to the private secretary to Sir Oswald Moseley, the British Fascist, that Austria would be taken over by Germany before spring. Hermann Göring, discussing his four-year economic plan with foreigners, had announced that the problem of paying cash for Austrian raw materials would disappear in the spring.

All this came to a head on January 27 in Vienna, when the Austrian chancellor, Dr. Kurt von Schuschnigg, discovered one of Captain Leopold's more devious plots: the overthrow of the Austrian central government by force. The discovery was the result of a raid on the headquarters of a group named the Committee of Seven; the premises were actually the office of the Austrian Nazi underground movement. The raid produced documents initialed by Rudolf Hess, Hitler's deputy, indicating that the Nazis in Austria were to stage an open revolt in the spring of 1938. When, as was expected, von Schuschnigg attempted to put down the revolt by calling out the Austrian army, the German army would march across the border "to prevent German blood from being shed by Germans," as Hess had put it. Ambassador von Papen could not have been very happy about the report, for the plan called for his murder by Austrian Nazis to provide another excuse for German intervention.

Then von Papen learned on February 4 that he had been fired from his job. It was part of Hitler's "cleanup" after the von Fritsch affair, part of the gathering into his own hands of all the power of the state. Von Papen had been an appointee of Baron von Neurath. Von Neurath had gone, and therefore von Papen had to go.

Von Papen scurried off to Germany on February 5, straight to Berchtesgaden, to see Hitler in order to find out what was going on. There he learned about the struggle with the generals from a Hitler who was almost exhausted from the strains of the recent weeks. Von Papen considered the problems and suggested to Hitler that von Schuschnigg be invited to Berchtesgaden to talk things over

with the Führer and perhaps to arrange something mutually agreeable for the future of Austria.

Hitler was intrigued by the idea, although his idea of something
"mutually agreeable" was not precisely what von Papen had in
mind. Hitler "unfired" von Papen immediately and sent him hur-
rying back to Vienna to arrange for the meeting.

Von Schuschnigg, von Papen discovered, was inclined to be coy.
He understood that should he go to Berchtesgaden, he would be
walking into the lion's den, so he made some conditions. First, he
said, the agreement of 1936, which guaranteed the independence of
Austria and noninterference by Germany in Austrian affairs, must
be reaffirmed. Off went von Papen to Germany again, to return with
Hitler's assurances that he only wanted to talk about "a few differences" that had arisen since the agreement was signed.

So on February 11, 1938, Chancellor von Schuschnigg set off on a
secret special train for Salzburg. The next morning he would drive
by car across the border to Hitler's mountain retreat at Berchtesgaden. The meeting at "the Eagle's Nest" promised to be fate-
ful for both sides.

Chancellor von Schuschnigg set out for Berchtesgaden. The Austrian section of the road was filled with "Austrian Legion" troops—
Nazi supported and Nazi supplied. There were 120,000 of them in the
area, outnumbering Austria's legal army by 2 to 1. Von Schuschnigg
was made well aware of this on his approach. When he entered Germany and reached Berchtesgaden, the SS sentry at the gate that protected Hitler's "eyrie" spoke with an unmistakable Austrian accent.
Von Schuschnigg arrived at the house. Hitler came down the steps to
greet him, the Führer in his usual brown jacket, black trousers, and
red swastika armband. He was accompanied by two of his fiercest-
looking generals. Hitler wasted no time in telling von Schuschnigg who
was boss. First he told the Austrian chancellor to get rid of the fortifications along the German frontier, "as otherwise [he] was going to
send a couple of engineer battalions to clear them up for him."

Hitler had a habit, once he started on an issue, of working himself up into a frenzy. He did so that day. Soon he began to shout:

You have done everything to avoid a friendly policy. The whole
history of Austria is just one uninterrupted act of high treason.

That was so in the past and is no better today. This historical paradox must now reach its overdue end. And I can tell you right now, Herr Schuschnigg, that I am absolutely determined to make an end of all this. The German Reich is one of the great powers and nobody will raise his voice if it settles its border problems.

At first they talked alone in the first-floor study. Or, rather, Hitler talked. Though von Schuschnigg had come to confer, he found himself being lectured like a schoolboy. Hitler told him frankly that he had planned to invade Austria on February 27 but that he had, for the first time in his life (this was anything but true), changed his mind. Now he had another plan. Austria would have a chance to work out its destiny. But von Schuschnigg had to come to terms that very day, or else. That morning von Schuschnigg objected strenuously to the whole idea.

At lunch Hitler brought out three generals who had been invited to Berchtesgaden for the day as window dressing, and he discoursed loudly about the new weapons of the Luftwaffe and the panzer armies he was building. Von Schuschnigg toyed with his food. Hitler then changed his tone and began to speak grandly of rebuilding Hamburg, of making all Germany a paradise of modernism. Skyscrapers taller than those in New York, a huge bridge across the river Elbe, all this was in Hitler's plans.

After luncheon the Austrian chancellor and his foreign undersecretary were left in a small room to wait. They waited two hours. Finally they were taken into the presence of German Foreign Minister von Ribbentrop and Ambassador von Papen. Von Ribbentrop handed the Austrian chancellor a two-page document. "These," he said, "are the Führer's final demands, and he will not discuss them."

The demands, von Schuschnigg discovered, called for him virtually to turn his government over to the Nazis. The ban against the Nazi party, imposed because of notable and proven disloyalty, had to be lifted immediately. All Nazis put in jail for any crimes at all (even murder) were to be amnestied. Seyss-Inquart was to be made minister of the interior, which amounted to putting the ministry into Hitler's hands, and would be in charge of police and security matters. Another Nazi, Edmund Glaise-Horstenau, was to be appointed minister of war. Preparations were to be made for the assimilation of the Austrian economy into the German economy.

(Small wonder that Göring was talking about suspending payments for Austrian raw materials.)

Not surprisingly, Chancellor von Schuschnigg did not like the terms, and he said as much. Von Ribbentrop was unsympathetic. These were the Führer's terms. They argued. Finally Ribbentrop went out to find Hitler. He had reached agreement with Schuschnigg on all points except the appointment of Seyss-Inquart.

Hitler said that if Schuschnigg did not agree, he would invade Austria that very day. At one point Hitler asked Schuschnigg to step outside; then the Führer bellowed for General Keitel. Keitel came into his office with an inquisitive look on his face, but Hitler told him only to sit down and say nothing. The dumb play went on for ten minutes, while outside von Schuschnigg wondered what Hitler was up to.

Finally, von Schuschnigg agreed to everything Hitler demanded. Then he and his foreign undersecretary drove back down the mountains to Salzburg. The road looked the same, but it was not. Nothing would be the same again. Austria had just been sold out.

The evidence of that was not long in coming, although Hitler insisted that the only report of the meeting be a simple statement that the two men had met at Berchtesgaden. Nothing else.

Meanwhile German preparations for an eventual invasion of Austria began in earnest. In case von Schuschnigg should have some second thoughts, Hitler staged what appeared to be preparations for immediate invasion. A military headquarters was opened in Munich, and troop units were moved around. The problem was that Chancellor von Schuschnigg had returned to Austria and conferred with Austrian President Wilhelm Miklas, who also did not like the concessions. By February 14 rumors were racing through Vienna to the effect that the Germans were preparing an invasion within the week.

Hitler had given von Schuschnigg until February 15 to announce that the Berchtesgaden agreement would be carried out by the eighteenth. On February 15 President Miklas gave in, and on the sixteenth the general amnesty for Austrian Nazis was announced and Seyss-Inquart was named minister of the interior. The next day he went to Berlin to get his orders.

On February 20, 1938, Hitler spoke to the Reichstag, and gave a very clear warning to the world regarding his plans for the future:

Over ten million Germans live in two of the states adjoining our frontiers.

Austria apparently had been a puppet; it was just a matter of time before Czechoslovakia's turn would come.

Still, the last acts of the Austrian drama had to be played out. Hitler was concerned lest Italy, which claimed a special relationship with Austria, decide to move to stop the takeover. This was quite conceivable, except that Mussolini would need the support of England and France to intercede, and his invasion of Ethiopia as well as his support of the Fascists in the Spanish civil war had eroded those relationships. For a little while it seemed that the Austrians might get their backs up. In a speech to the Austrian Bundestag on February 24, von Schuschnigg indicated that Austria would make no more concessions to Germany. But no more concessions were really needed. For even as von Schuschnigg spoke, a crowd of 20,000 Nazis swept through Graz, tore down the Austrian red, white, and red flag, and raised the Nazi swastika banner. Since the police were under the command of the Nazi Seyss-Inquart, no attempt was made to do the slightest thing to stop the rioting.

Von Schuschnigg was ruing the day he had ever driven across the mountains from Salzburg. What could he do? He decided on one final desperate step: he would call for a plebiscite to decide one question, one question alone: "Are you in favor of a free, independent, Social, Christian and united Austria, or not?"

On the evening of March 9, Chancellor von Schuschnigg announced the plebiscite. It would be held in four days, on Sunday, March 13.

When Hitler learned of the von Schuschnigg plan, he was furious, although not particularly surprised. He knew that the terms he had insisted on were going to mean the end of independent Austria, and he knew that Schuschnigg and the president were not fooled. He had hoped that the indications of force majeure would carry the day, but he had to be prepared to carry his bluff further and, if nec-

essary, to actually pull together his resources and stage an invasion, risking all the dangers such an act would lead to in terms of
the big powers of western Europe.

Hitler called for Göring and Keitel. He decided that the German
army, unprepared as it might be, must move into Austria before that
Sunday vote. The generals began work, drafting orders to move fast.
On the night of March 10, Thursday, they sent out mobilization orders to three army corps and to the Luftwaffe. The invasion was
set for March 12.

The key figure was Austrian Security Minister Seyss-Inquart. A
telegram for his signature was drafted in Berlin appealing to Hitler
to send troops to restore order because of bloodshed in Vienna. The
telegram was sent to Vienna for Seyss-Inquart to send back to Berlin. Also, a speech was prepared and sent down for Seyss-Inquart
to make on March 11, stating that the plebiscite was unconstitu-
tional. Hitler capped it all by drafting a threatening note to Chancellor von Schuschnigg.

Hitler's real fear was that France and Britain might step in to
help Mussolini stop him.

But the plans went ahead. There was no way of stopping them
and still maintaining the momentum Hitler had generated. Further,
all this came at a most dangerous time—in the middle of the von
Fritsch scandal. The Austrian crisis gave the generals something to
think about, something in which they could submerge their griev-
ances over their loss of political power. It was, as Hitler knew, still
conceivable that the army could regain its power by rebelling openly
against him. In that case his chances of survival were no more than
fifty-fifty. The army still had the organization and the weapons to
enforce its will. But Hitler had sapped that will with the successful
bluff he had run at the Rhineland, when every general predicted disaster. Now he would keep the generals off balance with another
thrust, this time at Austria.

*   *   *

Even if the western democracies had been less feeble at this moment, they still might not have been able to take any action to stop
Hitler. France was suffering one of the innumerable crises in confidence that bedeviled the Third Republic in the 1930s. On March
10, when events were moving rapidly in Berlin and Vienna, there

was no government in office in Paris. A caretaker foreign ministry was not empowered to act. There was no one to order out the troops.

In London the British politicians were quarreling about the Chamberlain government's appeasement of Mussolini, who was continuing to seize territory in Africa. Anthony Eden, the Tory foreign secretary, had just resigned in protest. Prime Minister Neville Chamberlain chose to look upon the bright side, although he knew precisely what was going on in Berlin. His embassy had provided him with details about the ultimatum given to Schuschnigg by Hitler and the fact that Austrian independence was certainly going down the drain. But in a public statement Chamberlain announced, "What happened at Berchtesgaden was merely that two statesmen had agreed upon certain measures for the improvement of relations between their two countries." So Hitler knew he had nothing to fear from France, which could not act, or from England, which would not act.

Really, the only fear Hitler had, and he was to allay it in a hurry, was that the German army would not march. He called in General Keitel, the chief of Oberkommando der Wehrmacht (OKW), and told him to be ready to move in two days. Keitel aroused General Beck, the chief of staff of the German land army. Beck went to see Hitler.

"I cannot take any responsibility for an invasion of Austria," General Beck said.

"You don't have to," Hitler retorted. "If you stall over this, I'll have the invasion carried out by my SS. They will march in with bands playing. Is that what the Army wants?"

Beck shuddered and went away. The army began working furiously; its last few teeth had been pulled.

On the night of March 10 Hitler issued a directive to the Wehrmacht. The purpose of the operation in Austria, he said, was to restore constitutional conditions. "I myself will take charge of operations," announced the Führer.

So the army knew who was now running Germany's military affairs. To ensure that it remembered, Hitler also assigned three SS regiments to the operation.

Hermann Göring was taking care of political events, operating from a telephone booth in Berlin where a line was kept open constantly to Vienna. He called Minister Seyss-Inquart almost hourly.

In Vienna Chancellor von Schuschnigg was trying to stave off disaster by stalling. The time for capitulation stipulated in Hitler's last ultimatum passed. Still Schuschnigg did not act. Göring was directed by Hitler to force the resignation of von Schuschnigg by nightfall.

In midafternoon Schuschnigg announced the postponement of the plebiscite. Seyss-Inquart telephoned Göring to tell him, and Göring told Hitler. It was not enough, Hitler said. Von Schuschnigg had violated the Berchtesgaden agreement, and he would have to go. He must resign. No less would do. By 5:30 Hitler wanted a report that President Miklas had asked Minister Seyss-Inquart to form a new cabinet. Otherwise...

Seyss-Inquart still had enough Austrian in him, although he was a Nazi, to ask whether Hitler proposed to allow Austria to remain independent after he took over and made it a Nazi state. He asked Göring. The field marshal, knowing precisely what was going to happen, gave him an equivocal reply.

At 5:30 came more bad news. Von Schuschnigg had resigned, but President Miklas was still jibbing at appointing Seyss-Inquart to the premiership.

Göring ordered Seyss-Inquart to find the German military attaché and take him to the president's office. They were to tell President Miklas that unless Seyss-Inquart was appointed to head a new government, the German troops would invade that night and Austria would cease to exist as a nation.

"Tell him we are not joking," said Göring.

But the Austrians were not quite that easy. At 7:50 p.m. Chancellor von Schuschnigg went on the air over the Austrian state radio:

Men and women of Austria, today has faced us with a difficult situation.... The government of Germany has presented to the Federal President an ultimatum with a time limit, demanding that the President nominate as Federal Chancellor the candidate specified to him, and to appoint a cabinet in accordance with the German government's proposals. Otherwise an invasion by German troops will take place at the appointed time.... The President has instructed me to inform the Austrian nation that we are yielding to force. Because we are resolved on no account even at this grave hour, to spill German blood, we have ordered

our armed forces, in the event of an invasion, to withhold resistance and to await the decision of the nation. I leave the
Austrian people at this hour with a heartfelt wish, May God protect Austria.

The Austrian army, as von Schuschnigg and everyone else knew,
was incapable of offering sustained resistance to the German forces
massed along the border. Schuschnigg's last action as chancellor
was to tell the Austrian commander, General Sigmund Schilhausky,
to withdraw his troops from the frontier to a line behind the Enns
River and to offer no resistance to Hitler's forces.

After von Schuschnigg's radio speech, Seyss-Inquart went on the air
and announced that he, as the sole member of the cabinet still in office, would assume executive power. But President Miklas paid no attention to him, the Nazi leaders of Austria paid little attention, and the
scene at the Austrian Chancellery was one of total confusion.

At 8 p.m. came word that von Schuschnigg had not resigned after all; he had merely withdrawn from Vienna. President Miklas used
that as an excuse to refuse to appoint Seyss-Inquart premier.

What was to be done? Göring counseled immediate invasion.
Hitler waited. But he waited only half an hour; then he suddenly
announced that it was time to go. The invasion was on.

As commander in chief of the German armed forces, Hitler
signed Directive No. 2:

1. The demands in the German ultimatum to the Austrian government have not been fulfilled.

2. The Austrian Wehrmacht has ordered its troops to withdraw
   before the entering German troops and avoid combat.
   The Austrian government has ceased to function.

3. To avoid further bloodshed in Austrian towns, the German
   entrance into Austria will begin, in accordance with Directive No. 1, at daybreak on March 12.

I expect the specified objectives to be reached by the fullest efforts, as quickly as possible.

At 10 p.m. came word from Vienna that President Miklas had dissolved the Austrian government and ordered the Austrian army not to resist the coming of German troops. Half an hour later Seyss-Inquart sent the telegram prepared earlier for him in Berlin, calling on behalf of the provisional Austrian government for German troops to restore order in Austria.

Prince Philip of Hesse, a special envoy of Hitler's, arrived in Rome and went to the office of Count Ciano, the foreign minister, bearing a letter from Hitler explaining and outlining his plans for Austria. Hitler did not know quite how Mussolini would take this move, because in the past Mussolini had been very much opposed to such a plan.

But Mussolini was buried deep in his own problems, and he had neither troops nor venom to spare on Germany. When the two men came to him, he put a good face on the matter and said he was perfectly pleased about it. Hesse went back to the German Embassy and called Hitler.

"I have just come back from the Palazzo Venezia," said Hesse. "The Duce accepted the whole thing in a very friendly manner."

"Then please tell Mussolini that I will never forget him for this. Never, never, never. No matter what happens...As soon as the Austrian affair has been settled I shall be ready to go with him through thick and thin, no matter what," Hitler said.

"Yes, my Führer."

"Listen, I shall make any agreement. I am no longer in fear of the terrible position which would have existed militarily in case we had gotten into a conflict. You may tell him that I do thank him ever so much, I will never, never forget him. I will never forget him."

"Yes, my Führer."

"I will never forget it, whatever happens. If he should ever need any help or be in any danger, he can be sure that I shall stick with him whatever happens, even if the whole world is against him."

"Yes, my Führer."

Then a relieved Hitler went to bed.

The generals were so nervous they kept bombarding the Chancellery with telephone calls all night long, until finally Hitler was aroused and he told them to stop it. The invasion was going to go on. There was nothing the timid generals could do about it.

On Saturday morning, March 12, Hitler left Berlin by plane at 6 a.m. He went first to Munich, where he was briefed by General Fedor von Bock, commander of the Eighth Army, which was stationed in Bavaria and which was entrusted with the invasion.

The "invasion," when it came, was more like a triumphal parade, von Bock announced. The troops were showered with flowers as they marched into Austria; old soldiers from World War I put on their uniforms and joined up. Even the Austrian army was falling in behind. And Czechoslovakia, about which Hitler had some fears, was doing nothing to impede the invasion. Nor were France or Britain. There was absolutely nothing to worry about.

At four o'clock in the afternoon Hitler crossed what had been the Austrian frontier at Braunau and drove to Linz. Seyss-Inquart had been summoned to meet him there. What a drive it was! The Führer stood up in the back of his blue Mercedes open limousine and gave the Nazi salute as he moved through the crowds along the road. So great were the crowds who came out to see the conquering heroes that it was dusk before Hitler's driver could force his way through to Linz. A million people crowded into the city to see the German leader. It was obvious that public opinion was very strongly in favor of alignment with Germany.

Hitler went into the Linz city hall and appeared on the balcony. He was home again for the first time in a quarter of a century.

If Providence once sent me out from this fine city, and called upon me to lead the Reich, then surely it must have had some mission in mind for me. And that can only have been one mission—to return my beloved native country to the German Reich.

That night Hitler stayed in Linz for the first time since leaving the country, and the next day he drove to Leonding to visit the graves of his parents.

The reception that Hitler received—overwhelming approval— put a new idea into his head. He had been thinking about an autonomous Austria under his control, but now he changed his mind.

Why not make Austria a part of the Greater German Reich, as it deserved to be? Was that not what he had been talking about in *Mein Kampf* and in all his early planning? The reunification of all German peoples under one flag? Of course it was. By the time he returned to Linz, he had decided that Germany would annex Austria. Everyone, from Göring to the Austrian cabinet members, seemed to agree with him.

In Linz he made a speech indicating just this. Then he got to work to set the wheels in motion. It was Sunday, March 13, the day that von Schuschnigg's plebiscite was to have been held, the day the Austrian people had been expected to vote for a free and independent Austria. Instead, plans were made that day for the annexation—the *Anschluss*. The plebiscite would be held on April 10, Hitler said. The first article would say, "Austria is a province of the German Reich."

And so, that day, to all intents and purposes, at the Hotel Weinzinger in Linz, Austria became the *Ostmark*, just another province.

The next day Hitler continued his triumphant tour. It was afternoon when he reached Vienna, accompanied by General Keitel. Outside the Imperial Hotel, where he was staying, the crowds gathered and waited for a glimpse of him. They began to chant: "We want to see our Führer. We want to see our Führer."

In Vienna the church bells rang and Nazi swastikas hung from the steeples. The only trouble was caused by the local Nazis, who, now that they had been granted amnesty, went looking for revenge against the Social Democrats and personalities of the late Austrian government. There were riots and murders that night in the back streets, and the foreign correspondents reported them faithfully. The world had a rather different view of Hitler's entry than did the people of Germany.

On March 15 Hitler went to the Maria Theresa monument to review an enormous military parade. Wehrmacht troops and Austrian soldiers marched by, bedecked with flowers, complete with flags and bands. A thousand war planes thundered overhead, the vast majority of them German. The show was enough to warn western diplomats that Hitler was no longer a petty dictator, but a very large one. Veterans of World War I stood by with lumps in their throats as the band played the "Prinz Eugen March." To such music German and Austrian troops had marched into battle together in 1914. The enthusiasm was real.

After the military parade Hitler made a little speech there in the Castle square. "I announce to the German people that my Austrian fatherland has now returned to the Greater German Reich," he said. The people swelled the square with their cheering.

That night Hitler and Keitel flew back to Munich. Hitler sat on the left so that he could see his beloved Austria flowing past beneath the wing of the plane. Keitel brought out a map, a clipping from a newspaper, showing the new territory that Germany had acquired. It closed in Czechoslovakia on three sides, like a vise. Hitler smiled as he looked at the map and fingered the newly shaded areas. "All that," he said, "all that is now German again."

For the next four weeks Hitler remained in a state of ecstasy. His main task was to drum up enthusiasm for the *Anschluss*—the union of Germany and Austria—which was to be decided by the plebiscite of both nations on April 10. He traversed both countries, speaking, speaking, speaking, and wound up the election campaign on April 9 in Vienna.

The election was rigged, of course. Nazi election committees had a good view of people as they voted at the tables. No one demanded the right to vote in secrecy; it would have called attention to any voter who did so. So the result was a foregone conclusion: when the ballots were counted, the "Yes" figure was 99.09 percent in Greater Germany and 99.75 percent in Austria.

But what if the election had not been rigged? Undoubtedly the Austrians would have voted for Hitler anyhow, for he offered something they had not enjoyed since the last days of the Habsburg Empire: a sense of belonging to a nation of destiny. The Habsburgs had fallen, and all those lands, Hungary, Serbia, Czechoslovakia, had broken away from the fold. Here came Hitler offering to restore the sense of dignity and glory, and the popular support he achieved was enormous. In the days after World War II it became popular in Austria to forget all about the Hitler years, but the fact is that during the war some of the most ardent Nazis of all (and I met a few of them in the Far East in 1945) were the youth of Austria. All their lives this generation had lived under the clouds of depression and instability. Hitler brought them a new sense of belonging, and they virtually worshipped him for it.

The Austrian Nazis, from the beginning, were the worst Nazis of all. Their orgy of sadism and persecution of the Jews began immediately and surpassed anything that was going on in Berlin, because so many more "ordinary people," not just the SS and the other professional bullies, were involved. The old town homes of the well-to-do were looted, young women were raped, and old people were beaten up.

So, just as Austria had ceased to be, Vienna became merely another German city, and not a very important one at that. Hitler actually did not like Vienna; he had spent too many miserable months there, half on the dole, fighting with the Social Democrats. Austria became the playground of the Germans, with prices lower than those in most other German cities and with unmatched scenery in the Alpine area.

But the Austrian political leaders of the past were to have no more freedom. Chancellor von Schuschnigg ended up in a concentration camp. Others were shot or murdered or imprisoned.

Without firing a single shot, the Germans had added 7 million people to the Reich, with many more soldiers and resources and a more important international position than before. Hitler had, in fact, restored the German Empire concept. Had France and Britain decided to stop Hitler on that March day when his troops crossed the Austrian frontier, it would have been no trick at all, as Hitler's generals were later to admit. But Britain and France stood by paralyzed. Italy had seen the light, and Mussolini cast his lot with Hitler.

"The hard fact is," Neville Chamberlain told the British House of Commons, "that nothing could have arrested what actually has happened in Austria unless this country and other countries had been prepared to use force."

And they were not morally so prepared. The tragedy was as simple as that.

After the *Anschluss* anyone who could look at a map and make sense of it could see what was coming next. It had all been laid out in *Mein Kampf,* in Hitler's words that all "racial" Germans must be united under one flag. The next state to feel the German jackboot would have to be Czechoslovakia. In Prague that could be seen very clearly. Only in Paris and London was the view clouded by fog; Paris and London and Washington, of course, but Washington still did not consider European problems to be of any importance to America. Never had the democratic nations of the west been more disunited, more confused, more unwilling to face up to the lessons of history and the unpleasant political realities of the day. As Hitler could see, Europe was decadent and rotting, ripe for his picking.

5

NIGHTMARE AT MUNICH

Case Green. The German generals called it "Deployment Green." It was the OKW plan for the military conquest of Czechoslovakia. No sooner had Austria been annexed than the generals were set to work on the Reich's next acquisition.

They were assisted vigorously by Dr. Goebbels's propaganda machine. For two years Goebbels had been building his propaganda campaign around the Prague government's "suppression" of the Sudeten Germans. The generals were also helped by the Sudeten German party of Czechoslovakia. This party received an outright subsidy from the German foreign office.

For months the German foreign office had been playing cat and mouse with the Prague government. At the time of the *Anschluss* Hitler and Göring had soft-pedaled the differences between the two countries because Hitler really was afraid that the Czechoslovak army might march and, if that happened, that perhaps England and France would be stirred to action. That would have been the end of his Austrian plans; the German army was still far too weak for a war on that scale.

Therefore, Prague was given many indications that the change in Austria was all that the Germans really cared about—that this would be the end of their territorial ambitions.

Nothing could have been further from the truth. Hitler and Göring talked frequently about the need to take over Czechoslovakia.

The moment that the *Anschluss* was completed, the Germans began to move. The first step was to be sure that the Sudeten German party would remain in parliamentary opposition, no matter how many overtures were made to them. Thus they could continue to complain that the Germans in Czechoslovakia were mistreated. On March 28, 1938, Hitler told a Sudeten German leader, Konrad Henlein, that he intended to settle the Sudeten German question in the near future.

The important fact about Czechoslovakia, which did not apply to Austria, was that the Czech government had alliances with France and with the Soviet Union. Thus, if Hitler moved against Czechoslovakia militarily, he might precipitate a general European war that he did not want just then.

What he did want was the support of Mussolini in this new enterprise. To get it, he went to Italy on May 3 with an entourage of 500 people, including Göring, Goebbels, Himmler, Hess, and von Ribbentrop—all the top Nazi political stalwarts.

They spent a week in meetings in Italy, but the time was wasted. Hitler had made an error: he could not count on Mussolini to help him in the matter of Czechoslovakia. It was hardly a fatal error, but an error nonetheless, and one that left a bad taste in the mouths of both sides. Hitler went back home to supervise the buildup of his armies.

On May 20, for no reason most Germans could ascertain, the Czechoslovaks suddenly ordered a partial mobilization of their army. It was a shock, but one that had to be borne. In truth, the Czechs had learned of Germany's contingency plan, presented for Hitler's signature that same day.

On May 21 two Czech policemen shot dead two Sudeten German farmers, and the Czech government went ahead with the mobilization of 200,000 troops in the belief that Germany was ready to attack. German troop concentrations in Silesia, Saxony, and Austria convinced them.

That night Hitler decided that the attack on Czechoslovakia must be made. The only question was when.

*

Meanwhile, Hitler was planning fortifications along Germany's western border. The goal was to build, within eighteen months, 10,000 concrete pillboxes and other structures along what Hitler called the "west wall," largely between Karlsruhe and Aix-la-Chapelle. Hitler himself designed the pillboxes and saw them tested in trials at Jüterbog, where the structures were fired upon by heavy field howitzers.

Such measures were Hitler's way of showing his many timid generals that he held them in contempt. In one speech he was so cutting that General Beck suddenly decided to resign as chief of staff of the army; General Franz Halder took his place.

But at that moment, so badly fragmented was the German General Staff that some officers sided with Hitler in his attitude toward the "defeatism" which he perceived in many of the generals. To the latter Hitler's plans were madness; to him the generals' reluctance to risk war was cowardice. What must be remembered is that at this stage Hitler *wanted* war. Everything that he did in the Czechoslovak crisis must be viewed in that light. He wanted to humiliate the Czechs and, through them, the British and the French. He was still living over the wretchedness of the Versailles years, and he would not, could not, forget them.

So in the summer of 1938 Germany prepared for the Czechoslovak crisis it intended to bring about. The primary method was to keep the Czechs off balance by holding one set of maneuvers after another in Silesia, Saxony, and Bavaria. In August Hitler took General Halder and several other high military men on his yacht to review the fleet in the Baltic Sea, and in the privacy of the voyage Halder brought out his situation map to brief the Führer on his plans for operations against Czechoslovakia when the time came. Hitler asked for another map to be prepared for him to peruse at his leisure, and for all the specifications of the operations, but then he refused to say yea or nay. He wanted to think it over, he told Halder. So the general gave Hitler all his notes and the map; he said he needed a decision soon because orders had to be drawn for the armies that would be involved.

Hitler then showed real brilliance in assessing military matters. He objected to the army plan because it did not make adequate use of the panzer groups, which he wanted to send toward Prague immediately to seize the capital. It was the sort of maneuver that the Germans would use again and again very successfully in months to come. Halder said the German artillery support was too weak. Hitler retorted that this was nonsense: the panzers would get so far ahead of the artillery that it would not matter anyhow. The blitzkrieg was being born.

The generals were not immediately impressed. They worried about such matters as the army's firepower. The new, heavy 15-centimeter infantry howitzers would not be ready until autumn. That summer Hitler had only twenty-three 21-centimeter howitzers, and eight of these were in East Prussia.

All plans were now speeded up. Admiral Raeder was told that he must finish the battleships *Tirpitz* and *Bismarck* by early 1940. He had expected to have until 1943. But they would be needed in 1940, said Hitler grimly. The battle cruisers *Gneisenau* and *Scharnhorst* would have to be more heavily armed. The submarine construction program was going to be stepped up. The Type VII 500-ton *Atlantik U-Boot,* the most effective killer of its kind, was to go into mass production.

The Führer then turned his attention to the plan for destroying Czechoslovakia. It must be done with lightning speed, he said—within four days so that the western Allies would not have time to think. It would take France at least four days to mobilize. By then it would all be over.

On May 30 Hitler spelled out his plan:

Day 1: The fifth columnists would sabotage Czech "nerve centers" while infiltrating troops seized fortifications on the border and the Luftwaffe bombed.

Day 2: German troops in Czech uniforms would secure bridges and road points along the German route.

Day 3: The army would move in trucks and take over the border fortifications.

Day 4: The divisions waiting on the frontier would move and drive straight for the heart of Czechoslovakia, led by the panzer divisions heading for Prague.

As the Führer dictated the details of his strategy, OKW completed its planning directive. Hitler signed it that day. General Keitel ordered the Wehrmacht to be ready to implement Case Green by October 1.

"It is my unshakeable resolve to smash Czechoslovakia by means of a military operation," Hitler said.

Having set the wheels in motion for the attack on Czechoslovakia, Hitler went to the Berghof for the summer and took life easy. He would get up at around 10 a.m., read the papers, have lunch with whomever was staying at the house, take a walk, watch a movie, eat dinner, and then go to bed between ten o'clock and midnight. Once in a while he went down to Munich, where he would lunch at the Osteria Restaurant, a few doors from the Nazi offices on the Schelling Strasse. He had a favorite table there, out in the Italian garden, under a tree next to the fountain.

Officers came and officers went at the "eyrie"—too many; they annoyed the Führer. Finally he gave orders that no one was to be admitted to the summer place without his special permission.

Göring came bustling up to inform Hitler of his preparations. The Luftwaffe planned bombing attacks on Czechoslovak cities. Hitler looked over everything and approved. But he did not always approve his generals' plans. He was particularly critical of the army engineers. He was forever correcting their specifications for bunkers and dugouts—and with reason: not for nothing had Hitler studied architecture in Vienna. His own experience in the trenches in the First World War had given him an almost complete contempt for huge defensive fortifications such as the new Maginot line, a deep disposition of blockhouses and bunkers on the French side of the border, designed to keep Germany at bay for a century. His troops would not sit in blockhouses and wait to get broiled, blown up, or smoked out. They would move out and fight in the open, overwhelming the enemy in *his* blockhouses. One of Hitler's real strengths (and weaknesses, as will be seen) was indicated by that Iron Cross on his chest. He knew firsthand the problems of the infantryman. Such matters as drinking water, places for men to relieve themselves, and the need for hooks and pegs for men to hang up their belongings inside blockhouses—all these things aroused Hitler's interest, and he issued orders about them.

Hitler was, said General Otto Förster, interested in all the big issues (annexation of Austria) and all the small issues (design of bunkers) but nothing in between. That was one of the Führer's major errors then and later. As Förster correctly put it, most decisions in this world fall between the two stools of grandiose plan and intricate detail. Much later, after Hitler had ordered the invasion of the Soviet Union, the effort would fail because Hitler neglected to pay attention to the supply and maintenance problems of an army organization in inclement weather in an enemy environment. That was the sort of detail his "incompetent generals" should handle, said the Führer at the time, quite forgetting that the failure to pay attention to such logistics matters had also brought down Napoleon.

Throughout that summer of 1938 Hitler played with Europe. He lazed around the Berghof, but he never missed a trick. Goebbels would come, and the two would sit down in Hitler's study and prepare a propaganda campaign to frighten the Czechs.

"Put the wind up them. Show them your teeth," he would say.

The Nazi-controlled newspapers of the Sudetenland were laced with articles predicting a German takeover. Hitler's information about what was going on, also, was extremely accurate. His intelligence agents had tapped the Czech Foreign Office telephone lines, so he had access to the reports on all the conversations between Czech diplomats and their Foreign Ministry. And, knowing the weak links in the international diplomatic and press corps, he carefully fed them information, or what a later generation would call "disinformation." Various dates were "leaked" for the invasion of Czechoslovakia, all of them different, all of them designed to keep Europe off balance. But he made sure that everyone in Europe knew that he was definitely planning to take over Czechoslovakia.

He talked tough, and took pride in this as an "old revolutionary." One day the British ambassador came while Hitler was at the luncheon table.

"Gott im Himmel," shouted Hitler. "Don't let him in. I'm in a good mood."

The Führer then proceeded to work himself up into another of his artificial rages. He went into an anteroom and met the Englishman. The diplomat brought his message and received a verbal trouncing for his trouble. Hitler began to scream. He yelled and howled and spat insults one after the other. The English diplomat was cowed and went away as soon as he could escape. Hitler returned to his lunch.

"I need some tea," he said. "That man thinks I am furious." And the Führer smiled his broadest smile.

Yet Hitler already had new worries. Some of the generals were beginning to do more than mumble; they had seemingly recovered their manhood and were conspiring to overthrow Hitler. In August the Führer had word of a recent meeting that was almost mutinous. General Beck had read an antiwar memorandum, and many of the senior generals seemed to agree with it. Hitler's response was not to call his commanding generals on the carpet for disloyalty, but to call their chiefs of staff to a meeting over which he would preside, and there to indoctrinate those chiefs of staff with a point of view entirely different from that expressed by their superior officers. Thus Hitler sowed dissension within the ranks of the generals.

All summer and fall Hitler saw to it that the military maneuvers were continued around the Czech border. Inevitably, the constant racket of the guns and the constant movement got on the Czechs' nerves. It was just what Hitler wanted.

Hitler went to the maneuvers, talked to the generals, and told them about his plans to invade Czechoslovakia, but he was always evasive about the date.

Hitler was also proving to be a political seer. His generals suggested that British rearmament would make Britain superior to Germany and that Britain would act.

"Nonsense," said the Führer. "The British will recoil from confrontation as long as the Germans show no signs of weakness."

He did not fear France, whose weaponry was obsolete. He did not fear Russia at all, because of her isolation and backwardness.

Allied officials were brought to Germany and shown the "works." For example, a French general was given a tour of Luftwaffe headquarters by Göring, who then arranged a totally deceptive display which indicated that aircraft only in the design stage were actually in full production. All available Messerschmitt (ME-109 and ME-110) fighter planes were moved from one airfield to another so that the French general could see them every time he landed at a different field. The impression given was that the Germans had thousands of fighter aircraft ready to go.

In such matters, Hitler and his associates were not always successful. Notable was the failure with Admiral Nicholas von Horthy, the regent of Hungary. Hitler wanted Horthy's help in the dismemberment of Czechoslovakia, and asked for it in a series of summer meetings. He took Horthy for a voyage on the state yacht and entertained Madame Horthy.

Hitler was his most persuasive in asking for the Hungarians' aid. All the while the conversations of the Hungarians were being monitored. And the monitors had some bad news for the Führer. His machinations had come to naught. Hungary decided against the use of force in dealing with Czechoslovakia.

At the end of this series of meetings relations between them were so cool that the Hungarian and German contingents returned south on separate trains.

Hitler's miscalculations could be enormous, although not all of them would be immediately apparent. One day Admiral Erich Raeder, the naval chief of staff, came in to see Hitler about the problems of fighting a naval war with England. Hitler listened for a while and then shut Raeder off.

"Herr Admiral," he said, "what you and I have been discussing is pure theory. Britain will not fight."

* * *

It was the end of August. Hitler devoted his efforts to persuading his generals that he could fight in the east against Czechoslovakia and not risk an attack in the west by the French and British. On August 26, with 2000 bodyguards, he made an inspection of the west wall, the German system of fortifications along the French border. At Aachen he was met by a number of generals who warned that the western defenses were only a third completed. It was no time for a war, they said. Hitler tried to convince them that the French would not fight because the Italians would menace them in the south and in Africa. Along the west wall Germany would have 2000 tanks, he said, and the superb German antitank mine. The generals were unconvinced. During the initial phases of the attack on Czechoslovakia, they said, the German west would have no reserve troops. What then?

"I will not call off the attack on Czechoslovakia," Hitler insisted.

It was a contest between the generals' opinion that Germany was not ready for war and the Führer's intuition that the taking of Czechoslovakia must come in 1938.

At this time, the differences between Hitler and the generals became so serious that the dissident generals put together a conspiracy designed to overthrow Hitler. General Beck was the leader. Other generals committed to the plan were Erwin von Witzleben, Count Erich von Brockdorf-Ahlefeld, Count Fritz von der Schülenburg, and General Erich Hoepner. The plan then was to seize Hitler just as soon as he gave the order for the strike against Czechoslovakia and to put him on trial before the People's Court. Ultimately the generals hoped to have him certified as insane and put into an asylum.

Many other generals were silent partners in the scheme, including General Halder, the new chief of staff. But all of the generals' plans hinged on one factor: *that the British and French would intervene if Hitler moved against Czechoslovakia*. And this became the vital flaw in their plans.

In August the generals sent an envoy to England. He was General Ewald von Kleist-Schmenzin, a member of the old guard of German nobility. Immediately he got in touch with Sir Robert Vansittart, chief diplomatic adviser to the British cabinet. He spoke very frankly about Hitler's war aims and the Führer's determination to attack Czechoslovakia. He told the British that the generals knew the plan, as well as the date of the planned attack, and that they were unanimously opposed to the attack. But, he said, the generals would have no power to stop the war unless they had help from the outside. He warned that unless Britain and France acted, the world was certain to have war. What it would take to set the conspiracy in motion, he said, was a statement from London that Britain would intervene in case of German attack on Czechoslovakia.

Von Kleist then went to see Winston Churchill and told him the same thing. Churchill told him that he was certain Britain and France would stand up and that the United States was also becoming very anti-Nazi. But in official quarters in London the German generals' warning was heavily discounted as propaganda from a group of "outs" against the "ins." Thus, at the moment that the German generals needed a real commitment from England, they did not get it.

The only concrete action was the recall to London of Sir Nevile

Henderson, the British ambassador to Germany, for "consultations." This was done with much publicity in an attempt by Prime Minister Chamberlain to give an indirect warning to Hitler. But Hitler was not listening to indirect warnings, and when Henderson reached London, he talked the government out of the idea of sending him back with a real warning. Instead, he went back to Germany with orders to prepare Hitler for personal contact—which meant a meeting—with Prime Minister Chamberlain.

The fact was that both Prime Minister Chamberlain and French Premier Daladier were committed to policies of peace, even if this meant appeasement. Their forces were unprepared for war and their nations were psychologically unprepared for it. They had been neglecting their national defenses since the financial crisis began in the late 1920s. They did not even want to think about military struggle, and they were willing to think about anything else.

Despite the unsatisfactory reaction of the British to the plan to get rid of Hitler, the German generals continued to struggle against the coming attack on Czechoslovakia. On September 3 generals Keitel, Halder, von Rundstedt, and von Reichenau met with Hitler and spoke of the difficulties of attacking Bohemia and Moravia. They did the same on September 9, in a conference that lasted from 10:30 p.m. until 3:30 a.m. Hitler lost his temper and accused the generals of faintheartedness.

Now, even without British help, the conspirators among the generals were ready to strike. But Hitler remained at the Berghof, surrounded by guards and friends. The planned putsch was to take place at the Reich Chancellery in Berlin.

Like a juggernaut, Hitler's plans moved forward.

The Czechs saw what was coming. On September 5 President Eduard Beneš called the Sudeten German leaders to Hradschin Palace in Prague and told them to write out their full demands on the Czechoslovak government. The government would accept those demands, no matter what they were.

"My God," exclaimed Sudeten leader Karl Hermann Frank. "They have given us everything we want."

But Hitler was having none of that. Who cared what the Sudeten Germans wanted? They were merely pawns in Hitler's game. From

Berlin came orders: the Sudeten Germans were to break off all negotiations with the Czech government. There was to be no agreement of any sort.

On September 7 the Sudeten leaders broke with the government
on the invented pretext that the police had been harassing their people.

On September 10 at the Nazi party's annual Nuremberg rally, Field
Marshal Göring made a belligerent speech, accusing the Czechs of sup-
pressing the Sudeten Germans. Two days later Hitler gave his speech
to the Nuremberg rally. As everyone expected, the speech concerned
Czechoslovakia. Hitler harangued against President Beneš and the
Czech government. He accused them of mistreating the German mi-
nority. He threatened that something would be done. But he did not
declare war. (He was reserving that action for October 1. That was
the date set for the actual invasion of Czechoslovakia.)

In Sudeten Czechoslovakia, Hitler's speech caused an uprising
that took the Czech troops two days to put down. The Sudeten Germans began saying that the only solution to the problem was the
cession of Sudetenland to Germany.

This idea was finding favor in London, where Chamberlain was
looking for any course of action he could pursue that would not in-
volve military action. But France had to be consulted.

On September 13 the French cabinet was in session all day long,
considering what action it might take if Hitler attacked Czechoslovakia. France had its treaty, which called for military support to the
Czechs. Should France honor the treaty? The cabinet was divided.

That night the British ambassador was called to the office of Premier Daladier, who suggested that he go to London to tell Chamberlain to make the best deal he could with Hitler.

Chamberlain was of like mind. He sent a message to Hitler announcing that he was coming to Germany.

"Heaven has fallen on me," Hitler exclaimed when he had Chamberlain's message. Here was the prime minister of the greatest empire
in the world coming to Hitler on his knees, seeking peace. Hitler knew
how to deal with that situation.

So Prime Minister Chamberlain made the long trip to Berchtesgaden,
and the German dictator did nothing to make it easier for him. The
British people, meanwhile, believed that Chamberlain was going to

warn Hitler of what would happen if he continued his aggressive ways. They had been completely duped.

Even as Chamberlain was in the air bound for Germany, Hitler knew that the British prime minister was coming to appease him. Hitler would apply a bit of psychology on his guest. Chamberlain had to fly to Munich and then take a three-hour train ride to Berchtesgaden. All along the route, Hitler managed to have troop trains passing on the opposite track. Nor did Hitler greet his guest at the station; he waited for the prime minister of the British Empire to come to him and walk up the long stairway to the top, where the German Führer stood.

They met that afternoon. Hitler began with a harangue about the problems of the 3 million Germans of Czechoslovakia. He threatened war, world war.

Chamberlain suggested that if this were so, he was wasting his time and might as well go home.

Hitler saw that he had gone too far. He calmed down then. He proposed that the Sudetenland be ceded to Germany. What did Britain think of that?

Chamberlain had been thinking about little else. The only concession Chamberlain could get from Hitler was the promise that he would not embark on military action until the two met again. Since Hitler was not planning to begin his military action until October 1, it was no concession at all.

On September 18 Chamberlain was back in London, preparing his cabinet and the French for the great act of perfidy. On September 20 Hitler's generals had their marching orders.

The British and French had been meeting in London, and they agreed to the partition of Czechoslovakia. The Czechs were not consulted. What the Allies had given in the Treaty of Versailles, the Allies now took away. Every bit of Czech territory inhabited by more than 50 percent Sudeten Germans would be ceded to Hitler.

But the Czechs rejected the suggestion when it was finally made to them. To do this, they said, was to put all Czechoslovakia under German control. The British warned the Czechs that if they refused, Britain would no longer be interested in the fate of their country. France also warned the Czechs.

President Beneš now knew that he was being deserted and thrown to the German wolves. He turned to the Russians. They said they would honor their treaty with Czechoslovakia. *But* their treaty called for them to come to the aid of the Czechs only if the French did too. And the French had now refused to honor their treaty.

So in the hour of need, Czechoslovakia stood alone. If the Czechs fought the Germans, they would fight alone.

On September 22 Chamberlain again left London for Germany.

Hitler had been working himself into a new frenzy. One observer said he had seen the Führer hurl himself to the floor of his office and chew the carpet. Perhaps. But there was no question about his being nervous. From London came reports that the British people were beginning to have serious doubts about the policy of their prime minister. There was talk in London about the need to stand up to Germany. Now, having promise of another coup in which he could achieve his whole aim without the firing of a shot, one would think that Hitler would have been happy. But he wanted war. He wanted fighting. He wanted to show the world that Germany was a major power. Hitler worried lest the opportunity slip away from him. For he could see that public opinion abroad was turning against Germany, and this might be deadly in the end. He asked Goebbels about American opinion, in particular.

Chamberlain was back in Germany, hat in hand. This time the two men met in the little Rhine River town of Godesberg.

Chamberlain said that the French, the British, and finally the Czechs had agreed that the future of the Sudeten territory was to be determined by a commission of three members: a Czech, a German, and a neutral. Hitler made new demands. It was too late for a commission, said Hitler. The Sudeten area must be occupied by Germany at once.

So Chamberlain went back across the Rhine into Switzerland and began making telephone calls to Paris and London.

Hitler had a real problem, although not one with which many people would sympathize. His whole plan had been to destroy Czech military might by force. The British and French were about to destroy Czechoslovakia for him, but without force. That was no good. Hitler must show the world that the German army was supreme. Therefore, the least he could accept, he said, was a military occupation.

That is how the matter stood the next day. Chamberlain wrote
Hitler a letter, asking for the Führer's final proposals, together with
a map. Later that day, September 23, they would meet again. Now
Hitler had the news that the Czechs had mobilized their army. When
Chamberlain came back across the Rhine to talk, Hitler gave him
the real ultimatum. The Czechs would get out of the territory, and
the Germans would take over on September 28.

Chamberlain recoiled. The ultimatum was not acceptable.

"It is not an ultimatum," said Hitler, "it is a memorandum."
And he pointed to the title at the top of the page. Sure enough, it
said "Memorandum."

They argued. Finally Hitler announced that he was making a great
concession. He said "X day" could be October 1, and he grandly wrote
that date into the memorandum in his own hand. X day, of course,
had been October 1 all along.

And so the meeting ended with this magnificent "concession."
Chamberlain left, saying he was pleased with the "relationship of
confidence" that had developed between himself and Hitler in those
few days. He looked forward to more discussions with Hitler in the
future to settle more international problems, he told the dictator.

Hitler could scarcely contain his laughter until after the British prime
minister had left. How right he had been all along. The British would
not fight.

But, then, the Czechs refused to make the necessary concessions and suggested that they would fight, even if they had to fight
alone. British public opinion swayed to the Czech side. Even Chamberlain had to agree to support the Czechs, and so did the French.
Chamberlain said that the Czechs would give Hitler the Sudeten areas and that a meeting should be held immediately. Hitler demanded
an immediate acceptance by the Czechs of the agreement with Chamberlain. It seemed that war would actually come, and reluctantly
the British and French agreed to support Czechoslovakia.

So Hitler appeared to make "concessions." A conciliatory letter was sent to London on the night of September 27. The next day
many people in Britain, and certainly the penny press, suggested
that war was about to break out. But Chamberlain wanted to do
anything short of war, and he did. A four-power conference was

set up: France, Italy, Britain, and Germany were to decide the future of Czechoslovakia.

At noon on September 29 the representatives of the other three powers came to Munich. Various solutions to the Czech problem were suggested. Hitler would permit no Czechs to participate, and the British and French meekly swallowed his new demands. Although these were for much larger chunks of territory than before, at 10 p.m. on the night of September 29 the agreement was reached. The Czechs protested, but the British told them that no one cared; they were to be sacrificed for the good of Europe. At one o'clock on the morning of September 30 the four representatives signed the agreement calling for the German army to march into the Sudeten territory and occupy it on October 1. Hitler had gotten most of what he wanted, a military occupation that would allow him to flourish his swords for all to see. The next day there were some formalities, but all had been decided. Czechoslovakia had been deserted by Britain and France.

That day President Beneš reluctantly surrendered, and he told the Czech army not to fight: "We were abandoned....We stand alone."

Not quite alone, but alone enough. Winston Churchill had a few words to say in the House of Commons:

> We have sustained a total, unmitigated defeat. We are in the midst of a disaster of the first magnitude....All the countries of middle Europe and the Danube valley, one after the other, will be drawn into the vast system of Nazi politics. And do not suppose that this is the end. It is only the beginning.

Having said that, Churchill was shouted down by the appeasers.

President Beneš, whose life had been threatened by the Germans, resigned and flew to London to live in exile. The Czech foreign minister, Dr. Kamil Krofta, said the requiem:

> We have been forced into this situation, now everything is at an end. Today it is our turn, tomorrow it will be the turn of others.

But it was left to Jan Masaryk, son of the founding father of the Republic of Czechoslovakia and now minister to London, to pose the really important question for Britain and the world.

On Black Wednesday, the day that Prime Minister Chamberlain announced that he would go to Munich to meet Hitler, Masaryk had listened to the debate from the diplomatic gallery of the House of Commons. With disbelief he heard Chamberlain tell the members and the world that he had brought peace in his time. Then Masaryk called on the prime minister and the foreign secretary at No. 10 Downing Street to discover whether the Czechs would be invited to Munich to participate in the discussion of their future as a nation. He learned that the answer was no.

Masaryk stopped talking and looked at Chamberlain and Foreign Secretary Anthony Eden, and their eyes dropped. "If you have sacrificed my nation to preserve the peace of the world," he said finally, "then I will be the first to applaud you. But if not, gentlemen, God help your souls."

Thus perished the new nation, created from the carcass of the Austro-Hungarian Empire by the western Allies in the flush of victory over their enemies of World War I. It had existed for less than twenty years. Now, although the land continued to bear its name, the soul was gone, sacrificed in the names of peace and freedom by men too frightened to realize that freedom is reserved for those who are willing to fight for it. The deed was done. And from that day forward the all-encompassing conflict that would be known as World War II was inevitable.

6

AND NEXT CAME
POLAND...

While most of the world marveled at the easy political victory Adolf Hitler had scored over the western democracies, and many mourned democratic Czechoslovakia, Hitler himself was not happy. General Keitel said that Hitler had really wanted a war so that he could add the whole of Czechoslovakia to his empire. As it was, the Germans got only about 20 percent of the country, at least in this initial go-round.

Worse, from Hitler's point of view, was that the sacrifice of Czechoslovakia and the supine show that Prime Minister Chamberlain had put on was now widely called "appeasement" in the west, and overnight it became a highly pejorative term. The democracies were beginning to get their backs up.

Hitler had hoped to put so much pressure on the Czechs that they would succumb to his wish that they join the Third Reich in military alliance. After Munich there was no hope of such a solution. Now, if Hitler wanted more, he would have to take it by force of arms, and as his generals knew, the possibility of general war increased with each passing day.

Late in October Hitler again began planning for war. The Oberkommando der Wehrmacht was instructed to draw up plans for the occupation of Memel and Danzig. General Keitel was sent north to get a picture of German readiness along the frontier with Poland. This "east wall" was the subject of several inspection trips by Hitler himself. He did not like what he saw and fired several commanders.

The Poles now came to Hitler's attention. Hitler had started something with the dismantling of Czechoslovakia. The Poles occupied Tesin and claimed possession of Moravian Ostrau and the largely German-speaking towns of Witkowitz and Oderberg. Hitler did not like that.

Admiral Horthy now raised his voice to claim Slovakia and the Carpatho-Ukraine areas of Czechoslovakia. Hitler was impatient about that; Horthy had lost his influence with Hitler when he refused to come to Hitler's side during the original Czechoslovak crisis.

As for the Czechs, under the new government that had replaced that of President Beneš, the country took a pro-German turn. OKW was pleased about that, because the Czech army was still strong enough to engage at least twenty-five German divisions should it come to a fight. In October the Czech minister to Berlin, Dr. Voytech Mastny, told Hermann Göring that his country had realigned its foreign policy on that of Germany.

On October 9 Hitler let the British prime minister know how greatly he valued the new friendship that Chamberlain saw in their relationship. In a speech to workers along the German west wall at Saarbrücken he announced that Germany was continuing her rearmament. He had been aroused by the announcement of British upgrading of their own rearmament program and by the resignation of Duff Cooper, first lord of the admiralty, in disgust over the Munich trouncing Britain had taken. Said Hitler:

> It only needs for Mr. Duff Cooper or Mr. Eden or Mr. Churchill to come to power in place of Chamberlain, and you can be quite sure that their aim would be to start a new world war. They make no bones about it, they admit it quite openly.

Hitler could orate all he wished. Germany's physical resources were severely strained just then, and there was no way he could undertake any more military adventures until the German economy caught up with his enormous expenditures. Still, he could plan, and he did. He anticipated that his war with England would begin in 1942. General Keitel was now operating on that assumption. Tanks, guns, and aircraft were on the list for stockpiling. Hitler told Göring, in the latter's capacity as economic czar, to launch a new giant Wehrmacht rearmament program. Göring responded immediately by ordering a fivefold increase in the Luftwaffe.

Keitel ordered all three services to submit, by December 1938, their plans for expansion.

The Luftwaffe's plan called for production of 500 of the new Heinkel 177 heavy bombers. These would be used to bomb Britain into shards.

The navy showed Hitler a conservative plan for two more battleships and more submarines. Hitler saw it and castigated Raeder. The new battleships *Bismarck* and *Tirpitz,* he charged, were underarmed and badly designed. Raeder admitted that, and he added that the whole German naval program was of very little use insofar as it was addressed to a possible war with Britain. When Raeder said that, Hitler lost his temper completely and went into a harangue, the gist of which was that the navy had to be ready to fight Britain. The outcome was the Z plan, under which the Germans would build by the end of 1943 six huge battleships (35,000 tons each) armed with 420-millimeter guns. Besides that, the U-boat fleet was to be vastly enlarged. All this would be a clear-cut violation of the naval agreement with Britain, but Hitler did not care. He knew that by 1943 he would have renounced the naval agreement anyhow. He had no intention of abiding by any treaties he had made once they were no longer of use to him.

As for the army, Hitler took a personal interest in its reformation. He remained furious with the generals because of their attitude before Munich, and he demanded of Keitel a list of senior officers who were candidates for retirement. On October 28 the chief of the *Landwehr* ("Land Army"), General von Brauchitsch, and Göring went over that list, and two days later it was given to Hitler. All the leading opponents of Hitler's policies, their names and positions carefully noted by the Gestapo, were retired at one time. Hitler did not know it, but one side effect of the upheaval in the army was that it broke up the conspiracy that might have led to open rebellion. Von Rundstedt and Beck, two of the conspirators, were now out of office and power.

*

In the fall of 1938 the world had a demonstration of what life would be like in a German world. Dr. Goebbels had gotten into trouble with Hitler because the propaganda minister was forever chasing women; in the summer of 1938 he was having an affair with a film actress, and his forcible seductions (some called them rapes) of dozens of women were a conversation topic at Berlin dinner tables. So Goebbels decided to do something spectacular to regain Hitler's favor. His opportunity came when a half-mad young Jew invaded the German Embassy in Paris and shot Counsellor Ernst vom Rath. Subsequently, vom Rath died. He was one of the party faithful, and Hitler thought so highly of him that he had sent his own physician to Paris to try to save the diplomat's life.

Goebbels got in touch with various elements of the SS and the Gestapo and started a national pogrom against the Jews on November 9. That day and the next, hundreds of Jewish businesses, synagogues, and homes were burned to the ground; Jews were beaten, ninety-one were killed, and many were injured. It covered all of Germany, and it shocked the world. It also shocked Hitler, who had known nothing about it and was furious that Goebbels had taken the law into his own hands. Afterward, however, he backed Goebbels. He imposed a fine of a billion marks on the Jewish community for the shooting of vom Rath, and the compensation due to the Jews for the property damage was confiscated by the Reich on the pretext that it was a part of the settlement for the murder of the counsellor.

In fact, this night of horror, *Kristalnacht* ("night of glass"), November 9, 1938, was the beginning of the Holocaust.

Hitler's feelings about the Jews had been well aired in *Mein Kampf,* but in recent years he had been too busy with problems of state to give much personal attention to the matter. His underlings, nevertheless, had been pursuing it with ardor. Goebbels's actions in November reminded him of this priority, and on January 30, in a major speech to the Reichstag, he warned the world and the Jews of what was coming:

I have very often been a prophet in my lifetime and I have usually been laughed at for it. During my struggle for power, it was primarily the Jewish people who just laughed when they heard me prophesy that one day I would become head of state and

thereby assume the leadership of the entire people, and that I
would then among other things, subject the Jewish problem to
a solution. I expect that the howls of laughter that rose then
from the throats of German Jewry have by now died to a croak.

Today I'm going to turn prophet yet again: if international
finance Jewry inside and outside Europe should succeed once
more in plunging our people into a world war, then the outcome
will not be a Bolshevization of the world and therewith the victory of Jewry, but the destruction of the Jewish race in Europe.

In the spring of 1939 the OKW came up with a new directive for
deployment and battle. General Keitel was promoted in grade as
chief of Oberkommando der Wehrmacht. Hitler was intensifying his
preparations for war.

For months Hitler had been bothering himself with the "problem" of Danzig. Another of the provisions of the Treaty of Versailles
was about to haunt the world. At Versailles the west had cut Germany in two. The creation of a corridor that separated East Prussia
from the rest of Germany and the establishment of Danzig as a
"free" city had been dreadful geographical and political mistakes.
East Prussia was an integral part of Germany and had been since
the nineteenth century when Bismarck put together the German Empire. In their vengeful spirit and their practical desire to give the
new state of Poland an outlet to the sea, the Allies had quite overlooked German revanchism. Now that national desire was melding
with the Führer's requirement for *Lebensraum*.

In April 1939 Hitler began renunciation of the treaty of nonaggression signed with Poland five years earlier. Still, the policy was
to go slow. General Keitel sent a message to the chief of the General Staff saying that expansion had to be completed by 1943. There
would be no mobilizations before that time, Hitler had ordered. Virtually all army weapons production was stopped in 1939 to allow
the naval and Luftwaffe programs to move quickly because by 1944
each of the services was to have been tripled in size and strength.
The Luftwaffe would consist of sixteen fighter wings and fifty-eight
bomber wings, mostly ME-109s, ME-110s, Heinkel 177s, and Junkers 88s.

On January 17, 1939, Hitler declared that the naval program had absolute priority over all others, and even Göring agreed to that. That month and the next Hitler devoted much time to a series of speeches to the Officer Corps, trying to undo the damage he felt had been done by Beck and his fellow generals who did not believe in their Führer's aims or methods. His first speech was made to 3000 army lieutenants. His second was made to 200 generals and admirals. His third speech was before several hundred army colonels. He laid out for them the past and the future. The Rhineland had been occupied in 1936, although the original timetable had called for 1937. The year 1938 had brought the triumph in Czechoslovakia. "It is only one step along the long path, gentlemen," he said.

Early in 1939 Hitler ordered all three armed services to prepare with all possible speed a new operations plan, this one for war against Poland. It would be called "Operation White."

Meanwhile, Hitler was preparing to end the life of the rump Czechoslovak republic. He had begun this process less than ten days after signing the Munich agreement and solemnly assuring the western Allies that he had no further territorial ambitions regarding Czechoslovakia. The question asked of OKW was, "What reinforcements are necessary in the present situation to break all Czech resistance in Bohemia and Moravia?"

*　　*　　*

In *Mein Kampf* Hitler had said that only after all the racial Germans in Europe had been assimilated into the Reich—only then—would it be possible to consider the expansion of the German Empire to include other peoples. There were yet ethnic Germans in a number of countries. Now, in deciding that most of Czechoslovakia would be absorbed, Hitler was already expanding his aims. He would include Czechs, a non-Germanic people, in his empire. But not Slovaks.

"An independent Slovakia," wrote one foreign office official, "would be weak constitutionally and would therefore best further the German need for penetration and settlement in the East."

In March 1939 Hitler induced the Prague government to grant "independence" to Slovakia and Ruthenia. The Czechs no longer had serious illusions about offering military resistance.

On March 14 President Hacha of Czechoslovakia asked to be

received by Hitler to discuss the problems of what was left of his
country. The Führer graciously assented. And so, on the night of
March 14, the Czech president and his foreign minister came in by
train from Prague to the Anhalt railroad station in Berlin. Their trip
was uneventful except that as their train moved through Czech territory, the president learned that the Germans had occupied the town
of Moravska-Ostrava and were already on the edge of the provinces
of Bohemia and Moravia, ready to move.

A new drama was about to begin.

Hitler had spent the evening in the music room of the Chancellery,
watching a movie: *Ein Hoffnungsloser Fall* ("A Hopeless Case").
How fitting a title! When Foreign Minister von Ribbentrop announced that the Czech party had arrived at Anhalt station, Hitler
examined his fingernails, which were spotless as usual, and softly
said that "the old fellow" should be allowed to rest a little. As everyone knew, President Hacha had a bad heart. What Hitler had in
store for him was not calculated to improve his health.

When the Czech president and his party arrived at the Chancellery, at about midnight, they were given a full military welcome by
the SS guard, the sort of drums and cymbals ceremony accorded
heads of state. But they were then kept waiting in an anteroom until 1:15 a.m. Finally, Hitler summoned them to his office. Foreign
Minister von Ribbentrop was there. So were Field Marshal Göring
and General Keitel.

After virtually no preliminaries, Hitler gave Hacha the word. On
Sunday, March 12, Hitler had decided that Czechoslovakia was to
cease to exist. It was to be incorporated within the German Reich.
The occupation would begin at six o'clock on March 15.

Actually it had already begun. General Keitel interrupted Hitler
with a note: Witkowitz had been occupied by the Germans, he said.
Hitler nodded with satisfaction. Before 4 a.m. President Hacha telephoned Prague and gave the bad news to his cabinet. He told them
resistance was futile; the Germans had a division for every Czech
battalion.

So Czechoslovakia died.

*

Keitel left the Chancellery and headed for the Czech frontier. From there he drove on in a long convoy of motor vehicles along the Prague road, and soon they came to the marching columns of German infantry. It was a cold winter's night; the troops were marching through snow drifts and black ice. They reached the outskirts of Prague the next day, just as dusk was falling, and Keitel drove down the Hradshin to his billet, Hradcany Castle, the president's own mansion. Hitler had already arrived on his special train. They had a cold supper that night: Prague ham, rolls, butter, cheese, fruit, and pilsner beer. Even Hitler, who almost never drank, had a small glass of beer. It was not every day that Pilsen became part of the Reich.

At about noon on March 16 President Hacha and his government came to Hitler's wing of the presidential palace to declare their loyalty to Germany. Hitler then declared an official "protectorate" over Bohemia and Moravia. Freiherr von Neurath would be the "protector" of the new entity.

Czechoslovakia? There was no such place.

From Prague Hitler traveled down to Vienna. At the Imperial Hotel he drafted a treaty with the new nation of Slovakia, another German protectorate. The map of Europe had once again been redrawn.

And it was to be redrawn again a week later. Hitler issued an ultimatum to Lithuania over Memel, another city wrested from Germany by the Versailles treaty. The Lithuanian government gave in immediately and transferred the city back to Germany. Hitler arrived in Memel aboard the German cruiser *Deutschland,* and he made a symbolic tour of the city. Another bit of old Germany restored.

But Hitler's action had other consequences. His ultimatum for Memel had aroused the Poles to mobilize their troops along the German border and to reject brusquely Hitler's suggestions about Danzig. They went further. If Hitler persisted in pushing them about Danzig and the corridor, it would lead to war, said the Poles.

Ernst von Weizsäcker, one of Hitler's close advisers, suggested that the Germans had now used up all their international goodwill, over Memel and Prague, and that the Danzig problem could no longer be solved by negotiation. "The only way we can deal with the Poles' insolent attitude...is by breaking the Polish spirit," he said.

*

At Munich, Britain and France had guaranteed Czechoslovakia against aggression. But they did nothing.

Small wonder, then, that Hitler had concluded that Britain would not fight and that little further attention had to be paid to London's views on European affairs. Not only the Führer held this view; Chamberlain and company had persuaded Mussolini that the British were finished as a world power.

But now the worm was preparing to turn. Anyone who had ever read *Mein Kampf* should have known what was going to happen next. The government in London certainly knew. And on March 31 Prime Minister Chamberlain spoke up in the House of Commons:

> In the event of any action which clearly threatened Polish independence and which the Polish Government considered accordingly it to be vital to resist with their national forces, His Majesty's Government would feel themselves bound at once to lend the Polish Government all support in their power. They have given the Polish Government an assurance to this effect. I may add that the French Government have authorized me to make it plain that they stand in the same position in this matter.

But Hitler was no longer listening to London. From there had come too much twaddle. His mind was made up: Poland was next on his list.

As we have seen, his immediate goal was to regain Danzig and the Polish corridor. In March 1939 Hitler had offered the Poles a deal: if they would agree to the return of the free city of Danzig to Germany and give Germany a secure corridor across the Polish corridor, linking Germany proper with East Prussia, Hitler would recognize the Polish western frontier and accept their corridor as permanent. (He did not mean a word of it, and the Poles knew it.)

But after Czechoslovakia, after the creation of Slovakia, after the Memel ultimatum—everything changed. The Poles told Hitler to go to hell.

At this point General Keitel hoped that Hitler would call a halt. He wanted that reprieve until 1943 which Hitler kept promising the army. The army's problem was training. The old Officer Corps had been broken up; the last act had been that forcible retirement of several dozen generals that winter. Hitler's answer—Nazi indoctrination—was no answer at all. One of Hitler's many fundamental errors, which would dog him in the years to come, was his failure to understand that training is the basis of a strong army. A strong Officer Corps and a well-trained noncommissioned officer cadre are essential. Hitler really believed that his elite troops of the SS were at least the equivalent of any of his army divisions. It was an illusion he would cherish until almost the end.

Certainly the German army's best units were excellent, and they would prove themselves in the early fighting. But these units suffered from a lack of depth. That would prove to be one great mistake, attributable to Hitler's basic inability to understand the elements of an army. A World War I corporal, no matter how brave, was not a general.

Much as Keitel wanted that four-year delay before combat, by April he knew in his heart that he was not going to get it. Hitler was forever mentioning Poland.

All that he had to do, Hitler said, was what he had done before: show a strong right arm and the silly British would collapse from fright.

Hitler did not want a war with Poland over Danzig and the corridor, he told Keitel, but strength was the basis of diplomacy; if he wanted to achieve peace, he would have to prepare for war.

The news that Britain had guaranteed Poland's security, which reached Berlin on March 31, sent Hitler into a rage. The next day he went to Wilhelmshaven to attend the launching of the battleship *Tirpitz,* and he made a speech so fiery that he later ordered that its broadcast, scheduled for that night, be canceled and that the speech be edited first. In it he warned the west of war to come.

On April 3 Hitler issued his directive for Case White, the attack on Poland. September 1 was the key day.

On April 28, replying to a message from American President Franklin D. Roosevelt asking for guarantees that Hitler's armies would not attack other nations, Hitler made a two-hour speech that was carried by the radio networks of all of Europe and the United States. He renounced the Anglo-German Naval Treaty of 1935. He denied that he had any intention of attacking Poland. But since Poland had violated the German-Polish nonaggression pact by calling up its troops, Hitler said, and by making a treaty with Britain that was obviously aimed at Germany, the German-Polish pact was now void. He devoted part of his address to ridicule of the American president, and his Reichstag listeners roared their laughter and approval.

Following this propaganda victory, which was regarded as the greatest he had yet achieved, Hitler retired to Berchtesgaden.

On May 22 Germany concluded the "Pact of Steel" with Mussolini's Italy.

On May 23, Hitler went to Berlin and called in his military leaders. He told them that war was coming, and he outlined the course of it: Poland, and then Britain and France. It might be a long war, he warned. "The aim," Hitler said, "will always be to force England to her knees."

So Hitler had declared himself. War was coming. There was no question about it.

The preparations were already well along. Spurred by forced savings and internal credit, the armament factories were working overtime turning out guns, planes, tanks, and warships. The Luftwaffe now consisted of twenty-one wings and 260,000 men. The armament industry was producing more than it had at the peak of World War I. Its output was greater than that of any other country. Germany was already the most heavily armed nation in the world.

Late in August, to strengthen his position in the east, Hitler concluded a pact with his old enemies, the Communists. The Nazi-Soviet pact, as published, simply guaranteed that in the case of an attack by another nation on either the Soviet Union or Germany, the other would not lend support to the third power. Thus, if Hitler attacked Poland and then Britain attacked Hitler, the U.S.S.R. would not join in on the side of Britain, regardless of its treaties with France or Poland.

But there were secret protocols to this treaty. One gave the U.S.S.R. German permission to attack Finland, Estonia, Latvia, and Lithuania. And both nations agreed to partition Poland between themselves, with the frontier at the rivers Narew, Vistula, and San.

So Hitler's way was cleared. Now he could start his war.

7

HITLER STARTS
HIS WAR

All summer the Wehrmacht had been studying the problem: how to invade and defeat Poland as quickly as possible.

All spring and summer the workmen on the west wall had labored at top speed to get the defenses ready so that Germany, when attacking Poland in the east, could not be struck in the back by France or England.

General Keitel spent much of the summer trying to persuade Hitler that the army was not ready for war. He, like most German generals, was particularly worried about the possibility of war on two fronts. Keitel kept telling Hitler of the risk, although he knew full well that the advice served only to make Hitler distrust his generals even more than he had in the past.

Early in August Hitler had made an egregious error. He called the chiefs of staff of the various military commands to the Berghof for a meeting. Because of his profound distrust of the senior commanders, he was again trying to woo their principal subordinates away from them. He spoke long and eloquently, but when he was finished, there was silence. He had not made a good impression. As if attempting to make up for it, a few days later he spoke to the generals of the eastern German armies arrayed against Poland. This time he tried to be conciliatory, but the generals were not overly impressed. Hitler's long-standing distrust was continuing to drive a rift between his entourage and the army. To say that this rift was a major cause of Germany's ultimate defeat would be overstating the case, but Hitler's attitude clearly was a major cause of difficulty all through the war.

All this while, the last ten days of August, Hitler was worrying about the impending German-Soviet pact that would help in his invasion of Poland, but he was also going full steam ahead with the invasion plans.

On August 24, 1939, Hitler arrived in Berlin. August 26 was P day— the date for the invasion of Poland. On August 25 Hitler summoned General Keitel to the Chancellery. He had just received some startling bad news. Under the terms of the Pact of Steel with Italy, Mussolini was bound to join Hitler in the war. He had written Mussolini a letter outlining the steps he was taking and specifying the August 26 invasion date. He had fully expected the news to leak from Rome to London, followed by another last minute action by Chamberlain to try to prevent the war. There was no question in Hitler's mind: he would face down Chamberlain and win another diplomatic victory beneath his guns.

But Mussolini had "betrayed" him, he discovered on the morning of August 25. Mussolini had replied to Hitler's letter that the king of Italy had invoked his one great power: he had refused to sign the mobilization order presented to him by Mussolini. Therefore, Mussolini could be of no assistance to Hitler in this venture.

The shock was enormous. There was no chance now of winning a diplomatic demarche. Hitler's anger against Mussolini was furthered by a thinly veiled blackmail demand that if Hitler could find such war materials as rubber, tin, copper, manganese, and steel to ship to Rome, then perhaps Mussolini could review the situation.

So important did the matter appear to Hitler that he wasted no time on recriminations, but instructed Keitel to find out if Germany could supply these materials to Italy.

For Hitler was now seriously worried. He recognized that he had miscalculated:

There's absolutely no doubt that London has realized by now that Italy won't go along with us. Now Britain's attitude towards us will stiffen—now they will back up Poland to the hilt. The diplomatic result of my letter is exactly the opposite of what I had planned.

And he told Keitel that the British government, which had been sitting on the Polish defense treaty, would now dust it off and ratify it posthaste.

Keitel went back to the War Ministry to try to find out if Germany could supply Italy. Early that same afternoon he was summoned to the Reich Chancellery once more. Hitler was even more agitated than he had been in the morning. He was, to put it bluntly, rattled.

He had just received a message stating that the British-Polish treaty was being ratified that very day by the British. He wanted more time to negotiate now, so he asked Keitel to pull back the troops, who were supposed to attack the next day. What Hitler had wanted, of course, was a last-minute plea by the British to call off the invasion; he supposed that he could then repeat the Munich performance, get back his Polish corridor and Danzig, and then conspire with the Soviets to partition Poland at his leisure.

So the invasion of Poland was postponed until August 31.

It soon became obvious that Mussolini's demands for strategic materials were so impossibly high that they could not be met. Even the Italian ambassador to Berlin thought there must have been some error in the figures. But no, Hitler knew: Mussolini had simply used this ploy as a means of getting out of his agreement to support Hitler in any military adventure he wanted to start.

For the next five days the diplomats in the European chanceries fluttered in a series of furious negotiations. But Hitler's demands were the usual ones: Danzig, a road across the Polish corridor immediately, cession to Germany of all former German territories with mostly German population, and a plebiscite to determine the future of the Polish corridor.

On August 31 the invasion was once more postponed for a day. Hitler was awaiting the arrival of a Polish envoy in Berlin who might be prepared to meet Germany's demands.

But no such eleventh-hour reprieve came, and this time Hitler was committed to action. As dawn broke on September 1, 1939, the Luftwaffe began bombing Polish railroad junctions and airfields. There was no declaration of war; the Germans simply invaded.

For three days various personages, including President Roosevelt, tried to persuade Hitler to stop his attack. He was obdurate. If he was not given what he wanted, he was going to take it.

Until the last, Hitler did not really believe the western democracies would actually declare war on Germany. On the night of September 2 everyone around the Chancellery was in a splendid mood, reported Hitler's army liaison officer, Colonel von Vormann. But at nine o'clock on the morning of September 3, British Ambassador Nevile Henderson came to the Foreign Ministry bearing the ultimatum from London. Hitler had until 11 a.m. to move his troops out of Poland. And at 11 a.m. in came the French ambassador bearing a similar ultimatum from Paris. Hitler had until 5 p.m. to move his troops out of Poland.

Hitler did not move his troops. He scoffed that the British and French were too effete to fight.

But Colonel von Vormann had another feeling:

> I'm not a grouser or a defeatist, but the future looks very grim to me. This is just what we didn't want. Until this morning the idea was to play for time somehow and to postpone the decision. Even today the Führer still believes that the Western powers are only going to stage a phony war so to speak. That's why I've had to transmit an order to the Army at 1:50 not to commit hostilities in the West ourselves. I can't share his belief. He's got the wrong idea of the British and French psyche.

And so on September 3, 1939, Britain and France, honoring their treaties with Poland, declared war on Germany.

Hitler dictated proclamations to the German people, to the Nazi party, and to the Wehrmacht. He signed them, and then he left the Chancellery. He boarded his special train and headed for the Polish front, where he would direct military operations himself.

The British and French might do a lot of talking, Hitler said, but they would not fight. And as the days went on, General Keitel and the others began to believe that Hitler might just be right. For there was no attack on the western front, where the Germans were completely vulnerable. Had the French attacked, they almost certainly could have broken through; Hitler would then have been forced to move troops from the east to the west. The pressure would have been off the Poles, and no one could know what would happen then. But the French did not move. Keitel in particular could not understand the failure of the French to attack, thus making the slaughter of the Polish army inevitable.

In this fighting, Hitler displayed one of the characteristics that tended to put the German people squarely behind him. General von Briesen, the commander of the Thirtieth Infantry Division, had been assigned a position on the flank of General Johannes Blaskowitz's Eighth Army, which had surrounded a Polish army. The Poles had launched attack after attack to break out, and most of them had come against the Thirtieth Division. After some heavy fighting Hitler visited this section of the front, still under the enemy guns, and found General von Briesen in a schoolhouse that had become his headquarters. Von Briesen was wearing a bandage on his left arm, and Hitler and Keitel learned that the general's left forearm had been shot off. Asked about it, von Briesen admitted that he had led his last reserve battalion into action himself, and had thus stopped the Polish breakout. When they left the command post, Hitler, who hated most Prussian generals of the royal school, praised von Briesen:

> That is a real Prussian general of the royal school. You can't have enough soldiers like him. He is a man after my own heart. Before today is over I want him to be the first divisional commander to get the Knight's Cross [of the Iron Cross]. He has saved Blaskowitz's army by his gallantry and drive.

Of course, within days the whole army knew of the honor given General von Briesen, and German morale went up several notches.

*   *   *

The war was real from the beginning, no matter what Hitler said. On September 3, 1939, U-boat skipper Fritz Lemp took sight on the British liner *Athenia* and sent a torpedo into the ship. It sank that day, taking down a number of civilians, including some Americans. Here, on the very first day of the war against Britain, the Germans had violated the rules of submarine warfare that they had accepted in the naval agreement of 1935, rules that were supposed to govern the actions of every country.

Then came another reminder that the war was real. Colonel General von Fritsch, he who had been so badly used in the scandal trumped up by Heinrich Himmler, was killed on the Polish front. Von Fritsch had wanted an army, but he had not gotten it. The fact was that Hitler did not want to employ these old-school generals. He had also promised Field Marshal von Blomberg that if war came, von Blomberg would be put back in harness, but Hitler had not wanted to put Blomberg back. Nor had he given von Fritsch his army but a staff post with the Twelfth Artillery Regiment as an observer for OKW. A stray bullet had struck von Fritsch while he was talking to some other officers, and he bled to death.

A state funeral was held, for von Fritsch had been ill-used by Hitler and all Germany knew it. Hitler did not attend; he was too busy at his little headquarters at Zoppot. But he sent a wreath, and von Fritsch got a grand send-off, with all the dignitaries of Berlin in attendance. The war had taken its first fatality among the generals.

The destruction of the Polish army was so easy it was almost startling. For the Germans were employing entirely new battle tactics. General Heinz Guderian had raced east across the Polish corridor with his panzers. The result would become typical of this war: the Poles attacked, but with mounted cavalry. Horses against tanks. Anyone could predict the result. It was a dreadful carnage. And the blitzkrieg, the "lightning war," was born.

Part of the technique was the racing tanks. Another facet was the screaming Stukas, the German dive-bombers that came down with such a screech that they terrified the whole area over which they attacked. The world had not seen anything like this: tanks lunging 40 miles a day, self-propelled guns keeping right up with them. The army of 1 1/2 million men was almost completely motorized, moving according to orders by radio, telephone, and telegraph, orders transmitted with what had to seem to the Poles to be lightning speed.

Within two days the Polish air force had been destroyed completely. Most of its 500 modern planes were blown up by German air attacks on their home fields before they could even take off. Cracow, the second city of Poland, fell on September 6. That night the Polish government fled Warsaw and went into exile. It was really all over then.

Much of this had occurred because the French had failed to take the pressure off the Poles. The Polish army was completely outmoded, and its strategy and tactics were those of World War I. So the defeat would have happened inevitably anyhow, the British and the French told themselves—although perhaps it would not have been quite so brutal or so swift had the British and the French been poised to go into action immediately. They had all sorts of excuses, but the fact was that if the British and the French had moved fast in early September 1939, they could have occupied the Ruhr and the Rhineland and knocked Germany out of the war. They had the matériel and the men, but not the will to do it. As Winston Churchill said, the battle had been lost at Munich. The Munich sickness was still endemic in western Europe; until it was cured, nothing could be done and Hitler would have his way.

In a week the Polish army was finished. Most of its thirty-five divisions were in shambles. The second phase of the war involved surrounding the remaining units and wiping them out. The entrapment of the Polish troops west of Brest-Litovsk and the River Bug was begun. On September 16 General Heinz Guderian's Nineteenth Corps reached Brest-Litovsk. The next day his corps met General List's Fourteenth Army a few miles south of Brest-Litovsk and closed the ring on tens of thousands of Polish troops. All Polish forces save a handful on the Soviet border were now surrounded. The military action was virtually ended.

Now Stalin became worried that Hitler would not live up to his bargain to let the Soviets have the eastern part of the country. So the strange partners, Germany and the U.S.S.R., each of whose leaders detested the other's social system, began to quarrel even before their alliance was cemented by action.

The bickering continued. Ultimately the Soviets and Germans split Poland, and the Soviets also took this opportunity to take over Estonia, Lithuania, and Latvia. This did not sit well with the Germans, although they had agreed to it in principle, because in Estonia and Latvia alone there were nearly 100,000 *Volksdeutsche* (ethnic Germans). The Germans got nearly all of populous Poland, including Lublin and the lands east of Warsaw. But on September 28 the map of eastern Europe was drawn again by the partners, and the big change was announced at a state banquet in Moscow.

And what had happened to Poland? One of the secret protocols of the new treaty told all:

> Both parties will tolerate in their territories no Polish agitation which affects the territories of the other party. They will suppress in their territories all beginnings of such agitation and inform each other concerning suitable measures for this purpose.

Poland, like Czechoslovakia, had ceased to exist.

One other secret protocol of this treaty pledged the two totalitarian leaders, Stalin and Hitler, to establish in Poland regimes of terror which were calculated to suppress Polish culture.

Even so, in the end the Nazi-Soviet pact of August 1939 turned out to be another of Hitler's shortsighted calculations. It has gone down in history as justified by the Germans to lull Stalin into a state of self-satisfaction while Germany prepared for her *drang nach Osten*—"drive to the east"—which appeared in the pages of *Mein Kampf*.

But the fact was that the Germans wiped out the Polish military forces in a week without any help from Stalin and that the Soviets, without firing more than a few shots, had secured control of the Baltic states and almost half of Poland, albeit the agricultural, nonpopulous half. Stalin now blocked Hitler's way to Ukrainian wheat and Romanian oil. Even Poland's fairly important oil region of Borislav-Drogobyz was taken over by Stalin.

The justification for paying this territorial price to the Soviets was that Hitler had to keep his rear protected while he dealt with whatever threat the western Allies might pose. But the Führer had neglected the fact that Stalin was in no position in the summer of 1939 to take on a war with the most powerful army in Europe; nor is it likely that Stalin would have honored the Soviet-Polish alliance that would have pitted him against Germany, particularly after seeing how the German army sliced through Poland like a knife through cheese. No, Hitler's deal with Stalin had to be counted as one of the Führer's basic errors, one that would lead him to an even worse error at a worse time because of his resentment of this bargain he had struck.

In the west, despite all the saber rattling of the British and the French, the war was nothing at all. Berliners, noting that it had not been so quiet on the western front since the autumn of 1918, joked and called the war in the west the great *Sitzkrieg,* or "sitting war." In London the people on the street began to refer to it as "the phony war."

It was indeed a strange war. France, which had the largest army in Europe, assigned that army to sit in the bunkers of the Maginot line, facing the German west wall, and wait.

So the French troops waited while the Polish army was wiped out. The German generals now reversed field and agreed with their Führer: the French, they said, did not want to fight and had no intention of carrying out an offensive war.

By September 6 General Halder had recognized that France, instead of being strong, was weak and badly led. He had begun planning to transfer whole divisions to the western front, making this recommendation, less than a week after the German troops had begun rushing through Poland.

On September 9 Hitler issued the order: air force and army units would be moved to the west. Hitler was immensely pleased with himself. Once again he had shown up his generals with their faint hearts. He had told the generals that the French and the British would not fight, and although both nations had declared war, they had not fought.

So the German troops began moving toward the west wall. The British finally got under way in the first week of October, but then sent only 160,000 troops across the Channel.

Worse, the French and the British could not agree on what was to be done. The British Royal Air Force wanted to bomb German targets. Göring agreed that if the British had struck hard at the Ruhr with their bombers in those first days when the Luftwaffe was concentrating its efforts against Poland, the German war effort might have been crippled. But the French wailed that if the British bombed German targets, the Germans would retaliate against French tar-

gets. This was hardly a war spirit. The British allowed themselves
to be persuaded to refrain from bombing.

And so, while there was a war in principle, following the occupation of Poland, there was no war in fact on the land of Europe.
Only at sea was the war real at the beginning; the U-boats were
sinking British ships by the score. During the first week of the war,
Admiral Karl Dönitz's submarines sank 65,000 tons of Allied shipping. But then Hitler intervened. He saw what France was doing,
and he felt that Britain, too, had no enthusiasm for the war. Would
it not be wonderful if a peace could be concluded that would take
France and Britain out of hostilities and give the German generals
those three and a half years, until 1943, that they wanted? The generals had promised that by then they would be prepared to go to
war against the world if necessary.

So Hitler had called in Admiral Erich Raeder, chief of his navy,
and told him to go slow on the sea, as the army was doing on the
land. No French shipping was to be attacked, and no more British
passenger vessels. Dönitz could continue to sink British merchant
shipping, but the surface raiders would not go out as had been
planned. The war at sea would be scaled down in the hope that the
whole effort could be brought to an end within the next month or
two. By September 20, when Poland was being absorbed, the talk
in the western press was about "peace." In Berlin, too, correspondent William Shirer noted in his diary entry of September 20 that
the man on the street was talking about peace, which most Germans expected to come at any moment, because Herr Hitler had
once again shown the world that Germany really wanted peace. The
day before, in a speech in the newly recovered German city of Danzig, Hitler had declared:

> I have no war aims against Britain and France. My sympathies
> are with the French *poilu* [soldier]. What he is fighting for he
> does not know.

And there in Danzig Hitler called upon God, whom he declared
to be on Germany's side, to make the western Allies understand
the realities of war, how useless it would be, and how blessed peace
would be.

What Hitler meant, of course, and he was joined in his pious mouthings by Stalin—who was digesting the other half of Poland, plus Estonia, Latvia, and Lithuania—was how blessed peace, German style and Soviet style, would be for those two parties. After all, Hitler was only talking about peace for three or four years, until his generals would be ready to drive France and Britain to the wall.

8

THE PHONY WAR

The war in Poland ended with an enormous German military parade through the streets—or what was left of them—of Warsaw. Hitler flew in from Germany for the parade, but when he saw that at the airfield a banquet had been laid out for him in a hangar, he turned on his heel and ordered his pilot to warm up the plane for takeoff.

"I never eat with the troops except standing at a field kitchen," he said. And he left immediately for Berlin.

The banquet over, General von Brauchitsch ordered the first divisions to move to the western front. The first soldiers arrived at Aachen, specifically because Hitler had ordered it. He had examined the western front and found that his forces on the Dutch and Belgian frontiers were far too weak.

The talk in Berlin continued to be of the prospects for peace.

Just as Warsaw fell, the German press and radio began a peace offensive. "Why do France and Britain want to fight?" was the question asked by Dr. Goebbels's propagandists. "Germany wants nothing from the west."

At the end of September Hitler told a Swedish diplomat that he had not given up his hope for peace. "If the British actually want peace, they can have it in two weeks without losing face," said Hitler.

But, of course, while Hitler spoke that way to foreign diplomats and the press, he was taking quite the opposite tack with his generals. When would they be ready to attack in the west? he demanded.

One thing Hitler did know: if and when Winston Churchill became the leader of the British government, all talk of peace would end. "Then," said Hitler, "we shall fight. There will never be another November 1918 in German history."

Early in October Hitler waited for some word from the western leaders. It came in the middle of the first week of that month in the report of an address by Chamberlain to the House of Commons. The prime minister argued that Hitler's talk was no more than talk and that it contained no hint of any intention of righting the wrongs Hitler had done in Czechoslovakia and Poland. No reliance could be placed on the word of the present German government, he said.

So Hitler knew at last that the performance of Munich could not be duplicated. He was already preparing for an attack on the west; now he doubled his efforts.

On October 10 Hitler issued a new directive to the generals he trusted so little:

> If it should become apparent in the near future that England and under England's leadership, also France, are not willing to make an end of the war, I am determined to act vigorously and aggressively without great delay. Therefore I give the following orders:
>
> a. Preparations are to be made for an attacking operation through the areas of Luxembourg, Belgium and Holland. These attacks must be carried out at as early a date as possible.
>
> b. The purpose will be to defeat as strong a part of the French operational army as possible, as well as allies fighting by its side, and at the same time to gain as large an area as possible in Holland, Belgium, and Northern France as a base for conducting a promising air and sea war against England.

Hitler was very much afraid of a long war. Time would be working against Germany, he said. Neutrals might be drawn in on the opposing side (and here he was thinking of the Soviet Union and the United States). Germany's limited food and raw material base would make it difficult to carry on a long war. And the Ruhr was terribly vulnerable to land and air attack. If this area collapsed, then Germany's war effort must follow very closely.

Thus Hitler revealed his reasons for wanting to end the war quickly. He indicated a grasp of the situation far greater than any other participant save Winston Churchill. Churchill knew that time would work on the side of Britain—if the country could sustain itself against the greatest danger: U-boat attack. A strong German submarine campaign, similar to that employed in World War I, would threaten the lifeline Britain must have across the Atlantic to Canada, the United States, and Latin America.

For weeks Hitler's troops moved westward as fast as the carrying capacity of Germany's railroads would allow. The talk of peace was so pervasive, however, that the army General Staff ordered a partial demobilization, and General Keitel had to step in, as OKW commander, to stop it. He still had to be prepared for a real war in the west, but the troops were tired after the fighting in Poland and needed a rest. And the Maginot line still seemed extremely formidable.

The French had sixty-five active divisions and forty-five reserve divisions. The Germans had only thirty-five divisions on the Siegfried line (the west wall) all during the Polish campaign. The generals did not believe the German army had the proper weapons to breach the French fortification line. It was apparent that when the time came to attack, Hitler's army would have to move through northern France, Luxembourg, and Belgium, where the permanent fortifications were few, weak, or nonexistent.

But the weeks went by and virtually nothing happened. Only along the Saarbrücken sector and in the Perl area south of Trier were there even outpost engagements. For weeks on end no shots were fired, and the civilian workers on the Siegfried line went on with their fortification efforts immediately behind the frontier.

By October the whole German order of battle in the west had changed. Instead of three armies, Hitler had eight in this area.

The Führer was impatient, holding that each day the army did not move gave the enemy time to strengthen its defenses. The British Expeditionary Force finally arrived on the continent in October. Hitler was also very much concerned that the French might make a lightning thrust at the Ruhr, and he knew that with their forces they

Adolf Hitler in the early days of the Nazi party. *(The Bettmann Archive / BBC Hulton.)*

Hitler and General von Hindenburg greet the Nazis just after Hitler became Chancellor. *(The Bettmann Archive.)*

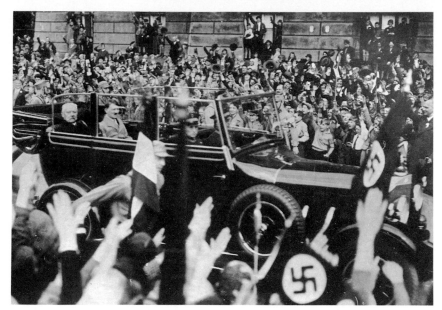

Hitler and President Hindenburg at a mass meeting of German youth, 1933.
(The Bettmann Archive.)

Generals of the old
school: General
Hans von Seeckt
and General Werner
von Blomberg.
*(AP/Wide World
Photos.)*

Hitler Mädchen on the march. These girls were part of the Nazi youth movement of the 1930s. *(The Bettmann Archive.)*

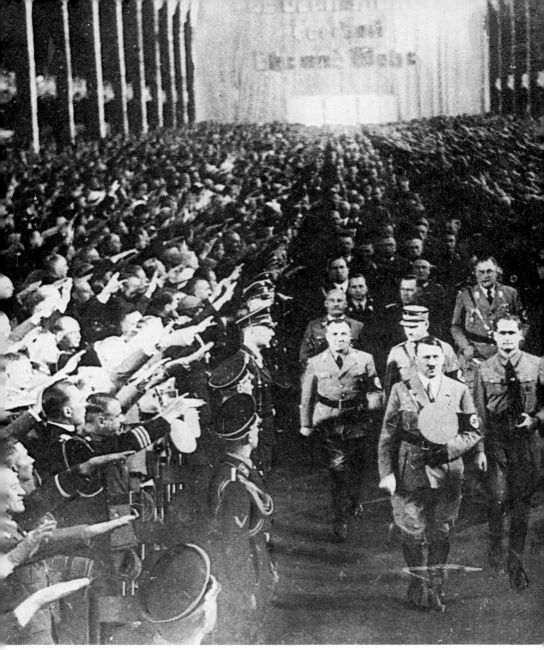

Hitler opens the Nazi Congress in 1935 as storm troopers salute. Hess is on the right. *(AP/Wide World Photos.)*

Franz von Papen. *(AP/Wide World Photos.)*

Chancellor Dollfuss at the time of the German takeover of Austria. *(The Bettmann Archive.)*

Hitler invades Austria. *(AP/Wide World Photos.)*

General von Bock with Austrian officers. *(AP/ Wide World Photos.)*

Hitler announces the annexation of Austria at a mass meeting in Vienna.
(UPI/Bettmann Newsphotos.)

The ranking officers review the troops: from left, Major General Hermann Göring, General von Fritsch, Admiral Raeder, and Field Marshal von Blomberg. *(The Bettmann Archive.)*

General von Bock, left, and Heinrich Himmler in the days before Himmler became really important. *(The Bettmann Archive.)*

Hitler takes a salute. *(AP/Wide World Photos.)*

Hitler at a horse show with General von Blomberg, left, and Goebbels, far right. *(AP/Wide World Photos.)*

Hitler and his Nazis. Hermann Göring is at top left.   *(UPI/Bettmann Newsphotos.)*

Hermann Göring gets his field marshal's baton from Hitler, 1938.   *(AP/Wide World Photos.)*

Hitler in Vienna, 1938. Behind him are two of his henchmen,
Hess and Goebbels. *(AP/Wide World Photos.)*

Hitler visits an art exhibition in Munich with Dr. Goebbels. *(AP/Wide World
Photos.)*

Goebbels, Hitler, and Mussolini with Italian and German officers in Rome.
(The Bettmann Archive.)

Hitler and Goebbels at the Reichskanzlerei.
(The Bettmann Archive.)

Hitler and his generals studying maps: from left, Halder, von Brauchitsch, Hitler, and Keitel. *(The Bettmann Archive/BBC Hulton.)*

General Feldmarschall Walther von Brauchitsch in the field with members of his staff. He served Hitler well but was finally cashiered. *(The Bettmann Archive.)*

Heinrich Himmler in 1938.
(AP/Wide World Photos.)

Hitler reaffirms his ultimatum to Czechoslovakia in an address at the Berlin Sports Palace. Seated in front, from left, are Goebbels, Göring, von Ribbentrop, Dr. Frick, and Heinrich Himmler. *(UPI/Bettmann Newsphotos.)*

In 1938, Hitler marches into the Sudetenland of Czechoslovakia. *(UPI/ Bettmann Newsphotos.)*

Studies of Hitler.   *(AP/Wide World Photos.)*

could do so. If they did, he counted the war lost. But he remained convinced that the French really would not fight. Even as he prepared, he exploited that feeling to the utmost; Hitler's fortunes had not risen so high by avoiding risks.

At this juncture, the Führer and his generals quarreled again. General Keitel had the definite impression that Hitler had no confidence in him, so he asked to be posted elsewhere. Hitler would not hear of it.

The disagreement was over the army's state of readiness for war. The generals argued that their forces needed much more training. During the Polish campaign, testified General von Brauchitsch, the infantry had been overly cautious and not attack-minded. The NCOs were not very proficient, nor were the soldiers in their basic tasks and skills. Also, the discipline of the troops was very poor. Von Brauchitsch said it reminded him of the terrible days in 1917 when the troops had rebelled.

All this talk pained Hitler enormously. At one meeting of Hitler, von Brauchitsch, and Keitel, the Führer jumped up in a fury and accused von Brauchitsch of defeatism. It seemed incomprehensible to Hitler that the commander in chief of the army would condemn his own troops just because of a little lack of discipline. Moreover, Hitler himself had been in Poland during the fighting, and none of the commanders had said a word about the fighting posture of the men that was anything but complimentary. Yet now, when the world was full of wonderment at the victory the German army had achieved, the commanders in chief of Oberkommando Wehrmacht (Armed Forces) and Oberkommando Heeres (Land Army) were being extremely pejorative about the whole thing.

Having tongue-lashed his chief generals, Hitler slammed out of his study, leaving them standing there looking at each other. Von Brauchitsch and Keitel separated immediately, each going his own way without a word.

About this time, Hitler began more closely examining the High Command's plans for war in the west. Generals Jodl, Halder, and Keitel were assembled to discuss the strategy. Halder did the talking. When he had finished, Hitler asked for his map, and Halder gave it to him and went out. Now the Führer spoke:

This is just the old Schlieffen Plan, you know, with a strong right flank along the Atlantic coast. You won't get away with

an operation like that twice running. I have quite a different idea
and I'll tell you about it in a day or two and then I'll talk it over
with the War Office myself.

Thus Keitel learned of Hitler's plan for the war in the west, which
was in fact the armored breakthrough at Sedan, striking up the Channel coast at Abbeville and then swinging around in the rear of the motorized British and French armies, which would be advancing on the
the Franco-Belgian frontier. The Germans would cut them off.

When Hitler advanced this plan to the War Office, it was almost
hooted down. Had he been any other than the supreme commander, the generals would have scoffed at him. As it was, they kept
their remarks to themselves when he was in the room, but on their
own they spoke scathingly of the "little corporal" who thought he
was a strategist. The only general who agreed with Hitler was von
Manstein, chief of staff to von Rundstedt's Army Group A. (The
aged von Rundstedt had been recalled from retirement.) Von Manstein saw immediately what his Führer had in mind; it was just the
sort of thing he had been considering himself.

What must be done, Hitler and von Manstein agreed, was to attack through Luxembourg, Belgium, and Holland, destroying all their
armies and the French and British armies. Thereby, the Germans would
gain positions on the English Channel and the North Sea from which
the Luftwaffe could be employed constantly against Britain to help
bring the country to its knees. Also, the establishment of U-boat
bases on the English Channel and the Atlantic shores of France
would be an enormous advantage in destroying British military shipping. Hitler saw all this, but his generals did not.

The prestige of the U-boat service suddenly soared, for all the wrong
reasons, when Oberleutnant Günther Prien penetrated the British
Home Fleet anchorage at Scapa Flow in northern Scotland on October 14 and sank the British battleship *Royal Oak*. The loss of this
vessel was a blow to British prestige, but not to the fleet's capacity.
But it brought to Hitler's mind the submarine service, and helped
Admiral Karl Dönitz get the enhanced building program he wanted.
What Dönitz knew and Hitler never accepted was that the most important task before the U-boats was to sink British merchant ship-

ping and thus destroy Britain's capacity to wage war. That view
was shared by Dönitz and Winston Churchill.

One of Hitler's major naval errors had to be his blindness regarding the proper use of the U-boats. Admiral Dönitz had wanted
to start the war with 300 submarines. Instead, he had fifty boats,
most of them the little 250-ton "canoes," which were capable of
only short patrols and really suitable only for use in the North Sea,
not in the Atlantic. Their greatest value was the laying of mines in
British coastal waters. In fact, during the early weeks of the war,
mines sank more ships than did submarines.

Had Dönitz been given those 300 submarines by 1940, he could
have won the war in six months, he claimed. But he was not given
the boats; in fact, it would be a long time before he would have that
many vessels.

So the struggle within OKW began. In the past, Hitler had given
verbal orders for the changes he wanted. That meant he bypassed
OKW and dealt personally with the commanders of the army, the
navy, and the Luftwaffe. But now he became edgy and insisted on
the formality of putting everything through OKW. Thus Keitel became for the first time the key figure in the German military mechanism, and not just the supernumerary and sounding board for Hitler
that he had been in the past. Hitler was tired of the arguments with
his generals, and he did not want to continue them. From this point
on the generals would appear at his bidding and at no other time.
He had completely broken with the old relationship.

Hitler and Göring were very much concerned about the war in the
west even though nothing was happening, except at sea. Göring was
worried about England. "God help us if we should lose this war,"
he warned one day.

The mobilization of Germany continued apace. Food rationing
was instituted in October; raw materials were rationed, as well. Military conscription continued. The plan was to have 136 divisions by
the spring of 1940 and then to keep on building.

Hitler had wanted to attack in the west on November 12, 1939,
but as we have seen, von Brauchitsch objected strenuously. Though

he now thought little of von Brauchitsch after their confrontation Hitler withdrew a direct order he had given to make the attack.

But Hitler now insisted that by November 20 the Germans had to launch their attack. "The British will be ready to talk only after a beating," Hitler said. "We must get at them as quickly as possible."

Hitler's determination on this score very nearly brought about his undoing in the autumn of 1939. General von Hammerstein, who had always opposed Hitler, had been given command of German forces in the west. He invited Hitler to visit him, with the intention of kidnapping the Führer and turning him over to the British, but Hitler was suspicious and refused to go.

The generals were keeping in touch with the British that fall, hoping for a break that would let them stage their coup against Hitler. Contact was maintained through the Vatican and through Switzerland. General Halder and General von Brauchitsch passed the buck back and forth. No one was willing to take the responsibility for the first act that would commit the conspirators.

Nothing happened. Hitler sent orders four different times in November 1939 for an attack in the west, but each time the attack was postponed. Finally Hitler seemed to understand that the generals were not bluffing; they really did not believe the army was ready to fight. Moreover, the Belgians and the Dutch seemed to have gotten wind of the German plan to attack through their countries.

The plan came to nothing that fall. Hitler put off the attack scheduled for December 27 until January. On January 10 he ordered the attack to begin "fifteen minutes before sunrise" on January 17. But January 17 came and went with no offensive. This time there was a very good reason for the delay.

On January 10 a German military plane got lost in bad weather and landed in Belgium. Belgian soldiers surrounded the plane; inside was a German major who carried the complete plans for the attack on the west.

*   *   *

The major later reported that he had burned the plans, but no one believed that they had been completely destroyed. The German generals shuddered when they contemplated execution of a plan of which the enemy might be aware. So for this reason—and another that was even more important—the plan to strike in the west was shelved for the winter.

The other reason was Hitler's perception that if he did not move into Denmark and Norway, the British would do so and prevent his use of the all-important ores of Norway. This would present him with a much more difficult war.

While Hitler dithered that fall, the Allies got ready. As Winston Churchill put it, they prepared for the last war. The defensive mentality of the British and French was very strong, the product of the horrors of the 1914–1918 war.

One reason the western Allies did not attack was the defensive orientation of the French. But another was a British assessment which showed that the German army would have a hundred divisions to throw against the west. The French, with their seventy-two divisions and fourteen reserve divisions, did not feel up to matching fire with fire. By Allied assessment, taking into account the French divisions needed to watch the Italian frontier, the Germans overpowered the Allies by a 4 to 3 ratio. In terms of air power, the Allies estimated that the Germans could concentrate 2000 bombers against them; the French and British had only 950.

So the Allies sat behind the Maginot line and waited.

The next action was generated from the sea, and by Winston Churchill, first lord of the British Admiralty, the chief political officer of the Royal Navy. Churchill had been first lord before—in 1914—but was rejected after the tragic Dardanelles campaign. Since then, Churchill had been regarded as a political "unguided missile" by a series of governments. But, with war, this man who had seen it coming was suddenly in demand. "Winnie's back" was the message throughout the fleet.

The Royal Navy was very much concerned about the Scandinavian peninsula, which stretches a thousand miles from the mouth of the Baltic Sea to the Arctic circle. The coastline is fringed with little islands that belong to Sweden, Norway, and Denmark, but by precedent (a thousand years of usage) these islands were available to the Germans. They could pass through the surrounding waters as they had in World War I, and this protection gave them a large advantage over the British blockaders. Furthermore, the Germans imported a great deal of Swedish iron ore as well as ores from Narvik, on the west coast of Norway.

Churchill proposed that the British cut off the German supply from Narvik. How this was to be achieved was debated at length, but in the end it came down to Churchill's recommendation for an invasion of Narvik and other ports to deny the Germans access to the ores.

Meanwhile, the German navy saw precisely the same possibilities, and Admiral Raeder submitted to Hitler a proposal called "Gaining of Bases in Norway." Hitler saw Raeder's memo and agreed wholeheartedly that Scandinavia presented a threat and an opportunity. And so, on December 14, Hitler ordered OKW to prepare for the invasion of Norway.

But on December 22, when Churchill presented a similar British plan to the cabinet, all he got was inaction.

The British cabinet was stirred to activity in January, with the capture of that German major whose plane had been forced down in Belgium with the plans for the attack in the west. The major had indeed lied when he said the plans were destroyed by fire. They were not destroyed at all, and the French and British governments were given copies of the plans by the Belgian government. Yet, surprisingly, knowing that the German plan called for the invasion of Belgium and Holland as well as France, the Belgian government still refused to make common cause with the Allies; Belgium stuck to its "neutrality."

So the British in France knew what was going to come eventually: the German attack. But reacting effectively was another matter entirely, for they had precious little with which to react, owing to the incompetence of military management in Britain between the two wars. The British had pioneered the development of the tank, that heavily armored vehicle whose task it was to lead the van of shock troops in surprise attack on the enemy. At the outbreak of war the British had only a handful of tanks available, and these were outmoded by German or Russian standards. The British Expeditionary Force in France had only seventeen light tanks and a hundred "infantry" tanks. The latter were virtually useless; most of them carried no weapon larger

than a machine gun. The numerous German panzers, with their 80-
and 88-millimeter cannon, were formidable.

The other problem in the west was the deterioration of the morale of the French army. Winston Churchill, a shrewd observer of
his French ally, noted that the French would have fought much better had the war begun in earnest in the fall of 1939. But the inaction
of the French generals, the corruption of the French political system, and the constant lethargy of that combination sapped the élan
of the French soldiers so that, as 1940 began, they were a very dispirited force.

Meanwhile, the Germans were preparing their moves. On January
27, 1940, General Keitel was ordered by Hitler to take over Study
N—the planning for the invasion of Norway.

On February 20 Hitler brought General Nikolaus von Falkenhorst to his study for an interview. Von Falkenhorst had been involved in Scandinavian military operations in the 1914–1918 war.

> Hitler reminded me of my experience in Finland and said to me,
> "Sit down and tell me what you did." After a moment, the Führer
> interrupted me. He led me to a table covered with maps. "I have
> a similar thing in mind," he said, "the occupation of Norway; be-
> cause I am informed that the English intend to land there, and I
> want to be there before them."
>
> Then, marching up and down, he expounded to me his rea-
> sons. "The occupation of Norway by the British would be a
> strategic turning movement which would lead them into the Bal-
> tic, where we have neither troops nor coastal fortifications. The
> success which we have gained in the East and which we are
> going to win in the West would be annihilated because the en-
> emy would find himself in a position to advance on Berlin and
> to break the backbone of our two fronts. In the second and third
> places, the conquest of Norway will ensure the liberty of move-
> ment of our fleet in the bay of Wilhelmshaven, and will protect
> our imports of Swedish ore."
>
> Finally he said to me, "I appoint you to the command of
> the expedition."

Hitler then dismissed von Falkenhorst and told him to be back
at 5 p.m. with his plans for the occupation of Norway.

Von Falkenhorst, who knew nothing about Norway, went out to a bookshop and bought a Baedeker travel guide. From Baedeker he drew up his invasion plans in about three hours. One division was to be allotted to each of the five principal Norwegian ports: Oslo, Stavanger, Bergen, Trondheim, and Narvik. That was it.

So Winston Churchill and Adolf Hitler were thinking along the same lines that winter of 1939–1940. The difference was that Churchill was constrained by the weaknesses of a not very well organized democratic government in London, while Hitler, his own master, had only to issue an order and his will would be done. Thus the Germans were quicker off the mark in Norway than the British, and that is basically the story of what happened there in the next few months.

The vital move began that very afternoon: Hitler once more summoned von Falkenhorst to the Chancellery, this time to meet with Keitel, Jodl, and himself. They went over the detailed (such as they were) plans for the Norway operation. Hitler was satisfied that von Falkenhorst knew what he was doing.

"What comes now?" asked Keitel. "Case Yellow, or this?" (Case Yellow was the German attack on France.)

Hitler did not reply that day. He pondered for a while; but he also learned that Churchill was pressing for British action, and he made his decision. On March 20 he announced to Keitel that "Exercise Weser," the new name for the Norwegian invasion, was to precede Case Yellow.

The way had already been prepared militarily and politically by the Germans. The groundwork had been laid by Admiral Raeder. He had been in touch for months with Captain Richard Schreiber, the German naval attaché in Oslo. That is how Raeder, and through him Hitler, had been in touch almost daily with the plans of the British for Norway. There was much loose talk in Oslo in those days and there was also a man who wanted to bring it all to Hitler's attention, a man named Vidkun Quisling, a member of the Norwegian privy council. Quisling came to Berlin, where he was greeted by Admiral Raeder. Quisling was full of information. He told Raeder the time and place of the planned British landings in Norway: at Stavanger and Christiansand. Quisling said he had a plan to seize power and preserve Norway for the Germans. So Raeder went to see Hitler and told him all this news, and Hitler called in Quisling for an interview. Hitler liked what he heard and ordered Keitel to devise a plan for working with the Norwegian traitor.

The German invasion of Norway was on.

Not so the British action. The best Churchill could do was get an agreement to mine the Norwegian territorial waters. This was to begin on April 4. He also secured permission to send a British brigade to occupy the port of Narvik.

But now what was to be done? The British had news that the Germans were massing troops at Rostock and that 200,000 tons of German shipping were concentrated at Stettin and Swinemünde with troops on board.

Then came April 19, 1940.

9

NORWAY

The British talked too much.

That's why, when Winston Churchill was trying desperately to persuade his colleagues in the Chamberlain government to move against Norway, the Germans were aware of the British moves and began working even faster. It was a simple matter when the constituency of Germany had been satisfied, and that did not take long since the constituency was one man: Adolf Hitler.

The German navy had persuaded Hitler that if the British got into Norway, they would be able to dominate the Bay of Helgoland and the exit channels for the German surface fleet and U-boats. Once the Führer was convinced, OKW established a special bureau to deal with Norway. The invasion would come from the sea, a bold plan in view of the British domination of the North Sea. It was so bold that Hitler and the navy concealed the plan from the German army and from Göring and the Luftwaffe. Here was the first instance in which the Oberkommando der Wehrmacht functioned as the German military High Command, without reference to the army and air force general staffs.

Vidkun Quisling sent a number of storm troopers down to Germany, where they were trained by Himmler's SS experts, although even these SS men were not completely aware of the reasons for the action. They did not have to know. It was enough for them that these were Nazis living up to Nazi standards, and they instructed the Norwegians in the tactics of violence and intimidation. The Norwegian Nazis were preparing to seize strategic points in Norway in connection with the German invasion.

One of Quisling's great values to the Germans was that he kept them informed on an almost daily basis of the British moves, so the Germans could plan ahead. Meanwhile, in the winter of 1939 Quisling was bribing whole sections of the Norwegian government in the coastal areas, using money given to him by the Germans. He bought railway officials, post office workers, communications experts, and army officers. In January Quisling was given 200,000 gold marks and a promise of 10,000 pounds sterling a month for three months beginning in March.

On March 1 the secret of Norway had to be let out of the bag, because Hitler demanded the assignment of army troops and air force units to the Norway operation. When General von Brauchitsch discovered that his General Staff had been evaded in the planning for four months and then presented with a fait accompli, he was furious. The atmosphere at army headquarters was downright deadly. When Field Marshal Göring discovered the fact, he was angrier still because he was the Führer's heir apparent and number one adviser as well as head of the Luftwaffe. He raged at Keitel until the OKW chief had to call on Hitler for support. Hitler issued a formal directive for the occupation of Denmark and Norway:

In view of our military and political power in comparison with that of the Scandinavian States, the force to be employed in Exercise Weser will be kept as small as possible. The numerical weakness will be balanced by daring actions and surprise execution.

On principle, we will do our utmost to make the operation appear as a *peaceful* occupation, the object of which is the military protection of the neutrality of the Scandinavian States.

Corresponding demands will be transmitted to the governments at the beginning of the occupation. If necessary, demonstrations by the Navy and Air Force will provide the necessary emphasis. If, in spite of this, resistance should be met, all military means will

be used to crush it. The crossing of the Danish border and the landings in Norway must take place *simultaneously*.

Since surprise was the key to the whole operation, the troops would
be taken into the secret only after their transports had put to sea.

The secret of the operation, confined for so long to so few heads,
was one of the best kept of the entire war. Ten days before the attack was launched one of the people who should have known how
to keep his mouth shut, a colonel of the *Abwehr* (army intelligence),
told a Dutch friend of the coming assault, and the Dutchman informed the Danish naval attaché. But the Danish government chose
to believe that the tale was just another of the many rumors that
had been floating about since the British first proposed a move
against Stavanger. On April 4, 1940, the Danish minister in Berlin
warned his government of the impending attack by the Germans.
Still the Copenhagen government did not believe. On April 5 the
Norwegian cabinet at Oslo was informed of an impending attack,
and scoffed at the tale. On April 7 German troop transports were
sighted from the shore, moving along the Norwegian coast. Still Norway did not act.

The lethargy was enormous, a true indication of the emotional
morass into which all Europe had fallen. On April 8 the British Admiralty informed the Norwegian legation in London that a strong
German naval force had been sighted approaching Narvik. That day
the Oslo newspapers reported the rescue of German troops from
the transport *Rio de Janeiro,* sunk by a Polish submarine operating
out of England. The Norwegians were given the name of the ship,
the fact that it was moving toward Bergen, and the statements of
rescued German soldiers that their mission was to land at Bergen
to protect Norway from British invasion. Still, the Norwegian government refused to act; it would not mobilize its army or mine the
ports. It was as if Norway had already accepted the fact of the German occupation.

Even the British cabinet failed to understand what was happening. The German ships were at sea, but Prime Minister Chamberlain was still talking about the German invasion threat as if it were
something amorphous, something planned for the future in case the

British tried to cut off shipments of ores to German ports. And it was just then—April 8—that First Lord of the Admiralty Winston Churchill finally received approval to act in Norway.

But it was much too late. The date for the German invasion of Norway was set for April 9, and those ships at sea were flying the Union Jack. To all appearances they were British vessels, and they would continue under that flag until just before 5:15 a.m. on April 9, when they would drop the British ensign and hoist the Nazi flag.

All challenges to the German ships were answered in English. When challenged, the German ships reported that they were chasing German steamers along the Norwegian coast.

Hitler was at his most efficient. Every day was devoted to conferences in the OKW headquarters in the German Chancellery. Generals Keitel and Jodl each had a study and an office for their adjutants and other assistants next to the former Reich cabinet chamber. At about noon Keitel would come in from the War Ministry in Bendlerstrasse. Jodl worked at the Chancellery all day long. So Hitler had someone there at all times to implement his directives. The Führer himself made all the decisions, including the very little ones. That was his way.

He coordinated the activity of the military and the diplomatic forces perfectly. At 5:15 on the morning of April 9, the ships began to land at the five big Norwegian ports, and German troops crossed the Danish frontier by land. Five minutes later the foreign ministers in Oslo and Copenhagen were awakened from their beds by German emissaries who bore messages: each minister received an ultimatum from German Foreign Minister von Ribbentrop: Norway and Denmark were to accept immediately the protection of the Third Reich.

> The German troops therefore do not set foot on Norwegian soil as enemies. The German High Command does not intend to make use of the points occupied by German troops as bases for operations against England as long as it is not forced to do so. On the contrary, German military operations aim exclusively at protecting the north against the proposed occupation of Norwegian bases by Anglo-French forces.

In Copenhagen the Germans did a remarkable job. General Kurt Himer, the chief of staff of the small German army force heading for Denmark, had arrived in civilian clothes two days earlier. He had made arrangements for a pier to accept the ship *Hansestadt Danzig*. All that would be needed, he said, was a truck to handle some supplies and a radio transmitter. And so the *Hansestadt Danzig* arrived off Copenhagen a little before dawn on April 9 and passed the guns of the fort guarding—but that day not guarding— the harbor. It passed the Danish patrol boats that were tied up at the Langeline Pier in the middle of the port, and the citadel of the army, and the royal palace. And soon the single battalion—all that the Germans deemed necessary to capture Copenhagen—moved against the citadel and the royal palace and captured them both in minutes. The transmitter that General Himer had brought in was used to broadcast the word to all Denmark that the Danish government had surrendered. Denmark then fell into the Nazi empire.

But in Norway, it was a quite different story.

At Narvik the German occupation looked easy. Colonel Konrad Sundlo, the Norwegian army garrison commander there, was a friend of Vidkun Quisling's, and he surrendered the garrison without firing a shot. The naval commander did not give in so easily; there was fighting, and 300 Norwegian sailors were killed. By 8 a.m. Narvik was in German hands. Down the coast, Trondheim also fell easily to the Germans. At Bergen, there was some resistance, but the Germans conquered. The real test was still to come, and it began that afternoon of April 9. British dive-bombers came over Bergen and sank the German cruiser *Königsberg* with bombs.

Everywhere the Germans moved fast, usually with successful results. By noon four of the five major Norwegian cities were in German hands. But at Oslo there was trouble.

When the demands came, and the Danes capitulated without a struggle, the news seemed to strengthen the Norwegians. The Norwegian foreign minister said he was aghast to learn that the Germans planned such action. He told the German minister that Norway would not submit.

*   *   *

Hitler's one defeat on the day of triumph came at sea. The German fleet was coming in to occupy Oslo, and members of the German legation were on the dock early in the morning to greet the conquering heroes. But the heroes never came.

At the entrance to the Oslo fjord the Norwegian minelayer *Olav Trygvesson* had challenged the German warships, which included the pocket battleship *Lützow,* the 10,000-ton cruiser *Blücher,* and the light cruiser *Emden.* The *Olav Trygvesson* sank a German torpedo boat and damaged the *Emden,* but the German squadron fought its way past and moved up the 50-mile fjord. Fifteen miles south of Oslo the fjord narrows to a width of 15 miles. There the Oskarsborg fortress opened fire on the *Lützow* and the *Blücher* with heavy guns and torpedoes launched from the land. The *Blücher* sank with a loss of 1600 men, including a Gestapo detachment that was scheduled to take over administration of Oslo. Rear Admiral Oskar Kummetz and General Erwin Engelbracht managed to swim ashore, where they were promptly captured by the Norwegians. The *Lützow* was damaged also. The German squadron turned back. It had failed to take Oslo, and the legation staff stood on the dockside in the cold all morning, waiting for "heroes" who were dead or fighting their way back to open water.

But the airborne troops and Field Marshal Göring's Luftwaffe did what the navy could not. The airfields around Oslo were captured in short order, and the troops landed and marched into Oslo behind a band. Oslo fell that day to the Germans without much of a struggle.

The Norwegian government had fled to Hamar, 80 miles north of Oslo, and later that day fled again to Elverum, near the Swedish border. German troops marched on Hamar, but they met resistance and had to fall back.

That night, in Oslo, Vidkun Quisling announced that he was the head of the new government of Norway. He ordered all resistance ended.

But King Haakon refused to submit, and the Norwegian resistance began. The king and his party now moved through the mountains to Andalsnes. For the first time, Hitler had been defied successfully by the victims he tried to claim. He might have captured most of Norway, but he had not conquered the Norwegians' spirit.

And for a time it seemed that Hitler might not have Norway for long.

On April 10 British destroyers moved in on Narvik, sank two of

the five German destroyers in the port, damaged all the others, and
sank all but one of the German cargo ships that had come in. Going
out, the British ships encountered the five other German destroyers of that squadron and managed a fight. One British destroyer was
sunk, one was beached, and one was damaged, but three destroyers got away. Three days later another British squadron came to
Narvik and wiped out all the remaining German warships.

When word of the defeat reached Berlin, Hitler became hys-
terical.

The Germans were lucky then because the commander of the British Expeditionary Force was a timid man. He did not move into
Narvik when he could have, but landed north of the city. And then
the British army bumbled and fumbled until the Germans were able
to get into action. The Luftwaffe bombed and strafed, and the German army came in with tanks and heavy guns. The British had lost
their heavy equipment and had to fight with infantry field weapons:
machine guns, mortars, and rifles. The Germans made short work
of them.

In Oslo the Germans tried to organize the government, but Quisling proved totally incompetent. Six days after he had proclaimed
himself head of the government, the Germans kicked him out. In
an attempt to secure local support, they appointed a council of six
leading citizens, including the Lutheran bishop of Norway and Paal
Berg, the president of the Norwegian Supreme Court. What they
did not know was that Berg was secretly organizing the Norwegian
resistance movement. When the results of this council's appointment did not bring immediate cooperation from the Norwegians,
Hitler decided to act.

The Germans had moved swiftly to capture the southern half of
Norway. Hitler then made an error so serious that it was to have
permanent consequences for the war: he took authority for occupation of Norway away from the German army and put it into the
hands of the Nazis. Hitler insisted that Terboven be called Reich
Commissioner for Norway. The German army was furious. General Eduard Dietl, the German army commander in Norway, was in
such bad military shape that Hitler called in Field Marshal Göring
and demanded that the troops be evacuated by air. It was impossible: Göring did not have the transport planes available for the job.

Hitler became even more upset. He recalled the German minister to Norway and said that force must be used to stop the Norwegians from resisting. The Gestapo obeyed by arresting twenty distinguished Norwegian citizens, including Paal Berg. Then General von Falkenhorst signed an order providing that they were to be shot if the Norwegians did not stop their resistance and sabotage of German installations immediately. The pattern of the Norwegian occupation was set, and it would not change. After that, the only cooperation the Germans could get in all Norway was from the handful of Nazis who knew that their own lives now depended on the Germans. On April 29 a British warship picked up King Haakon and his government and took them to Tromso, far north of the Arctic circle. There they established a provisional government.

At the end of May an Allied army of 25,000 was still fighting in Norway. The Germans could have been defeated, and for a time Hitler thought they were defeated. But then the German army made its swift move into the Low Countries and France, and suddenly the British found themselves with their backs to the wall and no time to think about Norway. The troops fighting in Norway were abandoned, and ultimately they had to flee or give up. King Haakon was taken to London by a British warship, protesting bitterly at the abandonment of his country by the western Allies. The plight of his own people precluded the king from understanding the full depth of the crisis then faced by the west. Now Norway became another occupied territory, a part of Germany's new, unwilling empire.

The capture of Norway had a serious effect on the British war effort, as Winston Churchill had known it would. First of all, the abandonment of Norway by the west was of a piece with the abandonment of Austria, Czechoslovakia, and then Poland. German prestige in the world rose to a new high, and Allied prestige fell to a corresponding new low.

Physically, the capture of Norway was enormously important to the German war effort. The iron ore and other natural resources were now easily available to the Germans. The Swedes, mindful of their own delicate position, refused to help the Norwegians. They would not sell them arms in their moment of need, nor would they sell them gasoline. Their refusal speeded the surrender of the Norwegian forces considerably. Hitler pressed Sweden to let German

troop trains and supply trains cross Swedish territory, and ultimately
the Swedes gave in. Thus Sweden's neutrality during the war became pro-German neutrality and remained that way.

Despite Hitler's errors and his occasional hysteria, the German
army proved itself both competent and resourceful in Norway and
the consequences of the dictator's political and military errors were
lessened by the troops on the scene.

The employment of the navy in Norway highlighted a serious
weakness, in fact, although it was not readily apparent. In the sea
battles with the Norwegian navy, the British navy, and the Royal
Air Force the Germans took a severe beating. The heavy cruiser
Blücher was sunk, a dozen destroyers were lost, the cruiser *Emden*
was damaged so badly it had to go into a navy yard for repair, and
so were the battle cruisers *Scharnhorst* and *Gneisenau* and the
pocket battleship *Lützow*.

Another grave failing of the German navy was also uncovered
in the Norwegian campaign.

The German U-boat force was pulled entirely from the Atlantic
and the North Sea around England by Hitler to participate in the
Norwegian campaign. All the U-boats were assigned to various
ports.

To the horror of Admiral Dönitz the German U-boat captains
began to report torpedo failure. They attacked one British battleship six times in one day; the torpedoes were defective and not one
of them exploded. The story was repeated a dozen times. At first
Dönitz believed the failures were those of his captains, but when
Günther Prien, the hero of Scapa Flow, reported torpedo failure,
the admiral had to take another look. He discovered that the firing
mechanisms were at fault (a defect shared by the Americans, who
had copied the German torpedo "pistol"). All the U-boats had to
be withdrawn from the Norwegian campaign and tied up at docks
while Dönitz and his staff produced a modification that would let
the torpedoes work properly. All this took many weeks at a time
when the German army was forging ahead in western Europe.

10

A STROLL ON THE CHAMPS-ELYSÉES

Aside from the military aspects, the German conquest of Norway turned out to be a major mistake for Hitler in the political arena. It caused the fall of the Chamberlain government and the rise to power of Hitler's implacable enemy, Winston Churchill.

The Labour opposition to the British government in power called for a debate on the Norway campaign. The object was to embarrass the Chamberlain cabinet and bring about its fall, if possible.

When the debate opened on May 7, it became apparent that Labour was not the only enemy of the Chamberlain government, not by far. Some fifty Conservative members of Parliament joined with the Opposition. On the second day of the debate, Winston Churchill took the floor and, as first lord of the admiralty, attempted to shoulder all the blame for the British failures in Norway. But the House was not having any of that. David Lloyd George, one of the architects of that earlier dreadful error, the Versailles treaty, got up to state the real case for change:

The nation is prepared for every sacrifice so long as it has leadership, so long as the Government show clearly what they are aiming at, and so long as the nation is confident that those who are leading it are doing their best. I say solemnly that the Prime Minister should give an example of sacrifice because there is

nothing which can contribute more to victory in this war than
that he should sacrifice the seals of office.

And then the vote of confidence was called. The government
won a majority of eighty-one, but the large number of Conservatives who sided with the Opposition lent a different interpretation
to the tally. As everyone could see, confidence in the Chamberlain
cabinet had seriously eroded.

Following the debate and vote, Chamberlain was so badly shaken
that he decided to give up the leadership of Britain in favor of a
national government. Such a cabinet would take in members of the
Labour and Liberal parties so that the war effort could be advanced
without any political overtones.

When the leaders of Labour were consulted, at first they seemed
to indicate that they would not cooperate in the realignment. They
wanted the Conservative party to have to take responsibility until the
Tories had failed so often that the people demanded a total change.
But then, on the morning of May 10, the Germans unleashed their long-
expected offensive against the Netherlands, Belgium, and northern
France.

Immediately the Chamberlain government resigned, and Winston
Churchill was asked to form a national government for Britain.
Within hours Churchill was meeting with King George VI. Before
dawn on May 11, the new government was formed and strong measures were being taken.

For months the OKW had been ready to launch the lightning strike
against the Allies. On May 8, as the British debated the future of
the Chamberlain government, General Keitel gave the order that
put the whole scheme into motion. The orders were rushed to the
three military services and to the German Foreign Office. At six
o'clock on the morning of May 10 a courier was to call upon Queen
Wilhelmina of the Netherlands and hand her a note from Hitler explaining that developments in the war had made it unavoidable that
German troops cross Dutch territory. The queen was asked to direct her army to permit the Germans to march unmolested across
Holland. She was invited to remain in the country.

But plans sometimes go awry, and in this case Admiral Wilhelm

Canaris, chief of the *Abwehr* (military intelligence bureau of the OKW), threw a monkey wrench into Hitler's plans. Canaris was one of Hitler's real enemies, and even as he was working for the Reich, he was conspiring to achieve Hitler's fall. In this particular matter, he managed to warn the Dutch.

The German government courier with the message for Queen Wilhelmina had secured a visa from the Dutch Embassy in Berlin. His credentials were impeccable. Still, through an agent, Canaris slipped the word and the courier was stopped as he crossed the border into Holland on May 9. The Dutch police who stopped him looked into his diplomatic pouch, quite illegally, but at the same time very effectively. They found the telling paper. Thus The Hague had a twenty-four-hour warning when Hitler had intended it have none. The Dutch master plan for defense was then set into motion. The major effect was that the Dutch began to flood the countryside by opening the dikes. Canaris could not have done more; he had given the Allies the small advantage of warning.

The results of the warning frightened Hitler. He had alarming news from Holland. The Dutch government had canceled all military furloughs. Roadblocks were going up all over the country. People were being evacuated from cities. Obviously someone had learned something. Göring was worried about his ability to bomb Dutch resistance and requested postponement of the operation until the twelfth or thirteenth of the month so that he could get his supply chain in order. Hitler said no. His intuition told him that he must attack by the tenth or the whole plan might fail. He could give them until the tenth and not one day longer.

No more could be done to buttress the physical preparations for the offensive. At noon on May 9 Hitler and his entourage left Berlin. They did not want to attract attention to their direction so they boarded the train at the small station of Grünewald. The train, said the officials, was headed for Hamburg, where Hitler was scheduled to make a speech the next day. But that information was for the foreign reporters and spies. Hitler was again going to war. Once dusk fell, the train's direction was reversed, and at 3 a.m. the Führer arrived at Euskirchen, not far from Aachen (Aix-la-Chapelle). By car Hitler and Keitel and the other members of the staff were then driven to Felsennest ("Rocky Nest"), the new bunker headquarters that the Todt Organization (Hitler's military construction agency) had blasted out of solid rock atop a wooded mountain.

The Führer's bunker was a windowless hive of concrete cells. Hitler had one large room to himself. On one side was Keitel's cell, which adjoined Jodl's. On the other side of the Führer were his military adjutants. The whole was air-conditioned, but so intense was the silence that Keitel could hear Hitler turning the pages of his newspaper as he read in the room next to him.

The entire bunker system was artfully concealed. So, indeed, were the operating headquarters of the OKW, a few miles away, and the headquarters of the commander in chief of the army, half an hour's drive away along forest lanes. The British Royal Air Force never did find the complex.

Hitler's direct participation remained a secret from the Allies too. They did not really believe that he was deeply involved in military operational planning. Writing in a compendium of Hitler's speeches that would be published in America as *My New Order,* Raoul de Roussy de Sales reinforced this belief. De Sales had very good credentials in matters European, for he had long been the American correspondent of *Paris Soir* and of Havas, the French news agency. But in this matter he could not have been more wrong. As Hitler said in one of his speeches, "I have already assured you and all of you, my friends, know that if a long time elapses without my speaking, or if things seem quiet, this does not mean that I am doing nothing."

No, as General Keitel said, Hitler was in charge of operations from the moment they began:

> The fact was that Hitler was familiar with every last detail of our tasks and operations. He knew the target set for each day and the plans of attack, and he often exercised close personal influence on them.

Back in October 1939, when German troops were mopping up in Poland, Hitler had taken several days off to interview all the army group and army commanders scheduled for this western operation about their plans. Said Keitel:

> With each one he had discussed all the details, sometimes asking awkward questions and showing himself to be remarkably

well-informed on terrain, obstacles and the like, as the result of his penetrating study of the maps. His critical judgment and suggestions proved to the generals that he had immersed himself deeply in the problems inherent in executing his basic orders, and that he was no layman. Afterwards he was furious about the superficiality of his friend Reichenau, who made a public fool of himself, while he particularly praised the detailed preparation and war game practice that had gone into the planning of the most formidable task confronting von Kluge's Fourth Army, the breakthrough in the Ardennes.

At this point, the beginning of the great battle, Hitler was particularly interested in the operations of General Ewald von Kleist's armored group, which was to lead the breakthrough toward Abbeville. He liked the planning done by the chief of staff, General Zeitzler. He remarked that the terrain was eminently suitable for a tank battle and that it must come without delay. And now he turned his attention to the plan of General Ernst Busch's Sixteenth Army, which would work on von Kleist's southern flank to shield that armored group from attack from that direction.

This attention, of course, put every general on his mettle, and some were surprised to learn just how much Hitler did know about the minute aspects of their military operations.

By warning the Dutch, Admiral Canaris had put a neat crimp in Hitler's plans. The first move was supposed to be the capture of the airfields near The Hague. Once that was accomplished, the Germans would occupy the capital and capture the queen. The German troops landed, but the Dutch began fighting and by the evening of May 10 had driven the Germans off the air bases.

The Germans also planned to seize the bridges over the Maas and Nieuwe Maas rivers, south of Rotterdam. Airborne troops took the bridges on the morning of May 10, before the Dutch could blow them up. The paratroopers hung on tenaciously against the Dutch for two days, until the Nineteenth Panzer Division drove through to them.

The Dutch resisted stoutly throughout the country, and the Germans grew desperate. Then on May 14 they brought the "new war" to Rotterdam. While operating under a flag of truce, German bombers wiped out the center of the city, killing 800 civilians, wounding several thousand people, and destroying the homes of 78,000. Europe would not be the same again, and ultimately German civilians would come to know the terror of enemy bombing.

After five days of resistance, Holland surrendered, but not its queen. She fled to England with her government, aboard a pair of British destroyers.

Meanwhile, the Germans had been moving on several fronts. On May 9, at 1:30 in the afternoon, General Heinz Guderian was alerted, and at 5:30 on the morning of May 10 he crossed the Luxembourg frontier near Wallendorf with the First Panzer Division of his Nineteenth Armored Corps. Guderian had already made a reputation for himself by the savagery of his attack in Poland, using tactics that would give rise to the term "blitzkrieg." Now Guderian's armor was driving toward France.

On this first day of the campaign, Keitel came to Hitler with a communiqué that he wanted to issue to the press: "In order to direct the overall operations of the armed forces, the Führer and Supreme Commander has moved to the front...."

Hitler objected to that statement. He preferred to remain anonymous, he said. "Let my generals have the glory."

But Keitel was insistent. The country, the enemy, and the world at large must learn that Hitler was a true genius, he said. It was important to the war effort. Whereupon Hitler succumbed and allowed Keitel to put out his communiqué. It was not a question of ego with him—his own was so immense that he did not need the praise of others. He was convinced only by Keitel's insistence that the announcement was for the good of the war effort.

That first morning of the spring offensive the atmosphere at the Felsennest headquarters was extremely tense: Had the Germans managed to take the enemy by surprise?

The answer was more yes than no.

Admiral Canaris had done his best to see that the Allies were warned, but the Dutch response was not perfectly coordinated. They had delayed in opening their dikes and delayed in authorizing their police and army to shoot.

The Germans moved swiftly into Holland and Belgium. The Allies sent the Anglo-French army northeast from the Franco-Belgian border to the Belgian defense line along the Dyle and Meuse rivers. They were moving into a trap.

The main German drive was coming on the Allies' right flank: advancing through Belgium and northern France, across the Seine River, and then turning north to encircle the Allied forces. *Fall Gelb* (Case Yellow) they called it.

As the drive began, the German and Allied forces seemed evenly matched—136 German divisions against 135 divisions of French, British, Dutch, and Belgian troops. The Allies had great advantages, it seemed. One was the "impregnable" Maginot line in the south. Another was a series of equally "impregnable" Belgian forts, as well as the "water lines" of the Dutch. But the great difference was that the Germans were under a unified command, headed by Adolf Hitler himself, while the Allies were fragmented. They had not had even a single staff meeting attended by all the commanders of the Allied forces. It was an alliance in name only.

And the Germans had something else in their favor: excellent planning, down to the company level.

*   *   *

In the defense of Belgium, the Allies had drawn a line along the Meuse River between Namur and Liege and along the Albert Canal from Liege to Antwerp. The key to the defense system was a series of fortresses built after World War I. The central fort, Eben Emäel, was the most powerful; it was defended by 1200 troops who lived in concrete bunkers that were completely impervious to shot and shell. They could, claimed the Belgians, hold out for a year under siege.

That's what they thought they could do.

On the morning of May 10 a German sergeant in command of ten gliders carrying a total of seventy-eight troops landed atop Fort Eben Emäel. They used a new technique they had developed in exercises in Germany. (At Hildesheim the Germans had built a replica of the fort, and studied the ways in which it might be assaulted.)

The sergeant and his men got out of the gliders. They had with them something new and special: "hollow explosive." They put charges into the gun turrets of Fort Eben Emäel, poking them inside. They also brought up portable flamethrowers. The charges exploded, putting the armored turrets out of action. The gas and flame spread around inside the fort, killing or wounding the defenders. Within an hour the Germans had penetrated the upper galleries, and the guns were finished. Then observation posts were blinded. Anyone who poked his head up had flamethrowers turned on him. After two hours a unit of Belgian infantry arrived; but the German sergeant called for help, and Stuka dive-bombers attacked the Belgians and drove them away. They came back, and this time the sergeant called for paratroops. They arrived and dropped. All night the Germans held out on the top and in the upper galleries of the fort.

On the morning of May 11 advance panzer units came up and surrounded Eben Emäel. The officer in charge suggested that the Belgians might want to surrender before the panzers destroyed the fort completely. The Belgian survivors then filed out, hands behind their heads.

That was the end of the "impregnable" fortresses. The same story could be told of all of them.

On May 13 the Germans secured four bridgeheads across the Meuse River between Dinant and Sedan. They captured Sedan that day, thereby threatening the center of the French-British line. The next day the French and British received a lesson in the new warfare.

The Germans had mobilized their tank striking forces in three columns that stretched back for a hundred miles, deep inside Germany. They were on the move. On May 14 they broke through the French armies and headed for the English Channel.

But the greatest and most devastating attack was that of General Guderian's Nineteenth Panzer Corps, around Sedan. On the night of May 13 the German combat engineers had bridged the river with a sturdy pontoon bridge. The next morning Guderian's tanks began pouring across. The British and French air forces came to destroy the bridge, but the Germans had surrounded it with flak wagons and fixed antiaircraft guns, and in one RAF attack 60 percent of the seventy-one attacking planes were shot down. The French sent armor, but by day's end seventy tanks had been destroyed. Once more the Allies faced the problem of trying to fight a war with the weapons of the war just past.

While this was happening, the attention of the Allies High Command was focused on General von Reichenau's Sixth Army and on the Sixteenth Panzer Corps, which was carrying out the conventional offensive in the north. On the evening of May 15 the Belgian, British, and French forces were holding very nicely on the Dyle River line from Antwerp to Namur, and General Gamelin, the French overall commander of ground forces, was very pleased with the way the battle was going.

The British and the French thought the whole German attack was the Schlieffen plan all over again, just as in World War I.

So, as General Halder, the army chief of staff, saw very clearly, the time was right for the trap to be sprung. The Allied armies numbered twenty-four British and French divisions and fifteen Belgian divisions in the north, against the German Sixth Army with fifteen divisions in the front and half a dozen in reserve. The German force here was strong enough to stop any enemy attack. And the British and French forces had nothing behind them except the English Channel. Meanwhile, the panzer forces were pouring through in the south and moving toward the French coast.

On May 16 an upset Prime Minister Churchill flew from London to Paris to find out what was happening. During the night he had been hearing very ominous rumors. When he reached the Quay d'Orsay to talk to Premier Paul Reynaud and General Gamelin, he got a shock. The Germans were 60 miles west of Sedan, rolling along with their tanks in undefended open country. There was nothing to stop them, either in the direction of Paris or in the direction of the Channel.

"Où est la masse de manoeuvre?"

"Where is the strategic reserve?" Churchill asked.

"Aucune," replied General Gamelin. "There is none."

But Hitler did not know that, and consequently he made an error that day that very nearly cost the Germans their initiative. General Guderian was more than a third of the way to the Channel when he received an order from Hitler to stop short. Göring's Luftwaffe intelligence unit had received a report that the French were about to mount a big new offensive to cut off the exposed panzer corps. Since it was unbelievable that the French would not have reserves, and a counterattack should be just what they would launch, Hitler believed the story. Hitler faced down General von Brauchitsch and General Halder, who wanted to go on. Later in the day General von Rundstedt, the commander of Army Group A, which had launched the breakthrough at the Meuse, sided with Hitler: a French strike would be coming.

"The Führer is terribly nervous," wrote General Halder in his diary on May 17. "He is worried over his own success, will risk nothing and insists on restraining us. He has brought only bewilderment and doubts."

Halder said the French had no forces in the south. Hitler disputed him and told him to get set for an enemy counteroffensive. Halder stalled. In the west, the panzer divisions, restrained for two days, finally got moving again under a directive that allowed them to make "reconnaissance in force." So they pressed forward, seven armored divisions, driving toward the Somme river, only 50 miles from the Channel. On the evening of May 20 the Second Panzer Division reached Abbeville at the mouth of the Somme. Thus they trapped the Belgians, the British Expeditionary Force, and three French armies.

When the great news was confirmed, all Hitler's doubts evaporated in a great burst of euphoria. He was already working on the peace treaty that would right the wrongs of 400 years, he said.

If the Allies had a chance, it was to break out of the pocket in Belgium and fight their way across northern France to the sea, to join up with the forces pushing up from the Somme. General Gamelin so ordered on the morning of May 19, but the government's confidence in Gamelin was gone. Before nightfall he was replaced by General Maxime Weygand, whose first move was to cancel Gamelin's breakout and linkup order. In so doing, Weygand sealed France's fate.

No French troops moved from the Somme; thus the forty divisions that could have saved the day were never employed.

And General Guderian and his fellows moved on. By May 24 Guderian had captured Boulogne and surrounded Calais. He had reached the coastal town of Gravelines, about 20 miles southwest of Dunkirk.

The British, French, and Belgian armies were forced into a triangle with one side along the English Channel from Gravelines to Teneuzen and with its apex at Valenciennes, 70 miles inland. There was no way of breaking out of this trap with Germans on all sides and the sea at their backs. The only possible hope was the sea. The Germans were poised for the kill when, suddenly, within sight of Dunkirk, the German armored force again was ordered to stop.

Hitler had just made his first major tactical blunder of the war. He had ordered the halt, backed by von Rundstedt but opposed by von Brauchitsch and Halder. It was all part of the same mystical feeling that Hitler had that something was not going right. Von Rundstedt's ultraconservative, not to say timid, attitude was certainly a major factor in Hitler's decision to stop the army on the lip of total annihilating victory.

But there was more to it than that. Part of the reason was Hitler's distrust, contempt, and fear of his own generals.

For four days, at Churchill's insistence, the admiralty had been rounding up every bit of shipping it could find in the British Isles to evacuate the army from Dunkirk. Now Hitler's enormous error gave them time to do so. It was as if a miracle had been ordered in the British hour of need. For had that army of nearly 350,000 men not been evacuated, the British likely would have fallen easily to virtually any German invasion and certainly they would not have been able to mount offensives in Africa or anywhere else for several years after 1940. The salvation of the army at Dunkirk was the salvation of Britain's war.

General von Brauchitsch and General Halder stood by and figuratively gnashed their teeth as Hitler refused to listen to reason. His error was compounded by cronyism and by the unbridled ambition of Field Marshal Göring, who somehow convinced Hitler that if he allowed the army to finish off the British, French, and Belgians, the army would supplant him. Hitler's distrust of his army generals was of long standing, so he allowed himself to be convinced that Göring's Luftwaffe could by itself wipe out the Allied troops trapped in the pocket.

The situation continued thus until the evening of May 26, while the British strengthened their defenses around Dunkirk, and ships and boats began coming in to take the troops off. That evening of

May 26 Hitler finally saw that he had duped himself and that the
chance to trap the Allied forces was fast disappearing. So he rescinded his stop order. But by this time the panzer divisions had
lost their momentum.

Britain's Operation Dynamo began. It involved the sea-lift of a
third of a million men from the French beaches by every sort of
craft that could sail. There were 850 such craft swarming around in
the waters off Dunkirk, from battle cruisers to catboats. Three British divisions held the German armored troops at bay as the evacuation continued. At the end of four days the ships and boats had
taken off more than 125,000 troops. The British were truly fortunate that the weather had closed in and the Luftwaffe could not fly.
So the evacuation continued under the eyes of the now astounded
German generals, who suddenly realized what was happening but
were powerless to stop it. On May 31 another 68,000 men were taken
off the French beaches; on June 1, 64,000 more. By June 2 only
4000 British soldiers remained on French soil, protected now by
100,000 Frenchmen who had nowhere to go, but whose staunch defense was proof that the French debacle in World War II was a result of the failure of the politicians and the generals, and not of the
poilu. They held out, although surrounded, until the last of the British were evacuated.

A total of 338,000 Allied troops had been taken out of Dunkirk.
It was a moment of seeming triumph for the British. But it was followed immediately by the sobering realization that wars were not
won by evacuating in the face of the enemy.

The truism was underscored on June 10, when the French government deserted Paris, and on June 17, when the new French government in Bordeaux, headed by Marshal Henri Philippe Pétain,
asked the Germans for an armistice.

Armistice? said Hitler. He would have to consult his ally, Benito
Mussolini, for Mussolini had recently entered the war, having decided that the Germans were going to win it.

On June 19 German engineers pulled the old railroad car in which
the peace of 1918 had been signed back onto the tracks on the edge
of the forest at Compiègne. There the vengeful peace of 1940 was
signed with France, thus reversing history. William Shirer, the cor-

respondent, was present. He watched Hitler go to the World War I monument on the site and read the inscription:

HERE ON THE ELEVENTH OF NOVEMBER 1918
SUCCUMBED THE CRIMINAL PRIDE OF THE
GERMAN EMPIRE—VANQUISHED BY THE FREE
PEOPLE WHICH IT TRIED TO ENSLAVE.

Then Hitler sneered and moved scornfully into the railroad car to present to the beaten French representatives his demands, which amounted to total submission to the Third Reich. And so the Germans came to stride up and down the Champs-Elysées. Mostly central and western Europe was now their arena—all but one small segment, a tiny island kingdom visible from the French beaches, a constitutional monarchy headed by Hitler's one most fearsome enemy, a small, fat man named Winston Spencer Churchill. He and his compatriots were determined to fight on.

11

THE BATTLE OF BRITAIN—I

After the armistice that took France out of the war was signed on the afternoon of June 22, 1940, there was a brief celebration in the dining room of the headquarters Hitler had taken over. A military tattoo was followed by the hymn "Nun danket alle Gott"—Now Thank We All Our God—because, of course, God was on Hitler's side. It was the Führer's signal hour of triumph. For years he had yearned for the moment when all the wrongs he had enumerated about Versailles would be wiped out by the pens of his enemies.

That evening his generals and party leaders gathered around him and congratulated him on his victory, and like the caesars, he took it all with smiling grace.

The next morning Hitler and his staff took off by airplane for Paris and landed at Le Bourget field. They arrived so early that most of Paris was still abed. The sleepy bakery deliverymen were out in their trucks and horse-drawn carriages. Shop owners were beginning to take down the grilles from the windows and sweep out their little stores. A few all-night cafes stood under the glaring fluorescent lights, and late workers stopped for a glass *sur le zinc*.

Hitler and his entourage were driven up to Montmartre; from there they looked down at the beautiful city, just awakening from its sleep. Then they went on a brisk tour, commanded by the Führer, of the architectural points of interest. They paused at the Arc de Triomphe, and dallied a bit at the Opéra, whose architecture had always fascinated Hitler. Then they went to Napoleon's tomb, where Hitler paused with a reverence that previous conquerors had reserved only for the pope.

"That was the greatest and finest moment of my life," he said.

At one point, toward the end of the French campaign of the summer of 1940, Adolf Hitler had considered destroying the Paris he hated because it seemed to symbolize the Versailles treaty. But he reconsidered when he realized that he could outdo the French at building beautiful monuments. He, Hitler, the new Napoleon, would make Berlin the most beautiful city in the world. He had just the man to do it: Albert Speer, an architect who had been drawn into Hitler's inner circle and who would serve in a multitude of ways including, ultimately, as minister of armaments.

Speer was put to work designing a model city, built around an avenue longer and broader than the Champs-Elysées and dominated by an enormous central railroad station with four levels of traffic. The station plaza would be 3300 feet long and 1000 feet wide and would be lined by captured weapons of war. Already—after Czechoslovakia, Poland, Denmark, Norway, the Netherlands, Belgium, and France—the weapons collection was huge. The Arc de Triomphe towers 160 feet over the Place de l'Etoile in Paris. Hitler's Arch of Triumph would be 386 feet high. The other buildings along this broad avenue would be equally enormous and, as architect Speer suddenly realized years later, equally monstrous: eleven ministry buildings along a 3-mile avenue. One of the dominant buildings, built early, was the Soldiers Hall, a huge cube, which was to house various exhibits. The first of those was the railroad car from Compiègne, where the armistices of 1918 and 1940 had been signed. Immediately after the signing ceremony Hitler had the car shipped to Berlin as a symbol of Germany's revenge.

A few days after the victory, Hitler moved to another headquarters built for him by the Todt organization. This one was in the Black Forest: "Tannenberg," it was called, located west of Freudenstadt. Here he oversaw the plans for his next adventure: coming to terms with Britain.

With the fall of France, Hitler was certain that Britain would seek an easy exit from the war. He was prepared to give one. "Britain can get a separate peace any time after restitution of the colonies," he told General Jodl. By "the colonies" Hitler meant German East Africa, which had become Kenya; German Southwest Africa, which had been placed under the rule of the Dominion of South Africa; the Kameroons, in northwest Africa; the Marshall Islands; the southern part of New Guinea, which the Australians had taken over; and half of Samoa, which New Zealand had taken. Hitler was prepared to be most generous, considering the beating the British had taken in Norway and France. All he really wanted, he told General von Rundstedt, was a free hand on the European continent, and since the British had no interests there, it seemed quite logical that they should agree.

So as of June there was no plan for the continuation of the war. Hitler did not have such a plan, nor did he ask for one. His major concern, brought from the generals, was about Soviet talk and activity in the Balkans and the Baltic Sea. The threat was from the east, not from the west.

So very logical was Hitler's thinking that most of the world expected Britain to withdraw from the war.

But that showed how little the world knew the British.

At five o'clock on the evening of June 13, 1940, Prime Minister Churchill reported to the British War Cabinet. He had just that afternoon returned from a final visit to Paris, leaving as the Germans entered the city, and had spoken with the French leaders to learn of their decision to surrender.

He told the cabinet of the French situation, and then he turned to the main issue before them. "We must now concentrate our efforts," he said, "on the defence of our island."

The defense was concentrated. Had Hitler been able to walk unobserved in a London street he would have been astounded to hear the people around him. For almost nowhere was there talk of giving up or of negotiated peace or of "some arrangement."

No, the talk was of war, and of defending the island and of winning. Churchill described the mood of the people:

Nothing moves an Englishman so much as the threat of invasion, the reality unknown for a thousand years. Vast numbers of people were resolved to conquer or die. There was no need to arouse their spirit by oratory. They were glad to hear me express their sentiments and give them good reasons for what they meant to do, or try to do.

Hitler still thought it almost certain that he could negotiate a peace with Britain, and he was spending most of his time drawing up his peace proposal. Thus he did not pay much attention to Churchill's speeches from the other side of the Channel.

"We will fight on if necessary for years," Churchill vowed, "if necessary alone."

On June 18, 1940, he spoke for his compatriots in what would become perhaps his most famous lines:

I expect that the Battle of Britain is about to begin. Upon this battle depends the survival of Christian civilisation. Upon it depends our own British life, and the long continuity of our institutions and our Empire. The whole fury and might of the enemy must very soon be turned on us. Hitler knows that he will have to break us in this island or lose the war. If we can stand up to him, all Europe may be free and the life of the world may move forward into broad, sunlit uplands. But if we fail, then the whole world, including the United States, including all that we have known and cared for, will sink into the abyss of a new Dark Age, made more sinister, and perhaps more protracted, by the lights of perverted science. Let us therefore brace ourselves to our duties, and so bear ourselves that, if the British Empire and its Commonwealth last for a thousand years, men will say, "This was their finest hour."

And so it was to be.

At the end of June the Pope offered to mediate the war. So did the king of Sweden. The German ambassador to Washington arranged an interview of Hitler by Karl von Wiegand, a war correspondent for the powerful Hearst newspapers. The gist of it was that Hitler was ready to make peace with Britain.

But Churchill was having none of it. He grimly told the king of Sweden that just as soon as Hitler was ready to restore the freedom of Czechoslovakia, Poland, Norway, Denmark, Holland, Belgium, and France, he would be willing to talk peace. Austria, for some unknown reason, was not mentioned.

Yet there was no comprehension of this determination in Berlin. Hitler believed the war was won, and that was the official line.

But July 1 came, and the British indicated no intentions of surrender or accommodation. From the far side of the English Channel Hitler could hear only the snarls of the British lion. Reluctantly, on July 2 Hitler issued orders to OKW to begin planning for the invasion of England.

On July 11 he met with Admiral Raeder to talk about the problems of transporting German troops across the Channel. Raeder skirted the real issue, which was the weakness of the German navy brought about by the losses in the Norwegian campaign. Raeder would rather talk, and did, about the results to be obtained by cutting off British international trade by means of the U-boat campaign. Hitler was skeptical.

On July 13 Hitler met with his generals at the Berghof. He was still puzzled by the British failure to accept his overtures, but was now convincing himself that the British were counting on the Soviets to take the pressure off them. This possibility could bring him to paroxysms of anger. On July 16 he worked himself up enough to issue a new OKW directive, this one planning for the invasion of England. He called it "Operation Sea Lion." It was to be carried out in the middle of August.

On the evening of July 19, 1940, Hitler made his ultimate offer to Britain by radio:

> In this hour I feel it to be my duty before my own conscience to appeal once more to reason and common sense in Great Britain as much as elsewhere. I consider myself in a position to make this appeal since I am not the vanquished begging favors, but the victor speaking in the name of reason.
>
> I can see no reason why this war must go on.

The world did not even have to wait for Prime Minister Churchill to respond. Within the hour, the British Broadcasting Corporation and the British newspapers were, on their own initiative, reading the pulse of the people and rejecting the German offer.

Three days later the British rejected it formally in a speech by Lord Halifax, the foreign secretary.

And so, at the apex of his victorious drive through Europe, Hitler suddenly found that he had on his hands a war that he could not comprehend. He might talk, as he would, about the destruction of the whole British Empire, but he had insufficient strength to bring it about. Germany was not a sea power, and since 1918 it had not even pretended to be one.

The lack of planning was the significant factor in Hitler's whole war approach. He had gone from one speck to the next, picking up old German territories and settling old German scores. Now the scores were settled. He was the master of Europe from the Pyrenees to the Arctic Ocean, from the Bay of Biscay east to the new Soviet border in mid-Poland. The Balkans seemed ripe for his plucking. But what did all this mean? Nothing, if he could not come to terms with Britain. And now he knew he could not, so he had to begin, from scratch, planning for an entirely different sort of war.

General Keitel, along with eleven other generals, had been made a field marshal. Keitel's new task was to prepare Germany for conquering England. It was to be done by the navy and the Luftwaffe. Admiral Dönitz, the submarine commander, was promised a greater building program than he had hoped for, although Hitler still did not listen when Dönitz said that the U-boats could bring Britain to its knees in six months if there were enough of them.

The navy was seriously concerned with Sea Lion. In the course of his planning Rear Admiral Kurt Fricke pointed out that the German navy had no landing craft. If the Germans wanted to invade England, they had better get some quickly.

OKW did not have much to offer in the beginning. General Jodl, Keitel's chief of staff, suggested a three-pronged approach to the problem:

1. Intensify the air war against England, including terror attacks against population centers by bombers.

2. Intensify the sea war against British shipping.

3. Land troops to occupy England.

All were easier said than done. As Jodl pointed out, troop landings could be accomplished only after the Germans achieved air control of the skies over Britain. That meant wiping out the British Royal Air Force's power to defend its skies.

The fact was, however, that the German generals never seriously contemplated a landing on the British shore, no matter what the propagandists said. They knew that the navy had been crippled at Norway. They knew there were insufficient transports and no landing craft.

So the whole preparation by the army during the late spring and early summer of 1940 was a sham. The generals convinced themselves that an invasion would not be necessary anyhow. As Jodl put it:

> Since England can no longer fight for victory, but only for the preservation of its possessions and its world prestige she should, according to all predictions, be inclined to make peace when she learns that she can still get it now at relatively little cost.

Jodl was speaking before the British flatly turned down the German offers. But even afterward, he and the other generals hoped that the air war, the knocking out of British air power, added to the intensification of the submarine and surface raiding of the waters sailed by British ships, would force the British to those terms. The generals so believed because they had no other frame of reference. The German general staff, in its most halcyon days, had never contemplated a *total war*. Suddenly, although they did not yet know it, that is precisely what the generals were facing.

Operation Sea Lion, then, was a German bluff, the generals knew; it was a will-o'-the-wisp that could never be brought off.

But the next step was not. Hitler worked himself up to believe that Field Marshal Göring could, as he promised, quickly destroy Britain's air power. Then, somehow, the resources would be assembled to move the German armies across the English Channel, even if it meant raping every European port of every vessel useful for the job. No, if the generals were not serious about Operation Sea Lion, the Führer was. The difference was that the generals operated within the bounds of feasibility, while such mundane matters had never before restricted Hitler. He saw no reason that they should restrict him now. So in July 1940 Hitler embarked on a new war, for the first time not knowing where he was going or how he was going to get there.

In his rolling of the dice, Hitler was gambling that he could force Britain to surrender, yet he was planning to employ the wrong weapon—that overblown instrument, the Luftwaffe—and still was not unleashing the single instrument that could have accomplished his purpose. Winston Churchill knew. His greatest fear was that the Germans would discover the full potential of the U-boat to quickly destroy England's commerce. Churchill always kept one eye on the reports of sinkings and on the ratio of ships lost to ships produced every month. That was the key to Britain's survival. She must have transport. Britain's shipyards were furiously building the instruments of war: Flower-class corvettes and destroyers to combat the U-boats. Some merchant shipping was on the ways, particularly ships that could be converted to carry guns and aircraft. From America, from Canada, from Australia, and from anywhere else, Britain must secure her merchant shipping. That was the real war that emerged in the summer of 1940, and Hitler was barely aware of it.

12

THE BATTLE OF BRITAIN—II

In Britain the months of July and August passed uneventfully. Of course, every day the German bombers came over some part of England and bombed. Of course, every day ships sailed out into the Atlantic, and ran or failed to run the gauntlet of the German U-boats. The radio waves were filled with the triumphant boasting of Hitler's propagandists. From neutral corners came reports of the fate of British soldiers and others left behind on the continent to struggle to survive or to fail in the attempt.

The war was never far from the consciousness of any man or woman who lived in England, but, at least, as Churchill sighed, the months passed "without any disaster," and the British settled down for a long war.

By mid-August the beaches of England bristled with defenses. The British had added to their shore artillery one 14-inch naval gun, two 9.2-inch railway-mounted guns, two 6-inch naval guns, and two 4-inch naval guns, and they were moving more. Two 13.5-inch naval guns from the old battleship *Iron Duke* were on their way to the shore, and four 5.5-inch guns from HMS *Hood,* a battle cruiser, were also coming. Churchill was making strong representations to his friend Franklin D. Roosevelt for the dispatch of at least two 16-inch coast defense guns. Churchill had also appealed for other help, and the Americans had responded by sending 250 new tanks. The Americans were beginning to build ships for the British, ships that would ease the pain of the losses to the U-boats.

On the shore and inland, the British army trained, and so did the territorial troops who had come from Australia, South Africa, Canada, and other faraway places to help in Britain's hour of need. The Home Guard rose to more than a million men and women. Some of them trained with rifles, some with sporting shotguns, and some with clubs. But they trained, and in their eyes was a look of grim determination. In the years since World War II ended, much has been made of the determination of the Japanese people in 1945, as well as of their government, to defend their homeland on the beaches with any weapons that came to hand. Little has been said of the British situation in 1940, but it was very much the same: an independent island people determined to defend their home soil to the death. Churchill had a slogan for it that he would use when the time came: "You can always take one with you."

The Germans, looking down from their Junkers bombers, thought they saw below a pastoral scene wherein, as Foreign Minister von Ribbentrop told Count Ciano, his Italian counterpart, "a single German division will suffice to bring about a complete collapse" of the British defenses. As Churchill said in his memoirs:

> I have often wondered, however, what would have happened if two hundred thousand German storm troops had actually established themselves ashore. The massacre would have been on both sides grim and great. There would have been neither mercy nor quarter. They would have used terror, and we were prepared to go all lengths.

In Berlin it was tacitly agreed that the Wehrmacht would not be employed for several months. Hitler had changed the chain of command again that summer. He then designated the *Wehrmachtführungsamt* (Armed Forces Operations Office) as his personal military operations staff, emphasizing his overall command of all German forces. He promoted Major General Jodl to full general. Keitel had already been made a field marshal at the July 19 session of the Reichstag. Hitler then moved his headquarters to the Berghof for the summer, taking Jodl and Keitel. Then he gave them the summer off, and Keitel went home to his farm at Helmscherode, bought some farm equipment, and played farmer for a few days. "I was," he said, "a farmer again—my lifelong dream—a farmer again for the last time in my life."

It was a lovely summer. It was a time, as Churchill said, "when it was equally good to live or die."

Marshal Göring was preparing the way for a great number of young men to die.

After the armistice with France was signed, Keitel had a visit from an old friend, Colonel Werner Kreipe of the Luftwaffe, who described the Luftwaffe's operations and adventures during the last stages of the campaign against France. Kreipe told how on May 28 the Third Group of Bomber Wing 2 had been flying Dornier 17 bombers over the disorganized remnants of the French army, having a field day and without any real opposition, because the French air force had been virtually wiped out. That night the bombers returned to their field at Rocroi near the Franco-Belgian frontier and found orders: the next day they would attack the British Expeditionary Force beginning to embark at Dunkirk.

The next morning the air group set off, all twenty-seven aircraft, to begin bombing the British. Below, as far as the eye could see, the beaches were crowded with soldiers, horses, vehicles, and equipment of all sorts. What an ideal target. The Dorniers prepared to go in by formation and bomb.

But just then came rattles on the radio sets: "Enemy fighters coming in from astern" was the report.

Within seconds the Dorniers were attacked by a squadron of British Spitfires. Despite the efforts of the Dornier gunners, the Spitfires attacked again and again and drove the German planes away from the Dunkirk beaches before they could bomb.

Back at Rocroi the staff officers waited, listening to the reports from the wing leader. The command leader, who was at the head of the formation, was attacked six times by one Spitfire. When he landed, Colonel Kreipe himself examined the Dornier. He counted eighty-six bullet holes in the fuselage. The planes, too, were counted. One was missing and two were seriously damaged.

The German planes were gassed up, given ammunition, and ordered to take off again. This time the target was Nieuport.

When the Dorniers came in to bomb, there, too, the Spitfires were at them, even though German fighters came to protect the bombers. The Dorniers managed to bomb, but their accuracy was questionable because of the severity of the British attack. When the German planes returned to base, three Dorniers were missing and five were so badly damaged that they were useless for the near future. The three missing planes had been forced down behind the German lines. But there had been many casualties among the aircrews. In one day eleven of the twenty-seven planes of one group had been put out of action. This was not the sort of war the Luftwaffe was used to fighting.

Colonel Kreipe told General Keitel all this. At that moment it did not sink in, because Keitel and the other generals still believed it most likely that the British would negotiate a peace. But as the weeks went on and the British stood firm, the generals began to have some doubts.

Not Reich Marshal Göring. When Hitler told him that before he would launch Operation Sea Lion, Göring must guarantee him air superiority over Britain, the Luftwaffe chief said it would be easy. To be sure, he asked his chief of intelligence, Colonel Josef Schmid, for a special report.

Schmid came up with the following: he credited Britain with an aircraft production of perhaps 300 first-line fighters per month and 150 first-line bombers per month. Actual British fighter production in July was nearly 500, and it remained at that level during August and September. The Germans still did not realize that Britain was putting forth its every effort to win this war. Churchill was well aware of those efforts:

> The entire population laboured to the last limit of its strength, and felt rewarded when they fell asleep after their toil or vigil by a growing sense that we should have time and that we should win.

Churchill knew that in July and August the British had maintained air superiority over England. The Germans thought otherwise. Schmid's report indicated that between August 12 and August 19, 644 British aircraft had been destroyed and 11 airfields put out of action. The real figures were 103 British planes destroyed and 1 airfield put out of action—temporarily.

So confident about his ability to smash the British did former fighter pilot Göring become that he paid little attention to German airplane production figures. In fact, the Germans produced only 227 fighters in July, and that figure would drop to 177 by the month of September. Hitler's staff was refusing to transfer materials for the air force's use, and the Air Ministry was not fighting hard enough to get them. The net result was that British fighter production was up 43 percent ahead of plan while German fighter production fell 40 percent short of its goal. The same sort of disparity existed in the fighter training programs. The British were moving heaven and earth to train fighter pilots that summer. The Germans were desultory. What was the hurry? They had already won the war.

This was not the way to win an air battle, let alone an air war.

In July the Luftwaffe operated under a directive to attack British shipping. The idea was to bring the Royal Air Force out to fight over the English Channel and the North Sea, where British planes would have less "fighting time" available, because of fuel considerations, and where downed British planes and pilots stood a much smaller chance of being able to make an emergency landing in order to be patched up to fight again. But the British would not come out. Churchill and his generals knew what the Germans were up to, and they wisely refused to commit the British fighter planes in great number to the battle against shipping. Thus the shipping losses for the summer months of 1940 were very high, mostly from air attack. The merchant seamen and the navy complained, but they were not in on the great secret. They did not know what Hitler had planned for Britain, but Churchill did. His Royal Air Force had about 750 fighters in July, and the number had to be increased, not diminished by losses, before the attack came.

The British also faced a new factor that summer. Admiral Dönitz lost no time in moving his U-boat operations center to the French coast. This saved his U-boat captains hundreds of miles when going out into the Atlantic to destroy shipping.

The total ship sinkings for June came to 260,000 tons, sixty-four ships. In July it was almost the same. In August it was 214,000 tons.

There was more bad news. The Italians, with 100 submarines, were now entering the war in the Atlantic. More trouble was coming.

But in the air war the results for the summer were better. By careful nurturing, the RAF had lost only 148 fighters in the sparring operations around Britain, while the Germans had lost 300 planes and another 135 had been damaged.

In July Hitler discussed the invasion.

> The decision as to whether the operation is to take place in September or is to be delayed until May 1941, will be made after the Luftwaffe has made concentrated attacks on southern England for one week. If the effect of the air attacks is such that the enemy air force, harbors, and naval forces etc. are heavily damaged, Operation Sea Lion will be carried out in 1940. Otherwise it is to be postponed until May 1941.

On August 1 Hitler sent a directive to Reich Marshal Göring, outlining the air war as he wanted it:

1. The Luftwaffe was to overcome the Royal Air Force as soon as possible.

2. Attacks were to be diverted from southern harbors, which the Germans would want for Operation Sea Lion.

3. The Luftwaffe was to exert all its effort for Operation Sea Lion.

4. Hitler would make the decisions about terror attacks.

5. The air war would begin on August 6. Eight to fourteen days later Hitler would decide what was to be done in the future.

Meanwhile, the army and the navy got into an argument over the length and breadth of the front on which the ground troops were to be landed in Britain. As a result, by August 16 Hitler was having serious doubts about the whole operation. Field Marshal Halder, the realist, wrote in his diary that there was no chance of making any landings in Britain in 1940.

Admiral Raeder generally agreed with this position; but the planning went on.

And in the air so did the fighting.

On August 15 Göring launched his campaign to bring Britain to its knees.

"I will smash their fighter defenses in four days," he had bragged in July. "To destroy the RAF completely will take a little longer—perhaps from two to four weeks." And he confided to his associates that all the quarreling between the generals and the admirals was useless. He, Göring, would bring Britain to surrender all by himself with his Luftwaffe.

To do this job, Göring had assigned three *Luftflötte,* air fleets, with a total of about a thousand fighters and about 1300 bombers. From the Low Countries, Field Marshal Albert Kesselring would lead the attack. Field Marshal Hugo Sperrle would attack from France; General Stumpff's air fleet, from Norway and Denmark.

The German name for Göring's air offensive was *Adlerangriff*—"Eagle Attack." It was launched on August 12 with a raid on British radar installations. Five of these were damaged and one was destroyed. For a time it seemed that the Germans were prescient, for radar was the key to British air defenses. Employing radar, the British could spot the incoming enemy flights and send fighters up to meet them. If the Germans had persisted in hitting the radar installations, the whole story of the Battle of Britain might have been quite different. But the radar attack was incidental and not deemed vital to the German plan. They did not pursue it, and thus threw away their golden opportunity.

On August 13 and again on August 14 the Germans sent heavy raids against British airfields. They claimed that five fields were destroyed, but actually there were only a few holes in the runways. The Luftwaffe lost forty-seven planes, the British thirteen.

On August 15 the Germans threw a heavy attack against Britain, with 1000 bombing missions flown. Eight hundred planes attacked the south coast of England, and another hundred bombers were sent against the northeast, which the Germans expected to find undefended. But the radar was their undoing. The British saw them coming: a hundred bombers from Norway and Denmark, escorted by thirty-four Messerschmitt 110 fighter planes. About eighty Spitfires and Hurricanes were sent up to meet them, and they shot down thirty German planes without losing one British fighter.

The German raids in the south did some serious damage. They hurt four aircraft factories in the Croydon area and damaged installations and runways at five RAF fighter fields. But the Germans lost seventy-five planes that day, against thirty-five for the RAF. Both sides exaggerated their victories and diminished their losses shamelessly. Had the rest of the world known the facts, the highly touted BBC would have lost its reputation when it claimed—or quoted the official British claim without question—that 182 German planes had been shot down and 40 more damaged. But nobody noticed, and nobody believed the German claims.

There were, in these early days of the air war, some notable instances of chivalry. For example, British Squadron Leader Douglas Bader was a heroic figure even before the war. He had lost both his legs in an accident but had overcome the handicap and was now a British fighter ace, with five kills. During the Battle of Britain he was shot down near St. Omer in France, and his aluminum legs were smashed. When he was entertained by the German officers at their mess, he mentioned his problem, and someone said he thought he might be able to get Bader's spare pair of legs delivered from Britain. So messages were sent over the international distress frequency, and sure enough, in a couple of days down onto the German airfield came floating Doug Bader's extra pair of aluminum legs, by parachute.

The British could thank God for Hermann Göring, for the August 12 attack on the radar stations was repeated only once or twice and with no great zeal.

"It is doubtful whether there is any point in continuing the attacks on radar stations," said Göring on August 15, "since not one of those attacked so far has been put out of action."

The battle seemed to be going in favor of the British. The Germans were losing many Stuka dive-bombers because they were relatively slow, so they withdrew them from the battle on August 17. That was another Göring decision. But the trouble with Göring's decisions was that he spent about half his time in Berlin on his other business, and only a portion of the remainder of his time directing the Luftwaffe. He was not always quite certain of what he was doing, and the results were sometimes ludicrous.

Yet not always. On August 19, during a lull in the fight because of bad weather, Göring reviewed the action up to that point. His week was not yet up, but he realized that he needed a bit more time.

He did understand the importance of the "sector stations," underground centers from which British Fighter Command directed operations. There were seven of these stations around London. Göring shrewdly ordered all of them attacked. All of them were hit on August 24, and some were badly damaged.

The Germans were coming perilously close to winning the air war, and Hitler seemed to sense it. He held his decision about Operation Sea Lion in abeyance.

In the next two weeks, between August 24 and September 6, Göring tried to flatten the British. He sent over an average of a thousand planes each day. They concentrated on those communications centers, and soon had six of them almost destroyed. They knocked out five fighter fields in the south of England. And they were tiring out the British fighter pilots. These men had been in the air steadily for three weeks, flying several missions every day. And in those weeks the British lost 460 fighters. The Germans lost far fewer, only about 215 fighters and 140 bombers. And worse, a quarter of the RAF fighter pilots were killed or seriously wounded during this period.

Winston Churchill for the first time began to believe there was a danger worse than the U-boat menace. In a few weeks, he told his associates, Britain would have no organized air defense.

But then came one of those strange quirks of warfare that could be meaningless in themselves but sometimes psychologically affect the whole course of action.

On the night of August 23 the Germans launched one of their rare night missions against British bases. The target for some twenty-five German bombers was an aircraft and fuel center on the outskirts of London. But the navigator miscalculated, and the lead bombardier dropped his bombs on the center of London. The other bombardiers followed suit.

The British had been expecting a terror raid, and this, said the morning newspapers, was it. A number of houses had been blown to splinters and a number of civilians had been killed. This was just the sort of warfare the British had expected from Adolf Hitler.

It was not just the newspapers. The British High Command also believed the bombing raid was deliberate. So the next night the British retaliated with a raid on Berlin. Eighty RAF bombers were sent to bomb the German capital. Only about half managed to penetrate the dense cloud cover over Germany that night, but they did bomb and they did do some damage. The effect on German morale was enormous, because Berlin had never before been bombed. The British had been bombed in World War I by aircraft and zeppelins; not so Berlin.

*   *   *

The bombings continued for a week. Still the damage was very slight. But Hitler had to make some decisions. What about Operation Sea Lion? What about the continuation of Göring's attacks on the British airfields? Knocking out those British fighters did not seem quite so important now, with all the furor in Berlin about the British bombings. After all, the first anniversary of the war was approaching. Hitler had promised peace, and the German people wanted peace. Some were beginning to grow cynical about Hitler's promises, and that was not good.

On September 4, Hitler felt it necessary to make a major speech to his nation to answer two questions: What was to be done about the bombings of Berlin? Was Britain going to be invaded?

Hitler addressed himself to the first question. If the British continued to drop bombs on Berlin, the Germans would retaliate by dropping ten times as many bombs on London. So enormous was the response of his audience, mostly women nurses, that the second question was for the moment forgotten.

And so, almost at the point where success would have been achieved by Göring, the decision was made—to please Hitler—to halt the attacks on Britain's fighter defenses and to begin the terror bombing of the British cities. Hitler undoubtedly knew by this time that he did not have the resources to carry out Sea Lion; certainly the navy and the army knew. But he had to get "off the hook" on which he had impaled himself with his directive setting up the operation. His reasoning now was that Göring could promise to raze

London for him, and the destruction of the British capital would undoubtedly bring Britain to the point of a peace accommodation.

On the evening of September 7 the bombing campaign against London began. That night the Germans sent nearly 1300 bombers and fighters to England. They struck the Woolwich arsenal. They hit the gas works, power stations, and miles of docks. Soon great fires were rising on the banks of the Thames. In two nights nearly 1000 people were killed and nearly 3000 were wounded.

Night after night the bombers came over and dropped their bombs on England's industrial centers. The attacks were so successful from the German point of view that on September 15, a Sunday, the Luftwaffe carried out an enormous daylight raid. In the first wave, 200 bombers were sent to bomb London, escorted by 600 fighter planes.

The British were watching on their mended radar sets. They saw the Germans coming and sent up the fighters, which intercepted the German raid. Most of the German bombers were turned away. A few hours later another wave came, and this too was repelled. At the end of the day, the Germans counted their losses: 156 planes lost and more than 100 badly damaged. The British had lost only twenty-six aircraft.

After all the propaganda claims were sorted out, one thing was clear to all concerned. The Germans had given British Fighter Command a little more than a week to recover from the terrible beating it had taken. In that hiatus the information centers had been repaired and the fighter pilots had been able to get a few good nights of sleep. The delay of the Germans had been disastrous to their hopes. Göring had come so close, within perhaps twenty-four hours of victory—one more immense raid on the fighter sectors might have done the job—but he had stopped; now it was impossible to regain the lost momentum.

On September 17, after consulting with his army and navy commanders, and having wrenched from Göring the admission that the Luftwaffe did not have air superiority over England, the Führer made his decision.

Operation Sea Lion was postponed indefinitely.

*

For the next two months London would be bombed night after night. So would other cities: Coventry, Liverpool, Portsmouth, Hull, Manchester. Thousands of women and children would be killed and many more thousands made homeless by the bombings. Nonetheless, the British knew now that they were safe from invasion. Hitler had suffered his very first significant defeat.

The bombing continued all winter, but it did not seriously hurt British war production. The main reason was that the Germans did not have a long-distance, heavily armed, four-engine bomber, capable of flying 1200 to 1500 miles and capable of operating at high altitude with heavy bomb loads. British aircraft production did not go down during this period; it increased.

In February 1941 Göring went to Paris to confront his two senior air commanders, field marshals Kesselring and Sperrle. With great fanfare he set up a meeting at the Sale de l'Horlage. What was wrong with the Luftwaffe, he demanded to know, that it could not defeat England? Kesselring and Sperrle mentioned the lack of heavy bombers, as well as the poor quality of training of the new aircrews. Excuses! shouted the Reich marshal. He wanted results.

But he did not get them. Sixty-five major raids were laid on London, sometimes with 800 bombers on a single raid. But the results were not compatible with the effort, and the war elsewhere was demanding more and more air power. Thus in May 1941, without fanfare, the gigantic assault on Britain came to an end, and Hitler's failure to bring Britain to its knees would not be reversed.

13

STRIKING SOUTH

By midsummer 1940, Hitler and his staff realized that the U.S. government was all but allied with Britain, in spite of strong antiwar sentiment in America. As Field Marshal Keitel put it, "I knew that there was no hope of ending the war with Britain, for the United States and all her unlimited resources stood behind her."

But the object was still the same, to force England to sue for peace. The means to that end had to be changed.

When Keitel returned to OKW from his brief sojourn as a farmer, Hitler told him to go down to Innsbruck to meet with Marshal Badoglio, the chief of the Italian General Staff. The object was to see what the Germans could do to further the Italian war effort against the British in north Africa. There the British were pushing the Italians back on the Tripolitanian frontier. Keitel offered Badoglio two panzer divisions. Badoglio declined, saying that tanks would be a liability in the sands of Africa, and thereby proving himself to be one of the worst field generals of all time. When Keitel remonstrated mildly, he did get an agreement to send a team of tank experts to north Africa under Colonel Freiherr Hans von Funck.

But Mussolini and Hitler had agreed that the Germans would send several Luftwaffe groups to southern Italy to combat the British in the Mediterranean. This was part of a larger agreement in which Mussolini offered his submarines to Hitler. Since Admiral

Dönitz was constantly complaining about not having enough U-boats in action, Hitler had agreed. But Dönitz was a Prussian through and through, and he was completely contemptuous of the Italians. He and his staff contrived to make them look very bad in northern European operations, and he later claimed that the Italian submariners were incompetent, although the record for the months in which they operated in the north and central Atlantic disproves the Dönitz claim. What Dönitz's attitude did prove was that the Germans were really incapable of working with allies on an even footing, an arrogance that was ultimately to cripple their relations with the Italians.

Hitler had another scheme up his sleeve. With the connivance of Spain, which he hoped to arrange with Franco, he proposed to seize Gibraltar, the British fortress on the Spanish side of the strait that separates the Atlantic Ocean from the Mediterranean. He also proposed, over the objections of Admiral Dönitz, to put a large U-boat force into the Mediterranean. Dönitz fought the idea because he considered the Mediterranean to be a trap, too shallow for safety and locked at both ends by British bases.

But Hitler's meeting with Franco ended in failure; he did not convince the Spanish dictator either to give him access to Gibraltar or to enter the war on the side of the Axis. The Italians, who invaded Greece that year, were jealous of the whole Mediterranean area and strongly preferred to see the Germans keep on their own side of the Alps. And so it seemed that Hitler was not going to move into the south—that is, it seemed that way to people who did not know Hitler.

With the abandonment of Operation Sea Lion, Hitler was at loose ends. There was no new policy, and he sensed that to stand still was to go backward. The course on which he had embarked, the conquest of Europe, must be ever onward. His thoughts at this point turned toward the east, which was his ultimate goal—to achieve *Lebensraum* for the Germans. To accomplish this, of course, he would have to fight the Soviets, but that idea had always appealed to him. As he now began telling his subordinates with growing enthusiasm, it was unthinkable that the two most inimical politico-social systems in the world could coexist for long. If he did not attack the Soviets, he was sure they would soon enough attack him. One system or the other was going to be destroyed. More and more in the summer and fall of 1940 Hitler came back to the opportunities and dangers of a war in the east. All his marshals save Göring shuddered at the idea of a two-front war. The German forces were already fully extended in Scandinavia, Poland, Czechoslovakia, and western Europe. That was all right, said Hitler. Probably some of those troops in France could be moved. The French seemed docile enough.

Late in August Keitel was so upset by Hitler's talk about war in the east that he wrote a long memo on the subject. For his pains he received such a dressing down from Hitler that the field marshal tried to resign his post. He asked for a field commission.

"Have I no right to inform you if in my view your judgement was wrong," Hitler demanded.

"I really must start forbidding my generals to go into a huff and ask to resign every time someone lectures them. In any case do you think *I* could resign?

"I want you to understand that it is nobody's right but mine to relieve a person of his office if I see fit, and until then that person will just have to put up with the job."

The Führer softened a little: "It was just last fall that I had to tell Brauchitsch the very same thing."

As Hitler admonished Keitel, both men rose to their feet. The field marshal then walked stiffly out of the room without saying a word.

Throughout the fall of 1940 and early in 1941 Hitler kept telling his staff that the Soviets were planning an attack on Germany. The generals did not believe it, and they continued to oppose a two-front war.

German military policy continued in the doldrums. Only Hitler wanted to expand the war. He ordered von Brauchitsch to double the number of armored divisions. He had not created this powerful mobile army to have it rot. There was no way he could use his army against Britain in the spring of 1941. The east was the answer.

The winds of change shifted to the Balkans. In June the Soviets seized Romanian Bessarabia. In late August the Romanians also were forced (by pressure from Berlin and Rome) to cede 16,000 square miles of territory to Hungary. A few days later the Romanian government collapsed and King Carol fled. General Ion Antonescu became head of state, and presided over the ceding of another 3000 square miles, this time to Bulgaria. Germany was not going to be left out of this game, so on October 8 German troops marched into Romania to "protect" the oil fields there. Against whom? Against the Soviets, obviously.

In the fall Hitler learned that Mussolini was planning to attack Greece, and he called for a meeting with his Italian partners. Il Duce knew what was on the Führer's mind, and he ordered his troops to march before the two dictators would meet on October 28. So when they met at Florence, the first order of business was to read the dispatches from the Albanian front, where Italian troops were already in action. Hitler was furious. "This new adventure," he predicted to his associates, "will come to disaster."

The terrain was dreadful; the weather was about to change for the worse; and Mussolini did not have enough troops ready to do the job. As far as Hitler was concerned, the only positive outcome of recent weeks was the request by the Italians for an armored division to be sent to north Africa. Colonel—now General—von Funck had convinced the Italians that tanks really would work on the desert sands. Hitler now had his entry into the Mediterranean.

So far, so good.

Even better, Romania and Hungary allied themselves with Hitler and Mussolini by joining the Rome-Berlin-Tokyo mutual defense alliance.

But Hitler's judgment about the foolishness of Mussolini's Albanian and Greek adventure was proved to be quite correct within a matter of days. The Greeks were a very hard nut to crack and they launched a stiff counteroffensive. In short order they captured Port Edda and 28,000 Italian prisoners. Before the end of December 1940 they had seized a quarter of Albania.

The weather changed for the worse, and the Italians found themselves bogged down. Now what? Mussolini was in difficulty, and Axis prestige was at stake. Something had to be done. Fortunately for Hitler, the winter brought an end to fighting, so he had the cold months in which to devise a solution. OKW spent the winter planning a Balkan offensive to save Mussolini from humiliation.

But that was not all Hitler was doing. In December 1940 he made the final decision to invade the U.S.S.R. As he told Keitel, it was only a matter of months before the Russians invaded Germany, so why not strike first? Keitel shuddered again, but he had the good sense to keep quiet. There was no gainsaying Hitler when he had his mind made up.

Nothing much had to be done that winter except to ensure that the railroads to the east were in shape to carry the troops when the time came. The attack was scheduled for May 1941.

One other plan was in the works. Hitler thought he had finally secured Franco's permission for German troops to cross Spain to attack Gibraltar. An impressive plan was prepared. But early in December 1940, when Admiral Canaris, who had special influence in Spain, was dispatched to get the Caudillo's signature on the dotted line, he came home with an empty paper. Franco had backed away. He was afraid that if he let the Germans in, Britain would declare war on him and send troops to invade Spain. Hitler was disappointed because he could see that if he took Gibraltar, he could cut Britain's line of communication with the Mediterranean. But there was nothing to be done, and he had more important matters to think about.

Chief among them was the coming attack on the Soviet Union. In the latter half of January 1941, General Halder came in to outline to the Führer the army's operations plans. His revelations about Soviet preparations confirmed all that Hitler had been saying about the Soviet buildup, and there could be only one reason for it: a planned attack on Germany.

At the end of March Hitler did what he did best: he made a speech to his generals about what was going to happen on the eastern front. He laid it all out for them: the inevitability of the conflict, the need to solve the eastern problem before the United States came into the war in the west on the side of Britain. From the day that the Americans had sent that first batch of tanks to reinforce the British army, which had lost so much equipment at Dunkirk, Hitler knew that the Americans would ultimately enter the war. He saw much more clearly than did the average American citizen just how steadily President Roosevelt was moving the United States to Britain's side.

*

The war against the Soviets would be a new sort of war, aimed at the destruction of a political system, above all. Certainly Hitler wanted the territory, and the access to the Caucasus and middle eastern oil, but even more he wanted to rid himself (and the world, he said) of communism. Since his boyhood days in Vienna, communism had been the blackest of his enemies, surpassed in his pantheon of demons only by the Jews, who, he said, were the inventors of communism in addition to all their other crimes against humanity. So now, also, there was the need to fight a war *a l'outrance,* with no silly notions of chivalry. The Soviets must be destroyed. The German troops in the U.S.S.R. must be ruthless. Soviet political commissars should be shot down and not taken prisoner. As long as territory in the east remained unpacified, there would be no courts-martial of German troops accused of excesses of any sort. There would be no transport of Soviet prisoners into Germany.

What would the German generals do with their prisoners?

That was their problem, said Hitler grimly. There would be no, repeat no, transport of Soviet prisoners to Germany. In the first place they would constitute a political danger to the German work force. And there need be no second place.

The generals were shocked, and Hitler knew it. "I do not expect my generals to understand me," he said as he closed his speech, "but I do expect them to obey my orders."

Among other changes, Hitler decided to give Heinrich Himmler total authority in the rear operational areas behind the Soviet fighting front. That meant Himmler would become more important than any of the generals, and Field Marshal Keitel protested. He was brusquely overruled. Hitler knew what he was doing, and he knew his man. If anyone could exercise the maximum of brutality in occupied Soviet territory, it was Himmler.

A few days after Hitler's speech to the generals, Keitel conferred with von Brauchitsch. The latter said that the generals detested the sort of war Hitler proposed to take to the Soviet Union. No one rebelled, but it had to be plain to Keitel that wherever possible the generals would do their best to subvert the intent of Hitler. They were, after all, primarily soldiers, and there were rules to soldiering. Hitler (whose campaign against the Jews had already proved his inhumanity) proposed to make warfare totally inhumane and to put the generals in the position of becoming accessories to pure murder. This prospect disturbed the generals in a way that the anti-Semitic outrages never had, for it struck home. Thus, even before launching his drive eastward, Hitler had further antagonized his generals; he ensured that when the chips were down, there would be little personal loyalty or feeling for him to cause them to "go the extra mile."

In the winter of 1940 the war in the west was conducted in the air and at sea. The Luftwaffe kept bombing London and other British cities day and night. At sea the German air force was cooperating with the U-boats, and the big Dornier bombers were ideal as observation planes, although not as good as the Focke-Wulf bombers, which were now going along on the attacks.

*　　　*　　　*

In March 1941, German troops massed on the borders of Hungary, Romania, and Bulgaria. Field Marshal List was prepared to cross the Danube into Bulgaria. All this was done to forestall the Soviets. Also, Yugoslavia's Prince Paul, regent of the kingdom, was negotiating to join the Rome-Berlin-Tokyo Axis and he signed up on March 25. The next day dissident nationalists began a political coup that threw out Prince Paul's government and Prince Peter was proclaimed King. A new cabinet announced that Yugoslavia would be neutral.

Hitler called for Field Marshal Keitel and General Jodl, and announced to them that he would not stand for this change. The German army would march at once. The attack would be made from the north by forces in Germany, and from the east by forces under Field Marshal List, which were poised on the Bulgarian border.

Keitel said it was impossible. The preparations for the attack on the U.S.S.R. could not be stopped. There were no troops available for such an adventure except List's and this force was not strong enough to do the job.

That was why Hitler had called them in, said the Führer. They must find a way.

He began issuing a stream of orders:

List's army was to encircle Yugoslavia on the east, and march on Belgrade. German and Hungarian units would move across the Danube and capture Belgrade. A new army, consisting of rear echelon troops from the massing against the Soviets, would strike from Austria. No further discussion would be permitted. And Hitler walked out of the meeting, leaving the smoke of his orders behind.

So the Germans marched and invested Yugoslavia. Hitler went south on his special train, accompanied by Keitel and Jodl. The train was put on a small siding; from there, Hitler personally directed the campaign.

After twelve days the Yugoslav government capitulated. The Germans also began pouring into Greece. General Jodl was sent down to take charge. Hitler was predisposed to be generous to the Greeks, for after all, Mussolini had started that war. All he really wanted was to drive the British out of Greece, where they had landed in March. So the Germans fought the Battle of Mount Olympus and defeated the British at Thermopylae.

On April 23, six days after the surrender of Yugoslavia, Greece capitulated. Four days later the Germans entered Athens. A British Expeditionary Force of 60,000 men had to be evacuated; 12,000 of them did not make it. They, and almost all the equipment of the British southern force, were captured.

Soon the British presence was visible only on the Isthmus of Corinth, and a handful of Aegean islands, including the big island of Crete.

The war in the south began to come together then, with its focus in the Mediterranean. The small German contingent that had started in north Africa had already been raised to a reinforced panzer division under General Erwin Rommel, an armored force commander who had made his reputation with a lightning dash to the sea in France. The problem now was to shield German-Italian communications in the Mediterranean, which were under sea and air attack by the British. Hitler had many suggestions for Mussolini, including the stripping of several old destroyers to turn them into fast transports. He was full of ideas. But, ultimately, he knew he would have to step in personally in the Mediterranean if he wanted to have his own way.

Rommel had just stopped the British drive against Tripoli. More such actions were needed. Hitler decided to strike a real blow against the British by seizing one of their major bases, either Malta or Crete. In the discussions in OKW, Keitel and Jodl opted for Malta as the more dangerous base. Either way, the job was going to be one for the Luftwaffe, using airborne troops, which the Luftwaffe controlled. But Göring, smarting from his failure against Britain, needed a success. He convinced Hitler that the assault should be made against Crete. The other generals were certain that Göring's decision was made because Crete was an easier nut to crack.

A successful assault against Malta would have crippled the British in the Mediterranean for years. Crete was only an incidental base, in no way a major part of British defenses. Hitler's soft spot for the feelings of his old Nazi associate caused him to make this error, which would ultimately cost him control of the Mediterranean.

The invasion of Crete was on.

Luftwaffe General Kurt Student was in charge of the Crete operations. He had assembled the finest airborne force then in existence. For years he had been studying the art of parachute warfare, and it was his genius that had led to the easy capture of the Belgian forts from the air.

Now he had a force of 500 air transports and 70 gliders, plus a large force of bombers. The bombers came first, to soften up the British defenses. After a week of bombing, the first German parachute troops dropped on Crete on May 20. Their mission was to capture the Maleme airfield, the only useful one on the island. On May 21 they took it. With control of the airfield, Student was able to reinforce his troops by glider and by transport. Nine days later the British position was seen as hopeless. The Royal Navy agreed. It had lost nine ships and seen seventeen more damaged by Luftwaffe bombing. The final effort had to be the evacuation of as many troops as possible; the last Allied soldier left Crete on May 31.

The Luftwaffe operation had been a brilliant success, yet Hitler quite ignored it. Student's paratroops would never again be employed in airborne operations, even in situations where their use would have made all the difference. Hitler's blind spots included the use of airborne troops, a military specialty he did not understand or appreciate. Particularly on the Normandy beaches, the outcome of those first desperate hours might have been quite different had the German advocates of airborne operations been allowed their way.

But in the late spring of 1941 Hitler was not very interested in anything as minor as Crete and how it had been captured. His mind was on the Soviet border, while his staff, of necessity, was actively supporting all the various German efforts in the south, which were politically and militarily extremely complicated.

Hitler was already a month behind in his plans for the attack on the Soviets. The new invasion date was set for the middle of June. To achieve it, many of the units used to attack Yugoslavia had to be rushed back eastward. So another problem was created. There was no time to "pacify" Yugoslavia properly. The consequence was the immediate rise of partisan warfare. There were not enough German troops in Yugoslavia to strangle the partisans at the beginning. So within a few weeks Josip Broz Tito had established a formidable army in the mountains, supplied by the British and joined by many deserting Italian troops. This force would harry the Germans from that time on. One more month of operations in the Balkans and the opposition might have been crushed, as it had been in Czechoslovakia and Poland. But Hitler was in too great a hurry, and he had too little realization of the consequences of his lightning strokes. The blitzkrieg was enormously effective, but it had to be followed by orderly mopping up. And in Yugoslavia that never happened.

In June 1941, then, the British remnants from Greece and Crete had been evacuated to Egypt to participate in the north African war. General Rommel had been making great strides, particularly after the British had moved those 60,000 troops out of Africa to fight in Greece. The remnants who came back stopped further Rommel successes. During the summer both armies regrouped on opposite sides of the Egyptian frontier. The British prepared for a counteroffensive in the fall. Rommel sought reinforcements from Germany, but Hitler was not really listening, for at that time all his senses were turned fixedly to the east. For that reason he was not even very conscious of what was happening in Germany and in Britain just then, nor had he been since the beginning of May.

It was Hitler's habit to hold forth at luncheon (which might last until 4 p.m.) on the matters that interested him and to encourage discussion among his intimates, who numbered about sixty people. (All of them had access to Hitler's table by the simple process of announcing to his adjutant their intention of coming for lunch.) However, because of Hitler's preoccupation with the Soviet attack, he was not often at the luncheon table in April and May, and therefore some of his intimates were not privy to the changes in his thinking. One such was Rudolf Hess, the loyal young party comrade who had served as Hitler's amanuensis for the writing of *Mein Kampf.*

By 1941 he was deputy führer and Hitler's principal personal assistant. He knew Hitler's mind—his hatred of the Soviet Union and his abiding respect for Britain. In the absence of Hitler's guidance during this period, Hess decided that he would personally strike a blow for the Führer by going to Britain on a one-man peace mission. He would meet with Churchill and the other British leaders, and he would persuade them to stop the war so that all Hitler's efforts could be devoted to the stamping out of bolshevism.

So Hess flew to England, piloting his own plane. He bailed out over Scotland and was captured, and the story became known. But instead of negotiating, the British slapped Hess into the Tower of London, and there they kept him as an oddity. Hitler was embarrassed and had to make an announcement that the Hess flight was completely unauthorized and would in no way affect the conduct of the war. Indeed it would not, for as Hitler had now concluded that he would have to beat the British, he could never make a deal with them. Except...

The exception might arise out of what he was now about to do. He was embarking on the subjugation of the Soviet Union. Once that was accomplished, Hitler believed, the British might be much easier to deal with.

14

PRELUDE TO DISASTER

In the middle of June 1941, Adolf Hitler called all his senior front-line commanders and the representatives of the military high commands to the Reich Chancellery. His purpose was something like that of a sports coach before a big game: to instill in his people an appreciation of the task before them.

They were now entering the "war of ideologies," Hitler said. Some of the people who were listening to him would remember his previous speech to the generals, in which he had outlined the policies to be pursued toward the population of the Soviet Union. Now they had a clear example, in the Balkans, where the pacification operation had not been vigorously pursued and where uprisings had occurred, uprisings that were still nettling the occupiers. This was an example of what might happen when conquered civil populations were treated too leniently, said Hitler. Let them all beware, lest it happen in Soviet Russia. Leniency was only regarded by such people as weakness.

In Russia, they could expect that the commissars would incite the people to acts of violence and terrorism. These must be countered with terrorism. "The mailed fist, will be, in the end, the kindest way," said Hitler. He continued:

One can only smash terror with counter-terror, not with military tribunal procedures. It was not with the lawbooks that I myself smashed the German Communist Party's terrorist tactics, but with the brute force of the S.A.

Field Marshal Keitel suddenly realized during this speech that Hitler had become absolutely obsessed with the idea of destroying communism. Then and later the dictator kept referring to his prediction that if the Nazis did not destroy the Communists, the Reds would destroy the Third Reich.

Here, of course, was the error that would ultimately destroy Hitler and his government. As a commander, Hitler was well aware of the dangers of a two-front war. He could even predict that the vast resources of the United States would be thrown into the balance at some point and on the side of those unlikely allies, the British and the Russians. He could predict all this, and yet commit Germany to a two-front war, knowing that the chances were great that his enemies would surround him and triumph. His decision had to be based not on reason but on the basic article of faith of his whole Nazi philosophy: that all the evils of the world came from Jews and Communists. He would risk self-destruction and the end of his Thousand-Year Reich to stop the Soviets before they could start.

The major problem with Hitler's assessment was his failure to understand two factors:

1. Stalin wanted nothing so much as time. He would have left Hitler alone for years, and perhaps forever, if the German dictator had allowed him to do so.

2. The Russians, no matter their politics, had a powerful feeling for their homeland and would fight to the death for it. They had done it before with Napoleon, scorching the earth behind them as they retreated, destroying their own cities and towns, and they would do it again. Hitler went to war to fight the Communists; he ended up fighting the Russian people.

Looking back on that day, Keitel marked it as the real beginning of the end:

He had wrongly assessed the reserves of Bolshevism and of the Stalin State, and it was thus that he brought about the ruin of himself and the Third Reich he had created.

The apparent industrial reserves of the Soviets were so slender that the Germans hoped to conquer in six months. But what the statistics did not show was the grim determination of a people against the wall. Nor did the German estimates take into account the outside aid that the Soviets would receive within the year. No one could predict that.

It was truly remarkable. Here was the man who venerated Napoleon, the man who had confided to intimates that his greatest glory came when he stood at Napoleon's tomb in Paris and knew that he had surpassed the great conqueror. Yet he was unable to learn the primary lesson of Napoleon's fall: his sacrifice of the major resources of his conquered Europe in the campaign against a Russia that was not even as well organized as was Stalin's in 1941. It was not that Hitler did not know what had happened to Napoleon in Russia, or why. It was simply that he had become so obsessed by the threat of communism that he chose to ignore the lesson of history.

So *Aufbau Ost*—"Buildup East"—was now complete. For nearly a year German units had been moved along the 2500-mile front from the Baltic to the Black Sea. All sorts of camouflage had been employed and deception practiced. All these troop movements were represented simply as an exchange of men, the older men being replaced and sent home while younger ones were brought to the fighting units destined to control Poland, Romania, and the south. Great pains were taken to reassure the Soviets that there was no threat.

The war against Russia, Operation Barbarossa, was designed to shatter the Soviet fighting ability in one powerful, long blow.

"Wiping out Russia's very power to exist. That is the goal!" Hitler exhorted.

One drive would be launched in the south, toward Kiev and the Dnieper River. The second drive would be staged in the north, through the former Baltic states, toward Moscow. Hitler planned to allocate 120 divisions to this task, keeping only 60 divisions for the defense of the west and Scandinavia.

On the night of June 21, 1941, Hitler's special train, with Field Marshal Keitel and the rest of the OKW staff aboard, reached the Führer's new headquarters in a forest near Rastenburg, East Prussia. Göring's headquarters were not far away, and the German War Office's headquarters were on the other side of it. Within an hour all the high officials of the Third Reich's land and air forces could be assembled by plane at Hitler's *Wolfsschanze* ("Wolf's Entrenchment").

The rules were then established.

At noon each day a conference would be held at the Führer's headquarters; war news and operational plans would be discussed then. Colonel General Jodl would outline the war situation for the Führer.

At 3 a.m. on June 22, 1941, the troops were ready to move. Fifteen minutes later the artillery opened fire. An hour later German troops crossed the Soviet frontier south of Brest-Litovsk.

Three army groups made the assault. In the south Field Marshal von Rundstedt drove toward Kiev. Above him Field Marshal von Bock drove toward Moscow. North of him Field Marshal von Leeb headed for Leningrad.

In the center General Guderian's tanks led the way. They had been waterproofed for Operation Sea Lion and that capability now came in handy. They splashed across the River Bug 600 miles west of Moscow.

All along the front the Russians were taken completely by surprise.

The Luftwaffe outdid itself. By the end of June, twenty-three of Göring's pilots had destroyed 1500 Soviet planes on the ground and most of the reserve planes flown in from central Russia. With mastery of the air, the Germans could now devote the efforts of the Luftwaffe to assisting the ground troops, knocking out whole columns of enemy infantry as they advanced to the front, and smashing the rail system.

An Italian journalist watched the Wehrmacht:

The exhausts of the panzers belched out blue tongues of smoke. The air is filled with pungent bluish vapor that mingles with the damp green of the grass and with the golden reflection of the corn. Beneath the screaming arch of Stukas the mobile columns of tanks resemble thin lines drawn with a pencil on the vast green slate of the Moldavian plain.

Hitler had promised terror. The Russians delivered it. On the first day of the campaign, a column of General von Manstein's troops came across a German patrol that had been cut off by the enemy. Every man was dead, and each one had been tortured and mutilated before he died. The tenor of the Russian campaign was set for both sides. It would be a war of horrors.

On that first day of the Nazi-Soviet war, Hitler issued a proclamation to the German people. It was long and rambling, dealing with every aspect of the war and Nazi-Soviet relations. But at the end he got to the point:

Today approximately 160 Russian divisions are standing at our frontiers. For weeks constant violations of this frontier have taken place, affecting not only us but from the far north down to Romania.

(In truth the Russians had behaved so properly that when the Germans swept across the border, the Soviets still refused to cross from their side because it would have been a violation of the agreements.)

Russian airmen consider it sport nonchalantly to overlook these frontiers, presumably to prove to us that they already feel themselves masters of these territories. During the night of June 17 to June 18 Russian patrols again penetrated into the Reich's territory and could only be driven back after prolonged firing.

This has brought us to the hour when it is necessary for us to take steps against this plot devised by the Jewish-Anglo-Saxon warmongers and equally the Jewish rulers of the Bolshevist center in Moscow.

German people! At this moment a march is taking place that, as regards extent, compares with the greatest the world hitherto has seen. United with their Finnish comrades, the fighters of Narvik are standing in the Northern Arctic. German divisions commanded by the conqueror of Norway, in cooperation with the heroes of the Finnish freedom, under their marshal, are protecting Finnish soil. Formations of the German eastern front extend from the banks of the Pruth along the lower reaches of the Danube to the shores of the Black Sea. The task of this front, therefore, is no longer the protection of single countries, but the safeguarding of Europe and thereby the salvation of all.

I therefore decided today again to lay the fate and future of the German Reich and our people in the hands of our soldiers.

May God help us especially in this fight.

And so Operation Barbarossa rolled along.

By the end of the first week, General Guderian's panzers had reached Minsk, 200 miles east of the Bug River, and linked there with General Hoth's Third Panzer Group. Six Russian divisions were trapped in two pockets near Bialystok and Vokovsk. West of Minsk another fifteen Russian divisions were surrounded by the panzers.

One of the Soviets' problems was Stalin's bad sense of timing. A few months earlier he had conducted a political purge of the army, a purge that decimated the middle ranks of command. The effects were felt in these first days of the war; the troops were badly led, and whole divisions found themselves without capable officers.

But no matter how fast the Germans moved inside the Soviet Union, they found an enemy with a spirit quite different from that they had encountered before. Most of Guderian's men were veterans of the French campaign. Here in Russia, as one of Guderian's panzer captains said, "there was no feeling, as there had been in France, of entry into a defeated nation." The Germans plowed through with their fast tanks, but all around them the following forces had to fight their way. There was no surrender. There was no quarter.

Almost immediately there arose a quarrel among the German generals. Guderian wanted to press on, leaving behind all the pockets of resistance. Time, he knew, was not on the side of the Germans. Soon the Russian winter would set in, and then there would be no more advance. But Guderian's superior was Field Marshal von Kluge, an infantry soldier of the broad-front school: move the front, clean it up, and move it again; do not let the forward elements get too far out in front.

Guderian claimed that if the Germans did not strike swiftly, the Russians would have time to regroup their defense. Von Kluge (with Hitler concurring) resisted the attempt to hurry ahead, leaving pockets of Soviet troops across the German lines of communication. Both sides had their points; the real problem was that the Germans were fighting on a 2500-mile front and did not have enough men and machines to cover it all.

Hitler stopped the unlimited advance. The armor bogged down.

On July 7 General Guderian had to make a major decision. He had brought his panzers up to the Dnieper River. Now, should he force the crossing, knowing that the infantry was two weeks behind him? He also knew that every day the Soviet defenses along the river were growing stronger.

Knowing full well that Hitler and OKW did not want him to move ahead, Guderian went ahead anyhow, not telling anyone until after it was too late to stop him. On July 10 and July 11 he made the crossings. He lost only eight men. It all looked extremely easy.

Just then Guderian's headquarters were at Tolochino, which had been Napoleon's headquarters in 1812.

Guderian wanted to push on, but on July 27 he had orders from Hitler to take his Second Panzer Group toward Gomel, which meant the group would swing around and head back toward Germany to encircle some ten Soviet divisions left behind by the fighting. Guderian and other officers believed the way to fight the Russians was to encircle huge armies and then leave them to the infantry. But Hitler did not believe in that; he wanted his troops to cut up the enemy units piecemeal and destroy them. The struggle of the conservatives and the adventurers continued.

Guderian and Hoth's panzers were more than three hundred miles from the Bug River now, halfway to Moscow.

On July 29 Colonel Schmundt, who was Hitler's adjutant, went to see General Guderian, bringing him a medal and some advice. He explained what Hitler had in mind:

1. Capture Leningrad. This would free the Baltic for German shipping.

2. Capture Moscow. This would deal a powerful blow to Russian morale and also knock out many important Soviet industries.

3. Take the Ukraine.

Guderian sent back a message. His advice, he relayed through
Schmundt, was to push ahead against Moscow. Forget the Ukraine
or any diversionary activity, and get to the heart of the matter.

On August 4 Guderian was ordered to report to Hitler at Novy
Borissov, the headquarters of Army Group Center. Hitler and
Schmundt were there, with Field Marshal von Bock and General
Hoth. Each officer was asked by Hitler to give his views, but pri-
vately, so that no one of them knew what the others had said. Von
Bock, Hoth, and Guderian all spoke up for the drive on Moscow.

But Hitler was of another mind. He assembled them all and told
them that Leningrad was his primary objective just now. Next might
be Moscow or the Ukraine; he had not decided which. He seemed
inclined to move toward the Ukraine because of the immense supply of industrial raw materials and agricultural products. He also
hoped to take Moscow and Kharkov before the winter set in.

Hitler was suddenly learning some of the facts of life. He had seriously underestimated the Soviets' military preparedness. Guderian
gave him some figures on Soviet tanks.

"If I had known," said the Führer to Guderian, "that the figures
for Russian tank strength which you gave in your book were in fact
the true ones I would not—I believe—ever have started this war."

He was referring to *Achtung! Panzer!,* which Guderian had published in 1937.

The general had given a figure of 10,000 Soviet tanks, knowing the
real number was 17,000. Hitler, who knew nothing about Soviet military strength, believed the figures to be much lower, and no one in
his entourage had bothered to either question Guderian or ascertain the facts elsewhere.

As summer wore along, Hitler was beginning to learn a good deal
about Russia that he had not known before. For example, Guderian
was complaining about tank replacements. The state of the Russian
roads was so bad that the tank engines filled with dust and finally broke
down. Guderian said he needed 300 new engines immediately.

The roads were indeed bad. Hitler learned that many roads marked
"good" on the maps did not even exist.

One problem was a simple lack of information. In July Field Marshal Halder, the army chief, suggested that there were only forty-six combat-worthy divisions in the Soviet Union. Three weeks later he said there were 360 such divisions.

As to the quality of Soviet weapons, for which Hitler had shown contempt, there was much to be learned. General Guderian was now convinced that the Soviets had a superb tank in the T-34. The German 88-millimeter shells simply bounced off its armor. And despite heavy initial losses in aircraft, the Soviet air force began to appear out of nowhere to challenge the Luftwaffe.

By August Hitler was planning the capture of Leningrad and Moscow. He issued a new directive to his generals:

> The Führer has decided to have St. Petersburg [his use of the czarist name for the city is typical] wiped off the face of the earth. The further existence of this large city is of no interest once Soviet Russia is overthrown. The intention is to close in on the city and raze it to the ground by artillery fire and continuous air attack. Requests that the city be taken over will be turned down, for the problem of the survival of the population and of supplying it with food is one which cannot and should not be solved by us. In this war for existence we have no interest in keeping even part of this great city's population.

Now came one of Hitler's major strategic errors of 1941 on the eastern front. The Soviets had concentrated their military strength in front of Moscow. The German generals wanted to move the central army group against that strength and overwhelm it immediately. Hitler refused. Leningrad was his first goal, the Ukraine his second, and Moscow could wait.

General Halder summed up the feeling of the generals in his diary:

> Thus the aim of defeating decisively the Russian armies in front of Moscow was subordinated to the desire to obtain a valuable industrial area and to advance in the direction of Russian oil. Hitler now became obsessed with the idea of capturing both Leningrad and Stalingrad, for he persuaded himself that if these two "holy cities of Communism" were to fall, Russia would collapse.

*

By September the Germans were claiming victory in Russia. The armies of Marshal Timoshenko, said Hitler, were surrounded in front of Moscow. The southern army of Marshal Budenny was virtually destroyed. The northern army of Marshal Voroshilov at Leningrad was also surrounded.

But Hitler still had to have his way. The greatest crisis of the war so far now developed between Hitler and his generals. General Guderian, for whom the Führer had much respect, was sent by Halder to try to persuade Hitler to take Moscow. He failed.

Hitler moved forces from the central army group to the south to help Marshal von Rundstedt. Guderian's panzer force was one of them. On September 19 Kiev fell to the Germans, giving them 665,000 prisoners of war. Hitler called the fall of Kiev the greatest victory in the history of the world. But while that battle was being fought, the central army group was stalled along the Desna River beyond Smolensk because its armor was in the south.

Finally, in September, Hitler was persuaded by von Brauchitsch to allow the generals to take Moscow. But it was very late.

"Move in ten days," Hitler ordered.

"Impossible," von Brauchitsch said. And it was impossible. It was not until October that the armored forces could be brought back up to the central front, refitted and prepared to fight again. On October 2 Operation Typhoon was launched—the drive on Moscow.

But Hitler was not content with this one major operation.

"Capture Leningrad at the same time," he ordered. Marshal von Leeb was told to take that city and then drive on and link up with the Finns to cut the Murmansk railroad. "Madness," whispered von Leeb.

At the same time von Rundstedt was to clear the Black Sea coast, capture Rostov, seize the Maikop oil fields, and push forward to Stalingrad on the Volga, cutting off the Soviets from the Caucasus.

Von Rundstedt explained that this would mean a drive 400 miles beyond the Dnieper River with his left flank exposed. Hitler said the Soviets could not have anything left in the area: there would be no serious resistance.

That remained to be seen.

*

The drive on Moscow moved very quickly. In the first two weeks of October the Germans encircled two Soviet armies and took 650,000 prisoners, 5000 field guns, and 1200 tanks. On October 20 the German armored spearhead was within 40 miles of Moscow. The danger was so great that the Soviet government evacuated to Kuibyshev on the Volga. Even the most skeptical of the German generals now expected to take Moscow before the Russian winter began.

But before the cold Russian winter came the wet Russian fall. The German army had taken over many French trucks. These began to fail. So did German trucks. The tanks were often delayed in their drive in order to pull wheeled vehicles out of the mud; as one junior officer reported:

> The infantryman slithers in the mud, while many teams of horses are needed to drag each gun forward. All wheeled vehicles sink in up to their axles in the slime. Even tractors can move only with great difficulty. A large portion of our heavy artillery was soon stuck fast.

Moscow was virtually in sight, but the Russian resistance had grown stronger. And in the woods and swamps behind the German army, the Russian partisan groups were beginning to take shape. No mercy, no quarter; those were the terms Hitler had laid down. They were already being visited on the Germans too. It was early November 1941.

In the south, Marshal von Kleist's panzers had entered Rostov, at the mouth of the Don river. They arrived on November 21.

"Hurrah," shouted Minister Goebbels's propagandist in *Völkischer Beobachter*. "The gateway to the Caucasus has been opened."

But if the Germans could see that, so could the Russians. Five days after the capture of Rostov, an enormous Soviet army descended on the leading German force, which as usual was far ahead of its infantry support. Von Kleist's panzers now turned around and raced back to the safety of the line at the Mius River, where the infantry waited. This was where von Rundstedt wanted to establish his winter line. Now it seemed doubtful if it could be held.

It was the first retreat for Hitler; he did not like it. He sent an order to von Rundstedt: "Remain where you are, and retreat no further."

Von Rundstedt replied immediately: "It is madness to attempt to hold. In the first place the troops cannot do it, and in the second place if they do not retreat they will be destroyed. I repeat that this order must be rescinded or that you find someone else."

That very night, the Führer answered von Rundstedt: "I am acceding to your request. Please give up your command."

So von Rundstedt was out. He was the first of many German commanders to feel the lash.

And the casualties were rising. As of November 26, German casualties in Russia were 743,000 officers and men, not counting the sick. That was a quarter of the total force of 3.2 million. Up north, on the Moscow front, snow was falling. The disaster was about to begin.

15

THE DRUMS OF AFRICA

Having set the wheels in motion for an expanded war by his capture of Greece and Crete, Hitler was powerless to stop the chain of events in north Africa. He had sent that first armored division to Africa eagerly; now he was bogged down there.

General Erwin Rommel had arrived at Tripoli on February 12, bringing the Afrika Korps, which started with two divisions. At the end of March he had attacked the British while their Africa force was cut back to send troops to fight in Greece and Crete. On April 3 he had retaken Benghazi, lost earlier by the Italians. He took Bardia and Sollum. So that spring and summer the Italians and the Germans advanced toward the Suez Canal. The Australian Ninth Division was sent to Tobruk and told to hold.

Tobruk then went under siege, a siege that would last until December 1941.

Rommel knew he could take Tobruk, if only he had the supplies and the tanks. But Hitler would not listen to his pleas. Actually Hitler could not listen; his situation in Russia was becoming more difficult every day. Like Rommel, Guderian wanted tanks and troops, but the way things were going in the east, Hitler realized there would be very few more tanks, troops, planes, and ships for Africa.

*

Ships? In the four months of summer the British had sunk a quarter of a million tons of Italian shipping that was carrying supplies, mostly for Rommel. The situation was so serious that Hitler decided to order his submarine commander, Admiral Dönitz, to make a major effort, together with Mussolini's forces, to destroy British sea and air power in the Mediterranean.

Now, after it was too late, Hitler could see that he had allowed himself to be misled by Marshal Göring; Malta, and not Crete, was the British base that should have been destroyed. From Malta the British bombers struck Mussolini's ships, killed Hitler's soldiers, and wrecked the tanks the ships were carrying. From Malta the British destroyers and submarines went out and sank more of those ships. Malta and Gibraltar were the British thorns in the Axis backside. Gibraltar was virtually impregnable from the sea, so well was the basin tended, and from the air it was one huge piece of granite, more formidable than any air raid shelter.

Late that summer of 1941 Admiral Dönitz was ordered to send six of his best U-boats into this fray. Marshal Albert Kesselring was ordered to send his Air Fleet No. 2 down to the Mediterranean, also.

The U-boats arrived early in October, having passed through the Strait of Gibraltar beneath the noses of the British. Although the British kept a careful watch, there was no way the submarines could be stopped entirely; by night the boats came through. Even so, the British air and sea patrols kept the U-boats on guard. Freiherr von Tiesenhausen, one of Dönitz's most skillful U-boat captains, wasted an enormous amount of time and several torpedoes trying to sink a 500-ton coastal steamer that was hardly worth a single torpedo. And then he missed! So many British patrol craft, escort vessels, and aircraft were overhead that a U-boat captain had to track, fire, and then run. He never knew precisely what he was accomplishing. And if that was true for von Tiesenhausen, it was also true for the other five U-boat captains. At the end of the first month, the U-boats had sunk two ships and damaged one patrol craft, and that was all.

Dönitz was terribly disappointed with the results. Those U-boats could have been employed in the North Atlantic all that time, and in the normal course of events would have accounted for 60,000 to

80,000 tons of shipping each. The boats in the Atlantic had Churchill so worried that he was calling on the Americans for more help. He had made a deal for fifty overage American destroyers, and he was urging the Americans to come into the war. Actually the Americans were in the war: U.S. naval craft were convoying British ships off Canada and moving as far afield as Iceland. In the next few months the Americans would have several encounters with German submarines. Dönitz already knew that the Americans were at war with his U-boats, and he had informed Hitler of every incident.

In the Mediterranean that fall, the U-boats finally did manage two spectacular achievements: they sank the carrier *Ark Royal* and the battleship *Barham*. But spectacular U-boat sinkings did not win wars or even battles. The morale of the Mediterranean U-boat crews went up, but it soon went down as the British began sinking the German submarines.

The war in Africa in the fall of 1941 meant that Hitler was fighting vigorously on two fronts. At a meeting with the Italians, the German General Staff had agreed that an offensive should be carried against the British in Egypt in the fall. Field Marshal Keitel was particularly eager to have Tobruk captured from the British, and he promised more heavy artillery for that purpose. That meant shipment by sea. The Afrika Korps demanded 40,000 to 50,000 tons of supplies per month, and that was not easy to deliver, given the dangers of British interference in the Mediterranean.

The same was true of the Luftwaffe, Kesselring reported to Berlin. In Libya the harbors of Benghazi, Bardia, and Derna all needed work to make them useful so that they could receive the maximum possible amount of fuel and ammunition for the air force. But the Italians were dawdling in their efforts at these ports, said the Germans, and thus the port of Tripoli became a bottleneck. And then there came some really bad news for Rommel. The change in the war in Russia, which had begun with so much success, meant that there could be no reinforcement of the Luftwaffe forces in Africa until victory had been achieved in the east. Keitel gave him the word.

Actually, Rommel was bogged down by his supply problems. After some brilliant victories in desert fighting he was unable to move. The German General Staff had said that fall that there could be no prospect of an offensive from Libya against the Suez Canal that year. Not without the Luftwaffe. Even if Rommel could take Tobruk, it would not help much. The problem was that every advance toward the east in Russia meant more trouble for the German supply train trying to move east in Africa, and an easier time for the British.

And Tobruk, the key to the Suez Canal, was holding out strongly against German encirclement. The port's antiaircraft defenses were very strong, and resupply was made possible by small ships and transport destroyers. This system allowed Tobruk to survive constant attack for 242 days.

In November 1941 the British were preparing an offensive against the Germans in Libya. General Sir Claude Auchinleck was to recapture Cyrenaica and then to attack Tripolitania. The Eighth Army was chosen for the job. This included the Thirteenth Corps, the Fourth Indian Division, the New Zealand Division, and the First Army Tank Brigade.

General Rommel was preparing at the same time to finally smash Tobruk, which stuck into his lines. He had about 560 tanks, from the Fifteenth and Twenty-first Panzer Divisions, the Ninetieth Light Division, and seven Italian divisions, one of them armored. The big difference was that the German tanks were heavier, better gunned, and better armored than either the British or the Italian tanks. Also, the German antitank guns were far superior to those of the British.

The Luftwaffe in Africa consisted of 190 planes, but because of supply problems only 120 were serviceable in November. The Italians had 300 aircraft, but only 200 were in service.

The British attack was to move west and north toward Tobruk, the armored units making a wide sweep to find and engage Rommel's armor.

On November 17, while the Germans were preparing for their attack on Tobruk, the British struck them. The main battle was fought south of Sidi Rezegh, a 100-foot-high ridge that dominated the Capuzzo track, Rommel's main line of communications from west to east. For three days the British seemed to be winning. Then on November 19 the Germans moved their armor and soon counterattacked at Sidi Rezegh. During November 21 and 22 the fighting was fierce at this point. The Germans had an advantage because their armor had been more heavily concentrated and their weapons were better. On the night of the twenty-second the Germans recaptured the ridge, and the British Thirtieth Corps lost two-thirds of its tanks and other tracked vehicles.

The Germans, with better guns, were simply more powerful than the British, and on November 22, after the retreat of the Thirtieth Corps, the way was open to Tobruk. Rommel staged a surprise night attack and disorganized most of the remaining British tank units.

On November 24 Rommel tried a brilliant movement. He planned to encircle the perimeter of the British forces and make his way east to the frontier, thus creating so much confusion that, he hoped, the British would withdraw from the battle. He went down the El Abd track to Sheferzen, just missing the headquarters of the British Thirtieth Corps and two enormous supply dumps. If he had captured either, the British would have been out of the battle. Rommel was superior in ability and in tactics. He was inferior in material supply.

Rommel moved fast and did disorganize several major British units. But his strike failed, because he had no air support and the British controlled the skies. So on November 26 Rommel returned to the Sidi Rezegh area, short of supplies, short of parts, and virtually bereft of air support from the Luftwaffe.

The struggle in eastern Europe was certainly making itself felt in ways that Hitler had never dreamed. Aside from the enormous casualties and difficulties he faced in the Soviet Union, Hitler's land war strategy was now shaken to its foundations. Only at sea was the German effort proving satisfactory. In the Atlantic battle he had the British badly worried, for they knew what the stakes were. Churchill had outlined the continuing problem for President Roosevelt in a letter at Christmastime 1940:

> The danger of Great Britain being destroyed by a swift, overwhelming blow has for the time being very greatly receded. In its place there is a long, gradually maturing danger, less sudden and less spectacular, but equally deadly. This mortal danger is the steady and increasing diminution of sea tonnage. We can endure the shat-

tering of our dwellings and the slaughter of our civil population by indiscriminate air attacks, and we hope to parry these increasingly as our science develops and to repay them upon military objectives in Germany as our Air Force more nearly approaches the strength of the enemy. The decision for 1941 lies upon the seas. Unless we can establish our ability to feed this island, to import the munitions of all kinds which we need, unless we can move our armies to the various theatres where Hitler and his confederate Mussolini must be met, and maintain them there, and do all this with the assurance of being able to carry it on till the spirit of the Continental Dictators is broken, we may fall by the way, and the time needed by the United States to complete her defensive preparations may not be forthcoming. It is, therefore, in shipping and in the power to transport across the oceans, particularly the Atlantic Ocean, that in 1941 the crunch of the whole war will be found. If, on the other hand, we are able to move the necessary tonnage to and fro across salt water indefinitely, it may well be that the application of superior air-power to the German homeland and the rising anger of the German and other Nazi-gripped populations will bring the agony of civilisation to a merciful and glorious end.

In the fall of 1941 Churchill's words of nearly a year earlier seemed as prescient as ever. In September, in spite of demands from Hitler for more boats to go to the Mediterranean, Dönitz's U-boat strength in the Atlantic was at a new high. Five wolf packs were ready to work the North Atlantic that month. The British shipping loss jumped to 210,000 tons.

But in the next few weeks Hitler panicked and ordered Dönitz to transfer his entire operational U-boat fleet to the Mediterranean. The submarine admiral now set out to get that policy changed; even so, at Hitler's insistence he had to keep building the U-boat force in the Mediterranean and the Atlantic off Gibraltar. And so bemused was the Führer with the way things were going in Russia that there was no chance of arguing with him about war in the Atlantic. The British were very lucky in October and November 1941. The number of sinkings went down, since so few U-boats were attacking the convoys.

But then came a move that would put the final stamp on both the American navy's attitude toward the Germans and Hitler's attitude toward the Americans. On October 31 the American destroyer *Reuben James* was working as part of the escort of British convoy HX-156, steaming south of Greenland toward England. The destroyer's participation in this effort was an outright violation of international law. The ship was sunk by a German submarine. Hitler, who had been holding Dönitz on a short leash for months regarding the Americans, now could have nothing more to say. The only person who might be at all happy about the sinking, as a matter of expediency in the service of a higher principle, was Prime Minister Churchill. It pushed the Americans that much closer to war with Germany.

In Africa, General Rommel had one great advantage: detailed knowledge of the movements and plans of his British enemy. It came from Cairo, where the American military attaché, Colonel Bonner Frank Fellows, was sending messages every day to the War Department in Washington. Colonel Fellows did not know that the "Black Code" he was using had been stolen by the Italians from the American Embassy in Rome in September 1941. The Italian secret service had copied the code books and returned them to the embassy, using as an agent an Italian citizen employed by the Americans there.

Colonel Fellows was an extremely efficient officer. He took thorough notes on General Auchinleck's briefings and on other information obtained from his British friends, and he transmitted everything in such detail that American military intelligence headquarters in Washington had a clear picture of the British position in North Africa. And so did General Rommel. Never has an intelligence system worked so well. In detail, if not importance, not even the American breach of the Japanese naval codes or the Ultra breach of the German OKW command code could compare to it. For those other codes covered hundreds of messages every day and the process of culling the valuable was extremely complex. In the case of the British in North Africa, it was as if Rommel were being briefed every day or two by a British operations staff officer.

So in the fall of 1941 Rommel knew what the British planned; if he had been able to act, he perhaps could have dealt them a mortal blow. But his hands were tied; Hitler had not given him enough support to do much with the intelligence he was receiving.

As the year 1941 neared its end, General Rommel assessed his situation. He had to have major support if he was to win in Africa. He had to have at least half that much support if he was not to lose. The consequences of the dreadful error of attacking Crete instead of Malta were now being driven home. The British were using Malta with enormous effectiveness as a fleet and air base. And from Malta Admiral Andrew Cunningham was raising hob with the Italian navy. In two attacks that year he had smashed much of the Italian fleet at Taranto and more at Cape Matapan. The remainder of the fleet was hugging its home shores and was of very little use to Rommel in his time of desperate need.

November came. On the twenty-fifth Admiral Cunningham sent a squadron out to find two German oilers that had been very effectively supplying Rommel. They found the *Procida* and the *Maritza* and sank them both that night.

The British moved against Sidi Rezegh and recaptured it. The garrison at Tobruk captured El Duda and enlarged their perimeter, and Tobruk itself was resupplied and reinforced by New Zealanders. That brought Rommel back from Bardia, and he recaptured Sidi Rezegh and dealt punishing blows to the New Zealanders. After heavy fighting the Tobruk garrison was again isolated.

But his own supply problems were too much for Rommel, and before the end of the month he was beginning a retreat.

On November 29 General Auchinleck reported to London that Rommel was in full retreat and that Indian troops and South Africans had taken El Adem and seemed to have raised the siege of Tobruk.

The Germans had taken very heavy losses in those last months of fighting: 13,000 German troops, 20,000 Italians, and 300 tanks. In contrast, British losses amounted to about 15,000 casualties among the empire forces and not quite 300 tanks. In terms of armor the situation was about even; but the Axis forces were taking heavy personnel casualties, largely because of the regional superiority of the Royal Air Force over the Luftwaffe.

At OKW at Rastenburg Keitel's staff was gloomy about the prospects. "The situation in North Africa demands the utmost effort to supply the German forces" said the staff report, "to replenish the considerable losses and to bring up first-rate reinforcements. With the present position at sea air transport must be the main carrier across the Mediterranean.''

Air transport. That meant the gasoline for the planes and the oil for the tanks must come by air. And what about replacement tanks? The Germans did not have aircraft suited for that sort of heavy supply operation.

*   *   *

On December 4 the situation was even more grave. Mussolini announced that it would be impossible to even talk about occupying Malta, a promise he had made offhandedly much earlier, in the Florence meeting with Hitler. He did not believe that the Italians in Libya could hold out much longer without more German help. The African supply situation was critical because the supply lines had not been kept open. And that had not been done because the Luftwaffe in the Mediterranean was crippled by shortages and could get no help from Germany. Every spare part, every new plane, was going to the eastern front.

On December 18 the Italians struck their most spectacular naval blow of the war. Three "human torpedoes" got inside Alexandria harbor and severely damaged the great ships *Queen Elizabeth* and *Valiant*. On the same day a force of British cruisers and destroyers, which had gone out to catch an Italian convoy headed for Tripoli, ran into a minefield. The *Neptune* and the two other cruisers were all damaged. Trying to rescue the *Neptune*'s crew, the destroyer *Kandahar* hit a mine and was stopped. The *Neptune* then drifted into two more mines and sank. Only one man of the crew of 700 survived.

This incident buoyed the German hopes more than it ought to have. OKW now spoke of the possibility of holding Tripolitania.

But something more had to be done. Rommel sent messages to OKW and finally received an invitation to come to see Hitler. At the end of December he prepared for his trip. He had high hopes that he could persuade the Führer of the importance of the African campaign and that he could secure the sort of assistance he needed.

16

AMERICA ENTERS

On December 7, 1941, a carrier strike force of the Imperial Japanese Navy attacked the American naval base at Pearl Harbor, Hawaii. Almost simultaneously Japanese forces moved against Malaya and the Philippines.

The Japanese attack was a complete surprise to Adolf Hitler and Benito Mussolini. The prospect of now having to fight America was more than an irritation to Hitler, who had been restraining his U-boat corps despite repeated provocations by American warships in the Atlantic. But once the die was cast there was nothing to do but join his ally, Japan, in declaring war on the United States, Hitler decided.

Field Marshal Keitel and General Jodl were in the OKW headquarters at Rastenburg that night of December 7, when Hitler came bursting in with a wireless message in his hand.

"I gained the impression that the Führer felt that the war between Japan and America had suddenly relieved him of a nightmare burden; it certainly brought us some relief from the consequences of America's undeclared state of war with us," wrote Keitel.

Like most of the world Hitler expected the United States to retaliate against Japan first. He was quite wrong. In meetings in America a few weeks later Winston Churchill persuaded President Roosevelt that the Rome-Berlin part of the Axis had to be defeated before it would be safe to turn the power of the west against Japan. After all, Japan's conquests in the Pacific were relatively unimportant compared with the war in Europe, Africa, and Russia. Japan could be, and would be, dealt with later. But for the first two or three years the emphasis had to be on the European-Mediterranean theater if England was to survive. And the survival of England was indeed the issue.

The United States and Britain were extremely fortunate in the early months of 1942 because Hitler's whole emphasis was on the war against the Soviet Union. His attention had to be there, for the war was going very badly for him on that front. The extent of Hitler's miscalculations about the Russians was beginning to become clear to him. By the end of 1941 he had lost a million men, a third of his eastern armies, and thousands of tanks, guns, and aircraft. His forces were bogged down, and everywhere there was trouble.

Just before Christmas 1941, Hitler fired Field Marshal von Brauchitsch as chief of OKH (Oberkommando der Heeres, i.e., the army High Command) and announced to the world that he had taken personal command of Germany's armed forces everywhere. Von Brauchitsch was simply the scapegoat. Hitler always had to have someone else to blame when his own errors became manifest. With the sacrifice, in Hitler's own mind at least, he had wiped the slate clean. It was a practice in which only an absolute dictator could indulge. In the Russian campaign von Rundstedt had been the first to fall, after Hitler's policies had led the southern army to disaster. Now it was von Brauchitsch. He would not be the last.

Outside Moscow and Leningrad, and in the south, the Soviets suddenly stiffened in the last weeks of 1941. The German generals had been talking about Christmas in Moscow and about the terrible defeats to be inflicted on the Russians once more. But General Georgi Zhukov had now taken over the defense of Moscow; his men had constructed a defensive position in depth, one which ran through the forests that bordered the Nara River, from Serpukhov, in the south, to Naro-Fominsk, protecting the western approaches to Moscow. The defenses consisted of blockhouses, wire entanglements, and minefields.

The remnants of the Russian armies decimated by the Germans

in those first lightning weeks were now reorganized into new units. New army corps were arriving from Siberia. Stalin welcomed them to Moscow. He and his staff remained in the Kremlin, although the diplomatic corps and part of the government had fled east. Stalin vowed that he would never leave Moscow alive. The Russian troops seemed to sense the new determination on the part of their leadership and to respond to it.

Conversely, the German army was tired. It had been moving at top speed since June. The machines were as tired as the men, and they broke down. The mud now became frozen ground, and snow began to fall daily.

Every sort of unforeseen problem arose. The Russian railroads were broad gauge and had to be relaid in order to carry the European narrow-gauge rail cars and locomotives. The amount of work necessary was enormous—like building a new railroad in every area.

And in the swamps and the woods of western Russia now appeared the partisans, local people who knew every inch of the terrain. The Germans had followed their leader's policy of determined brutality, and there was not a friend in sight anywhere. A German soldier alone on a road at night was already as good as dead, just waiting to be harvested by the partisans.

If the mud of October was unbelievable, what was to come was even worse. By the end of October the German forces outside Moscow were positioned along the Oka River, north from Aleksin, and then along the Nara to Naro-Fominsk, northeast across the main road, and to the Moskaw River, toward Ruza and Volokolamsk. At night the German troops could see the star shells bursting over Moscow as the antiaircraft guns blasted away at the night-raiding Luftwaffe. But the troops could not move. Rain, then snow, and exhaustion had them stuck fast.

In November Marshal Keitel summoned the chiefs of all the army groups to a meeting at Orsha on the Dnieper. The question was whether or not the German armies should dig in where they were for the winter. The final decision was to try one last attack on Moscow. It would have to take place at the end of the rains, when the ground would be frozen hard. The force chosen for the honor was Field Marshal von Kluge's Fourth Army.

By mid-November the mud had hardened.

Von Kluge's attack began. It went well for several days, with the Fourth Panzer Group leading the advance. To the north, General Reinhardt's Third Panzer Group also was attacking. Then on November 20 the Russian winter arrived. The temperature dropped to −30°C. Snow began to fall constantly. And the Russians counterattacked with fresh troops.

By December 2 it was apparent that the Germans did not have the force necessary to take Moscow. On that day the reconnaissance battalion of the 258th Infantry Division managed to reach the southwestern outskirts of Moscow, but there it was attacked by Russian tanks and by workers from the Moscow factories, who downed their tools and took up guns to fight the enemy.

Field Marshal von Kluge called off the German assault. One day before the Japanese attack on Pearl Harbor, Marshal Zhukov launched the first great Soviet winter offensive. That was the end of Hitler's hope of taking Moscow and knocking Russia out of the war by the end of 1941.

At the end of that year Hitler's whole mind was turned to the disasters that were shaping up in the Soviet theater of operations.

Thus when Admiral Dönitz wanted to open a powerful U-boat campaign against the American Atlantic shore, Hitler was not listening. Dönitz was located at Lorient, the big French submarine base, and often in Paris. Hitler was at Rastenburg and sometimes (very rarely these days) Berlin. Wireless messages could not convey the excitement Dönitz felt about the "opportunity," and there was no way that the admiral could wangle a visit to Rastenburg at this time.

And so Dönitz began the submarine campaign against the United States with only six U-boats, when he might have had twenty or thirty had not Hitler insisted on stationing them in the Mediterranean, where they were doing little good.

The first captains to return from the American station urged their admiral to send many more submarines across the Atlantic. The Americans had absolutely no defenses, they said. It was true; when the war came to the Atlantic coast of the United States, the country had no antisubmarine organization at all. The chief of antisubmarine warfare in Washington was a chief petty officer. Rear Admiral Adolphus Andrews, chief of the U.S. Navy Eastern Sea Frontier, did not have a single antisubmarine craft larger than a 160-foot Coast Guard cutter, and he had only one of those. There were no aircraft capable of carrying depth charges, and there were almost no depth charges to carry. Never in the history of warfare had a major nation been so completely unprepared for war as were the Americans.

Nor, despite many instructions and warnings and examples from the British, did the American naval authorities believe in the convoy system for the safety of merchant ships. Therefore, ships continued to sail alone up and down the American coast, and the German U-boats began to sink them. By the fourth week of January 1942 the U-boat campaign was in full sway, and not a single U-boat had even been damaged by American efforts. So seriously did Prime Minister Churchill deem the crisis that he peeled twenty-four precious trawlers off his own British defense system and sent them to America to fight the Germans. But it would take time to get them there. In the interim the Germans wreaked havoc. Their specialty was tankers, carrying the lifeblood of Britain's war effort. By February the beaches up and down the east coast of the United States were black with oil and covered with the bodies of fish and birds that the oil had killed.

In those first two months of war the Allies lost 600,000 tons of shipping. At the rate at which tankers were being sunk, Britain would soon be out of oil. The American oil industry council warned that the same was true of much of America. If things did not improve, before spring the northeast would run out of heating oil. At the rate of sinkings, the council predicted, by the end of 1942 the industry would have lost 125 of its 300 tankers that served the east coast, and there would not be enough fuel to carry on the American war effort.

On April 20 the U.S. Navy suspended the sailing of all tankers up and down the east coast, because of the rate of sinkings. With only a handful of submarines, Admiral Dönitz was preventing the American war effort from going into high gear. If he had possessed thirty operational boats to send to America just then, he might well have knocked Britain out of the war in Africa. But Hitler did not realize that the solution to the African problem lay in the western Atlantic, so the boats in the Mediterranean remained there, accomplishing virtually nothing.

Even Hitler was impressed with the Dönitz score, however, and he took a few minutes from concern over his worries on the eastern front to consider the admiral's requests. He made a slight concession: some of the boats scheduled for the Mediterranean were returned to the Atlantic, which meant more pressure on the American station.

But the Americans began to learn. The first U-boat to be sunk was *U-85,* which was sent to the bottom by the destroyer *Roper* on April 13, 1942. Soon the U.S. Army Air Corps and the U.S. Navy began to learn how to use depth bombs, and some of the newer planes coming off the assembly lines gave them better air control of the coastal seas. The PB2Y and PBM flying boats improved matters more than a little. These were much like the Pan American Airways Clipper planes that had been flying the Pacific for several years—extremely reliable aircraft with long range.

By April the British trawlers began to arrive in the United States, and it was possible for Admiral Andrews to begin coastal convoys. By this time Admiral Ernest King, the American chief of naval operations and the principal detractor of the convoy system, had begun to learn a few things about Atlantic warfare. Convoys were accepted then. The convoys across the Atlantic had never stopped; these were managed by the British and Canadians, who had been doing it for more than two years quite successfully. The Americans were beginning to learn how to play the game.

The second U-boat to be sunk off the American shore was *U-352,* which went down on May 3. Then the sinkings began to come more quickly. What was most remarkable was the speed with which the Americans, who had started from scratch, began to pick up the technique of anti-U-boat warfare, and how they began to put together the ships and weapons to do the job. The British had developed a forward-firing, multiple-barreled depth charge gun called the "Hedgehog." The Americans developed a smaller weapon, called the "Mousetrap." Both were effective because they made it possible for a destroyer or an escort, steaming at full speed up to a submarine contact point, to fire its charges as it approached, rather than waiting until it had passed over the U-boat and its propeller noises had alerted the submerged enemy.

There were many such developments. Most important in the antisubmarine campaign was the increase in the number of planes made available for that purpose from the vastly stepped-up production of the American aircraft industry. Another development was the perfection of the small aircraft carrier, which could carry about thirty airplanes. This was quite enough for convoy escort. One such carrier traveling with a large convoy could keep submarines down throughout all the daylight hours of flying days, and its presence was a constant threat to the U-boat captains.

By the summer of 1942 the tide had begun to turn. Churchill could breathe more easily as he saw the ship-sinking figures decreasing noticeably.

There were other aspects of the war against America that should have worried Hitler, had he been able to wrench his attention from his problems on the Russian front. One was the growth of an enormous American military machine, which meant tanks, planes, field guns, trucks, and the wonderful "jeep," the American "general purpose vehicle," which proved to be the handiest command car of any army anywhere and which was ultimately copied by the Russian and other armies.

In the early months of 1942 the Americans began sending air force units to England. Soon there were enough to begin bombing raids. Month after month the American force would expand, until the Eighth Air Force, with its B-17 bombers, became a major factor in the strategic destruction of Germany. The U.S. Navy began patrolling as far as Iceland with aircraft, and the B-24 bomber became well known as an antisubmarine aircraft. The British were allocated scores of these and found them extremely useful off Iceland and in probing the inner reaches of the Bay of Biscay, where many of Hitler's submarine pens were located.

Also, the British and the Americans in that spring of 1942 were already planning for the first joint military operation on land against the Axis powers. It would happen in north Africa, and the purpose would be to drive General Rommel into the sea.

Meanwhile, Hitler was getting very little value out of his declaration of war against America, and some of his generals wondered why he had done it. One important reason was to befriend the Japanese, for Hitler was hoping that Japan would open a new front in

Siberia against the Russians, thus helping take the pressure off his operations in front of Moscow. General Hideki Tojo, the chief of the Japanese military oligarchy, was known to be a strong Russophobe, and he had in his vault a plan to attack the Soviets, driving them west until he linked up with the Germans in the Caucasus.

But in the spring of 1942 the Pacific war began to change. Even with limited resources, the United States managed to mount two offensives in the Pacific—one in the central Pacific, managed by the navy, and another in the South Pacific, under the control of General Douglas MacArthur. The Japanese suddenly found that their victories were easy no more and that they were beginning to feel the pinch of the war. Any plan to attack the Russians was put off indefinitely.

So Hitler had reaped the worst possible harvest from his decision to declare war on the United States. Part of it was a question of bad luck. Part of it was a matter of Hitler's failure, as was also true of the Japanese, to appreciate the enormous productive potential of American industry or the speed with which it could be harnessed.

By the late spring of 1942 the United States was on a war footing and was becoming proficient at the war business. Lord Ismay, the chief of the British General Staff, accompanied Churchill to America that summer and said he was appalled at how badly trained the American troops were. He saw soldiers using tree limbs for "machine guns" and tree trunks for "field pieces" and pilots throwing bags of flour ("bombs") out of their cockpits as they "attacked." Certainly the Americans did not yet have their military hardware in order, but that was not the important matter. It would come. Those American troops could not stand up to any European army, Lord Ismay said. But Churchill disagreed, and as events were to prove, after a certain amount of faltering at the beginning in Africa (the disaster of Kasserine Pass, first of all), the Americans would go into battle that year and prove their worth as soldiers in the field.

All this Hitler had brought upon himself by his failure to appreciate the American potential.

But who could blame him? Certainly not his generals or associates. For they were much busier blaming him for the terrible mess he had created in Russia.

17

RUSSIAN WINTER

On December 8, 1941, in Berlin, a government spokesman had to admit to the German and neutral press that there was no prospect of reaching Moscow by the end of the year, as Hitler had promised his people he would.

If the Germans needed any further proof that something awful was happening to their war machine, they had the broadcast of Dr. Goebbels, propaganda minister and intimate of Hitler, who was more or less holding the party together in Berlin while the Führer was off fighting the war against the Russians. Goebbels called for public donation of furs and warm woolen clothing for the soldiers at the Russian front. It was hardly the sort of appeal that would inspire the confidence of the people.

Russian winter. The beginning of the Soviet offensive on December 6 caught the Germans totally by surprise. Somehow, it seemed, Hitler had made no preparations at all for this war. He had not considered the weather pattern. He had not considered the physical requirements of meeting Russian winter conditions. The German plan had called for victory before November. But Hitler could not even make up his mind what objective was most important in Russia. For political purposes he wanted to take Leningrad and destroy it. For economic purposes he wanted to take the Soviet southland.

What about Moscow? His generals told him this was the most important target of all; if he could take the capital and disorganize the Soviet central government, he would have won the war. Hitler scoffed, but Stalin did not. He knew that the battle for the life of the Soviet Union would hinge on the fate of Moscow, and his major effort was devoted to that front.

Marshal Zhukov was bringing in troops from Siberia and the Urals and preparing for a winter offensive. It was going to take every resource the Russians could muster, but it was that important. First would come the winter; then the Russians would strike the Germans a real blow.

Winter came early that year. By mid-November the mud had turned to frost.

From Warsaw, from Germany, and from Czechoslovakia replacements were rushed in by air to fill the German gaps. Although the temperature was well below the freezing point, some of these men arrived without overcoats, so swiftly had they been mustered. Some of them were rushed from a well-warmed barracks in the hinterland to the below-zero front within twenty-four hours.

Hitler simply had not expected to be fighting in Russia that winter, and *none* of his troops had winter clothing suitable for that front. That is why Dr. Goebbels made that strange *Winterhilfe* appeal for public donations of furs and woolens. Yet even after the appeal produced thousands of garments, most of the German troops that winter were still dressed in summer uniforms, with a greatcoat, perhaps, and a single blanket. When Soviet troops were captured, the first thing the Germans did was strip off the Russians' winter uniforms. Naturally, many of those Russian soldiers froze to death in short order, but the Germans did not care. After all, their Führer had told them that their enemy was barely human.

Russian winter. The water froze inside the boilers of the railroad locomotives. Each engine could at best draw only half the number of wagons it could pull at home. Many freight cars were stuck for weeks in the snow and ice on the sidings.

The temperature fell to $-40°C$. Someone shipped a trainload of red wine from France for the thirsty troops. When it arrived at the front, all the bottles had frozen and burst; all that was left were chunks of red ice.

Russian winter. The lubricant in the artillery pieces froze, and the guns could not be trained. The machine guns froze and would not fire, but the gunners could not open the breaches to fix them. If a man touched a gun or any other piece of metal, his skin froze immediately to the surface.

Glycerine was the answer to the lubricant problem, but there was no glycerin. The troops built fires under the tanks every night to keep the engines warm. In daylight operations tanks often slipped off the road into the ditches, and there they stayed. They would be there until the frost lifted. Other tanks were sent to dislodge them, and many of these, too, were at least temporarily lost to service.

Marshal Zhukov's offensive began north of Moscow, crossing the Moscow-Volga canal at Klin and striking the left flank of General Reinhardt's Third Panzer Group in the area south of the Volga lakes. The Soviet troops also attacked the front of the Fourth Panzer Group. The panzers could not withstand the pressure. The 37- and 57-millimeter shells of the infantry antitank guns simply bounced off the armor of the T-34s. Slowly the Germans began to withdraw, fighting all the way. Much of the German heavy equipment, the frozen field guns, even the frozen tanks, was left by the wayside as the troops moved wearily back. Frostbite was the biggest enemy now. The men's boots froze to their feet. Their hands froze. Their noses froze. Their ears froze. Their generals asked Hitler for permission to make planned, strategic withdrawals. Permission was denied. So the men fought on, but the "racially inferior" Russians were too powerful. Mile by mile the panzer units were moving back, losing most of their equipment.

It was at this point that Hitler sacked von Brauchitsch, looking for a scapegoat upon whom he could unload his own errors. Ultimately, as the new commander in chief, Hitler would have to give the panzer generals the order to retreat if it came to that.

By late December the desperate situation of von Kluge's Fourth Army was apparent. Marshal Zhukov had widened his offensive, north and south, aiming to surround the Fourth Army and cut it off from the rear. Von Kluge had no reserves to send back to clear and protect his supply lines; soon those lines were confined to only the Yukhnov-Medin-Maloyaroslavets-Podolsk road. All the other routes were covered with 6 to 10 feet of snow. If the Russians could cut this one road, it would be the end of the German Fourth Army.

Shortly before Christmas 1941, Army Group Center decided to establish a winter line of resistance. The line was to run from Velev through Yukhnov on the Ugra River to Gzhatsk and then north. The Fourth Army would withdraw to this line. Field Marshal von Kluge had already moved a motorized division to Yukhnov to cover the retreat. He called a meeting of his staff officers at his headquarters in a wooden cottage in Maloyaroslavets. They examined the maps and got ready to move the men out. Then came a telephone call from General Hans von Greiffenberg, chief of staff of Army Group Center. He spoke to General Günther von Blumentritt, chief of staff of the Fourth Army.

"You'd better make yourself comfortable," said von Greiffenberg. "A new order has just arrived from Hitler. Fourth Army is not to retreat a single yard."

And so, even as the retreat was in progress, it was stopped, and the weary troops turned around and came back to face the enemy they knew they could not defeat.

Back at Rastenburg, Hitler was fuming. His soldiers were retreating. Did they not know that if they withdrew even a few miles, they would sacrifice all that heavy equipment? The tanks, the guns, the heavy trucks, all were irreplaceable. Did they not know the value of munitions?

Hitler had to return to Berlin. The Reichstag session of December was about to begin, and he had to show some interest in the conduct of his government, as well as in the management of his war. The consequences of Japan's entry into the conflict, the initiation of war against the United States—these matters had to be dealt with. But almost as soon as Hitler arrived in Germany, his war again took ascendance over all else.

The Russian winter began; the temperature dropped. The generals asked again to retreat.

"Stand fast. Not one step back" was the order that went out from the Führer that December evening.

A night or two later Field Marshal von Kluge telephoned the Führer. Colonel General Erich Hoepner, he said, had ordered his army front to be withdrawn in defiance of the Führer's order. The Second Army could cause the downfall of the Fourth Army.

Hitler flew into a rage. He ordered Hoepner's immediate dismissal from command and his discharge from the armed forces for deliberate disobedience. All night long the Führer raged in the OKW headquarters reading room, cursing his generals.

Back in Berlin Dr. Goebbels was planning action against all the generals and other officers of the eastern front and the OKW and the OKH, "who are guilty of fostering defeatism. The Führer has called for such a written report from me, so that he may take proper measures."

Hitler, having lost the confidence of many of his generals, now was losing the loyalty of more of them day after day.

The confusion grew worse. On December 20, 1941, Heinz Guderian, Hitler's favorite among the panzer generals, was in command of the Second Tank Army, which had attacked Moscow from the south. But that army was now frozen solid in Tula.

Army Group Center had ordered Guderian to withdraw west into the gap south of von Kluge's Fourth Army—the object being to sacrifice the Second Tank Army, if necessary, to save the Fourth Army. Guderian saw it differently. He wanted to save his men. He proposed to withdraw along his line of advance, stage by stage, blowing up all his abandoned equipment as he went—including the tanks that were frozen in 2 and 3 feet of solid ice.

Von Kluge argued with Guderian, but to no avail. The panzer general said the order was impossible and he would not obey. So von Kluge complained to the Führer. Hitler fired Guderian and ordered him to come to headquarters immediately for a meeting.

Hitler started by indicating that Guderian could have his command back if he would listen to reason.

It was not reason, said Guderian stubbornly. It was suicide. He was interested only in the fate of his men.

For once Hitler did not lose his temper. Perhaps it was because he had already sacrificed half a dozen generals. He prescribed a rest for Guderian and told the general that he should go somewhere to "convalesce from this enormous strain on his nerves."

So Guderian went into retirement. The matter was dismissed without comment, and the German people did not know that one of their own favorite war heroes had been sacked for trying to save the lives of his men.

The situation of the Germans in Russia was virtually impossible. They faced men who were used to the severe winters, who had the clothing and equipment to survive them, and whose vehicles were adapted for the cold. The Soviet supply lines were short. The German supply lines were long. The Soviets had comrades at their backs. The Germans had enemy partisans at theirs.

In January 1942 Colonel General Adolf Strauss's Ninth Army was on the left flank of Army Group Center. Now came another incident. The commander of the Sixth Army Corps, General Förster, and one of his divisional commanders refused flatly to obey an order that would have cost them half their men. They were sent back in disgrace. Hitler would have no interference with his demand that the armies stand fast, no matter the cost.

Field Marshal Keitel agreed thoroughly with Hitler that the armies must stand fast. Otherwise, he said, all that equipment would be lost and thereafter the men. But Keitel knew that this decision was costing the loyalty of many officers. So it was with heavy hearts that the OKW staff held their cheerless Christmas celebration at Rastenburg. Keitel made a little speech about the importance of the struggle on the Moscow front, which Hitler now admitted, and they all sang "Silent Night, Holy Night." God, they hoped, was still on Germany's side.

The days went on. The Germans regrouped and withstood the Russian offensive. The Russians would break through the lines, but the Germans would throw them out again.

But the cost was enormous. Early in January 1942 the Fourth Army took stock of its headquarters artillery situation. Its original strength had been 48 heavy howitzers, 36 mortars, 48 100-millimeter guns, 9 150-millimeter guns, 84 assault guns, and 252 tractors. It was now down to 5 heavy howitzers, 8 mortars, 17 100-millimeter guns, 2 150-millimeter guns, 12 assault guns, and 22 tractors. That was the sort of attrition that no army could sustain indefinitely.

Russian winter. The only positive note was the fact that the German army had survived that first dreadful impact of Soviet counteroffensive. Field Marshal Keitel gave Hitler full credit for that survival. He still agreed that if the army had retreated, it would have been lost before it ever reached the borders of Germany. Perhaps he was right. The cost in casualties and lost equipment was already enormous. A million men dead, wounded, or missing by the end of the year—to say nothing of the men put out of action by illness, and sickness became endemic on the cold eastern front. The Germans faced such misery because they had brought arrogance with them instead of proper equipment. It is a measure of Hitler's megalomania that he would launch a war against 250 million people without considering that perhaps it would last more than four or five months.

Russian winter. In January the thermometer sank to −42°C. Many of the German soldiers still did not have greatcoats or proper boots. The standard issue jackboots worn in temperate climates were too tight to admit a second pair of socks, and the men who had those boots suffered immeasurably. Army Group North reported that in the Twelfth Panzer Division 63 men had been killed by the enemy and 325 had died from frostbite.

One German officer recalled that time:

We had no gloves. We had no winter shoes. We had no equipment whatsoever to fight or withstand the cold. I think this became a very, very big problem right away. We lost a considerable part of our equipment, guns, heavy and light equipment in general. Due to the cold we lost a lot of people who got frostbitten, and we had not even the necessary amount of ointments, or the most simple and primitive things to fight it. We cut strips off our overcoats to wrap them around our hands instead of wearing gloves. As it became colder...most of our artillery had become completely unusable. Guns didn't fire any more. Even our wireless equipment didn't work properly anymore because the batteries were frozen hard. So there was no way of communicating even between the advancing lines and the artillery batteries in the background. It was, of course, a very, very bad thing if you got wounded. We could hardly take care of our own wounded, not to speak about the enemy. We were afraid to become wounded and to become just the prey of a very bad winter climate or the prey of the enemy. And we had seen enough of the enemy to know that in cases like that prisoners were hardly ever taken.

Hitler did know, of course, that the Russians had suffered enormously in those six months of fighting. They had lost 4 million men, two-thirds of their coal production, and three-quarters of their iron ore production. And yet they still launched that winter offensive of 1941.

By the first of January the Soviets had opened two large gaps in the German line. One was at the northern end of Army Group Center's territory; the other gap was at the southern end. General Zhukov intended to surround Army Group Center and destroy it. To Hitler that would mean the loss of another million men at least. For a time the northern situation looked desperate. The gap had widened to 150 miles. Then, on January 15, Hitler finally had a change of heart. He ordered a retreat. He had to. The commander of Army Group Center had reported on the state of his forces:

The reason why it is doubtful whether the units can hold a new, unprepared defensive line is clear: because of the shortage of fuel and because of the icy roads I am not getting my motorized units back. I am not even getting my horse-drawn artillery back because the horses cannot manage the weather. Today, for example, the 267th Division had to leave its artillery behind. There is therefore a grave danger that as we retreat we may reach new positions, but without artillery. *On the other hand an order to stand and fight would induce in me the fear lest the soldiers would, somewhere or other, retreat without orders.* (Italics added.)

Indeed, units were retreating without orders.

Hitler had driven his men to the brink of rebellion. At least he had the good sense to realize that and on January 15 to order the retreat that saved Army Group Center from disaster.

*

At the end of December an irritated Hitler had replaced Field Marshal von Bock, commander of Army Group Center, with Field Marshal von Kluge. General Ludwig Kübler took over von Kluge's Fourth Army. But Kübler could not stomach the desperate situation into which Hitler had thrown that army, and he lasted only a few weeks. He was replaced by General Gotthard Heinrici, who was more amenable to Hitler's direction.

Russian winter. Everything was a mess. Hitler had estimated that the Russians could produce only 5000 aircraft a year. Actually they had been producing 10,000. The Russians started the war with 10,000 aircraft and a production rate of 1300 per month. From July to December the Russians produced more than 5000 new fighters, most of them of the new Yak-1, MiG-3, and LaGG-3 designs, as compared with only about 1600 Luftwaffe fighters produced in the same period. By midwinter the Russians were outproducing the Germans in aircraft by 4 to 1.

It was true that the Germans destroyed many Russian aircraft on the ground in the early stages of the war. But by winter the Luftwaffe in Russia was in terrible shape. As had Hitler, Luftwaffe chief Göring had expected victory in three months. The German air force had made no preparations for flying in a cold winter. In December 1941 there were only 500 serviceable Luftwaffe aircraft in Russia. The Russians had 1000 aircraft on the Moscow front alone.

The German losses now made themselves felt in every area of German society. Field Marshal Keitel had to force Albert Speer, the minister of armament and munitions, to give back to the armed forces a quarter of a million troops who had been discharged from the service after the fall of France to work in arms factories. These men were now desperately needed on the eastern front. The strength of German divisions was reduced from nine to seven battalions. The various support echelons were cut hard. But somehow the Germans held out through the Russian winter, and as spring came, the Germans were telling themselves that they could, indeed, still win this war.

Hitler had an entirely new idea. He had completely forgotten his own dreadful errors that had brought the German army to such a pass in the east. He had convinced himself that all his troubles came about because of the incompetence and unwillingness of his generals. All he needed, he said, was a few good generals and he could win this war before the next Russian winter set in. That was his goal and his firm belief in April 1942.

18

STALINGRAD—I

Sometimes it has been asked why Hitler declared war on the United States a few hours after the Japanese attack, and the traditional answer is that he was badly misinformed about the American industrial potential. Otherwise, say the responders, he never would have taken an action that would cause the Americans to begin sending enormous quantities of material to the Soviet Union. For the Americans began doing just that. The Arctic convoys to Russia soon started, and they were to carry 17,000 aircraft, 50,000 jeeps, 40,000 trucks, tanks, field guns, torpedo boats, fuel oils, gasoline, 5 million tons of ammunition and explosives, and all sorts of food and other materials.

Hitler knew all about American industrial potential. He had spoken of it several times in connection with Britain, and one reason he had restrained Admiral Dönitz's U-boats from sinking American ships in 1939 and 1940 was to ensure that America stayed out of the war.

Hitler had failed to achieve victory in the Soviet Union. It was, however, a cost that Germany could bear. As 1942 began, Hitler still had every hope of winning this war and forcing Britain to negotiate peace in the west. The United States would certainly follow Britain's suit and concentrate its efforts on defeating the enemy at which it was most aggrieved, the Japanese in the Pacific. Then Hitler's fondest hopes would have been achieved. Soviet communism would have been destroyed, and all continental Europe would either be his or be controlled by his allies.

In the spring of 1942 Hitler proposed to concentrate his efforts against the U.S.S.R., with a lesser effort in north Africa. Germany held the Atlantic coast of Europe from the North Cape to the Bay of Biscay. German troops were not far from Leningrad and were on the banks of the Don and the Volga rivers. The Balkans were controlled by Germany and its allies. German and Italian troops were poised to begin a new offensive in Africa as soon as Hitler could give them the material support they needed. Germany's U-boat force was growing stronger every month and threatened Britain's lifeline to the west. The German army was enormously powerful; only the Luftwaffe had begun to falter, and this largely because of the bad planning of its chief, Marshal Hermann Göring.

By late February the Soviet offensive from the Baltic to the Black Sea had figuratively run out of gas. By mid-March the rains had again turned the roads and fields into quagmires, and no army could move. By this time both sides were temporarily exhausted.

To Hitler this meant that only half a dozen of his 160 combat divisions were actually ready for action. His sixteen armored divisions had virtually no more tanks. Only 140 tanks were found to be serviceable. This was the minimum complement for a single division.

As the weather in Russia began to grow warmer, the Germans gained strength and by April had halted the Soviet winter offensive altogether. Hitler's plan was to concentrate in the south and conquer the Caucasus, the Donetz industrial basin, and the Kuban wheat fields. He would also take Stalingrad on the Volga River. All this would deprive Stalin of oil, food, and industry, all essential to the continued Russian war effort.

Hitler had to have that oil. "If I do not get it," he told General Friedrich von Paulus one day, "I will have to end this war."

So in the spring the Germans counted noses. Their casualties were almost 1.2 million for the year, not including the sick. Keitel was sent off to Romania and Hungary to find new divisions of Axis troops for the east, and he was successful. Göring went to Italy and got Mussolini's promise to send Italian troops to the Russian front. Altogether the German High Command secured promises for fifty-two Axis divisions: twenty-seven Romanian, thirteen Hungarian, nine Italian, two Slovak, and one of Spanish "volunteers."

General Halder, the chief of the army, expressed grave misgivings regarding this heavy addition of troops about whose fighting qualities there was more than some question. If nothing else, the differences in language and military custom were going to create a lot of confusion. But Hitler would not listen. So the commitments were made, and the foreign divisions began to come in to fill the holes in the German ranks.

The Germans were busy clearing up the many small penetrations that the Soviets had made through their lines, and reestablishing their long perimeter in Russia as an attack line. One major Russian penetration was at Cholm and Demyansk, where German units had been surrounded but had held out. Another was at Isyum, south of Kharkov, where the Soviets had run a spearhead through the German line but had been unable to widen it. The third major salient was the Soviet beachhead at Feodosia in the Crimea.

By April new units were coming from Germany and the tired troops were being sent home to rest and be formed into new, powerful units with new equipment. Much to the disgust of the army, the Waffen SS was brought onto the scene.

The Waffen SS was the despair of the old-line army officers. At the top it was composed of "party" men whose loyalty was directly to Hitler and not to the army system. Therefore, nothing was too good for the Waffen SS, and that organization began skimming the cream of German youth off the manpower pool.

> With the Führer's support, the Waffen S.S. had enticed the most valuable sections of German youth into its ranks by means of open and concealed, legal and illegal propaganda methods, and by indirect pressure tactics too; the best elements of youth, who would have been perfect future commanders and officers for the Army, were thereby lost to us.

So wrote Field Marshal Keitel, ever the army man, in analyzing the war campaigns. Like all the other army generals, Keitel was now suffering from Hitler's open contempt for their system. At one point in the running battle with von Rundstedt that had led to that field marshal's dismissal, Hitler had flown to Mariupol in the south to see General Sepp Dietrich, commander of the First SS Panzer Division (*Leibstandarte* Adolf Hitler), to see if he could learn anything compromising about von Rundstedt. Hitler expected Dietrich to tell him all, because Dietrich was first a Nazi and then a general. But in this instance Hitler was disappointed; Sepp Dietrich showed himself more general than Nazi. He stood up for von Rundstedt in the argument so successfully that Hitler, who had already ordered von Rundstedt fired at that point, visited him and came as close to apologizing to him as Hitler ever had or would to a general. Yet the healing had been only momentary. Hitler's hatred and fear of his Officer Corps never left him, and one by one, starting with von Rundstedt, the generals were sacked.

Now, in the spring of 1942, Hitler was encouraging the Waffen SS because he trusted those men more than he trusted his army. It was, said Hitler, an elite corps that was being politically trained in the way he had always wanted and in the way the army would have been trained had the officers not resisted his every importunity. So, Hitler told Keitel, he was going to move as many young men as possible into the Waffen SS. There would be no limit on the number of volunteers who could be accepted by this organization.

Keitel protested that the Waffen SS methods of recruiting were highly suspect, including bribery and intimidation. Hitler became enraged and demanded proof. But Keitel was too smart to put the necks of his informants in the Gestapo's noose. He shut his mouth tight, and never did reveal their names. Without proof Hitler refused to believe that his beloved Waffen SS was riddled with corruption. And so another little crack appeared in the structure of the Thousand-Year Reich. Ultimately the Waffen SS consisted of thirty-eight divisions, and the army men hated every one of them.

Hitler's first move in the spring of 1942 was against the Soviet wedge driving from Orel toward Poltava in the south. Field Marshal von Bock's Army Group South would make a breakthrough on its northern flank to Voronezh, on the Don River. It would roll up the Russian front along the Don and advance on Stalingrad. At the same

time the southern element of Army Group South would move into
the Caucasus, overrunning the oil fields.

To manage this, Hitler would have to move all available forces from
static positions on the eastern front. The tank armies were particularly
vital. The Crimea was also to be occupied to prepare a crossing from
the Kerch peninsula into the oil regions of the Caucasus. Germany's
petroleum problems would then be solved.

Hitler's first move was designed to fool the Russians about his
real intentions. He began moving troops toward Voronezh, halfway
between Moscow and the Donetz basin, to persuade Stalin that he
was wheeling up for an attack on Moscow. If they were convinced,
the Russians would hold their reserves up there.

Before the Germans could do anything, they had to get their logistics in order. The army and the air force in Russia required 120
trainloads of supply every day, but the transportation system was
producing only 100 trainloads a day. Therefore, somebody was always in short supply. One reason was the efficacy of the partisan
operations against the long German lines of communication. It was
a constant battle: the partisans would blow a rail line; the Germans
would repair it; the partisans would blow it again.

As Hitler's demands for the beginning of the spring offensive
grew more strident, Field Marshal von Bock tried to hold the Führer
back. Hitler wanted to launch the attack so that it cut right across
the enemy bulge at its root. Von Bock, expecting a Soviet counterattack, wanted to go slower and to use many of the troops for
defensive purposes.

But Hitler insisted. He ordered that the operation be carried out
as he had indicated, with no argument permitted. Von Bock, who
privately thought the whole scheme mad, did as he was told.

Hitler was proved right. The Poltava operation was an immense
success, and the Germans captured tens of thousands of Russian
prisoners. They had neatly severed the bulge that stuck into their
lines that winter.

Now the Germans began to suffer from intelligence leaks, which
cost them dearly in men and material. Hitler suspected all his generals. Several disaffected Luftwaffe officers had indeed become enemy agents, and were passing the secrets of the OKW to the British.

Or so the Germans thought, and it was true to some extent. But the real culprit was a Pole.

In the 1930s the Germans developed further an old coding and decoding machine called "Enigma," which had been invented in 1919 to protect trade secrets. The German government bought up the patent and perfected the machine for its growing communications network as Hitler rearmed. Later in the 1930s the Poles got wind of this development, and fearing that Poland was on Hitler's list of countries to be conquered, they set to work to break the codes. Somehow they secured a broken Enigma machine, and after the conquest of Poland in 1939, someone was brave enough and astute enough to get the machine to England and hand it over to the British government. By the summer of 1940 the British had fixed the machine and learned how to use it. After that, the Germans had no more vital secrets, *but the Allies had to go slow and be very careful lest they let the cat out of the bag*. That is why it was always important to the western Allies to have a few agents in the German ranks; it was good concealment for the most important and best kept secret of the war.

On the southern front, the Germans moved against Voronezh and began the battle for the Don. Hitler very quickly lost confidence in Field Marshal von Bock. Not liking what he heard, the Führer and Keitel flew out to meet with von Bock. They met, but nothing was decided. Hitler returned to Rastenburg and continued to complain about von Bock's management of Army Group South. A few weeks later von Bock was out, and Field Marshal Freiherr Maximilian von Weichs had replaced him.

For operations in the deep south of Russia, a new army group, Group A, had been assembled. Halder and Keitel agreed that its commander ought to be Field Marshal List. Independently they proposed the name to Hitler. The Führer hesitated. That should have been enough of a clue for the two to offer another name, but they did not. They persisted in forwarding List's name, and finally Hitler reluctantly agreed to appoint him. But from the beginning the Führer disliked Field Marshal List. The pattern of his relationships with his generals seemed to be set: any general who in any way stirred his antagonism was soon finished, and that antagonism was amazingly easy to stir.

Some have said that Hitler went insane. Certainly the old adage "Those whom the gods would destroy they first make mad" seems to have some validity when applied to Hitler's behavior beginning in the winter of 1942.

To understand what was going on in Hitler's mind, one must remember that he was both an old soldier of World War I and a founder of the National Socialist party. He was now playing soldier—commander in chief—but he also remained intensely political, and the Nazis were the focus of his ultimate loyalties. That meant that as his distrust of his generals grew, he depended more upon his party faithful. These were Göring, Goebbels, Himmler, and a new, ambitious Nazi, Martin Bormann. Himmler was busy with "special tasks" in the occupied east, which meant that he was in charge of the terror there. That terror included torture, murder, and wholesale shipment of populations to slave labor areas. These men had Hitler's ear, and if they made charges against the generals or others, Hitler was always ready to believe them. Field Marshal Keitel believed that Himmler was personally responsible for what happened to Field Marshal List.

As noted, Hitler had not been eager to appoint List as the chief of Army Group A. When the army began to move that spring, past Rostov into the Caucasian countryside, many charges of error and wrongdoing were brought against List. One of the charges was that he had prevented the armored units of the Waffen SS from breaking off toward Rostov, thus denying them a share in the glory. That charge certainly had all the earmarks of Himmler's work. Whatever the facts, Hitler believed the charge because he wanted to believe it, even though Keitel said that List was following his orders precisely.

By this time Hitler had moved his headquarters to Vinnitsa in the Ukraine. This complex was called "Werewolf." The hot, humid climate was dreadful, and Professor Morell, the quack doctor whom Hitler had favored for years, said that the climate had a very bad effect on Hitler's health and disposition.

That must have been so. In the summer of 1942 List came to Vinnitsa to report to Hitler. A few months earlier a plane carrying an important Wehrmacht officer had been shot down over Russian territory; the officer had been captured, and so had the spring war plan and the maps that went with it. Hitler had then ordered that no officer was to travel with detailed maps on his person. So List had come to the meeting with only a 1:1,000,000 scale map of his operational area. When he produced the map, Hitler raged at him for concealing information. Hitler's remarks were seconded by Göring, and List left quickly, thoroughly confused and discomfited. Field Marshal Keitel had been in Berlin at that time, and when he returned he reminded Hitler of his own orders on the subject of maps. Hitler blew up again, quoted Göring to substantiate his position, and refused to listen further.

The military situation in the Black Sea area deteriorated rapidly that summer. A Mountain Korps, appropriately, had been given the task of taking the mountain passes that led to the Black Sea, but the terrain and the Russian defenses were just too stout for the forces at hand. General Konrad, the chief of the Mountain Korps, said as much to List and proved his point satisfactorily. List then agreed, and told Jodl the same thing when Jodl came down to see what was wrong. Jodl went back to Vinnitsa and told Hitler, who erupted again. All his generals were conspiring against him, he raged. Keitel would one day call Hitler's delusion "pathological." The Führer had become obsessed by the idea of capturing the coast road running along the Black Sea and then over the western spur of the Caucasus Mountains. His generals had discovered that the logistical problems of fighting in the mountains made this impossible. Hitler would not see that point. He sent Keitel down to tell List that he was fired. He raged at Jodl all the time Keitel was gone, and said it was Jodl's trip to see List that had brought the matter to such a pass.

When Keitel returned to Rastenburg, Hitler would have very little to do with him. Jodl and Keitel had frequently eaten their meals with Hitler. Now their Führer would not eat with them, and he would hardly speak to them. He would not shake hands with them or carry on any but official conversations.

*   *   *

List had been fired for telling Hitler that he was going too far, too fast. The field marshal said that the reserves and logistics of the German army could not support this swift movement in the south. Hitler could not encircle Moscow.

On July 13 Hitler felt that he was nearly victorious. Nothing was holding him back except his generals. That day he fired von Bock, who was in command of the entire southern offensive, because that field marshal was not moving fast enough.

At that moment, July 13, Hitler could have sent the Fourth Panzer Army into Stalingrad, which was virtually undefended. But Hitler did not see this until it was too late. By the time he awakened to the possibility two weeks later, the Russians had also seen the problem and had rushed thousands of troops to Stalingrad. Now it was very strongly defended. By moving the Fourth Panzer Army again, this time away from von Kleist, Hitler also deprived that field marshal of the power to complete his drive into the Grozny oil fields. Von Kleist could have used the Fourth Panzer Army. But not now.

Then, on July 23, Hitler decided that he would capture both the Caucasus and Stalingrad at the same time. General Halder told him it was impossible, and for that Halder got a dressing down. General Directive No. 45 ordered that Hitler's decision be carried out.

Meanwhile it appeared that the German land forces were making great strides in Russia. On August 8 the Germans captured the Maikop oil fields, the greatest in the area, which normally produced 2.5 million tons of petroleum per year. But the Russians had burnt them. They were useless.

On August 21 the Germans had taken Mount Elbrus, the highest peak in the Caucasus. On August 23 the German Sixth Army reached the Volga River north of Stalingrad. On August 25 German tanks rushed into Mozdok, another oil center, a hundred miles from the Caspian Sea. Hitler believed that victory in Russia was now almost in his hands. He ordered the Sixth Army and the Fourth Panzer Army to move north along the Volga, take Stalingrad, and move on in an encircling movement that would allow him to surround Moscow. He was even talking about pushing through Iran to the Persian Gulf, to then link up with the Japanese in the Indian Ocean. The Japanese were sitting on the edge of India.

The events of the spring and summer—the initial effectiveness of the German blockade of the American coast and the success of

Rommel, who was making great strides in Africa—had convinced Hitler that in a few months the British and Americans would be ready for a negotiated peace. And in a few more weeks he should have Russia by the throat, and the *Lebensraum* that he had always wanted. It was simply a matter of killing off the Russians who had lived there.

Halder came to Vinnitsa to argue against overconfidence. Hitler informed him coldly that the Russians were "finished."

Halder read him a report. It showed that Stalin still would be able to muster from a million to a million and a quarter fresh troops in the region north of Stalingrad and that Stalin could raise half a million men in the Caucasus. Further, the Russians were building tanks at the rate of 1200 a month, he said. That hardly indicated that they were finished.

Hitler had rushed up with clenched fists and foam at the corners of his mouth and forbidden the reading of any more "such idiotic twaddle."

Halder insisted on making the point: What would happen when Stalin unleashed these troops?

So the struggle went on: in the field the German generals fought the Russians, at headquarters the German generals fought Hitler.

In the south the Russians changed tactics. They did not attack, and the Germans found that they were taking very few prisoners. The Russians were evading the traps the Germans set for them. Only in Stalingrad and in the mountain passes was the resistance heavy. The Russians were up to something. Halder and Keitel were certain that they were massing troops for a major blow.

The problem in later summer was that the German troops were again tired. If the Sixth Army under General von Paulus did succeed in driving to the Stalingrad area, aided by those uncertain troops from Hungary, Romania, and other allies, the forces were too slender for offensives in the oil fields. The front was overextended.

Halder warned Hitler that September that the Don River flank, held south of Voronezh by the Hungarians and Italians and west of Stalingrad by the Romanians, was badly exposed. Hitler replied that he knew it, but the Don itself was his best line of defense. Until it froze over, he was willing to take the calculated risk.

General Georg Thomas, the author of the report that Halder had read to Hitler, continued to amass his statistics on the strength of the Russians. Hitler forbade the circulation of "these defeatist reports." He also told Halder that it was really time for him to go. What was needed, said Hitler, was no more of the tired generals, but a strong infusion of National Socialist philosophy. This is what he proposed to bring to the army.

So Halder was the next general to relinquish his post, and the new chief of the army General Staff was General Kurt Zeitzler, chief of staff to von Rundstedt, who had been given a new job as commander in chief, west. The old field marshal would defend *Festung Europa* ("Fortress Europe") from the expected American and British attack.

Keitel and Jodl, now virtually ignored by Hitler, had hoped that Zeitzler would be the new link for them to provide the German military organization with proper management. But as soon as Zeitzler arrived, they realized that someone had gotten to him and that he was not going to pay any attention to them.

"Zeitzler not only disassociated himself from us, but was intent on excluding us to an increasing degree...from the decision-making on the eastern front by means of briefing Hitler [frequently] *a deux*," recalled Keitel.

General von Paulus did reach Stalingrad. All through October he attacked. The fighting reached into the streets of the city, and the Germans made block by block progress, if one could call it that, for their casualties were enormous. Zeitzler now had to warn Hitler that the troops were becoming exhausted. But fresh divisions were thrown into the fight, and were ground up one after the other.

The Germans controlled the river above and below Stalingrad. They did not have to occupy the city. But Stalingrad had become a symbol to Hitler. He would have the city that was named for his archrival.

One day General Zeitzler suggested that it would save many lives and much equipment if the Germans would withdraw from Stalingrad to the elbow of the Don River.

Hitler flew into another rage. "Where a German soldier sets foot," he said, "there he remains."

On October 25 General von Paulus informed Hitler that he expected to have completed the capture of Stalingrad by November 20. That was good, said the Führer, because it was about time. At this point he was completely confident of the future. After taking Stalingrad, he told his commanders, the Fourth Panzer Army and the Sixth Army would push north and south along the Volga.

Then Hitler picked up his papers and moved back from the Ukrainian command post to *Wolfsschanze* in Rastenburg. The Moscow and Leningrad fronts needed his attention. The southern front was entirely under control.

The war was winding down, he had decided. In the Atlantic the Germans had done great damage off the American coast all spring. The Americans had begun to pull themselves together in May, but by that time Dönitz had moved his U-boats back into the mid-Atlantic with super–wolf pack tactics, and the British were losing shipping faster than it could be built.

In Africa the Afrika Korps commander was moving ahead very quickly and should capture Egypt quite soon. He had suffered a few reverses in the fall after a vigorous spring, but Hitler was sure they were only temporary. Malta was under siege and should soon fall. The Germans seemed to be ascendant everywhere. They had hit their high point of the war.

19

THE RISE OF ROMMEL

By the middle of the summer of 1942 Hitler's relationships with his generals had grown so terrible that Field Marshal Keitel, the nominal chief of *Oberkommando der Wehrmacht,* and thus Hitler's chief operating officer in the whole field of defense, felt that he was completely out of Hitler's confidence. He dreaded the days he and his Führer would have discussions because they would almost always end in Hitler's shouting and screaming, and the results would make no sense whatsoever.

In the army that summer, the conspiracy against Hitler took bud and began to flourish. One of the hotbeds was Army Group Center, which had spent such a dreadful winter that some of the most ardent exponents of nazism had now been converted to the opposite pole. Major General Henning von Tresckow, Colonel Fabian von Schlabrendorff, Count Hans von Hardenberg, and Count Heinrich von Lehndorff were the ringleaders. All of them were closely associated with Field Marshal von Bock. They were trying to persuade him to arrest Hitler and lock him up as a dangerous lunatic. But von Bock would not yield, and so the conspiracy, in Russia and at home in Germany, smoldered but did not catch fire.

The problem was that the top generals had been given good chances for fame, glory, and promotion by Hitler. That is why no general would commit an overt act, although many were aware of the plotting and were also aware that if they did act, they would have the support of a great majority of the Officer Corps. Only the Nazis—the Himmlers, the Bormanns, and the other jackals—could be expected to stick with Hitler. But there was simply no single figure in the army with the determination, courage, and ability to take the reins.

Keitel was aware of the conspiracy. How could he not be? He took no active part in it, but neither did he expose it to Hitler and his Gestapo. By this time Keitel and Jodl would have been very happy to see Hitler unseated. But who would replace him? That was a question that no one could answer and another of the reasons that nothing happened.

In the winter of 1942 General Erwin Rommel in Africa had held on by his teeth, so to speak. His problem was supply. The German garrison at Halfaya had to surrender late that winter, not because of inability or unwillingness to fight, but because the troops ran out of food. The RAF and the Royal Navy continued to sink the supply ships that should have been bringing Rommel all he needed. The material and ammunition had been produced, and there was no problem getting it down to the bottom of the Italian boot; but once it went aboard ships and out into the open Mediterranean, it was fair game for the British. Too often the supplies went from the bottom of the Italian boot to the bottom of the sea.

On the other hand, the Italian sinking of those major warships in Alexandria harbor and the campaign of the Stuka dive-bombers and the U-boats against British shipping had left their marks, letting the Germans and Italians get some supply convoys through to north Africa. Rommel had received enough supplies by the late spring of 1942 to gain a false sense of euphoria about his position there. Now something had to be done to put those resources to good use, or there was no reason for his remaining in Africa. And he was willing to do it, although he had only one light infantry division and two panzer divisions under his command, plus the cooperation of a number of Italian divisions that he could not completely control. With the new supplies in hand, he decided that he had a better-than-even chance of capturing Tobruk, and this became his objective. Kesselring's renewed Luftwaffe support was made possible once again by an increase in supply that had come down through the Alpine passes to Italy.

Rommel's first task was to organize the defense of the sector that he had taken at the end of his previous drive, not far from Alexandria. Kesselring, who was in overall command of the entire south, agreed with Rommel and the Italian High Command that the moves should be:

1. Capture Tobruk.

2. Capture Malta.

3. Roll up the British in Egypt and drive them from Africa.

This was a logical plan. The capture of Tobruk would weaken the British position in Egypt and keep open the Nile River valley to Rommel. The capture of Malta would eliminate the air bases and sea base from which the British so successfully attacked the Axis convoys. With Tobruk and Malta in Axis hands, Rommel could drive the British from the land, while Kesselring's Luftwaffe assaulted them from the air. The result should be a quick victory.

That is how it started, with many victories.

On May 26 Rommel attacked with his three divisions and three Italian armored divisions. He was attempting to envelop the British from the south. By midafternoon of the second day he had reached a position behind the British at Gazala. One by one, for the next three weeks, his army overcame the British strong points. It was not a question of manpower, but really of Rommel's drive and determination. He pushed the Axis forces, and he pushed them again until they did his bidding. The hardest battle was fought at Bir Hakeim, a fort held by French soldiers and a Jewish battalion of the British army. It resisted stoutly but finally fell on June 9. Ten days later Rommel began the assault on Tobruk, backed stoutly by Kesselring's Luftwaffe.

Rommel's first move was to pretend to bypass the city, as he had done in 1941, and to pursue the British troops into Egypt. But on the second day the German forces wheeled and attacked Tobruk. The fighting was fierce but brief. By the evening of June 20 the Germans broke through the British lines, and the armor led the way into the port. Rommel took 30,000 prisoners, and an incalculably valuable store of supplies that would last his men for months.

Here, although Rommel did not know it, the Germans reached their apogee in Africa. The war was about to turn around.

On June 30 a triumphant Rommel crossed the Egyptian frontier and approached El Alamein, where the British were determined to make a stand. They had to stand there, for if they did not, the whole Nile delta would be open to Rommel, and that meant Alexandria, the great port.

With all those supplies back at Tobruk, Rommel now faced a logistical problem once again. The Royal Air Force harassed his supply trains. And since the British did not use weapons such as the 88-millimeter gun, much of the ammunition he had captured was valuable only if he used British weapons. What should have happened next was the capture of Malta, which would have solved Rommel's problem. But Kesselring did not have the planes to fly support for Rommel's land operation and to blast Malta at the same time, so the capture of Malta had to be put aside. What the Germans did not realize was that Malta was so beaten down and so short of supplies that three or four days of intensive bombing would have brought its surrender. But Kesselring could not manage, though he tried valiantly.

In mid-August the British staged Operation Pedestal, designed to relieve Malta. On August 9 Admiral Syfret entered the Mediterranean with the battleships *Nelson* and *Rodney,* three large aircraft carriers, seven cruisers, and thirty-two destroyers. They had come all the way from England; that was how important the salvation of Malta was seen to be by Prime Minister Churchill. On August 14 the warships picked up fourteen fast merchant ships loaded with supplies for Malta. The carrier *Eagle* was sunk by a U-boat, but her planes were flown off to Malta. On August 12 Kesselring's planes sank a merchant ship and damaged the carrier *Indomitable.* But the British shot down thirty-nine Luftwaffe planes and sank an Italian submarine. That night the battleships withdrew as the convoy approached. In the night battle, the U-boats and German torpedo boats sank seven merchant ships and the cruisers *Manchester* and *Cairo;* two more cruisers and three more merchant ships were damaged. But the surviving ships pressed on for Malta.

At dawn on August 13 the Luftwaffe attacked in strength. The American tanker *Ohio* was hit and stopped, and so was another merchant ship. But by this time the remains of the convoy were within the air umbrella of Malta. Five of the thirteen merchant ships made the passage successfully. It may not seem very successful, but the operation saved Malta and restored its fighting strength. The cost to the Royal Navy was very high: one carrier, two cruisers, and several destroyers sunk, many ships damaged, and 350 officers and men killed. But it was worth the price to keep Malta the dominant base in the central Mediterranean. The cost to the Germans was even higher.

Two Italian cruiser squadrons had come out on August 13 to attack the convoy near Malta, but Kesselring refused to give them air support because of an unpleasant experience with the Italian fleet in the past (when the Italians shot down many German planes). So the Luftwaffe would not fly cover, and the Italian fleet turned around and did not attack. Two of the Italian cruisers were torpedoed by British submarines in the Sicilian narrows. The Luftwaffe attacked alone, and fifty-two German planes were shot down. The loss made it impossible for Kesselring to continue his attacks on British shipping and support Rommel at the same time, until he got more planes and pilots.

Rommel camped outside El Alamein and made one foray after another, trying to break through the British line. On August 30 he nearly succeeded: the German troops pushed through a spearhead, but then the armored units ran out of fuel. A convoy that was supposed to be bringing new supplies was sunk almost on the edge of the Tobruk roadstead. The tankers that carried Rommel's fuel went up in flames or down to the bottom of the Mediterranean. For six days Rommel's armored units were stalled in the desert.

All during August, as Rommel tried to break through to Alexandria, General Bernard Montgomery prepared for the big battle the British knew was coming.

Rommel was quite right. Hitler had been so impressed with the general's performance in Africa that he had promoted him to field marshal. Now he ordered Rommel to break through to Alexandria. Troops intended for the assault on Malta were sent instead to Rommel as reinforcements. At a conference on August 27 Field Marshal Kesselring and Italian Field Marshal Cavallero guaranteed Rommel 6000 tons of fuel; 1000 tons would be flown in and 5000 would be delivered by tanker.

"The outcome of the battle will depend on the delivery of this fuel at the proper time," Rommel told them.

"You can begin the battle, Field Marshal, this fuel is already on its way," Cavallero assured him.

On August 30 it began. That night Rommel's two German armored divisions penetrated the mine belt the British had built around their line and moved into the Ragil depression. As planned, the British Seventh Armoured Division withdrew steadily before them, fighting as it went, and stopped on Rommel's eastern flank. North of the Germans three Italian divisions tried to move forward but got stuck in the minefield, but the German Ninetieth Light Infantry division made it through. From the Ragil depression the Germans could strike either north against the Alam Halfa ridge or northeast toward Hammam. The British wanted Rommel to go for the ridge, and to that end British military intelligence a few days earlier had arranged for Rommel's troops to "capture" a map showing a good tank fighting ground on the ridge and a very bad one in the direction of Hammam. Rommel fell into the trap and chose the ridge for his attack, just as Montgomery wanted him to do. On the evening of August 31 the British repelled a thrust to the north, and the Germans bivouacked for the night.

On the morning of September 1 the Germans began to advance against the center of the British line. They ran into heavy sand, just as Montgomery had known they would. The attack failed. The Italians had gone completely to pieces, which left Rommel with only three divisions in action instead of six. His tanks began to run out of fuel. Then he learned that three tankers coming his way had just been sunk. So on September 2 Rommel took up defensive positions. Montgomery refused to engage, so Rommel had to withdraw. As he moved back, the British harried him from the flanks and destroyed most of his unarmored vehicles. On the night of September 3 the British attacked the German infantry and the Italian Trieste infantry division. The British fought well and the German panzer divisions slipped through behind them and were saved. But Rommel had suffered a very serious defeat.

Back at his camp, Rommel knew that the Americans were soon going to come into action in Africa, and he sent a message to OKW:

Unless the supplies to Africa are placed on a firm basis, the Panzer Army will not be able to withstand for any length of time the combined forces of two world powers. Sooner or later it will be in danger of suffering the same fate which befell the Halfaya garrison.

Hitler did not deign to reply. Instead, to show his displeasure, he ordered Rommel home to Germany "for medical treatment." It was true that Rommel was sick and had needed treatment for fever for a long time, but that could not have been the real reason for his recall. It was typical of Hitler to show his displeasure with a general in this way.

General Georg Stumme was transferred from the eastern front to act as Rommel's deputy during his absence. Rommel went home, first traveling to the east to confer with Hitler. There, at Hitler's headquarters, he was astounded at the air of calm confidence. He attempted to puncture it.

Rommel had brought with him a 40-millimeter, armor-piercing shell, manufactured in the United States. It was the sort that had been fired from RAF guns and had destroyed many of his tanks in the African desert. He showed it to Hitler and Göring, who was present for the conference, and told them how effective this munition was against his armor. He also told them the Americans were about to come into the war in Africa.

"Quite impossible," said Göring blandly. "Nothing but latrine rumors. All the Americans can make are razor blades and refrigerators."

"I only wish, Herr Reich Marshal, that we were issued with similar razor blades," Rommel replied.

Hitler promised that the Afrika Korps' problems would be solved in short order. He was sending Siebel ferries, a sort of craft that was said to be immune to air and torpedo attack.

It sounded very good. It was true that tanks and weapons were arriving in Africa in great quantities—but not for Rommel. The first American Sherman tanks were arriving in the Nile delta, for Montgomery. The guns and trucks and supplies were coming, to Montgomery. None of Hitler's promises produced any weapons at all for the Afrika Korps.

The Germans and Italians were now at El Alamein, between the Mediterranean and the Qattara depression, the only defensive position in the western desert that could not be outflanked from the south. The British would have to make a frontal breakthrough, or they would fail.

The British had control of the air. They had immense supplies of ammunition. The Afrika Korps had very little ammunition and so little fuel for the tanks that its major tactic, the mobile defensive battle, could not be fought here. So the Afrika Korps built a huge minefield around its positions.

British intelligence now contributed again to the war. Montgomery convinced the Germans that he could not attack in October. His tanks were concealed beneath dummy vehicles. Dummy trucks were parked in the gun positions. When tanks and guns were moved from rear areas they were replaced by dummies. In the south huge dummy supply dumps were created, giving the Germans the impression that the British could not possibly move before November. A radio network was set up in the clear, its sole purpose to fool the Germans with fake messages. The British also brought in two new divisions with 150 tanks and 240 guns, and the Germans did not know it.

Montgomery also had a new battle tactic. The traditional armor battle called for destruction of the enemy's tanks and then of its infantry. Montgomery decided to do it the other way around.

The battle began on the night of October 23 with a British artillery barrage. The shooting started at 9:40 p.m. against the Alamein position. Twenty minutes later the British guns switched to the advanced infantry positions. The Australians and the Scottish Highlanders then moved westward through the minefield, north of the Miteirya ridge. The New Zealanders and the South Africans attacked from the northeast, captured the ridge, and cleared a second lane through the minefield. The Indians attacked the Ruweisat ridge. And in the far north the Australians attacked between Tel el Eisa and the sea. By dawn most of the first objectives had been taken by the British. Now up came the First and Tenth Armoured Divisions, with 700 tanks, to drive along the corridors cleared in the minefield. The Tenth Armoured Division was halted by German fire at the top of the Miteirya ridge, but the New Zealand armored brigade moved west over high ground until it got caught in a minefield and withdrew.

*   *   *

The British had broken through the German line and had managed to hold their positions. They now continued the attack.

At noon on October 24 Hitler telephoned Rommel at his sanatorium in Germany. "Do you feel capable of returning to Africa and taking command of the army again?" the Führer asked.

"Yes," said Rommel. The next morning he flew to Rome to confer with the Italians and to demand from the commander of U-boats in Italy the use of all his submarines to transport fuel to the Afrika Korps. He also demanded that the Italians use every available destroyer and submarine for the same purpose. Then he flew to Crete, and on the evening of October 25 he reached the battle headquarters in the western desert. General Stumme had disappeared, and General Wilhelm von Thoma was in command. (Stumme had died from a heart attack after he had been ambushed on the road during the battle.) Von Thoma told Rommel the grim details. Stumme had forbidden the Afrika Korps to destroy the British jumping-off bases because of the ammunition shortage. So the British had captured much of the minefield with light casualties. The German armored counterattacks were badly battered by the heavy British artillery fire and the RAF. Worse, the Afrika Korps was almost out of fuel.

On the night of October 25 the British bombardment killed hundreds of troops, and the British captured Kidney ridge. On the twenty-sixth the British widened their position west of the minefield. The Germans counterattacked and after a day of heavy fighting recaptured all of the ridge except the summit.

Rommel committed his troops to another attack. As they were making it, Italian bombers came overhead, moving toward concentrations of British troops beyond. The bombers were attacked by fifty British fighters, and in desperation unloaded their bombs. The bombs fell on the Axis troops, doing enormous damage. By late afternoon the British had broken through the German line south of Kidney ridge. Their attack was aided greatly by RAF fighter-bombers and fighters, which attacked the Afrika Korps troops again and again.

At sea the British were sinking the Italian supply ships.

"We shall lose this battle unless the supply situation improves at once," Rommel informed Hitler that night. Hitler did not reply.

On October 27 Rommel had so little fuel that he could not use his tanks as a unit. He had to commit them in small groups. The Ninetieth Light Infantry Division again recaptured Kidney ridge from the British, but the British bombed and bombarded the position. Three times in fifteen minutes bombers hit the assembled German and Italian troops at Miteirya Ridge and broke up that attack. The German armor also tried an attack, but it was driven back by intense British artillery fire.

That night Rommel again sent messages to Rome and to Hitler, pleading for help. Again there were no replies.

On October 28 the British resumed the attack. They had not yet committed all their forces. The Italians now brought some fuel to Africa, but they discharged it at Benghazi, 600 miles behind the front. The battle would be over before the fuel arrived. That night Rommel decided that he would have to withdraw or the British would be upon him.

Toward noon on October 29 Rommel learned that the last tanker on which he had relied had been sunk. The main British armored attack had not yet come. By October 31 Rommel had withdrawn to Sidi abd el Rahman. On the night of November 1 the British launched an enormous barrage on Rommel's main defense area, and night bombers softened up the lines of troops. That night the British armor and infantry attacked and broke through the Axis lines. The German ammunition and fuel situations were desperate. Rommel sent his aide de camp to see Hitler. The general instructed his aide:

> Explain our situation clearly to the Führer and suggest that the African theater of operations is probably lost to us. Ask for complete freedom of action for the Panzer Army.

The aide flew off. Rommel went to the front. He returned to headquarters at about noon. There was a message from Hitler:

> I and the German people are watching the heroic defensive battle waged in Egypt, with faithful trust in your powers of leadership and in the bravery of the German-Italian troops under your command. In the situation in which you now find yourself, there can be no other consideration save that of holding fast, of not retreating one step, of throwing every gun and every man into the battle. Important air reinforcements are being transferred to the Commander in Chief, South, during these next few days. The Duce and the Commando Supremo will likewise

strain every sinew to insure that you are supplied with the means
to continue the battle. Despite his numerical superiority the enemy too will reach the end of his resources. It would not be the
first time in history that the stronger will has prevailed against
the stronger battalions of the enemy. You can show your troops
no other way than that which leads to victory or to death.

"What we needed was guns, fuel, planes," said Rommel. "What
we did not need was an order to hold fast."

And so the battle was lost. General von Thoma was captured.
Finally, when it was too late, Hitler agreed to withdrawal to the
Fuka position, which Rommel had wanted to do three days earlier.
And then, on November 8, the Americans landed in Morocco and
Algeria.

Rommel must have wondered what Reich Marshal Göring thought
about that.

20

STALINGRAD—II

By the time that General Zeitzler took over as chief of the General Staff of the army, the armies had advanced to Stalingrad and into the Caucasus, and there they were, virtually exhausted.

In September 1942 Army Group North under Field Marshal von Kuechler and Army Group Center under Field Marshal von Kluge were static. The Leningrad and Moscow areas had not figured in Hitler's summer plans. There were serious danger points at Lake Ladoga, northeast of Leningrad, and the Demyansk pocket, where the Germans were encircled except for a narrow corridor that connected them with the rear.

But the real trouble was in the south.

Northwest of Stalingrad, the left flank of Field Marshal von Weichs's Army Group B was guarded entirely by units from Germany's allies, and none of the German generals had any confidence in them. Furthermore, the distance between the Stalingrad army and the Caucasus army was so great that they could not be of any assistance to each other.

In Stalingrad the fighting continued, building by building, as the Russian defenses were strengthened.

After General Zeitzler took over, he studied the eastern situation and then reported to Hitler. He had found the following:

241

1. Too few German soldiers occupying too much territory.

2. The most dangerous sector of the front was the long flank line that stretched north from Stalingrad to the right flank of Army Group Center. It was held by Romanians, Hungarians, and Italians, none of whom could be considered to be reliable.

3. Each month, troop and equipment losses were exceeding replacements.

4. The Red Army was vastly improved in training and weapons.

5. The railroad situation was completely unsatisfactory. There were not enough trains to do the job.

Knowing what had been happening to other generals who raised their voices in criticism of anything at all, Zeitzler expected Hitler to erupt after he had presented the report. But Hitler was benign that day, and he merely chided Zeitzler for being too pessimistic:

> The German soldiers are outnumbered, but they are far superior in quality to the enemy. Our weapons are better, too. And in the near future we shall have new weapons that will be better still.

This statement seems to have marked Hitler's point of departure from reality in regard to the reliance he would begin to place upon superweapons. He had always been fond of military gadgetry, but that was a different matter. Now he was listening when inventors and promoters talked about rockets, new submarines, atomic weapons, and other devices that would bring the war to an abrupt end, in Germany's favor, of course.

By repeating his arguments many times in the next few weeks Zeitzler managed to convince Hitler that there was danger above Stalingrad. But what to do about it?

Zeitzler suggested that the Germans withdraw from Stalingrad for the time being, pulling in the endangered flank and thereby freeing many divisions that then could be employed in other threatened areas.

Hitler flatly refused to do this.

"Where the German soldier sets foot, he remains." Hitler had told that to his generals. He had told it to the Reichstag. So now he was entrapped by the idea.

"You may rest assured that no one will ever drive us away from Stalingrad," he said. Nothing could make him change his mind.

The second solution might be to stay in Stalingrad, but to make preparations for a rapid withdrawal if the military situation should deteriorate. But Hitler refused to act; he would "let the situation mature," he said.

The third possible approach called for the withdrawal of those unreliable foreign divisions from delicate sectors and for their replacement by German soldiers and plenty of reserves. There was the catch. The German forces were so overextended that Hitler did not have the men to move around. To put more Germans on the Stalingrad front would be to take them away from the north and central fronts, and Hitler would not do that.

So the status quo remained, growing more dangerous every day.

Hitler did create a small reserve, which was placed behind the threatened Stalingrad left flank. It consisted of a single panzer corps, one German and one Romanian armored division. The German division had no confidence in the Romanian division.

Small German units, such as antitank battalions, were mingled with the foreign divisions. This was done to stiffen the non-German resolve to fight.

To deceive the Russians, the Germans set up a whole campaign of the sort the British used so effectively in north Africa, with paper divisions and much radio traffic. But the Germans were not expert enough, and the Russians were not fooled. Stalin was preparing for his winter offensive, which was going to be an attack on the weak left flank of the Stalingrad line.

If German deception was poor, German intelligence at the army level was not. By mid-November Field Marshal von Kluge, opposite Moscow, and General von Paulus, in Stalingrad, knew that the Soviet attack was going to fall on the sector held by the Romanians.

Week after week Hitler repeated his orders: there was to be no cessation in the fighting in Stalingrad. The house-to-house struggle was to continue, no matter the cost. At the end of the month the situation had become so bad there that the last reserve, several combat engineer battalions, was flown to Stalingrad, where the troops were ordered to use "new storm tactics" to clear the city of the enemy. The battalions were wiped out in short order.

Back in Germany for a brief visit, Hitler made a speech that showed the manner of his thinking very clearly:

> I wished to reach the Volga at a certain point, near a certain city. That city happens to bear the name of Stalin himself. I wished to take that city; we do not make exaggerated claims, and I can now tell you that we have captured it. Only a very few small parts of it are not yet in our hands. Now people may ask: "Why does the army not advance faster?" But I do not wish to see a second Verdun, I prefer to reach my objectives by means of limited assaults. Time is of no importance.

This Hitler said just when time was running out for his Stalingrad army.

Then, in mid-November, the Russian winter joined the battle with one of those terrible snowstorms that seem to come out of nowhere, blanketing a green land with white.

On the morning of November 19, 1942, Stalin was ready with his offensive. It began with a heavy artillery bombardment of the whole Romanian front, northwest of Stalingrad.

Field Marshal von Kluge got ready to meet the storm.

Back at army headquarters General Zeitzler asked Hitler for permission to release Panzer Corps H, that single reserve unit, from its position in reserve. But Hitler was not in East Prussia just then; he was traveling to Munich accompanied by Keitel and Jodl. Zeitzler telephoned the special train. Hitler did not like the idea, but ultimately he let Zeitzler have the corps.

Now, from the Romanians, came a flood of contradictory reports, always the sign of panic. Finally Zeitzler ascertained that the Russians had broken through the Romanian line at two points. Panzer Corps H was rushed to the larger breakthrough to stem the Russian advance.

Almost hourly, Zeitzler kept Hitler informed of the progress of the battle. He suggested from the outset that the German Sixth Army

Hitler steps down from his Fokker airplane after a flight from Berchtesgaden to Berlin. *(AP/ Wide World Photos.)*

Hitler and Eva Braun, with her terrier and his dog Blondi, at the Eagle's Nest in Bavaria. *(The Bettmann Archive.)*

Field Marshal Albert
Kesselring (seated) and
General Heydrich of his
Luftwaffe staff in
Italy. *(UPI/Bettmann
Newsphotos.)*

Vidkun Quisling, the
Norwegian politician
who became a Nazi
collaborator and
added a new word
for traitor to the
English language.
(The Bettmann Archive.)

Hitler's nemesis, General Georgi Zhukov of the Red Army. *(AP/Wide World Photos.)*

Himmler with his aide, Reinhardt Heydrich, who became the "protector" of Bohemia. *(AP/Wide World Photos.)*

French Prime Minister Edouard Daladier and British Foreign Secretary Anthony Eden in 1938. *(AP/Wide World Photos.)*

Hitler with Marshal Pétain of France. *(UPI/Bettmann Newsphotos.)*

Hitler's moment of triumph at the Eiffel Tower after the fall of France.
(AP/Wide World Photos.)

Hitler inspects a French tank destroyed in the blitzkrieg of 1940.   *(AP/Wide World Photos.)*

Hitler appeals to Britain for peace in 1940.
(UPI/Bettmann Newsphotos.)

Hitler greets General Harold Ohquist of Finland at his headquarters in East Prussia. They are flanked by General Keitel, left, and Foreign Minister von Ribbentrop. *(The Bettmann Archive.)*

Colonel General Ewald von Kleist visits Hungarian allies. *(AP/Wide World Photos.)*

General Guderian talks with tank crew members. *(AP/Wide World Photos.)*

Hitler, back to camera, talks to Field Marshal Karl Rudolf Gerd von Rundstedt. *(AP/Wide World Photos.)*

Field Marshal Erwin Rommel at Tobruk with Italian officers after the capture of the city. *(AP/Wide World Photos.)*

Hitler and his generals: from left, von Manstein, Ruff, Zeitzler, and von Kleist. *(AP/Wide World Photos.)*

Admiral Karl Dönitz.
(AP/Wide World Photos.)

Reichsmarschal Hermann Göring with Lieutenant Commander Günther Prien after Prien's spectacular sinking of a battleship in Scapa Flow, the British fleet base. *(AP/Wide World Photos.)*

Admiral Erich Raeder in 1928. *(The Bettmann Archive.)*

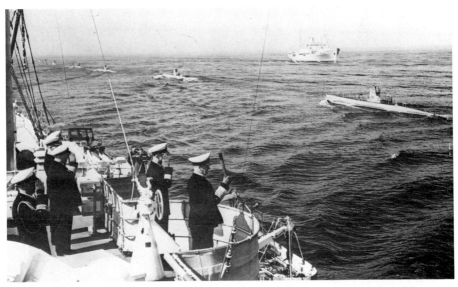

Admiral Erich Raeder and Admiral Dönitz inspect the newest in submarines. *(UPI/Bettmann Newsphotos.)*

Field Marshal Rommel with his staff at the Atlantic sea wall in 1944.   *(UPI/Bettmann Newsphotos.)*

Marshal Pietro Badoglio of Italy in three poses.   *(AP/Wide World Photos.)*

Hitler, Field Marshal Hermann Göring, and Propaganda Minister Dr. Josef Goebbels during the singing of the national anthem. *(UPI/Bettmann Newsphotos.)*

An aircrewman and General Heinz Guderian on a flight over the eastern front. *(AP/Wide World Photos.)*

Ready for the invasion: top, von Rundstedt and staff; and, bottom, Rommel and line officers. *(AP/Wide World Photos.)*

Field Marshal Rommel, left, and Field Marshal von Rundstedt, right, during a pre-invasion inspection of Atlantic Wall defenses. *(AP/Wide World Photos.)*

After the bomb plot of July 20, 1944, failed, here are Mussolini, Martin Bormann, Admiral Dönitz, Hitler, Göring, Otto Skorzeny, who rescued Mussolini after Italy surrendered and Il Duce was imprisoned by the Italians, and Air General Loerzer. *(UPI/Bettmann Newsphotos.)*

Hitler in his study in 1935.   *(UPI/Bettmann Newsphotos.)*

now be withdrawn from Stalingrad, while there was yet time. The front was going to be rolled back.

Hitler insisted that Panzer Corps H was going to win the battle for him. Zeitzler replied that Panzer Corps H could, at best, slow the Russian advance. There was no way, without many more German troops, that the advance could be stopped.

Hitler lost his temper over the telephone and began to berate his army chief of staff.

Zeitzler turned from the telephone to his reports. The Russian breakthroughs were growing larger. Soviet tanks were deep in the rear of the Romanians. Panzer Corps H was attacked by the Red Army tanks before it could launch its own attack.

The weather grew worse, blinding snow, frigid cold, and the Germans were hampered by roads clogged with fleeing Romanians.

Zeitzler telephoned Hitler again. He told him that Panzer Corps H was about to become fully embroiled and could be considered as good as lost. He again asked to remove the Sixth Army from Stalingrad. The Sixth Army could wheel about, move behind its own lines, and roust the Russians.

Hitler rejected the idea out of hand.

"Where the German soldier sets foot..."

But even to Hitler it was becoming apparent that there was serious trouble. He had his train's westward journey stopped. The train was turned about, and Hitler, Keitel, and Jodl headed back to Rastenburg.

Zeitzler said "good," he would be glad to see them, but Hitler said he would not see the army chief of staff until noon the following day, although the train would arrive at Rastenburg at midnight. Zeitzler was aghast; the armies were in battle, and Hitler was acting as though it were a tea party. He showed up at OKW headquarters at midnight. Hitler was furious at being interrupted, but he put on a smile, greeted Zeitzler with hand outstretched, and reminded him that they must remember Frederick the Great. Of course, this was another reference to the stand-fast policy.

Zeitzler brought out his maps. He showed Hitler that if they did not move the Sixth Army from Stalingrad, it was going to be encircled. This was his own judgment, but it was backed by Marshal von Weichs and the field marshal's chief of staff, General Georg von Sodenstern.

Generals and their opinions! Hitler raged. No, he wanted to transfer a single panzer division from the Caucasus to reinforce the Sixth Army.

This would take two weeks, said Zeitzler. The situation would not wait two weeks.

"In that case we shall bring up two divisions," said Hitler.

"By the time they would arrive, Sixth Army will be encircled," said Zeitzler.

Hitler lost his temper again.

Zeitzler repeated his earlier idea: "You must immediately order the Stalingrad army to turn about and attack westwards. This will save it from encirclement, will inflict great damage on the Russian armies that have broken through..."

Hitler crashed his fist onto the table. "I won't leave the Volga. I won't go back from the Volga."

And that was the end of the meeting. Nothing had been decided.

General Zeitzler went back to his quarters and went to bed for the night. When he got to his office the next morning, there was bad news.

On November 20 the Russians had launched their second attack, this one south of Stalingrad. Once more they chose to hit the Romanians. They broke through. Now the threat of encirclement of the Sixth Army was real and immediate. It was only a question of hours before the two Soviet pincers would meet. The services of supply troops in the rear were no match for the Red Army assault divisions.

The counterattack by Panzer Corps H was destined to fail, and the generals knew it before it ever began, but Hitler would not listen to reason. The Romanian armored division had never seen action and was equipped entirely with captured Russian tanks, most of them outdated. The German Twenty-second Panzer division was understrength. And coming at them were hundreds of new Russian tanks. Of course, the counterattack failed.

When Hitler learned of it, he turned to Field Marshal Keitel. "Send for the corps commander," he shouted. "Tear off his epaulets and throw him into jail. It's all his fault."

*   *   *

All day long General Zeitzler tried to convince Hitler that he should let the Sixth Army fight its way out of Stalingrad. The more he argued the more stubborn Hitler became. General Zeitzler believed his Führer had been persuaded to this position by Keitel and Jodl, but he was wrong. Here is what Keitel had to say on the subject:

> When the [Russian] counter-offensive began in November, perfectly positioned from the strategic viewpoint, first bowling over the [Third] Rumanian Army and thereby opening up deep into the flank of the Sixth Army, and when it was then on the point of surrounding von Paulus' army in Stalingrad, only one decision could possibly have staved off disaster: giving up Stalingrad and using the entire Stalingrad army to fight its way out to the west.
>
> I am in no doubt whatever that that would have worked out, that the Sixth Army would have been saved and the Russians probably defeated—admittedly at the cost of giving up Stalingrad and our position on the bank of the Volga.

So the generals suspected one another, and their combined suspicions were played upon by Hitler to support whatever position he wished to uphold.

On the evening of November 22, the third day of the battle, General von Paulus sent a message to OKW that his army was surrounded. The pincers had met. Hitler replied by radio: he ordered the commander and his staff to move to Stalingrad, and the Sixth Army to take a defensive hedgehog stance.

The Russians, who were now familiar with Hitler's stand-fast tactics, decided that they would not try to rush Stalingrad, but instead would prevent the Germans from breaking through to relieve the city. And so in late November and in December, the Russians pressed relentlessly against the whole German line, moving it steadily westward, away from Stalingrad, leaving the whole Sixth Army entrapped in that pocket.

Hitler seemed to relish the whole struggle. "The forces of the Sixth Army encircled at Stalingrad will be known as the troops of Fortress Stalingrad," he announced to the world from OKW headquarters.

This polemic was of a piece with his advice to Rommel on the eve of the battle of El Alamein, a bit of rhetorical propaganda that was supposed to do what his armies could not. He wanted to persuade the world and the Russians that Stalingrad was a real fortress, not just an army of Germans encircled in a city. It may have convinced the German people, or some of them, but it did not convince the Soviet generals—or the German generals.

The encircled area was 25 miles from east to west, and 12 miles from north to south. The steppe countryside was wide open with virtually no cover. Its eastern boundary was the right bank of the Volga. Inside were twenty German divisions and two Romanian divisions, plus services of supply troops, and some Luftwaffe troops. Stocks of ammunition and food were low. Altogether there were about 300,000 men in the pocket, and they were not going to be able to last very long without relief. The only means of communication were radio and airplane, for there were three airfields within the pocket.

Outside, at OKW and at army group headquarters, everyone waited for Hitler to change his mind and agree to let the Sixth Army fight its way out. General Zeitzler fought the battle every day with Hitler. Finally Hitler agreed that relief of the army was impossible at that point.

Then Hitler called in Keitel and Jodl. According to General Zeitzler, both Keitel and Jodl played Pollyanna to Hitler's opinions (a charge also levied by others against these two officers). According to Keitel's memoirs, written just before he was hanged in October 1946, Keitel believed and said that the whole Stalingrad operation was a grievous error, one which he opposed. In any event, the responsibility had to be Hitler's, and he flatly refused to bring the Sixth Army out of Stalingrad.

"I will not leave the Volga" became his battle cry.

21

DEFEAT IN THE
DESERT

In Africa Field Marshal Rommel's position was desperate. After El Alamein, not a single convoy reached the Libyan ports. The only supplies Rommel got came in by air, submarine, destroyer, or the occasional lone steamer that somehow escaped the RAF search planes or the Royal Navy's sharp eyes.

The Allies now had all the advantages. The American supply train was enormous; it served the British direct from American ports, as well as serving the American army that had just landed in Morocco and Algeria in November 1942. Not only was the British Eighth Army well supplied, but it was also an extremely efficient fighting force. "The Desert Rats," the troops were called. They had learned their trade the hard way, during the days when Field Marshal Kesselring's Stukas and ME-110s had total control of the air above the African battle zone, when Rommel's sleek tanks were more powerful and faster than those of the British. They had come through adversity, these Englishmen, Australians, New Zealanders, South Africans, Highlanders, and Indians. They had fought when the odds were against them, and now the odds had been reversed.

Neither the Germans nor the British had a great deal of use for the American soldiers. "The Amis," as the French and Germans called them, were a totally untried commodity. There was a good deal of British resentment over the selection of General Dwight D.

Eisenhower, an American, to be overall commander of the Allied southern theater, but it had to be swallowed if the British wanted American help. It was not a question of President Roosevelt's ego, but of the ego of the American people and the American military, whose basic distrust of the British went back to the American Revolution and the War of 1812.

The arrival of the Americans did not catch Rommel by surprise. He had known they were coming and he had tried to warn OKW in Rastenburg. That was the occasion on which Reich Marshal Göring had been so sarcastic about American abilities. But Göring was not alone. The feeling was shared by many very senior British officers. It was to be one of the real difficulties of the Anglo-American alliance.

But that did not help Rommel. Even from the eastern front it was possible in November 1942 to see that Rommel was now caught between two fires, the British on the east and the Americans on the west. Earlier, Rommel had warned Hitler that the Afrika Korps was finished and that all he could hope to do was to extricate it from Africa to fight again in Europe. Hitler's attitude hadn't changed. After all, "German soldiers had put their feet down in Africa, and..."

The American landings in French north Africa accomplished almost what the Allies wanted and what the Germans had feared. After the fall of France in 1940, the country had been partitioned. A French government was established at Vichy to govern the south and central areas, which were not essential for total German occupation. This government also controlled the French colonies in north Africa. The Vichy French there fought a little; but then, no longer so sure that the Germans were going to win the war, they turned around and embraced the western Allies once again. Hitler was forced then to take over unoccupied France or see it turn around to the Allies as well. What remained of the French army in Europe was now totally disarmed. The colonial army in Africa went over to the Allies.

The western Allies had missed one bet, and that gave Rommel a new lifeline of a sort. The Americans and British had not seized Tunisia, which they might have, and by failing to do that they had left the Germans some north African territory in which to maneuver. On November 11, 1942, the day that the French stopped their hostilities against the Americans in north Africa, there was enormous activity at the Luftwaffe bases in Naples and Trapani. Junkers 52 transports began taking off, one after the other. They were carrying all the German troops that Marshal Kesselring could muster, and their purpose was to dash to Tunis to capture that forgotten place before the Americans remembered it was there. This first contingent was one of the best fighting forces Germany had: Parachute Regiment No. 5. It had been scheduled to invade Malta, before that operation was called off.

Forty transport planes flew the regiment across the Mediterranean to Africa. At Tunis they landed—no one had to jump—and they looked around. The airfield was already crowded with German aircraft: Stuka dive-bombers and ME-110 fighter planes.

In Italy, in a matter of hours, Field Marshal Kesselring rounded up all the German fighting troops within call and all the mechanized equipment he could find. General Walther Nehring just happened to be in Italy. One of Rommel's best officers, he had been wounded by a British mine in August and had come back to Italy for treatment. He was just about ready to go back to Rommel when Kesselring intercepted him. Nehring, said the field marshal, was to fly immediately to Tunis and take command of the Ninetieth Army Corps.

And what, pray tell, asked General Nehring, was Ninetieth Army Corps? No such unit existed in the German army order of battle.

That was true, said Kesselring, because the Führer had just invented the Ninetieth Corps.

General Nehring flew to Tunis. There he discovered that the Ninetieth Army Corps did not exist except in Hitler's mind, where so many other wonderful weapons existed these days. It consisted of the paratroopers at Tunis and a handful of parachute engineers and a few soldiers landed from the sea. Nehring's command car would be a commandeered French taxicab. His communications depended on the French telephone service.

But by the end of the first week Nehring had captured Tunis and Bizerte and had disarmed the French, rounded up all the foreigners and all the Allied sympathizers, and was preparing to attack the Americans, who were advancing from the west. There were 5000 German troops in Tunisia by this time.

In the last week of November, the new German unit came up against the Americans. The First Battalion of the U.S. First Armored Division was trying to move toward Bizerte under the overall command of the British Seventy-eighth Division. The Americans had M-3

Stuart ("Honey") tanks, armed with 37-millimeter guns. These tanks were also armed with machine guns. But in the first Stuka bombing attack the Americans learned that their machine guns vibrated so badly that they worked loose every fifth or sixth bullet, and then the guns would jam as the empty belt sections went through. The Americans won first blood against the Germans. They came upon a German airfield and the tanks rushed through it, destroying scores of Stukas and fighter planes. But on Thanksgiving Day they met the German Mark IV tank for the first time. The 37-millimeter guns of the Honey tanks fired, but the shells bounced off the German armor.

The Germans could hardly wait to meet the Americans in force.

The first major encounter came at a spot named "Longstop Hill" by the British. It overlooked the Tunisian plain. The British tried to take it from the Germans, and the American First Armored Division helped. But they failed. The next event pitted the Germans against the American Second Corps, which included most of the First Armored Division. By this time, Hitler had reinforced the Tunisian area as much as he could. Colonel General Jürgen von Arnim succeeded General Nehring in command of what Hitler now named the Fifth Panzer Army. And, because it was closer and easier to reach from Italy, Tunisia was getting almost all the help from von Kesselring in Italy while Rommel was getting virtually nothing.

On the last day of November, Rommel flew to Rastenburg to see Hitler again. Reich Marshal Göring was with Hitler at the time, and the two top Nazis, as was their habit, placed the full blame for the failure at El Alamein on the local commander. This time it was Rommel. He had run away from the battle, they charged. They paid no attention to the fact that he had run out of fuel because of Hitler's failure to supply him, that he had run out of tanks because Hitler had not lived up to his promise to deliver more, that he had run out of ammunition because Göring's Luftwaffe had not provided it, and he had run out of air support because Göring's planes were not up to that challenge either.

Rommel finally became angry enough to speak his mind; he told Hitler that the Germans were finished in Africa. Unless they moved their forces out of north Africa they would lose them, and the Americans would begin moving up the Italian boot.

As usual when confronted with facts and frank opinions contrary to his own, Hitler lost his temper completely. He rose, screaming.

"Field Marshal," he shouted, "I don't want to hear any more of that kind of nonsense from your mouth! North Africa will be defended like Stalingrad is being defended. Eisenhower's invasion army must be destroyed at Italy's door, not in the Sicilian living room."

"Fine," Rommel said. Then let Hitler and Göring provide him with the men, tanks, fuel, ammunition, and air support to do it. Instead, Hitler provided him with a new title: supreme commander, German-Italian Panzer Army.

Hitler did not deign to reply to his demand: "North Africa will be defended. This is an order."

So Rommel flew back to Africa with empty hands, told to defend to the last man, but knowing there would be no fuel, no ammunition, no tanks, and no air support. "It would need a miracle for us to hold on much longer," he wrote to his wife. "What is to happen to us now lies in God's hands. We will go on fighting as long as it is at all possible."

And then Hitler compounded the insults. He took away the Twenty-first Panzer Division, one of Rommel's best, and gave it to von Arnim.

In January General von Arnim's army in Tunisia had enjoyed considerable success in limited actions against the Americans. The Germans had encountered the American 168th Infantry Regiment and had knocked it apart, capturing more than 600 prisoners. After interrogating the Americans in some depth to find out what sort of soldiers they were, the German intelligence officers came to the conclusion that they were pretty soft. The Americans were not politically indoctrinated, said their report. They did not know what they were fighting for except such things as "Mom's apple pie." They knew virtually nothing about the geography and politics of Europe. Most of them did not like their British allies. In a crisis their morale should disintegrate rapidly.

Field Marshal von Kesselring read this report with unusual interest. He had the overall responsibility for victory in Africa, and he knew how Hitler felt about the matter. Now he had not one but two Allied armies to combat. The best course was to take on one of them and whip it soundly. The best bet was the Americans.

*

On February 9, 1943, von Kesselring called together General von
Arnim and Field Marshal Rommel. They met at the Luftwaffe base
at Rennouch, Tunisia. The subject was the attack to be made on
the Americans.

The senior intelligence officer of the Twenty-first Panzer Division made a report. Most important to von Kesselring was the fact
that the GIs were badly led. Indeed, the French and British continued to refer to the Americans as "our Italians."

Then Kesselring outlined his plan. The Americans had pulled
back to Sbeitla and Kasserine in southwestern Tunisia, near the Al-
gerian border. Rommel would attack the Americans in the south,
near the town of Gafsa. Von Arnim would attack in the Sbeitla area, in the north. Once the Panzer divisions had swept through the
mountain passes, they would head for the port of Bône in Algeria.
This movement would eliminate the American threat to the Afrika
Korps flank, and it would give Hitler a victory.

But the two German commanders knew there wasn't enough fuel
to do what Kesselring asked. What they could do was inflict such
heavy damage on the Americans and the French that they would be
paralyzed. Perhaps they would even capture enough fuel to change
the odds.

So the attack date was set for February 14.

The British knew the attack was coming. Messages derived from
the German Enigma coding machine, and picked up and translated
in England, told all about it except where.

That became clear at 4 a.m. on February 14, Valentine's Day. The
shooting started on the road between Faid and Lesouda. The Tiger
tanks of the German Tenth Panzer Division led the way, 60-ton tanks
moving through Faid Pass, driving the Americans ahead of them. The
Americans sent forth their Honey tanks with the 37-millimeter guns.
The 75- and 88-millimeter guns of the German armor knocked the American tanks apart in no time. Then in came von Kesselring's Messerschmitt fighters to strafe the American infantry. The Americans sent
in their heavier Sherman tanks. But the Sherman tank had a fatal weakness, and the Germans had already discovered it in the few days since

the Americans had been in action. The Sherman's fuel tank (the vehicle burned gasoline, not diesel fuel) was located just off the rear sprocket of the track. The American tankers called the tank "the Ronson" after a cigarette lighter, because a shell glancing off the sprocket would smash the gasoline container and turn the Sherman into a blazing torch. So the German gunners aimed and fired, and one by one the Sherman tanks were incinerated.

The 168th Infantry was hit again by the Germans. This time a whole battalion, 600 men, was cut off and had to try to make its way through the German lines. Not all of the Americans made it, by far.

So the Germans came rushing up Kasserine Pass, having inflicted a dreadful defeat on the Americans. Between Faid Pass and the crossroads on the Sbeitla road lay forty-four American tanks, fifty-nine half-tracks, twenty-six field guns, and twenty-two trucks, abandoned by the Americans.

On the second day of the battle of Kasserine Pass Rommel's troops moved into Gafsa. They did not have to fight for it. British General Sir Keith Anderson's First Army had evacuated. Rommel then planned to move on to the northeast to Thelepte and Kasserine, where he would join up with von Arnim. The British, seeing what was happening in the pass country, sent 10,000 troops to support the sagging Americans. But the Germans were on the move. They passed an abandoned American airfield and counted sixty American aircraft. They captured six American half-tracks. And they could see Kasserine Pass ahead of them. They made the heights, and there below them was the 10-mile-wide Kasserine valley. Rommel had come to the point of departure at which the Germans could wipe out the Americans.

But General von Arnim did not send his three panzer divisions to link up with Rommel. So Rommel radioed von Kesselring, and before he was finished with the messages, he, Rommel, was in command of the Tenth and Twenty-first Panzer Divisions again. He ordered an all-out attack on Kasserine Pass.

But there was one aspect of the American army about which the Germans knew very little—the artillery. American artillery was the best in the world, and the men who used it knew what they were doing. In the end, the German advance at Kasserine, having run through the armored forces and the infantry, was stopped by the

American artillery and the British armored corps and infantry. And then, on the other side, General Montgomery began an attack against Rommel's Mareth defense line, forcing the German field marshal to abandon the assault on the Americans and rush eastward to save the situation.

Two weeks later Rommel was again in Germany, back in the sanatorium, undergoing medical treatment for his fever. Why he was recalled just then is not quite clear. In the February conference Field Marshal von Kesselring had given Rommel complete command of German troops in Africa for this new attack on the Americans, but then he had privately told General von Arnim that after the Kasserine Pass battle, he would send Rommel back to Germany and that von Arnim would take command. Another story has it that after the British and Americans began to move their pincers against Tunisia, Hitler saw the coming results and ordered Rommel back to Germany so that he would not be captured by the Allies, since "the Desert Fox," as he had come to be known, was Germany's most popular military commander.

Whatever the reason, Rommel did get out of Africa that winter of 1943 and he did go back into the sanatorium for treatment of ailments that were real.

The Americans reshuffled their commands, brought in fighting generals named George S. Patton, Jr., and Omar Bradley, and brought in ever more troops, equipment, guns, planes—more everything. In the spring, the inevitable happened, just as Rommel had told Hitler it would. After several losses even Hitler could see the signs, and on May 8, 1943, he ordered Africa abandoned.

But he was too late. Bradley's American Second Corps and Montgomery's Eighth Army drove on into Tunisia, toward Tunis (British) and Bizerte (American). They forced the German and Italian soldiers to the shores of the Mediterranean, capturing 150,000 prisoners. All Africa was in Allied hands. The Sicilian narrows was now open to Allied shipping and closed to the Axis powers. The land war in western Europe was about to begin once again.

22

STALINGRAD—III

Shortly after the Russian pincers had enclosed more than a quarter of a million German soldiers in a vise at Stalingrad, General Zeitzler made another attempt to persuade Hitler to pull General von Paulus's Sixth Army out of the besieged city. The army had adequate stocks of food and ammunition then and was in good enough condition to fight its way out successfully.

At that time, Reich Marshal Göring was once again visiting OKW headquarters, a situation General Zeitzler knew would not help matters, since Göring's principal talent was his ability to play Pollyanna to Hitler.

Zeitzler suggested that they had to get the Sixth Army out very quickly, because it would soon run out of supplies and it would not be possible to supply the army by air.

"The Reich Marshal has assured me that it is possible," said Hitler.

"No," said Zeitzler. "It is not."

"Very well," said Hitler, "let him tell you himself."

He sent for Göring.

"Göring, can you keep the Sixth Army supplied by air?" Hitler asked.

Göring gave the Nazi salute, raising his right arm out in front of

him, and replied, "My Führer, I assure you that the Luftwaffe can
keep the Sixth Army supplied."

"The Luftwaffe certainly cannot," said Zeitzler.

"You are not in position to give an opinion on that subject,"
Göring shouted.

Zeitzler then turned to Hitler. "My Führer, may I ask the Reich
Marshal a question?"

"Yes."

"Herr Reich Marshal, do you know what tonnage has to be flown
in every day?"

"I don't, but my staff officers do."

Zeitzler then said that allowing for all the stocks at present in
the hands of the Sixth Army, and given minimal needs and opti-
mum flying conditions, the Luftwaffe would have to deliver 300 tons
a day. But flying conditions would not always be optimal, so on
every flying day the Luftwaffe would have to deliver 500 tons of
supplies to the Sixth Army.

"I can do that," said Göring.

Zeitzler lost his temper. "That is a lie," he said.

Whereupon the discussion degenerated until Zeitzler walked out
of the office.

The situation at Stalingrad was even more desperate than Zeitzler
had thought. Von Paulus radioed that he needed 750 tons of supply
each day if he was going to hold out.

What Göring did not know at that moment was that the Soviet
air force had just established air superiority over the region. Thus,
when the Luftwaffe began flying supplies into Stalingrad, the opposition in the air was intense. In the last days of November 1942
everyone waited. The next move was Stalin's.

Zeitzler kept count of the daily tonnages flown into Stalingrad
by the Luftwaffe: The first day: 110 tons; the second day: 120 tons;
then, sometimes, 140 tons, but never more than 140 tons—perhaps
a quarter of the tonnage needed by the Sixth Army—that's all there
ever was. Some days no supplies got in at all. So by the first of
December von Paulus's situation had deteriorated seriously.

One of Hitler's habitual moves when situations threatened to get
out of hand was to change the chain of command. Now he established

a new group of armies: "Army Group Don," he called it. It was located between Army Group A and Army Group B. Field Marshal von Manstein was appointed commander. His responsibility would be to relieve Stalingrad. To do it, he had the Fourth Panzer Army and the two Romanian armies.

Von Manstein realized from the beginning that he would be unable to make an attack into Stalingrad to relieve the Sixth Army. But the Führer would not want to hear that. Von Manstein would have all the troops he needed, Hitler said airily. But the troops did not come. Yet von Manstein planned an attack for the eighth or tenth of December, knowing that it was impossible to succeed with the forces at hand.

After a few days of watching the Luftwaffe's fumbling attempts to supply the Sixth Army, General Zeitzler again went to Hitler. But Göring had already been there with his excuses. In a few days it would all be different, he had told Hitler.

"The Reich Marshal is bringing in more planes," said Hitler. "The Reich Marshal is developing a better organization. The Reich Marshal has given me his word."

But every day the Russians advanced farther westward, capturing more of the airfields from which the supplies could be flown into Stalingrad. So the lines of communication grew longer and longer. Every day, too, more Luftwaffe planes were shot down.

"Operation Winter Gale" was the name given to the attempt to break through to Stalingrad. By the end of the first week of December the Germans were as ready as they would ever be. More troops had been brought in from Germany. General Hermann Hoth, commander of the Fourth Panzer Army, had some new equipment. He had three panzer divisions, up to strength, and a weak force of infantry to cover his flanks. He also had a battalion of the new Tiger tanks, yet untried in Russian winter conditions.

From the beginning, General Zeitzler knew the attempt was hopeless. The German force was not strong enough. The starting point was Kotelnikov, 60 miles from Stalingrad. This was the only vulnerable point in the Russian line. But if the Germans knew it, the Russians must know it too, and they might be pretending that this point was vulnerable, only to have placed behind it very strong forces.

The attack moved as scheduled on December 12. In the begin-ning, in spite of the below-zero weather, the Fourth Panzer Army advanced rapidly. On December 18 the army was only 40 miles from Stalingrad. On December 19 the troops reached the Myshkoa Riv-er, and on December 20 they crossed it. Stalingrad was only 30 miles away. At night the troops of the Sixth Army could see the signal flares sent up by their would-be rescuers.

On December 21, with Stalingrad less than 30 miles in the dis-tance, the German attack came to a halt. The Soviet resistance had increased, but this was not the real reason for the total stoppage. The troops were dead tired, and their supply line was much too long and too indefinite. The vehicles and the men just stopped. Despite a flood of exhortation from Hitler, they did not start up again. The attack had lost its momentum.

Again Zeitzler tried to persuade Hitler to order the Sixth Army to break out of Stalingrad. A week earlier Hitler had said he wanted to wait and see what the Fourth Army attack accomplished. Now he had seen: it had accomplished little. But Hitler did not view it that way. He was full of enthusiasm. He spoke of reaching Stalingrad and holding the whole Volga line. He seemed to believe that he was about to reestablish the front as it had been before the Russian of-fensive began.

When the attack stopped, Hitler said that it would be resumed the next day. But on December 22 the troops did not move. On De-cember 23 they did not move either. At the end of that day OKW called off the attack. It was not to be resumed.

Now General Zeitzler secured the help of Field Marshal von Man-stein to talk to Hitler. The Führer liked von Manstein. The field marshal had acquitted himself admirably on the eastern front in the battle for Leningrad. These two senior officers now tried again to persuade Hitler to break out the Sixth Army. It still could have been done, even at this late date, particularly since the Fourth Panzer Army was only 30 miles away.

Hitler began to vacillate. At one moment he would tell Zeitzler to draw up an order directing von Paulus to break out. The order would be drawn, but then Hitler would refuse to sign it.

He made impossible conditions. He told von Paulus that he could break out if he could guarantee to hold the line of the Volga. Von Paulus could not. Hitler then said that von Paulus could break out if he could guarantee that all the men and all their weapons would get through to safety. No one could guarantee that, so the discussion was again closed.

From Stalingrad now began to come tales of misery and hopelessness. The troops had lost confidence in Hitler and in the ability of OKW to rescue them.

Zeitzler decided to take Hitler to see for himself what was happening in the south. Hitler refused to go. Zeitzler suggested that a group of officers be flown out of Stalingrad to come to OKW headquarters. Hitler could interview them and decide for himself what was happening there and what the prospects were. Hitler refused.

Zeitzler took matters into his own hands. He ordered General Hans Hube to be flown out and brought to OKW headquarters. Hitler liked Hube and seemed to have some respect for his judgment. Zeitzler hoped Hube could persuade the Führer.

Hube came to headquarters, but before he saw Hitler, he spoke with Zeitzler. Could he tell Hitler the truth, Hube asked. The rumor in Stalingrad was that Hitler did not want to know the facts— that no one could tell him the truth.

Zeitzler protested that this was not so. But he warned Hube that if he told the truth, which he ought to do, he ran the risk of incurring Hitler's anger and possible military disgrace.

So General Hube went to see his Führer. Hitler was at his most charming. He described the difficulties of the eastern front in detail and explained why it was important that Stalingrad be held. Hube listened for half an hour, and finally he had his turn to talk. He described the Stalingrad situation succinctly.

Hitler was not moved. Hube grew excited, so excited that he suggested that because the airlift had failed, one of the Luftwaffe generals ought to be executed. Hitler did not like that, and Hube's cause was lost.

All that came out of the meeting was a demand by Hitler for the establishment of a special committee to control the Stalingrad airlift. But that accomplished nothing, because it was beyond the power of the Luftwaffe to supply the Sixth Army. It was apparent to most of the Luftwaffe officers that Göring had not known what he was talking about when he had made those promises to Hitler.

*

The weeks went on. The year ended. Army Group Don was forced back, away from Stalingrad. The Fourth Panzer Army was pushed back 30 miles, then 60 miles, from Stalingrad. Up north the Russians extended their winter offensive and overcame the Italians, who were fighting between the Romanians and the Hungarians there. The Hungarian army in the north was imperiled by a flanking movement.

As the Luftwaffe airlift into Stalingrad continued to fail, the rations of the troops in the "fortress" were cut once, then again, and again. The ration was below the minimum needed for men to survive for more than a few weeks.

The Russians did nothing. They maintained their tight circle around Stalingrad but sent no more than a few patrols against the German lines.

At OKW headquarters General Zeitzler made sure that Hitler had every bit of negative information about developments at Stalingrad. Hitler now told anyone who would listen that he had been right all along, that it was important that the Sixth Army hold out at Stalingrad, and that, *as long as they could,* they were keeping large formations of Soviet troops occupied.

As long as they could...Even Hitler was beginning to see that the inevitable was now going to occur, although he would not directly admit it to anyone.

Zeitzler countered that argument. The Russians, he said, would leave only minimal forces around Stalingrad. They would not attack. They would wait, and ultimately the Sixth Army would be forced by starvation to surrender. Thus the Russians would get their quarter of a million prisoners and the Germans would have suffered a dreadful disastrous defeat, and it would be done without firing a shot. All those Russian troops Hitler spoke about could easily be used elsewhere.

At New Year's Hitler drafted a message saying that the Stalingrad troops would soon be relieved; he promised that, he said. Zeitzler refused to sign and forward the message, saying that it was untrue. Hitler's adjutant told Zeitzler he would report the failure to send the message, but Hitler never said a word about it. He sent the message through other channels.

Nor was Stalingrad the only disaster impending that winter. The success of the Russian winter offensive was also threatening the German line in the Caucasus. Army Group A in the Caucasian Mountains now came under threat, particularly after the failure of the Fourth Panzer Army move into Stalingrad.

The way the Russians were moving, it would not be long before they reached Rostov. Once they took that city, the Germans of Army Group A would be in real danger. Another encirclement was in the offing.

Secretly, General Zeitzler arranged with Army Group A to draw plans for the withdrawal of the Seventeenth Army and the First Panzer Army. The whole matter was concealed from Hitler, who undoubtedly would have stopped it.

Zeitzler then began pressing Hitler to withdraw the troops from the Caucasus. Hitler wavered, but at one point he authorized the withdrawal. Thereupon Zeitzler told Army Group A to put the plan into effect. It went like lightning. Later that same day Hitler reversed himself and decided against withdrawing the troops, but Zeitzler told him the orders had already gone out, and Hitler agreed to leave matters as they were. Thus, only by concealing matters from Hitler had Zeitzler saved two armies from the fate that was to face General von Paulus's Sixth Army.

On January 8, 1943, the Russians sent an officer with a white flag into Stalingrad. His mission was to demand the surrender of the German army. The long document he brought accurately detailed the difficulties of the Sixth Army, and the Soviet general promised that if the Germans surrendered, they would be sure of life, security, and their return to Germany or whatever country they came from at the end of the war. If they did not surrender, they would be annihilated, the Russian general promised. They must reply by 10 a.m. on January 9, 1943.

Von Paulus immediately sent the facts to Hitler and asked for freedom of action.

Hitler refused.

The Soviet deadline passed. Early on the morning of January 10 the Russian artillery began a barrage against the Stalingrad pocket. Two hours later the Russian infantry began the assault, supported by tanks. The fighting was fierce all day long. The Germans knocked out many tanks and fought very vigorously, but at the end of the day von Paulus had to report to OKW headquarters that the Soviets had broken through on the north, west, and south and that the Germans had been unable to close the gaps. In the next few days large areas of the pocket had to be abandoned without any orders from the Sixth Army. They simply could not be held.

On January 16 the pocket was 15 miles long and 9 miles deep, about half the size it was originally. The worst loss was that of Piomnik airfield, which had been the major supply link to the German rear.

On that same day the communiqués emanating from Hitler suddenly changed tone. For the first time he spoke of the serious difficulties and the attacks on all sides of Stalingrad. And every day from this point on Hitler reiterated his new catchword: "The Sixth Army is keeping strong Russian forces engaged and inflicting heavy casualties on them." It was as if this had all been planned by Hitler.

By January 16 supplies had stopped coming into Stalingrad, except in a trickle. Only one airstrip remained. The soldiers were fighting without hope. Every day some unit fired off the last of its ammunition and then destroyed its weapons. Truck drivers ran out of gas and then set fire to their trucks. There were no aid stations for the sick and wounded, no medicines, no bandages. The doctors had nothing to work with.

By January 24 the pocket was split in two. On that day the last plane took off from the pocket and flew west. Now the only supplies that came in were air-dropped, and just as often as they reached the Germans, they reached the surrounding Russians.

On January 24 the Russians again called on General von Paulus to surrender. Once again von Paulus radioed Hitler for permission. He described the plight of his exhausted troops. Further resistance was senseless, he said.

Once again Hitler refused. He radioed von Paulus that he must fight to the last man: "Congratulations...heroic defense...saving the Western World from the Bolsheviks..."

Von Paulus refused the Russian surrender offer. The fight went on.

In the north the Hungarians were attacked and defeated by the Russians. Farther north, the German Second Army was smashed.

In Stalingrad the end drew near. One division commander refused to obey von Paulus's orders and surrendered his division. A

Romanian division surrendered. Junior officers and noncoms secured permission to try to work through the lines and head west.

Inside the pocket men died of cold and hunger as often as from fighting. On January 28 the pocket was further split into little groups. Von Paulus predicted to OKW that the end would come on February 1.

Hitler could have saved part of the force by ordering von Paulus out, even then. But he refused. Instead, he sent messages ordering medals for the besieged.

On January 31 von Paulus radioed OKW that the final collapse could be expected within twenty-four hours. That day Hitler promoted von Paulus to field marshal, a final attempt to stiffen the general's resolve, since no German field marshal had ever surrendered since the Reich's unification under Bismarck. But the pocket was now divided into three pieces. One by one that day they surrendered, each sending a last message before it fell.

"Long live Germany," said Field Marshal von Paulus's radio.

And then the radio was silent.

23

THUNDER IN
THE WEST

On February 2, 1943, Hitler met with his generals and the rest of his staff in the situation room of OKW headquarters at Rastenburg. Field Marshal von Paulus and his Sixth Army had just surrendered. So Stalingrad no longer appeared on the map. The conference turned to a new problem, the possibility of withdrawal from the Donetz basin, where the Russians were threatening.

Hitler turned back to Stalingrad, however. He was particularly angry with von Paulus. All day long the German-language Soviet radio broadcasts beamed toward Berlin had been trumpeting the news of the surrender of von Paulus and his army. Hitler accused the field marshal of ingratitude, treason, and cowardice. General Jodl chimed in. He wondered if von Paulus had really been captured or if it was simply a Soviet propaganda trick.

"No," said Hitler. "I am sure he surrendered. How can one be so cowardly?"

Jodl said again that he doubted the story.

"Sorry," said Hitler, "but I don't. You know I don't believe in those wounds that Paulus was supposed to have received either. That doesn't seem to fit. What hurts me most personally is that I promoted him to field marshal. That's the last field marshal I shall appoint in this war."

He went on rambling. He wondered why von Paulus had not

committed suicide: "He could have freed himself from all sorrow and ascended into eternity and national immortality, but he prefers to go to Moscow."

He predicted that soon the captured German generals would be making anti-Nazi propaganda broadcasts over the Russian radio. (A few months later von Paulus and others were doing just that.)

In the winter of 1943 Hitler was interested in seeing how the Tiger tank would respond in the severe Russian climate. So he ordered a demonstration. The place chosen was a bit of no-man's-land, a long road, between the Soviet and German armies. Six Tiger tanks moved out onto the road. The Russians let them all go well out onto the road, and then they targeted the front and rear tanks and stopped them dead in their tracks with armor-piercing shells. So the four tanks in the middle were stopped too, unable to maneuver. One by one the Russian antitank gunners picked them off.

The next day, General Zeitzler related the incident in the situation meeting. Hitler did not bat an eye. But he did not mention the Tiger tank again for a while.

Stalingrad was the turning point. It was the culmination of Hitler's grievous error in attacking the Soviet Union in the first place.

One day, on the way to Munich, as Hitler's private train was stopped on a siding so that the telephone system could be hooked into the radio telegraph system to send the latest batch of messages from the Führer, a German troop train, consisting almost entirely of boxcars, came up and stopped on the siding next to it. Hitler was in his rosewood paneled dining car, sitting at a table with fresh white linen and gleaming silver. The soldiers began pouring out of the boxcar, wounded men, bandaged and in rags, skinny, hungry-looking men with cracked boots and wrinkled greatcoats. Hitler took one look and ordered the shades pulled down. This was the leader who had told his generals in Poland that he would not come to their victory party because he ate only at field kitchens when he was with the soldiers in the field.

Every day at noon, no matter where he was—and that might be Rastenburg, or the Reich Chancellery in Berlin, or the Berghof—

Hitler held a conference. He sat down in a plain armchair and his officers and toadies clustered around him and the map table. When Göring was there, Hitler had a special stool brought in; because the fat Reich marshal was getting more and more corpulent as the war went to his nerves, Göring found it hard to sit down anymore.

The maps came out. First was the map of the eastern front, which in the early summer of 1943 showed the Soviets getting ready for a new offensive. Starting at the top, on the Leningrad front, Hitler listened as the day's activity was read off to him. He wanted to know about every patrol, every act. Nothing was too detailed for him, no part of the "big picture" was too vast.

Hitler had already embarked on several disastrous policies. In defiance of the generals, he had built up the SS until it had a life of its own. His appointment of Hermann Göring as Reich marshal, economic czar, and minister of aviation had proved to be the undoing of the German Luftwaffe, which was now in deep trouble and would never recover. Göring had made a hash of the aircraft industry. Not enough aircraft were being produced, and Germany did not have a heavy bomber comparable to the U.S. B-17 or the British Lancaster. It was too late. Germany never would have a heavy bomber now.

The Russians had completely revamped their air force, producing the MiG-1 and the Yak series of fighters. In the west the trusty Spitfire was still very useful for short-range work, but the Americans were providing the best fighter aircraft, the P-47, designed as a high-altitude fighter but discovered to be a natural antitank weapon in low-level attacks because of its 75-millimeter cannon. For high-altitude work the Americans delivered to Europe the P-51 Mustang and the P-38 Lightning twin-engined interceptor.

The Germans still depended on the ME-110 and the ME-190. They were developing the ME-210, but it was a messy process, again because of Hitler's mistake in letting Göring take charge of something about which he knew virtually nothing. The German armies east and west were already feeling the pinch that went with loss of control of the air above the fighting fronts.

The Luftwaffe now was concentrating its efforts on protection of German cities, for the heavy bombing of Germany had begun.

*

At home in the Reich, the war was being seen by the German people with different eyes. It had begun so nicely, with one victory after another. But by the summer of 1943 virtually every family had lost someone near and dear to them. Food was rationed. Coffee was virtually something out of the past. Few people were giving away any more clothing for the eastern front; they were keeping it to wear themselves. The Allied air attacks against Fortress Europe, and particularly against the German cities, were becoming more and more frightening.

On June 10 the western Allies came up with a new bombing policy designed to cripple Hitler's war effort. The British would bomb strategic city areas of Germany by night, and the Americans would bomb by day. On the eleventh of June 168 American heavy bombers flew to Wilhelmshaven to blast the U-boat yards there. Or they tried to. It was not a successful raid because the Americans did not have fighter escort; the German fighters kept most of the bombers away from the target. The Americans had the same trouble on June 13, when their B-17s bombed Bremen and they lost 26 of the 102 bombers. The answer at that time, until the new American fighters could be brought into play in force, was the conversion of some B-17s into "flying fortresses." This was done by modifying the aircraft to carry many more machine guns. The result, the YKB-40, was indeed a flying fortress and deserved the name. Meanwhile, the British night bombing was more effective than the American daytime efforts, but both were giving the Germans a taste of the terrors the British populace had suffered.

At Hitler's headquarters all sorts of new problems were beginning to bedevil the OKW staff. Admiral Dönitz was complaining bitterly because not enough submarines were being built. "Steel shortage," he was told. The eastern front was complaining, too, for the steel shortage made it impossible to build railroad cars any faster, the officers were told. Weapons and munitions that couldn't be transported to them were of no use at all.

With the collapse of the German and Italian forces in Africa in May 1943 it was apparent in Rome and Berlin that western Europe would be the next target of the Allies.

Mussolini was desperately unhappy. The enormous defeat in Africa had hurt the Italians much more than it did the Germans, in terms of casualties, loss of equipment, and, above all, loss of self-esteem.

The Italians had begun to hate the war and to hate their allies, the Germans. Mussolini was also a frightened man. He saw his empire slipping away from him. There were mass strikes in Milan and Turin that summer.

Il Duce was calling on Hitler to make peace with Stalin so that the Führer could send all of his armies to the western front to fight off the Americans and the British. Hitler and Mussolini met at Salzburg in April, but the results of the conference were inconclusive. Hitler deluged Mussolini with a waterfall of rhetoric crafted to convince the faltering Duce that the Axis was winning the war.

At this point Hitler was duped by a remarkable feat of British intelligence. The British dumped a corpse, dressed in a British officer's uniform, off the Spanish coast. The corpse was picked up by the Spaniards. It bore papers that indicated that the British invasion was going to hit Greece. The German ambassador in Madrid and German intelligence soon had all this information and passed it along to Hitler. He believed every bit of it. Marshal von Kesselring and Mussolini tried to tell him that it was a ruse, that Sicily was the objective, but Hitler refused to be convinced. So he shipped the First Panzer Division to Greece to support three German infantry divisions which were doing nothing but enjoying themselves and which could easily have gone to Sicily. Another panzer division was sent to Sardinia to reinforce four Italian divisions. Two parachute divisions were sent to the south of France to watch for Allied landings there.

Hitler then traveled to Zaporozh'ye not far from the eastern front's Crimean line, and spent three days with General von Manstein there. Von Manstein had retaken Kharkov and Hitler was now talking about another offensive to go back to the Volga line.

Some of the senior officers were by now convinced that their Führer was perfectly mad. On March 13, 1943, the previously mentioned General von Tresckow and Colonel von Schlabrendorff arranged to place a bomb in a brandy bottle aboard the plane that would take Hitler from Smolensk back to Rastenburg. The bomb failed to go off.

On July 5 Hitler's new offensive against the Russians began. Seventeen panzer divisions started forward with Hitler's order of the day:

Soldiers of the Reich. This day you are about to take part in an offensive of such importance that the whole future of the war may depend on its outcome. More than anything else, your victory will show the whole world that resistance to the power of the German Army is hopeless.

Indeed, even many of the generals agreed this time. Hitler was right. A half million men were involved in this offensive, the cream of the German army, led by General Guderian, who had been restored to favor and ordered to produce a victory.

Then, on July 10, five days after Hitler started the summer offensive in the east, the British and Americans landed in Sicily. General Montgomery's well-tested Eighth Army was to be the key force in the invasion. The Eighth Army landed between Syracuse and the southeastern tip of the island. The American Seventh Army, led by General George Patton, was to have a secondary role, landing in the Gulf of Gela between Licata in the west and Scoglitti in the east. The Americans were to protect the flank of the British, but Patton so hated that role that he decided he would abandon it and race his allics to Messina, all the way across the island. When the two allied armies reached that point, they would control Sicily.

Montgomery moved steadily along the beaten track. He took Syracuse on July 11 and Augusta on July 12.

In this tense atmosphere, Hitler summoned Mussolini to another meeting. It occurred on July 19 at Feltre in northern Italy. Hitler did all the talking, as was usual for him these days. They met for five hours.

Il Duce was extremely depressed. Sicily was about to fall, he said. Then what?

Nonsense, said Hitler. They must fight on. Sicily could be held if Mussolini's men had the will to do it. Let them not give up. "Where the German soldier sets foot..."

And German panzer troops had set their feet on Sicily. Now they were fighting hard, Field Marshal von Kesselring reported. They would stop the Allies with Mussolini's help. He, Hitler, would send more German troops to Italy.

Admiral Dönitz had developed a startling new U-boat that was going to turn the war·around. The British would never know what had hit them at sea. (This was the Type XXI U-boat, equipped with snorkel, but it would be another year and a half before it would become operational.)

Mussolini's depression was not eased with a report of the first big Allied daylight air raid on Rome.

Il Duce left the meeting and went back to his capital, where he learned that terrible things were happening in Sicily. There he also found his Fascists in a rebellious mood, and they were joined by a revolutionary cabal led by no less a person than the king of Italy.

On July 22 Palermo fell to the Americans. The race for Messina was now on.

General Montgomery did not have so far to go, but he faced the very tough panzer divisions of von Kesselring's southern defense force. The field marshal had been ordered by Hitler not to give in, and he was doing his best, but the odds were impossible.

In Rome events moved with great speed. The Fascist Grand Council demanded restoration of a constitutional monarchy and return of the command of the armed forces to the king. Mussolini was out. The next evening, July 26, he was summoned to the royal palace by the king, arrested, and carted off to jail.

When Hitler learned of this turn of events, he was shocked. His first thought was to move into Italy, seize the rebels, and restore Mussolini to power. That very night Hitler fortified the Alpine passes. Field Marshal Rommel, now well again, who had fought the Italians in the Alps in World War I, was given command of Army Group B and told to defend the passes against all comers.

Hitler had big plans. He wanted to move into Italy in force, and Rommel was his man. A council of war was held on July 27, attended by Göring, Goebbels, Himmler, Rommel, and Dönitz. (The admiral was the new commander in chief of the German navy, since Admiral Raeder had resigned when Hitler expressed contempt for his surface navy.) They discussed ways of rescuing Mussolini and putting control of Italy back into his hands.

Then, on August 17, Patton's men streamed into Messina, winning the race against Montgomery by a nose. Von Kesselring had been busy evacuating his troops and those of the Italians; he took

110,000 of them off the island to the mainland to fight again. It was a brilliant move and would cost the Allies dearly in times to come.

So north Africa and now Sicily were occupied by the Allies. Even Hitler could no longer doubt that the Allies' next move in the west would be against the peninsula of Italy.

24

CRACKS IN THE
COLUMNS

Suddenly, with the fall of Mussolini, Hitler became far more amenable to what his generals in the east had wanted for months: to shorten the lines. Hitler's reason was that he wanted some of those eastern troops for western Europe now that the Allies were posing a threat to Italy. But he had embarked on an offensive, and Field Marshal von Kluge warned him that it would be impossible to move troops back immediately. The generals had a plan for a staged retreat, but to disturb the plan would be to threaten the entire German position in the east. It would be September before they would free any substantial body of troops.

That would be too long to wait, said Hitler, who was planning to send Rommel down to Italy to take control. He must have troops before that.

But there were no troops available just then. So, although Hitler wanted to act quickly, he was persuaded to begin negotiations with the new Italian government, headed by Marshal Pietro Badoglio. Von Kesselring said he needed that "negotiating" time to round up and move more divisions from Germany into northern Italy.

Hitler was very lucky. The Allies gave him six weeks, while they negotiated in Lisbon with representatives of Badoglio's government. If they had done what Badoglio wanted, invaded in the north, they might have avoided the whole attenuated, painful, and expensive Italian campaign. But they were not ready. They were planning a step-by-step walk up the Italian peninsula, and they had scarcely enough troops for that purpose. Indeed, two American divisions were about to move back to England from Sicily to prepare for the cross-Channel invasion of the continent. Before they went, however, their ranks were thinned by the snatching of thousands of men to fill the ranks of divisions scheduled for the Italian assault.

The assault began on September 3 in Calabria, the toe of the Italian boot.

Early in September Hitler was in Zaporozh'ye in the Ukraine, trying to instill some life into his sagging southern offensive in the east. Suddenly, on September 8, his remarkable intuition told him to turn around and get back to *Wolfsschanze,* his lair at Rastenburg. He followed his intuition. There, awaiting him, was the terrible news that "that traitor Badoglio" had signed a separate peace with the Allies. Moreover, two Allied armies had landed on the Italian peninsula at the same time the armistice was announced. The Rome-Berlin Axis had come apart at the seams.

The news had to have been expected, but it was still a shock. Mussolini was being held in secrecy somewhere in Italy. The repercussions of Mussolini's fall weighed on Hitler, but Goebbels finally persuaded him of the need to make a public statement about the event. So the Führer made a speech to the nation on September 10 in which he dared the Allies to try to find "traitors" in Germany. But he was nonetheless worried enough to begin draconian measures to ensure his personal safety. His bodyguard was enlarged, and his contact with the German people diminished.

The previous day, September 9, the British and Americans had landed again, this time at Salerno. Hitler was fortunate. The Allies had botched a chance. In the very beginning they might have landed nearer to Rome. The Italians, who had already joined the Allies secretly, had five divisions in that area. The Germans had two. The Americans had paratroopers who were eager to be employed. Had the U.S. fleet landed the troops near the capital, and had the paratroopers been dropped in, the southern Italian campaign might have been won right there. On September 10 Hitler told Goebbels that southern Italy was gone and a new line would have to be established north of Rome in the Apennine Mountains.

But at Salerno the Allies floundered, and the German defenders held them. The American paratroopers were misemployed, and the Allies made no attempt to use the Italians. The Americans had inherited the contempt the Germans said they felt for Italian troops. But the Allies forgot that the Italians now would have been fighting in their own country to save the city they loved—Rome—from the Nazis they hated.

But at that time no one could accuse the Americans of being long on international strategic knowledge. They were still very new to the war and had much to learn. They were learning, but the process was costly.

In Italy this shortsightedness cost the Allies a quick capture of Rome. General Eisenhower literally handed the capital back to the Germans. Hitler rushed eight more divisions into Italy.

The Führer's next problem was the rescue of Mussolini from the clutches of Italy's new government. Hitler felt a personal obligation to Mussolini that dated back to the period when Mussolini was *the* dictator of Europe and Hitler was a convicted felon who had tried to stage an abortive revolution. But, more than that, Hitler felt the need to bolster Mussolini and use him to set up a new government for northern Italy. That way the Rome-Berlin-Tokyo Axis would continue to exist.

At the daily situation conferences in the Führer's headquarters, various plans for the rescue were offered. But the Italians kept moving him around. One day Dönitz reported that one of his U-boat captains had spotted Mussolini on an island. A few days later he was gone. Finally Mussolini was taken to a hotel in the Abruzzi region of the Apennine Mountains.

The only way to get to this mountain retreat was by funicular railroad. Or so the Allies and the Italian government thought. The railroad was well guarded, and Mussolini had an enormous guard at the hotel. But a resourceful Waffen SS colonel by the name of Otto Skorzeny came up with a plan. He would fly in with glider troops, overwhelm Mussolini's guards, and fly him out in a small plane. On September 13 he did just this.

Mussolini was rescued; he proclaimed the new Italian Social Republic and set up at Rocca delle Caminate near Gargagno, on the shores of Lake Garda. It is not well known that at this point Hitler forced Mussolini to cede to Germany Trieste, Istria, and the South Tyrol. Had Hitler won the war, Germany would have gained a new sea outlet on the Adriatic. He also had plans to take over Venice. So much for the Führer's promise to Il Duce, at the time of the *Anschluss,* that Germany coveted nothing south of the Brenner.

Contemplating the western situation that fall, Hitler could be relatively content. The Allies had so botched their strategy that they had handed a lost Italy back to the Germans, and had thus guaranteed the stability of the Balkans, which had been in the balance. For had the Allies made a proper arrangement with Badoglio at the proper time, the Italians would have been fighting on their side, not just in Italy, but in Greece, Yugoslavia, and Albania. But the Americans did not seem to know that these places existed, and Winston Churchill, who did know, had sacrificed his own notions in favor of Allied unity.

Therefore, Hitler, from *Wolfsschanze* in Eastern Prussia, could contemplate with a measure of equanimity the developing situation: the Allies were tied down in an enormously costly attrition campaign that the Germans could manage with relatively few troops.

In midautumn 1943, then, Hitler's war looked like this:

Western Europe: Hitler's big problem was the rapidly building Allied campaign of bombardment of German cities and industries. The U.S. Eighth Air Force had yet to become a full partner in the effort, which still was not very effective. For example, on November 13, 115 B-17s set out to bomb Bremen, but bad weather caused 100 of them to abort the mission. They were escorted by P-38 fighters all the way to the target. It was the longest mission yet for American fighter planes. But the P-38s were badly mauled by German fighters.

Even so, the American bombers were getting to their targets. On November 25 the first P-47s were used to bomb and strafe tactical targets in France. That meant going after trains, trucks on the road, and small factories. The campaign of harassment of the Germans in France had begun. On that day the Americans brought their twenty-second heavy bomber group into action in Britain. The B-

17 bombing raids were becoming more effective, too, with increased fighter support and the confidence that gave. The Luftwaffe was now relegated almost entirely to a defensive role within the Reich.

Italian front: Field Marshal von Kesselring was pursuing a policy of attrition. The first stand had been made at the Volturno River, which runs down from the Apennine Mountains into a gulf north of Naples. He held this line for a month. Then he retreated to another line, where the Allies would have to cross the fast Sangro, Rapido, Garagliano, and Liri rivers. The Americans got bogged down at the Rapido River, where the Thirty-sixth Infantry Division was shattered by the Germans. Mountains were on the Allied right, a swampy coastal plain was on their left, and mountains and rivers were ahead of them. They were in the wrong place, but there was nothing to be done about it. The Germans had a powerful winter line. Von Kesselring established the Gustav line, which ran from Pescara on the Adriatic to the Gulf of Gaeta with Monte Cassino as its hinge. It dominated Route 6, the road to Rome. The Germans could hold up the Allied advance here for months. If there was anything Hitler did not have to worry about that winter, it was the Italian front.

At sea: The navy found that things had changed from the early days when the pickings were so easy for the Germans in the Atlantic and even from the days when the conditions along the North American coast were the same.

In August 1943 Admiral Dönitz achieved one of his goals: he had 300 U-boats. Before the war he had said that if he had 300 submarines, he could win the war in six months. But times had changed. He sank 500,000 tons of shipping that month, but with America in the war, he estimated that he had to sink 700,000 tons of ships each month to keep ahead of the Allied shipbuilding program. At the end of 1942 Hitler could count nearly 8 million tons of shipping sunk in the year, with only 7 million tons of new shipping added, or a net loss to the Allies of a million tons.

But more changes were in the offing. The most important occurred in April 1943, when the small American carrier *Bogue* escorted its first convoy across the Atlantic. The day of the escort carrier had arrived, and that meant the setting of the sun for the U-boat, particularly when combined with the development of long-range aircraft that could cover the eastern approaches to America and the western approaches to Britain. By the fall of 1943 there was no more midocean "gap" in which the U-boats had complete safety from attack. In May, Dönitz had admitted defeat in the mid-Atlantic and had temporarily withdrawn his U-boats from the convoy runs. By the end of November 1943 it was clear at *Wolfsschanze* that England was not going to be starved out of the war and that the war at sea was not going to change matters much. Indeed, from this point on the Germans were on the defensive, and they would begin looking to superweapons at sea and in the air to tip the scales for them.

Occupied Europe: The situation here was quite well illustrated by Heinrich Himmler's speech of October 14, 1943, to a group of SS officers at Posen, in Poland:

> What happens to a Russian, to a Czech, does not interest me in the slightest. What the nations can offer in the way of good blood for our type we will take if necessary by kidnapping their children and raising them here with us. Whether nations live in prosperity or starve to death like cattle interests me only insofar as we need them as slaves to our Kultur; otherwise, it is of no interest to me.
>
> Whether 10,000 Russian females fall down from exhaustion while digging an anti-tank ditch interests me only insofar as the anti-tank ditch for Germany is finished.

This was the German policy all over Europe. The worst treatment was reserved for the Jews, of course. The Nazis called their Jewish policy "the final solution to the Jewish question."

And that policy was extermination.

Hitler had given the basic order: exterminate Jews everywhere. The policy was being followed up. There were 5 million Jews in Russia. The Nazis planned to kill every one of them. There were 1.5 million Jews in the Ukraine. The Nazis would destroy them all. There were 3.3 million in Poland, 350,000 in France, 600,000 in Romania, 650,000 in Hungary, 240,000 in Germany itself. The Nazis were prepared to kill nearly 12 million people. It was going on right at that moment, in the fall of 1943.

The extermination camp at Auschwitz was the most modern; it could gas at least 2000 people at a time. Treblinka was very old-fashioned. Each of its ten gas chambers accommodated only 200 people.

The Polish Jews and many others were now sequestered and sent to the gas chambers. The Warsaw ghetto was leveled after the uprising of April 1943. Millions of Poles had become slave laborers.

In Russia captured partisans were killed on the spot. Prisoners of war were sent to slave labor battalions. All Europe lived in terror of the Gestapo and the Third Reich it represented. Hitler had created an empire for Germany, but it was a slave empire, burning with hatred for the Germans, ready to revolt at any time.

Eastern front: On the eastern front the Russians were mopping up the Luftwaffe day after day, with vastly superior air forces.

In the winter of 1943 the Red Army had retaken Voronezh and occupied a large salient 100 miles deep and 150 miles wide, centered on the town of Kursk. It stuck out into the German lines.

It was, in effect, a deliberate provocation by the Soviets to encourage Hitler to commit suicide. Every day in the winter and early spring Hitler had looked at the situation map and that salient had annoyed him. He wanted it removed. In April 1943 he gave orders to that effect. The tactical aim was first to open the road from Orel, at the northeast corner of the salient, and then to open it all the way to Moscow.

The Operation Citadel attack had begun on July 4. Within two weeks the Germans had been so decisively defeated—the "panzer divisions had been bled white," wrote General Joachim von Mellenthin—that Hitler ordered a retreat. He needed those troops in Italy, but that was not the only reason. The Germans had learned a few things in those two weeks.

For one thing the Germans had introduced a new tank, the Ferdinand. It was beautiful, but it had no machine gun and was thus prey to Red Army soldiers who climbed on top and dropped incendiary bombs down the air shafts. And the Germans had made the same mistake with their Panther tank that the Americans had made with the Sherman. It ran on gasoline and thus was a mobile torch just waiting to be ignited.

The Russians, on the other hand, had brought into the battle two new tanks that would mean much in the future. One was the SU-122, which mounted a 122-millimeter gun on a T-34 chassis. It weighed only 30 tons, but it had the destructive power of a much larger vehicle. The second tank was the SU-152, which mounted a 152-millimeter gun and weighed only 40 tons (as opposed to the 73-ton weight of the German Ferdinand).

After the battle of Kursk even Hitler seemed to realize that he could not win in the east. He was now turning more of his attention to the western front. For as well as anyone in the world, Hitler knew that everything the western Allies had so far done was yet preliminary. The battle for Fortress Europe was going to be fought in France or the Lowlands. Just now, Hitler's task was to preserve his nineteen panzer divisions on the eastern front and await developments.

During the summer of 1943, the Russians had launched a whole series of swift brief attacks on the German lines. By fall the Germans had fallen back to the Dnieper River. The Soviets had recaptured Orel, Bryansk, Kharkov, and Smolensk. By November the Germans had been pushed back 150 miles toward Poland in the north. They still held the Crimea, but they had evacuated the Caucasus.

At this point, the fall of 1943, the Soviets had 5.5 million soldiers under arms on the front against the Germans. The Germans had 2.4 million troops there. The Russians had 8500 tanks, the Germans 2300. The Russians had 21,000 field guns, the Germans 8000.

The Red Army was ready for offense or defense, and that defense was organized into eight zones that extended back 200 miles from the front. That was the secret, the reason that a salient or any other area could be defended by the Russians. There was no "crust" through which the panzers could break. The fighting would be just as hard at the end of the 200-mile zone as it was at the beginning. That was what had happened at Kursk. That was what was going to happen from then on.

On November 23, 1943, Hitler was truly impaled on the prongs of a two-front war. For political reasons the Soviets would not admit that there was a second front, but there was no doubt about it. Italy was that second front. Hitler's fifty-first war directive, issued on that day, was dedicated to the proposition that the western invasion of Europe, which had already occurred, was more dangerous to the Third Reich than the sapping of Germany's strength in the east. Hitler stated:

It is very different in the west. Should the enemy succeed in
breaching our defenses on a wide front there, the immediate consequences would be unpredictable. Everything indicates that the
enemy will launch an offensive against the Western Front of
Europe at the latest in the spring, perhaps even earlier.

And so, Hitler's eyes turned west. Antitank guns were to go to
Denmark, where the attack might materialize. (The Allies were creating a huge "disinformation campaign" to convince Hitler that the
attack was coming in Scandinavia.)

Yes, Denmark. In November and December 1943, Hitler was bemused by Denmark, so millions of marks were spent sending tanks,
guns, coastal artillery, and troops to that nation. The troops were employed building minefields along the coast. Denmark was to be made
invasion-proof.

December: Hitler was forced to turn his attention back to the eastern front, where more disaster was befalling the Germans. On the
last day of the year Zhitomir fell. Now not only the Caucasus but
the Donetz basin was lost to him. But who was to recall to Hitler
the words: "If I do not have the Caucasus and the Donetz basin I
cannot win the war."

Who, indeed? Certainly none of the generals who still served. The
word was out; if the news was bad, no one would tell Hitler. He had
made one of his most grievous errors here. He had lost all of his worth-
while confidants; none but the Nazi toadies now clustered around him.
He was isolated from his army and from his people.

25

CROSS-CHANNEL ATTACK

In 1943 Goebbels had come to see Hitler after a considerable absence, and he had been much affected by the new lines in the Führer's face and by his gauntness. Reich Marshal Göring observed that Hitler had aged fifteen years during the first four years of the war.

Hitler spent most of his time in the somber headquarters at *Wolfsschanze,* poring over maps, listening to his generals and interrupting constantly, growing grimmer and grayer, tightening his lips as he surveyed the decline of his empire. He was counting on the Allied landings in the spring. But would they come in Scandinavia, in the low countries, across the Channel, in the Bay of Biscay, in the Balkans? All these possibilities were suggested to him.

Admiral Dönitz was ordered to supply him information. Dönitz was to send his submarines to Scandinavia to stop any invasion there. The submarines might as well be useful for something, the Führer calculated, since they spent most of their time lately underwater, evading enemy attack. The old days—when Skipper Otto Kretschmer had astounded the world by inventing the night surface attack on convoys, from *inside*—were no more than a memory. A U-boat skipper who tried to surface inside a convoy by late 1943, day or night, was committing suicide.

There was no longer any talk of the sort of victory that would give Hitler a clean sweep. There was really no longer any talk of

victory at all, but of a policy of attrition: make it so hard for the
enemies to win that they would exhaust themselves and then peace
could be somehow managed. An enormous difficulty had been raised
by the British and Americans early in the game: the policy of demanding "unconditional surrender," to which President Roosevelt
and Prime Minister Churchill had committed themselves. "Unconditional surrender" had taken the starch out of the German generals' cabal against Hitler in 1942. In the spring of 1943, when peace
was on the mind of many Nazis, the reiteration of the unconditional
surrender policy put it right out of mind again, as Goebbels indicated in his diaries. By not differentiating between the fair-weather
Nazi-supporting Germans and the hard-core Nazis, it seems quite
clear (after forty years) that the Allies placed an extra burden on
themselves in Europe as they certainly did in the war against Japan. There was no way that Hitler could think of surrender; there
was no way the German generals could get the support they needed
until the situation grew a great deal more desperate than it was in
the end of 1943.

In a staff meeting at *Wolfsschanze* on December 20, 1943, Hitler
gave a good indication of his thinking at the time. He told General
Zeitzler that he was considering various ways to improve the western defenses. Always—but more so in recent months—Hitler's mind
had turned to the novel, the surprising, the bizarre, and this day
was no exception.

"Perhaps we can use automatic flame throwers," he said, speaking of the moment that the western Allies would land on the beaches
of *Festung Europa,* "and oil cans that can be thrown into the sea to
burn, thus hampering the movement of the enemy on the beaches
and endangering their ships."

He talked about a new invention: a mine that exploded when
approached by a mine detector. Thus the enemy engineers moving
across a minefield would be blown up. Such inventions, he said,
would have to be saved for the west.

One of Hitler's new problems was his failing ability to distinguish
between reality and fantasy. In the early years he had been truly
awesome in his ability to read the men around him and the international statesmen with whom he dealt. He knew precisely how to

treat von Schuschnigg, the Austrian chancellor. He had known how to handle President Hacha of Czechoslovakia. He had recognized the essential timidity of British Prime Minister Chamberlain and had known how to squeeze every concession from him before going on with his own plans and ignoring all the promises he had made. Hitler had been surprised that England actually went to war over Poland, but he had recovered from that major error of judgment. With a brilliant, innovative plan he had smashed the Allies in Belgium and Holland, causing the fall of France and the isolation of England.

He had, however, erred in his assessment of the Russians all the way along. Military experts such as General Heinz Guderian, who had studied Soviet armor, had an excellent appreciation of the Russian potential and accomplishment. Hitler never asked the experts for advice. He preferred to rely on his intuition: communism was the devil's tool; therefore, the Communists could not be competent. Once invaded, the Soviet Union would collapse like a house of cards because the Russian people had to hate their government as much as Hitler did. Thus fortified by his prejudices, Hitler had refused to see the facts. His increasingly bad judgment became even worse, fed by his penchant for isolating himself from all but "yes" men.

He still retained a measure of the old prescience. "If they attack in the west," he said one day, "that attack will decide the war."

But knowing that the attack was now coming within months did not necessarily provide the key to defeating it. A great many people, even laypersons with command of none of the military intelligence apparatus Hitler had, were predicting an imminent invasion of the continent in the spring of 1944.

In the winter of 1943–1944 the German military position was beginning to become desperate. Hitler had 300 divisions in the field, outside Germany. Inside Germany he had virtually no reserves. All his armies were totally committed. Without denuding one front he could not reinforce another. One hundred seventy-nine of his divisions were in the east, twenty-six in the Balkans, twenty-two in Italy, fifty-three in France and the low countries, sixteen in Scandinavia, and eight in Finland. If he wanted to move several divisions west, he had to take them from somewhere; if he took them from the east or south, he simply made the Allies' task easier.

*

In that spring of 1944, Hitler fretted. He needed only about six more divisions, he said, and then he could turn defeat to victory in the east. He did not ask General Zeitzler what he thought of that notion. By that February the important sources of raw materials that Hitler had spoken of in 1941 as the economic reason for his move against Russia were beyond his reach. The Donetz basin was gone, as was the black dirt country of the Ukraine. The Caucasus oil promise had never been realized. After two years of exhausting warfare the German army was back close to the old Polish-Russian frontier. The Russians were growing stronger every month, buttressed by a steady supply of arms and ammunition, machinery, and food from the United States. The winter campaign of 1943–1944 had taken another staggering toll of the best German fighting men. And in the spring of 1944 the German Seventeenth Army was cut off in the Crimea.

In May 1944 the western Allies launched their spring offensive against the Germans in Italy. There were no troops to send to Marshal von Kesselring to shore up the defenses, so the Anzio beachhead, once threatened by the Germans, was saved and the Americans and British forged on in Italy.

Von Kesselring decided at the end of May that he would evacuate Rome without a fight. He could not possibly win the battle; all he could do was go down in history as the man who destroyed Rome, not an epitaph he particularly coveted. So Rome was evacuated on June 6, 1944.

And elsewhere something even more important was occurring on that day.

For two years the Allies had been planning steadily for the day they would invade Fortress Europe across the English Channel. Long before a commander for the invasion was chosen, a staff under British General Frederick Morgan had begun putting together the basic plan. The problem with invading Hitler's Europe was getting through that first week or so, when the enemy ought to have every advantage because of short supply lines and troops in place behind stout defenses. That was the time when the invaders would have to locally outnumber the defenders by about 4 to 1, according to the figures compiled by the Americans from their experiences in the Pacific. The principal problem after the foothold was established was going to be logistics.

In the beginning the Allies talked about one or two ports. But, looking at the map of France and the Low Countries, it became apparent that the most sturdy German defenses existed and were being built around the available ports. Le Havre, and everything northeast of it, stood in the Pas de Calais (pass of Calais) region, the zone where the cost of invasion would be highest. The Pas de Calais area was a logical invasion point because the English Channel was narrowest there. Another likely invasion area was between the mouths of the Scheldt and Seine rivers. The Germans, too, recognized the attractiveness of this area, and Hitler called it a *Schwerpunkt,* a crucial point. The Allies would not be allowed to move off the beachheads, he vowed. They would be thrown back into the sea.

So the thinking in London passed to another area, that sector of Brittany and Normandy that faces southwestern England. The beaches were not bad, all things considered. The route inland was harder, but it could be managed. The greatest problem would be securing a port, and the only really suitable one in the area was Cherbourg on the Cotentin Peninsula. The Germans had fortified Cherbourg, and they could be expected to blow up the port facilities when the time came. So for practical purposes, if the Allies were going to invade the Normandy coast, they would have to bring their port with them. And that is what they decided. They began the construction of two artificial harbors that were designed to get troops, vehicles, and supplies ashore in short order.

It took a great deal of effort, but by the spring of 1944 the planning and training tasks were far advanced. But there remained a shortage of landing-ship tanks (LSTs) and other landing craft. It was a problem that seemed to linger on and on. The Pacific war was taking most of the available landing craft until the autumn of 1943, but after that more were earmarked for Europe.

The secret of the artificial ports was one of the best-kept Allied secrets of the war. The Germans saw the enormous structures from the air, but they believed the Allied propaganda, artfully placed, that these were some sort of storage silos. In this, as in so many other matters, the Germans were badly hampered by the absence of an effective espionage organization inside Britain. At the outset of the war the British had rounded up almost all the German agents and "turned" some of them so that they became agents for British propaganda. This, ultimately, was another of Hitler's failures: in the prewar years he had not fully appreciated the value of military intelligence and had not pro-

vided the *Abwehr* with the resources to put talented espionage agents
in place for when they would be needed.

As seen from Germany, the Allied plans were more than a little con-
fusing, which is just what Winston Churchill and General Eisenhower wanted. But all the Germans were not fooled all of the time.
The man in charge of the western defenses was a wily old fox, Field
Marshal von Rundstedt, the same man who had been fired by Hitler
in the east because he would not undertake the foolish campaigns
the Führer insisted upon, those same campaigns that had brought
the Germans in Russia to the brink of disaster.

Marshal von Rundstedt had been preparing for the enemy cross-
Channel attack since the fall of Stalingrad in 1943. His western army
was spread out in a great semicircle, with most of the forces dis-
posed near the coast. The primary defense line ran from Holland
along the English Channel and the Bay of Biscay to the Pyrenees
and then along the Mediterranean coast to Toulon. There the Italians took over the defense, until the fall of Italy that year. In 1943
there were not enough divisions in the west to stem any sort of major attack. The most serious problem, however, was that behind the
front there was no reserve. Whenever von Rundstedt managed to
get hold of a few extra units and prepared to put them in reserve,
Hitler snatched them away for the eastern front. It was no exag-
geration, according to General Bodo Zimmermann, von Rundstedt's
operations officer, to say that the muscle of the western army was
constantly weakened to send troops east, where they were gobbled
up in the Russian annihilation machine.

In 1943 OKW transferred twenty of von Rundstedt's divisions
to the eastern front. In return Hitler promised the field marshal sixty
divisions of "Eastern volunteers," most of them former Russian prisoners of war who had decided that anything was better than slave
labor under the SS.

Hitler had begun the construction of the "Atlantic wall" in 1942 to
convince the Allies that the coast was impenetrable. Giant concrete
structures began to appear along the shore. They were usually left
unfinished, but there was a certain propaganda value to having their

construction under way. Most of the material for this new "wall" was not new. It came from some of the old German defenses that were being dismantled along the Franco-German frontier.

In the summer and fall of 1943 the Allied air forces began to do serious damage to German communications in France. The American P-47s destroyed hundreds of locomotives and trains. They shot up convoys, and ultimately they made German defense building extremely difficult. Hitler was very much interested in the new V-1 and V-2 rocket weapons that were supposed to turn the war around for him, and he approved the "theft" of thousands of von Rundstedt's workers. They would stop building defensive fortifications and build instead rocket-launching sites.

Hitler's OKW War Directive No. 51, issued on November 3, 1943, announced that the English Channel coast would be the focus of the west invasion. He would, he promised, send all available material and personnel to the west. That comforting news was not all, however. He also ordered von Rundstedt to stop the enemy from landing. The enemy must be thrown back into the sea immediately, said Hitler. There would be no retreat. The coast must be held under all circumstances.

Von Rundstedt's reply to Hitler's new directive was a report which told of officers with artificial limbs stationed in the line, of a whole battalion of men with ear complaints, of a whole division, the Seventieth Infantry, that was formed of men who had stomach trouble and thus needed special diets. The report spoke of too few tanks, too few guns, too few light weapons. Only a handful of panzer divisions and paratroop divisions were even theoretically fit for combat, von Rundstedt reported.

Further, the Luftwaffe had grown so weak in the west that it could not possibly control the skies even for a day. The naval forces, emasculated as a consequence of Hitler's shifting priorities, consisted of a handful of small craft, mostly E-boats, suitable for raids across the Channel and not much else. The 500-ton Atlantic U-boats could not operate in the Channel because it was too shallow. The old 250-ton U-boats ("canoes") had all been relegated to training or sent to the Black Sea, where they were destroyed. The western defenses, in other words, were a sorry mess.

Hitler for once read what someone had to say and read it again. He promised von Rundstedt all sorts of improvements.

The Führer's major change was to send Field Marshal Rommel to inspect the defenses in the west. Rommel then was given command of Army Group B, which was to cover the invasion front. He then set up headquarters and began to build defenses. His concentration was on Normandy and Brittany. He built antiglider traps called *Rommels-pargel* ("Rommel's asparagus"), tall posts armed with mines. And his troops built beach obstacles that were designed to blow up or skewer landing craft.

Meanwhile the Allies were carrying out several disinformation campaigns. One indicated that the landings would be in Norway, and this impressed Hitler so greatly that he wasted enormous resources there. Another campaign indicated that the invasion would be along the English Channel east of the Seine. This was backed by the formation of a dummy army group under Lieutenant General George S. Patton, Jr. This nominal First U.S. Army Group consisted of a headquarters, a number of transmitters sending fake radio messages about troop movements and the like, and the establishment of "camps" on the southeast coast of England—camps which were really made up of dummy tanks, dummy trucks, dummy guns, and dummy troop housing, even dummy landing craft in the rivers and estuaries. All of this was to tie down the German Fifteenth Army at the Pas de Calais.

By the spring of 1944 the Germans calculated that the Allies had seventy-five divisions in Britain, with sixty-five of them useful for invasion of France. They also estimated that another forty-five divisions were available in the United States. Luftwaffe strength was so reduced that von Rundstedt believed that the ratio of Allied aircraft to German was 50 to 1. And all von Rundstedt had was a single immobile defense system with no depth and with only a handful of real fighting units.

In May 1944 the German order of battle in the west consisted of three divisions holding the critical area of the Normandy coast, the 716th, 352d, and 709th Infantry Divisions. The latter was also responsible for the defense of Cherbourg. The 243d Infantry Division was split between Normandy proper and the Cotentin Peninsula. A few other units, not very well equipped or manned, made up the rest. The defending divisions held sectors averaging 25 miles in breadth. Rommel did have the 231st Panzer Division stationed east of the Orne River, with most of its troops at Caen.

The Allies, after a false start, landed at Normandy on the south-eastern portion of the Cotentin Peninsula. Most of the strong German defenses were much farther east. The landings occurred on June 6, preceded by a drop of paratroopers and gliders. The American airborne divisions became hopelessly confused because of poor flight management by the troop carrier commands, but the misfortune had a silver lining because the confusion was so complete the Germans could not figure out what the Americans were trying to do. In the end, enough American troops managed to take and hold enough positions to assist the landing forces. The three major landings were at Gold and Juno beaches in the British sector, at Sword beach near Caen, and at Omaha and Utah beaches. There was relatively little trouble at Utah beach, but at Omaha, where the Germans were much stronger, the situation was in doubt for the first day. But the Americans did secure their foothold there. Despite a terrible spring storm that blasted the two artificial harbors, the Allies managed to hold on. And the Germans made one serious error. They sent virtually their entire available armor against the British "desert rats" who were fighting in the Caen area, leaving the area farther west, being attacked by the Americans, without much defense.

But the most important aspect of the Allied landings was the success of the disinformation campaign, which continued to convince the Germans that the real major landing would occur later and elsewhere.

When the news of the landings came in, Field Marshal von Rundstedt was ready to take action.

*   *   *

Two strong German divisions were available elsewhere in France. One was the SS *Hitlerjugend* Panzer Division, and the other was the Panzer *Lehr* Division. Hitler had given orders that these two formations should not be moved without specific permission from him. But von Rundstedt sent the orders to move them into action at Caen anyhow.

When Hitler learned of this a few hours later, he was furious. He upbraided von Rundstedt: "One cannot yet say for sure where the main invasion will come."

And so, on June 6, because the Germans could not make up their minds, the Allies got their beachheads in France. They were also lucky in another matter: Field Marshal Rommel, not expecting any action because of the bad weather predicted for this period, had taken a few days off to go home to Germany to see his family. Thus, when the Allies struck, the man who was supposed to throw them back into the sea was not on hand. It was hours before he could get to his headquarters by car, delayed by confused traffic on the roads.

So, as of June 7, 1944, the Allies were ashore. There would be plenty of fighting yet, and it would be fifty-nine days before they would break out of Normandy, but the invasion of western Europe was on.

26

SUMMER OF
DESPAIR

For the first few days after the Normandy invasion, Hitler's participation in the strategy of defense consisted entirely of issuing orders
through OKW to von Rundstedt and Rommel: "Throw the invaders
back into the sea," and "Refuse to give up a foot of ground."

That was all very good, but an indication of what was happening was to be found in the adventures of the *Hitlerjugend* and Panzer
Lehr Armored Divisions. Although they started for the battle area
of Caen, they never arrived. First they were stopped by Hitler's
direct orders. When he relented, the division commanders discovered that the Allies held air superiority, preventing the panzers from
traveling by day. At night the trains—if running at all—were badly
off schedule. The roads were clogged with traffic. So the divisions
broke up into battalions and trickled piecemeal into the Caen area,
thereby radically reducing their effectiveness.

After the first few days Rommel and von Rundstedt agreed that
Hitler would have to make some decisions before they could organize
any sort of effective defense. The two marshals agreed that the only
wise course would be to seal off the whole Cotentin Peninsula and then
bring up enough force to push the Allies back into the sea. But Hitler
would have to decide, so they called for a meeting.

Hitler came to the old 1940 command post at Margival, between
Soissons and Laon. There they met. The field marshals laid out the

problem. Hitler promised that he would issue the orders to bring up adequate troops and equipment for the job. But then Rommel suggested that it was time for the Germans to consider making peace. Hitler blew up and accused Rommel of interfering with political matters. In any event, he said, the Allies would not make peace with him, so the idea was worthless.

Perhaps this was the conversation that pushed Field Marshal Rommel into the arms of the conspirators who were trying to get rid of Hitler. Now that the Allies had landed in France, the conspirators were beginning to become desperate. For months some of the principals had been trying to persuade Rommel, but he had resisted. Now he no longer resisted. He had been convinced by the Führer's own words that until Hitler was gone, there would be no hope of peace for Germany. And the two field marshals could see just how desperate Germany's situation was becoming.

But Hitler soon enough went back to Berchtesgaden, and from OKW headquarters came the usual stream of messages. Nothing was new. The defenders were not to give up a foot of ground. Cherbourg was to be held to the last man.

It was not. On June 29 Cherbourg fell, and the first stage of the Normandy battle was over. The Allies had a port. It would take them some time to put it into usable shape again, but they had a real port.

At that time, the generals were trying desperately to get Hitler to issue a comprehensive defensive program. The piecemeal defense was simply sacrificing their best forces.

General Freiherr Leo Geyr von Schweppenburg, the commander of panzer forces, protested that the manner in which his armored units were being used was destroying them before they ever got into battle. They were going against the British around Caen, and the British had support from offshore naval guns and heavy support from the air. The Germans could not match any of this, and their supply situation was tenuous. The roads continued to be mostly useless in the daytime, and at night they were jammed with traffic.

Just before the first of July von Rundstedt and Rommel went to Berchtesgaden to see Hitler once again. Obviously he was reluctant to see them at all. He kept them waiting for several hours, a stratagem he earlier had perfected to unnerve his diplomatic opponents. But these two field marshals were not about to be unnerved. They waited patiently hour after hour. What they had to say was important, and it concerned Germany's destiny.

Finally Hitler summoned them.

The result: nothing. The field marshals left empty-handed. After they left, von Rundstedt telephoned Keitel at OKW headquarters and told him he was sick of the war, he was too old to continue to deal with Hitler, and he wanted Keitel to get a new commander for the west.

Keitel asked von Rundstedt what he thought ought to be done to save the situation.

"End the war, you fool," von Rundstedt shouted into the telephone.

A few hours later the word came: von Rundstedt was relieved again. So was General von Schweppenburg. They were too pessimistic, said Hitler. He had just the man. Hitler had brought Field Marshal von Kluge from the eastern front and had spent several days indoctrinating him with the theory that both von Rundstedt and Rommel simply lacked the resolve to win the war. That was all that was needed—a little optimism, said Hitler.

It took von Kluge almost a week of inspecting the lines to discover that the two field marshals had not been pessimistic at all, just realistic. The Allies had overwhelming power to throw against the Germans. Moreover, the German lines in the west were thin, manned with inferior troops whose weapons also were inferior. In mid-July Rommel submitted another negative report. Von Kluge was reading it when he received the news that Rommel's staff car had been attacked on the road by an Allied plane; the car had crashed and Rommel had suffered severe head injuries. So the actual defense of the west wall was now without a commander.

What was to be done? Hitler insisted that von Kluge do it all himself, take on Rommel's duties as well as his own. So von Kluge moved to Rommel's headquarters.

Then came July 20, 1944.

For several weeks the conspirators of the German Officer Corps had been waiting for a good opportunity to kill Hitler. They also hoped to kill Himmler and one or two of the other leading Nazis, but this was not essential. The man with the bomb was Colonel Claus von Stauffenberg. The Allies' policy of unconditional surrender was anathema to the generals, but they knew that as long as Hitler was alive there was no hope of changing that policy.

The High Command was now talking about a defense against a Soviet invasion of the Reich. So far had the Russians progressed that it was only a matter of time before they would cross the German frontier. Plans were being drawn to confront that threat.

Bialystok, on the Russo-Polish frontier, had fallen to the Russians, and they were poised to break through into the Ukraine. In France and Italy the generals had really given up any hope of containing the enemy.

Von Stauffenberg was convinced that even an additional week's delay would be too much. The strike against Hitler must be made the next day, July 20.

And so on July 20 the colonel left a suitcase bomb under Hitler's *Wolfsschanze* conference table, and the device exploded. The Führer was very lucky; his trousers were ruined, but he was not badly hurt. Immediately the major known conspirators—many had identified themselves by their actions when Hitler was erroneously reported dead—were rounded up and shot. Von Stauffenberg was one of the first. The hunt was on for any and all others. Among the names mentioned by one of the known conspirators was Rommel. That posed an extremely ticklish problem for Hitler, since the "Desert Fox" was Germany's most popular war hero. He must not be allowed to go unpunished, but a scandal would rock the nation. So the field marshal was given the option of a trial and execution (there was never any doubt about the outcome) or an "honorable" death by taking poison. He took the poison.

The fighting on the Normandy front continued. The Germans were unable to launch an effective counteroffensive, and one of the main reasons for this failure was the success of the disinformation program that had been carried out for so many months, persuading the Germans that the Normandy landings were just a feint and that the real landings would be made later at the Pas de Calais area. The whole program was aimed at just one man: Adolf Hitler. If the Allies could convince him that the Normandy landings were not important, they need do no more to convince anyone else.

The Führer was deceived. He would not commit the reserves to the Normandy front because he was convinced that there still were many more Allied divisions in England, poised to cross the Channel. For one whole month Hitler's invaluable reserve troops remained uncommitted when they might have changed the balance of the war on the western front.

After the assassination attempt, Hitler withdrew almost completely from contact with his generals except to issue orders. He deluded himself that all the failures of the past could be attributed to the plotting of his generals. Nearly everyone who had been around him in the recent past was now gotten rid of. General Zeitzler was dismissed. Two hundred people were arrested following the assassination attempt: two field marshals, seventeen generals, fifty other military officers, and scores of others in high places—people whom Hitler had trusted. He trusted virtually no one any more. Closest to him now were Goebbels, Himmler, and Bormann, his secretary.

Naturally, Hitler turned to his old Nazi comrades. The Gestapo was everywhere. No government official was above scrutiny. Armaments Minister Speer, who had always had Hitler's trust, was also suspected of involvement in the generals' plot. The Gestapo investigated him; Hitler turned very cool toward him. He was saved by a question mark.

The Speer investigation began because, when the conspirators were planning for the future, Colonel von Stauffenberg kept a notebook. After his execution the notebook was found, and the names in it served to spur a whole new round of investigations. Speer's name was in the book, on the list of potential members of the new cabinet.

"Minister of Armaments" read the entry, "Albert Speer...?" and the words "if possible."

Speer was brought in for questioning. He denied any complicity. He could prove that he had nothing to do with the men involved, and he could prove his whereabouts at any of the times about which the Gestapo agents had questions.

Oddly enough, although Germany was collapsing from within, the German war production effort was doing very nicely in the summer of 1944, knowledge that would have come as a distinct shock to the Allied airmen, who boasted that they had bombed Germany nearly into submission. Speer's armaments program was in high gear and producing more than ever before. The war materials were being produced, but they couldn't be efficiently delivered to those who needed them.

Hitler sensed the disorganization. He began to lean on the Nazi party organization rather than his government. He went from one place to another, meeting with his *Gauleiters,* telling them that all the failures of the past could be laid at the feet of the disloyal officers of the army. Only the party and its military apparatus, the SS, could be trusted.

In Berlin, the People's Court was robbing Germany of more generals, as one after another was implicated in the plot against Hitler and was executed. General Fritz Fromm, who had been responsible for killing many of the July 20 conspirators and who had just been appointed commander of a special "replacement army" that was being assembled from among men on leave, was himself implicated and eventually executed. Heinrich Himmler took command of Fromm's special army.

The existence of this unit was but one manifestation of Germany's worst problem: the manpower shortage. In future the "replacements" would be children and old men, the sick and the weak and the unfit.

On July 27 the Americans, who had been building steadily since June 6, attacked in force at Saint-Lô. Once that town was taken, the city of Avranches was threatened and, beyond that, the French plain. On July 31 Avranches fell, and the Germans failed to blow the bridge at Pontaubault.

The Allies were preparing to roll. They were taking an enormous toll of the German forces. In mid-July German casualties on the western front were 97,000, and 225 tanks had been lost. The replacements amounted to 6000 men and 17 tanks.

The Americans moved while the Germans contained the British. By August 7 Army Group B had lost 3200 officers, including 14 generals and 200 regimental commanders, and 148,000 enlisted men.

Then came the assault on Avranches.

"The enemy will not be permitted to break out into the open country" came the order from Hitler. "The Führer orders that all available panzer forces will be withdrawn from the front, will be placed under the command of General Eberbach, and will counterattack with the objective Avranches.''

That was the sort of order Hitler was giving then. The available panzer units were scattered all over; many of them were engaged against the British and could not possibly be withdrawn, and there was no way they could get to Avranches in time to halt the drive of the Americans.

Yet on the night of August 7 the Germans did manage to launch a counterattack. It was stopped cold by something new: the force of Allied bombing.

Through the Avranches gap poured George Patton's new Third Army, a mechanized force more powerful than anything in the war since Guderian's heyday in the east. The German Seventh Army was now in grave danger of encirclement by the American First Army coming from the south via Le Mans and the American Third Army moving against it from the east. The Allied plan was enormous: it called for cutting all German communications west of Paris and encircling the German Seventh and Fifth Panzer Armies. The only thing that saved the Germans was the tardiness of the British and Canadians in helping to close the encirclement.

The American army had broken through into the open plain despite all that Hitler had demanded of his troops. Patton was driving toward Paris. The Falaise pocket was closing in on hundreds of thousands of German troops. German defenses were totally disorganized. Yet this was only half the problem that faced the beleaguered Adolf Hitler that summer. The other half was in the east.

27

THUNDER FROM
THE EAST

In the west the British and Americans were driving on Paris. Rome
had fallen and Marshal von Kesselring had retreated to a defensive
line north of Rome, across the Italian boot to Pescara. Behind that
was the Gothic line, which ran along the course of the Arno River
from Leghorn to the Adriatic coast near Ancona. Hold, ordered Hitler. And von Kesselring retreated to the Gothic line. After that there
was a third defense line, north of Florence and north of Rimini. Here
the Germans would dig in for the winter of 1944–1945. The terrain
and the weather militated for this, but more important, the Allies
had denuded the Italian front of reserves that summer in order to
launch the second invasion of France—Operation Anvil.

This occurred on August 15, between Cannes and Nice. The troops
then headed through southern France toward Bavaria.

Following the invasion at Normandy, Hitler believed he had a wonder weapon in the Type XXIII submarine, a small U-boat equipped
with a snorkel. These vessels could operate nicely in the shallow waters of the English Channel, and some of them were sent there to try
to help stem the tide of invasion. They were not notably successful.
The Allied hunter-killer teams of aircraft and escort vessels were after
them every moment. What Hitler was waiting for now was another
wonder weapon, the homing torpedo. A U-boat would be able to fire
it in any direction from a submarine on the bottom of the sea, and it

300

would home on a vessel on the surface. The U-boats would not have to come to the surface for weeks, given their snorkel breathing devices. Dönitz was working on this weapon.

But for every wonder weapon the Germans developed the Allies seemed to have a counterweapon. The "squid" was a British device that could throw lightweight depth charges a long distance. Powerful searchlights and improved radar helped the Allies.

On the eastern front, beginning at Christmastime 1943, the Soviet forces went over to the offensive and from that time forward were almost always on the offensive. By February 1944 they had surrounded a larger force of Germans at Krivoy Rog. At Cherkassy Marshal Zhukov captured 30,000 German troops and another 30,000 escaped when Army Group South sent most of its tanks to open the way for them.

By spring 1944 the Russians had grown so strong that they no longer had to characterize their offensives by seasons. The offensive was constant. In March 1944 the Soviets began three main thrusts. One was aimed at the German line south of Krivoy Rog. The second was aimed at Uman. The third advance moved toward Shepetovka. In six weeks they advanced 160 miles. In tempo it was reminiscent of the early weeks of the war, when the front was moving the other way.

Hitler had dreamed of destroying Leningrad to prove to the world the futility of trying to oppose the German juggernaut. But the siege of Leningrad was lifted. No German had set foot in the city.

Hitler fired von Manstein, the fair-haired von Manstein, who was, next to Rommel, his favorite general of days past. He also fired Field Marshal von Kleist.

In the summer, while Hitler's attention was focused on Normandy, Marshal Zhukov launched a new vigorous attack near Bobruisk and captured most of the twenty-five German divisions in two weeks. What he didn't capture he destroyed. It was an enormous blow to Hitler, both in prestige and in the physical loss of so great a segment of his waning forces.

By the end of July the Russians reached the sea at Riga. Army Group North was now isolated and subject to encirclement. Ultimately it would have to be rescued by sea from the Kurland Peninsula.

South of this area, where von Kluge's Army Group Center had

once operated, the German line was in shambles. The Russians had advanced through Brest-Litovsk through Lublin, which they reached on July 24. This was only 100 miles southeast of Warsaw. One column moved that way. Soon it was only 50 miles from Warsaw. Then it was on the outskirts of the Polish capital.

Hitler's Greater Reich was crumbling before his eyes, but resolutely he turned his eyes away from the wreckage.

Everywhere Hitler played the same cracked record: no retreat.

The Americans and British were launching new offensives. The British did not keep up, and Hitler might have drawn a strong defense line at the Seine River, but he insisted on waiting until the last moment to decide. His commanders were given no chance to move back to catch their breath, to regroup and dig in. His hard line forced them into continuous, furious backpedaling. "No withdrawal" meant fight until it was too late to run away to fight again another day.

Late in July Hitler told von Kesselring that he would have to prepare an Alpine defense line. A few days later, Hitler was talking to his intimates about the "Home Theater of War." At that point the whole civilian population was to be called upon. The front line for von Kesselring, said Hitler, would be the area between the Swiss frontier and the Adriatic. Hitler laid down the conditions for the construction of defenses, designated the lines of authority, and even addressed himself to the growing problem of fighting the partisans.

Here he was again—the Hitler of old—the man who was not too busy to design a bunker, making sure that there were plenty of pegs for the soldiers to hang their clothing on, the man who thought nothing of ordaining the genocide of the European Jews. Yes, here was the man who did not cavil at destroying nations or planning the interior of museums. But he could not come to grips with what von Kluge had called "the intermediate problem" of managing armies so that they could fight and win, and not just "hold firm."

The greatest enemy of the German soldiers at that time was Adolf Hitler. Their Führer cared nothing for his soldiers' lives or welfare. "Hold the line" was his watchword. Hold the line no matter the cost, no matter whether it was worth holding or what holding it would mean for the future.

*

On July 21, 1944, Hitler appointed General Heinz Guderian as the new chief of the army General Staff. Guderian was a professional soldier, and he had been responsible for much of the brilliance in the creation of the panzer units.

One result of the attempted assassination of Hitler was the almost total disruption of OKH, the High Command of the army. Several officers were killed or wounded, and several others were either executed or disgraced. It was going to take Guderian some time to reorganize the army.

Hitler did not make it easy, for he now trusted no one, not even the men his duties ordinarily would force him to trust. He insisted on approving every detail of the work Guderian did. Guderian was allowed no powers of decision. The general asked to be allowed to give instructions to the eastern army groups on routine matters, but Hitler refused. Guderian asked to be able to issue instructions to the General Staff Corps officers on matters concerning the general welfare of the army. Hitler refused.

Field Marshal Keitel and General Jodl at OKW had long been accused of toadyism. Guderian now echoed those charges. No matter what Hitler said, he noted, those two insisted that Hitler was right.

When Guderian took over, the situation of the German army was as outlined above. Worst of all, there were very few reserves on the eastern front. Guderian would have to perform magic if he was to save the situation. His magic consisted of finding the only forces available in the east. These were troops in Romania behind Army Group South Ukraine. Guderian proposed to Hitler that all the divisions that could be made available in Romania be moved away from there and used to plug the gap in the line between Army Group Center and Army Group North. Surprisingly, Hitler agreed. Thus the Russian advance was halted in the Doblen-Tuckum-Mitau area.

Guderian then planned the evacuation of Army Group North before it could be surrounded and annihilated. He proposed that all the armor be brought down to a bridgehead in the Riga area, and there moved back to defend Germany. But here once again Hitler interfered. The commander of Army Group North did not want to give up his armor. He was convinced that the Russians would not

attack again in his area for a while. The field marshal went over
Guderian's head to Hitler, and the Führer, saying nothing to
Guderian, let the commander have his way. Thus Guderian did not
get the armor.

At this point the Germans faced another danger. They had established a line just east of Warsaw after Field Marshal Walther Model
won a victory in that area. Army Group Center was holding there.
Suddenly came news that behind the Germans, the Poles in Warsaw
had rebelled under General Tadeusz Bor-Komorowski. Communications with the German Ninth Army were broken. The possibility
existed that the Russians and the Poles in Warsaw would link up.
Guderian insisted that he must be allowed jurisdiction over military
affairs in Warsaw. But there he ran straight into the Nazi party and
Heinrich Himmler.

Himmler complained to Hitler and was upheld; the army did not
get control of a major sector of the fighting front in the east. The order
to put down the Polish rebellion was given to the SS, and Himmler
was in charge. The SS carried out its instructions with enormous brutality. Atrocities were commonplace. Guderian became so disgusted
that he demanded the removal of the SS from the army's fighting fronts.
Hitler refused. He now began to show signs of a brutality that had to
be guided by an unsettled mind. Furious with the Poles and egged on
by Himmler, he announced a new policy toward the Polish people:

> Senior Group Leader von dem Bach has been entrusted with
> the task of pacifying Warsaw, that is to say he will raze Warsaw
> to the ground while the war is still going on and insofar as this
> is not contrary to military plans for the construction of strong-
> points. Before it is destroyed, all raw materials, all textiles, and
> all furniture will be removed from Warsaw. The responsibility
> for this is assigned to the civil administration.

That meant that the SS, not the army, was in control of all events
in and around the Polish capital city. Guderian did not even know
about the order. But he had heard rumors, and he told Hitler that
Warsaw was important to the German defenses and must be pre-
served. Hitler was noncommittal, knowing what he had ordered the
SS to do.

While the Warsaw uprising was occurring, the Russians, who were very close to Warsaw on the north, suddenly stopped their drive. The Germans at the time thought they had forced the Russians to halt. But the Russians had stopped to let the Germans and the Poles in Warsaw kill one another off. They only resumed their drive once the SS had destroyed the independent military forces inside Warsaw. The Soviets did not want any independent military forces anywhere around them.

As the summer of 1944 wore on, army chief Guderian tried to assess his problems and meet them as he could. Hitler had created total confusion by refusing to establish fortified positions. In the west Hitler had expected that he could rely on the Atlantic wall, even though it was never completed. In the east he had flatly refused to allow the German armies to establish prepared defense positions, on the theory that if the generals had a fortified line, they would not fight as hard as they would if they had to fight in the open. With the front line now dangerously close to the German border, Guderian asked for permission to reestablish the old German fortifications along there—the ones that had existed before Hitler expanded toward the east. Hitler finally approved the planning, and the work began. It was August 1944. Time was growing very short.

28

DEFENSE IN THE EAST

All Hitler's major errors in the east now came home to confront the Germans. His underestimation of Soviet power, the considered policy of barbarism against the civil populations, his contempt for his Balkan allies, his destruction of the command structure of the German army—all these militated against a defense as the Russians plowed westward. And now Hitler was forced by circumstances to turn his entire attention to the deteriorating western front. Further, Hitler's growing paranoia prevented him from trusting anyone around him save those he ought not to have trusted, Nazi stooges.

General Guderian saw that the only possible way to defend the German borders was to enlist troops totally unfit for mobile warfare: the disabled, the overaged, and the youngsters. He got Hitler to agree reluctantly to his program of fortification. Hitler's major objection was that he hated to admit that the eastern front had become a totally defensive operation and that there was no chance of doing anything more than stopping the Russians somewhere in German territory. For a man who had dreamed of an eastern empire, this was a heavy defeat.

Guderian, the professional soldier, had no time for such sentimentality. The defenses had to be built, and immediately, or there was no chance of saving Germany from the Soviet drive.

All along the west wall the earthworks began to go up. Most of them were built by volunteers: women, children, and old men. This was the only untapped labor source in Germany by the summer of 1944. Hitler had wasted his human substance in several ways: by murdering the Jews and other minorities and by throwing away millions of men in the east in one ill-begotten campaign after another.

Members of the Hitler Youth also were dragooned into the building of the fortifications, and some of them into defending them. For there were no garrisons left in the east. All serviceable units had been rushed to the western front, where in August the Americans were dashing through France, bound for Paris. General George Patton had turned the panzer tactics—many of them perfected by General Guderian—against the Germans, and the Americans now had the equipment, the fuel, and the troops to forge ahead.

The only troops Guderian had for his eastern defenses were the dregs left over from the western battle zone. So old soldiers and sick soldiers and men who were not soldiers at all were rushed to Danzig, to Königsberg, to Breslau, and to other cities along the eastern wall to defend against the oncoming horde of Russians. Guderian formed 100 fortress infantry battalions and 100 artillery batteries. But then, even before he could get them into position, the needs of the western front were such that 80 percent of these units were rushed to the west. This was done by OKW with Hitler's approval, before Guderian could even learn about it. The units were thrown into one breach after another and were slaughtered in the west, instead of having that little training time in the east that might have made at least half-soldiers of them.

When Guderian asked OKW for weapons for the eastern fortresses, Hitler, Keitel, and Jodl said no. There were no weapons, they said. But in this regard Keitel and Jodl did not know what they were talking about. There were thousands of weapons stored in Germany, left over from the western European campaign early in the war, before Hitler took entirely into his own hands all decisions regarding the armed forces.

In the late summer of 1944, a picture of a sharply divided German military establishment emerged. As commander of OKH (the German army) General Guderian was actually relegated to management of the German war effort in the east, and to that alone. OKW, which was wherever Hitler was, concerned itself almost exclusively with the campaign in the west. It was as if the war against the Russians suddenly had ceased to exist, at least in Hitler's mind. He had given up thinking about the eastern war, because it was apparent that it was hopeless. If he had thought about it, he would have realized that the only thing that might possibly save him and his country from the Russians would be for the Americans and British to get to Berlin first. Yet Hitler was unable to see that. He still clung to the hope for a miracle that would change the growing certainty of ignominious defeat into sudden victory. He was planning to throw the last of Germany's resources into a sudden strike against the western Allies. To what end? Did he really believe that he could defeat them? Not if his mind were working properly.

His lack of balance showed itself in an unreasoning preoccupation with the west. Guderian found weapons for his eastern bastions, and ordered them shipped there. Keitel and Jodl stopped the shipment and diverted everything larger than a .50-caliber machine gun to the western front. The guns arrived there too late to do any good and without men to use them, so they were worthless. They would have been invaluable in the east, Guderian said.

Even in manning the defense of the east, General Guderian ran into Hitler's distrust, so the general suggested that a *Landsturm* ("Land Army," or militia) be formed and put under the direction of the old SA. SA Chief of Staff Schepmann was a man Guderian understood and could trust. At first, when he suggested the idea to Hitler, the Führer seemed to accept it. But a few days later Hitler said he would not agree to a force under the SA. Instead, he would establish a *Volkssturm* ("People's Army") under Martin Bormann, his own secretary, who would become *Reichsleiter* (national director).

So the *Volkssturm* was built on the Nazi pattern. More attention was paid to the proper way to deliver the "Heil Hitler" Nazi salute than to weapons training. At this late stage of the war the "Heil Hitler" salute became mandatory in every branch of the German military service. Hitler seemed to believe that by demanding this sort of show of loyalty he was drawing the German people around him; quite the reverse was true.

Nor was that all. Heinrich Himmler had suddenly emerged more powerful than ever before. After the assassination attempt Himmler had shown that he was able to put his finger on many of the conspirators, and this elevated him enormously in Hitler's esteem. So

Hitler had placed Himmler in command of the replacement army. He created new formations called *Volksgrenadiers* and *Volksartillerie Korps*. Earlier Hitler had spoken of ridding himself entirely of the normal army organization and creating a nazified army, entirely responsible to political controls. Now he had done so. The Volks organizations were entirely politicized. National Socialist control officers were appointed to every unit. They made sure of the political purity of the Volks organizations. The idea spread to every element of the services, until Guderian finally put up a fight against the politicization of his army units.

Every day the war worsened for Germany. All the troop units trained in Germany were diverted to the western front. Hitler kept talking about the west wall, but he was dreaming. Much of the old west wall of 1940 had been broken up and the fortifications moved to the Atlantic wall, which had now been breached irremediably.

While Hitler was dreaming of victory in the west, as if that would save the Reich, Guderian was trying to shore up the east as well as he could.

In August Marshal Ion Antonescu of Romania suggested the evacuation of the Germans in Moldavia and the establishment of a new defense line by Army Group Center in the Carpathian Mountains. But just about then came word of political difficulties in Romania. Foreign Minister von Ribbentrop suggested sending a German panzer division to Bucharest. Guderian had no such unit available, but he suggested the dispatch of the Fourth SS Polizei Division from fighting guerrillas in Yugoslavia. Hitler said he would consider it all, but he did nothing. He could not make up his mind. It was a process that grew ever more difficult for him as the war prospects darkened.

At this time General Guderian had serious negative reports on the situation in Bulgaria, where morale was very low. Guderian had the impression that his Bulgarian allies were about to pull out of the war. He suggested that no more military equipment be sent to Sofia and that a request be made for return of some already in the pipeline. Keitel and Jodl scoffed and refused to consent.

On August 20, 1944, the Russians launched a new attack against Army Group South Ukraine. The Romanians began to desert in large numbers and turned against the Germans. In order to avoid a complete collapse of the front, Guderian ordered a retreat and the seizure of the Danube bridges. But the Romanians got to the river first, seized the bridges, and thus left sixteen German divisions at the mercy of the Russians. Those divisions were entirely lost, and all because Hitler had refused to act when Antonescu and Guderian had pleaded for the immediate establishment of a defense line in the Carpathians. The line would not have prevented the Romanians from deserting, but it would have left the Germans in a tenable position.

As it was, the southeastern front was in shambles. Early in September the Red Army moved into Bucharest. Bulgaria went over to the Soviets on September 8, and the Russians took over the just-delivered consignment of eighty-eight Panzer IV tanks and fifty assault guns that Guderian had tried vainly to get back.

So the Balkans were lost. But that was not all that was happening in the east. At the end of August Finland sued for peace, putting that Axis partner out of the war and releasing Red Army divisions for the final thrust on Germany. Hitler now issued orders for the defense of "Fortress Crete," and he ordered fortifications for southern Austria, as well as fortification of Slovakia against the Russian advance.

The difference from the past was that now all responsible action was to be taken by the *Gauleiters,* the Nazi political commissars. In the southwest they were responsible for construction of the fortifications. They would supply the labor, and they would report directly to Hitler. It was, of course, a totally impossible situation for the army—being told to defend an area and then having political hacks come in to manage the defenses.

All these events along the eastern line had their effect on Hungary, the most strongly cemented of Germany's southern allies. Guderian went to Hungary to assess the situation and was not very well impressed. The Russians had reached Transylvania and were very near the Hungarian border. They were, in effect, very close to the soft underbelly that Winston Churchill had always yearned to attack.

29

THE WEST WALL BREACHED

On July 23 the Red Army was moving toward the Baltic, and Hitler perceived this as the greatest immediate threat. He then issued Directive No. 59, appointing Colonel General Schörner, a confirmed Nazi (one of the handful in the high ranks of the army), as commander in chief of Army Group North:

> This will empower him to employ in the overall area under his command all available forces and materials of the Armed Forces and the Waffen SS, of nonmilitary organizations and formations, of Party and civilian authorities, in order to repel enemy attacks and preserve our Baltic territories.

Thus was the northeast, the territory around Estonia and Lithuania, to be defended.

So in August 1944 Hitler was beset in the southeast and northeast and along the eastern line by three Soviet offensives. In Italy British General Harold Alexander was driving north. In southern France the Americans were pushing toward Bavaria. In northern France the Americans and British were driving toward Paris. In the air the Allies were dropping supplies to the French resistance, bombing French airfields used by the Germans, and bombing the Germans in the Rouen area. The heavy concentration of attacks of both

311

the Eighth and Ninth Air Forces was in tactical support of driving Allied ground operations. Still, on some days the Allies found time to bomb oil refineries, aircraft factories, and the Peenemünde rocket establishments. The Eighth Air Force had made arrangements for shuttle bombing, which meant bombing targets deep inside Germany, flying on to Soviet territory, landing, taking on bombs, and bombing Germany again on the return trip to British airfields.

At sea Hitler's U-boat campaign was almost totally disrupted. In July it cost Dönitz twenty-three U-boats to sink twenty-five Allied ships. It was not the sort of exchange that could be continued if one hoped to win the war. In August the Americans captured Brest, La Pallice, and Lorient—all the major western U-boat bases. The submarine menace in the Bay of Biscay ceased to exist. The U-boats had to move to Norwegian bases. In August Dönitz again sank twenty-five Allied ships, but this month he lost thirty-six submarines. That included the losses at Toulon and the Bay of Biscay bases, as well as submarines on operations at sea.

Following the escape of elements of the German Seventh Army and the Fifth Panzer Army from the Falaise pocket, the battle along the Seine River from Paris and Rouen was left to the Fifth Panzer Army. The Seventh Army troops were ferried across the lower Seine. Army Group G was responsible for the defense of southern France. On August 15 the Allies landed east of the Rhone and then began to push toward the mountains on a line parallel to the river valley. The German Nineteenth Army was supposed to hold the French Mediterranean coast, but that was impossible in the face of this new invasion. The commander in chief, west, now tried to persuade OKW to evacuate southern France as indefensible. It took Hitler two days to agree.

The Allies were pushing hard against Paris and southern France. The Americans and Free French had advanced to Rambouillet, and on August 24 they penetrated the outskirts of Paris. Other American troops had pushed across the Seine and moved toward the Marne River and Rheims. Field Marshal Model ordered the Germans to cross the lower Seine and defend the northern bank. The Fifth Panzer Army did cross, but it lost most of its equipment. The old Rommel headquarters at La Roche Guyon fell to the Americans. Soon Paris was engulfed. Hitler then went quite mad for a time. He ordered Paris destroyed by air attack. Told that the Luftwaffe could not gain air ascendance to do the job, he ordered the use of giant mortars to destroy the city. Fortunately Generals Hans Speidel and Günther von Blumentritt, the chiefs of staff of Army Group B and of commander in chief, west, managed to countermand the orders before they could be carried out.

On August 24, Hitler ordered the building of a new west wall. Three sets of special orders went out in the next two weeks covering this development. The primary responsibility was to be that of Martin Bormann and the Nazi *Gauleiters* in the west:

> Gauleiter Groh, Reich Commissioner for Belgium and Northern France, will be responsible for the line Scheldt-Albert Canal to east of Aachen....

> Gauleiter Simon will be responsible for the line of the Moselle from the West Wall southwest of Trier to the boundary between Gau Mosselland and Gau Westmark.

> Gauleiter Bürkel will be responsible for the line of the Moselle from the boundary of Gau Westmark via the Arsenal of Metz-Diedenhofe south of St. Avold to Saaralben.

> Gauleiter Wagner will be responsible for the Vosges position from Saaralben to Belfort, as previously planned.

There it was, the new west wall. And it was to be in the hands of the Nazis.

The only German army still intact in the west was the Fifteenth Army, which manned the coastal defenses of the west. It had to be withdrawn piecemeal and taken north along the coast.

East of Paris the Americans were breaking through the German First Army positions. The Americans missed one excellent opportunity: had they sent an armored force south across the Plateau de Langres, they might have destroyed Army Group G, which was retreating up the Rhone valley. The Americans failed to see this.

As the Americans and British moved forward, they were constantly and pleasantly surprised to discover that the Germans had no prepared positions in areas where they had been in control for four years. The reason, as any German general could have told them, was that for an officer to suggest such an idea to Hitler was to court disgrace. Such talk of defense was defeatist, Hitler had said from the beginning. And now it was too late.

*

On August 26, Paris fell.

Around the first of September Field Marshal Model told Hitler that the situation was such that the only possible defense was going to be at the west wall, the old Siegfried line, with its new additions. So Hitler issued a directive calling for a fighting withdrawal to the west wall, which skirted the border of Alsace-Lorraine. The plan was to close the gap that existed between the German First Army in Luxembourg and the remnants of Army Group G. What was left of the Fifth Panzer Army and the Seventh Army had moved across the Meuse.

Hitler's Directive No. 64

1. Our own heavily tried forces, and the impossibility of bringing up adequate reinforcement quickly, do not allow us at
   the present moment to determine a line which must be held,
   and which certainly can be held.

   Therefore it is important for us to gain as much time as
   possible for raising and bringing up new formations, and for
   the development of the Western defenses, and to destroy enemy forces by local attacks.

2. I therefore issue the following orders for the conduct of operations. The right flank and center of the Army in the West
   (including 1st Army) will dispute every inch of ground with
   the enemy by stubborn delaying action. The likelihood of local penetrations must be accepted, but these must not lead
   to the encirclement of large German positions....

On September 3 Brussels fell.

On September 4 the British entered Antwerp. But General Montgomery failed to move in time to close off the port, so the German Fifteenth Army was able to escape intact across the mouth of the Scheldt River to take up positions behind the Albert Canal and the Meuse River.

Now, when it was very late, Hitler decided that the parachute troops should be employed. The American First Army was on the

Meuse. General Patton's Third Army was on the Moselle near Metz, less than 100 miles from the Rhine. Hitler rushed five divisions to hold the Moselle. General Patton, who had been racing ahead for weeks, literally ran out of gasoline and diesel fuel and had to stop for resupply. Now the British in Antwerp and Patton threatened the industrial Ruhr from two sides.

Colonel General Kurt Student was now ordered to move with the First Parachute Army to the Albert Canal to hold Holland. Student obeyed, but he did not move an army in the normal sense of the word. The First Parachute Army consisted of 18,000 boys of age 16, old men, policemen, sailors of the merchant navy, soldiers on leave, and convalescents. There was in this organization one panzer detachment: twenty-five tanks and self-propelled guns.

Considering the overall German position, this armor complement was quite handsome. On the whole western front the Germans now had 100 tanks opposing the 2000 tanks of the Allies. The Luftwaffe could put about 600 planes into the air in the west; the Allies had 14,000 there.

The front was very ragged and the troops were dispirited. But at least, for the first time since the invasion, the Germans had a defense line in the west. Several generals suggested that Hitler now recall Field Marshal von Rundstedt to carry out the defense. Field Marshal Model, who was in effect commander of Army Group B, also approved of this plan. And so on September 5 von Rundstedt came out of retirement for the third time and took command at his new headquarters at Ahrenberg, opposite Koblenz.

The field marshal was at the west wall. But the west wall was still a shadow of its former self. What was to be done? Hitler turned the problem over to Himmler. The result was chaos. In a few days von Rundstedt told that to Hitler in no uncertain terms. The plan was scrapped, and von Rundstedt took over the building of the defenses. But not much was possible. There were no trained fortress troops. Von Rundstedt warned that the Allies could break through at any time. Actually, only one American armored division made a breakthrough, north of the Moselle toward Bitburg, and this was stopped because the Americans ran out of fuel. The Germans wondered why the Americans did not press the attack, but the Amis could not continue until their supplies caught up.

Von Rundstedt now had some time, but his forces were physi-

cally inferior. The Allies, he estimated, had fifty-three divisions on
the western front, while the Germans could put together only the
equivalent of twenty-seven. Certainly there were more divisions in
name, but the strength of an average German division was now under 5000 men—a full-strength American division might have 15,000.

Hitler now decided that his salvation was "fortresses." It was
really nothing new, this preoccupation with holding every foot of
ground on which a German soldier had trod. But it was incredibly
destructive of German resources, as it always had been. The clearest
example that summer was Hitler's insistence on holding the Channel Islands. After the Allies invaded successfully, he continued to
waste troops there instead of evacuating them.

September found the western front relatively quiet. Paris had fall-
en. France was being invested, city by city. In the south the new
invasion forces were moving into the Vosges Mountains.

There was one area of the fighting so serious that it sent Hitler
into flurries of activity. This was the American drive against Aachen.
U.S. forces were threatening German territory: the industrial Ruhr
and the whole west wall. Should they capture Aachen and take the
Ruhr, it would be impossible to prosecute the war for much longer.

The British were clearing the area around Antwerp, which would
be the new supply base for operations closer to and inside Germany. Germans still held the islands around the mouth of the Scheldt
River, which feeds Antwerp. Every garrison was ordered to hold to
the last man, and the fighting was intense, if ultimately futile. The
Germans did manage to hold the Allies for a long time, and it was
not until bombers broke the dykes at Walcheren that the flooding
caused Germans and Allies alike to seek the high ground. Then the
Allies captured Walcheren, and the long battle was over. But it had
delayed the Allied occupation and use of the port of Antwerp.

It is odd how differently the events of the war at this period were
seen from the opposing points of view. To the Allies their airborne
assault on the Low Countries was enormously important; it has been
celebrated in many books, telling of the viciousness of the fighting,
the near miss at the Rhine bridges, and the ultimate victory. To the
Germans it was one of those battles that could not possibly be won.
The most notable effort, from Hitler's point of view, was Field Mar-

shal Model's scraping together of miscellaneous troop units, including men on leave and units just back from the eastern front, to stop the British First Airborne Division at Arnhem. It was a gallant German attempt, but as Model knew, it was doomed to eventual failure. The problem, even more in the west than in the east, was the enormous backup resources that the western Allies could throw into any breach to turn around any small victory that the Germans managed to achieve. It was a case of too much and too many, and everyone but Hitler and his most ardent Nazis now shared von Rundstedt's view that the sooner Germany could end the war the better off she would be.

But Hitler was still entrapped by the unconditional surrender bugaboo, and he could not surrender even if he had wished to do so. Given all the propaganda devoted to the subject, there was no way the western Allies could reverse themselves either. So the drama had to be played out, although the ultimate results were already clear. Germany had lost the war. Now it was a question of when the fighting would come to a stop, how many men would be killed, and how much of Germany would be destroyed before it was over.

The Germans wondered why the Allies did not move in the Moselle area or against Army Group G. But Eisenhower's strategy was to take Aachen and then roll up the Ruhr and make a beeline drive toward Berlin.

So the Allies stopped before the west wall and waited. And the Germans wondered why they waited. The failure to take Antwerp on schedule was one reason. The others were the exhaustion of the Allied troops, who had been moving at top speed since June 6, and the inability of the services of supply to keep up with the front line.

This surcease of action stimulated Hitler to a new dream. He envisioned a sudden lightning movement, aping the drive of the summer of 1940, which would push the whole Allied army into the sea as the Germans had pushed the British at Dunkirk. Of course, the Führer's dream did not take into account the vastly different situation, the ability of the Allies to throw another thirty-five divisions from England into the fight, and the Allied armies fighting in the south of France. But Hitler by this time was no longer capable of sustained reason. OKW rushed troops along the whole west wall, as if it could be defended forever.

*

And so the year 1944 was drawing to an end. The Germans were holding along the west wall, but the Allies were not attacking vigorously just then. In the south the Germans were holding in Tuscany, so the Italian front was still active. On the eastern front the Russians took over Romania and advanced into Hungary, forcing the Germans to evacuate Greece, which the British then occupied. At the end of October the Soviets took Belgrade.

So Germany was quickly becoming Fortress Germany, and Hitler was entirely preoccupied with the minutiae of defense. He was fast getting down to the bunker level, and his attitude was already a bunker attitude, as his war directive of November 25, 1944, makes clear:

> Should a commander, left to his own resources, think that he must give up the struggle, he will first ask his officers, then his non-commissioned officers, and finally his troops if one of them is ready to carry on the task and continue the fight. If one of them will, the commander is to hand over command to that man, regardless of his rank, and himself fall in. The new leader will then assume the command, with all its rights and duties.

Imagine, if you will, a besieged fortress on the Rhine, defended by a thousand men. The commander knows that he is surrounded, that the Allies are ready to blast his position with bombs and artillery and then to overwhelm it. He decides to give up. His officers all agree that this is the only course. So do the noncommissioned officers. But from the rear rank steps Private Schultz, with thirteen weeks of military training and a secondhand, captured Czech rifle.

"I will take command," says Private Schultz.

And so the colonel is supposed to hand over command to the private and step to the rear rank.

This is the level of warfare to which Hitler had reduced himself by November 25, 1944.

How far off could the end now be?

30

THE EASTERN
DEBACLE

On the eastern front the Russians advanced steadily. In the south the Germans were completely unable to stop the Soviet drive; Romania, Bulgaria, and much of Hungary were occupied, though Colonel General Johannes Friessner's Army Group South had waged a desperate battle. After Belgrade was lost by Field Marshal von Weichs, the German command structure in the whole area degenerated into confusion. For example, OKW controlled one part of the battle zone and OKH controlled another part. The Red Army crossed the Danube and moved into the territory of the OKW, which was paying virtually no attention to the area. So the Russians moved swiftly toward Budapest and on November 24 took a bridgehead across the Danube at Mohacs. There were still German troops in Salonica, but German troops were being pushed back everywhere. On December 5 the Russians rolled up Army Group South's line along the Danube and reached the southern outskirts of Budapest. The same day they crossed the river north of the city, pushed on to Vac, and were stopped only east of the Gran River. By Christmas eve they had encircled the Hungarian capital.

In the area of Colonel General Josef Harpe's Army Group A the Russians reached the line of the Vistula River near Warsaw in the fall and moved up to a point between the San and Visloka rivers. This army group consisted of the First Panzer Army, Fourth Panzer Army, and Seventeenth Army. In September the Russians took several bridge-

heads across the Vistula. The Germans held there, however, helped
by the difficult mountain terrain.

Army Group Center, which once had been at the gates of Moscow, consisted of the Ninth Army, Second Army, Fourth Army,
and Third Panzer Army. They were all situated around Warsaw,
but so were the Russians. The Soviets were advancing north of Warsaw and on either side of Ostenburg. The Germans moved back,
past Memel, to East Prussia, and the Russians attacked again. Fighting now on German soil, the Germans rallied and drove the Russians back a little.

General Schörner's decision to keep his armor around Riga instead of sending it out set up the Russian victory that let the Soviets break through at Schaulen, where his armor ought to have been.
Only part of Schörner's force was evacuated.

During the late fall and winter the Germans held a front in this area
that was 750 miles long. Their plan was to set up a front line, the
Hauptkampflinie, which was to be manned to stop any ordinary enemy attacks. Twelve miles behind that line, the generals wanted to
build the *Grosskampflinie,* the last line of defense. They wanted authority to move from the first line to the second when it seemed to
them essential. General Guderian, the chief of the army, was given
this plan. He approved it and then sent it on to Hitler for his necessary affirmation. Guderian pointed out the great advantage:

The Russian method of attack consisted of first unleashing a heavy
and lengthy artillery barrage on the point the Soviets wished to strike.
After the area had been thoroughly softened up for hours, the tanks
then came streaming through, followed by more artillery and the infantry. By moving back 12 miles from the front line when the artillery
barrage began, the Germans could force the Russians to waste an enormous amount of ammunition and effort, only to discover when they
arrived at the *Hauptkampflinie* that there was nobody there. By the
time the Russians came to the second line, they would be half-
exhausted; the Germans, fresh, would be able to repulse the Russians and perhaps drive them back far beyond the original line of
defense. It was, said Guderian, an excellent scheme.

Hitler saw it and raged. Why should anyone sacrifice 12 miles in
a defensive operation, he said. No, the second line must be built a
mile behind the first. Guderian tried to argue but was told to shut

up. He went away grumbling. Hitler was fighting World War I again, when conditions were such that a 1-mile difference between defensive lines was meaningful. In 1944, with the new tanks and air power of the Russians, as well as the artillery power they had developed, the 1-mile gap meant nothing at all. The Germans would serve themselves better by not having two lines, rather than situating them as Hitler ordered.

At the beginning of the war Hitler's grasp of tactical and strategic matters had appeared enormous. But as every general knows, armies tend to *start* to fight wars with the weapons and the ideas of the past. The Germans were way out in front in 1939 with the new U-boats, the new tanks, the new artillery, and the new panzer techniques. But by 1944 the Stuka bomber was totally outmoded; the 88-millimeter gun was superseded by the 100-millimeter (and larger) guns of the Russians and the western Allies; the Soviet tanks were superior to the Germans' best (although the western Allies' tanks were not); and the tactics and strategy of the war had changed completely. (For example, the Americans had a great deficiency: their standard infantry antitank gun, the 37 millimeter, was useless. But by 1944 they were using 75-millimeter pack howitzers, and the P-47 fighter plane had become the nemesis of German tanks in the west. That is how adaptable the Americans were.) Despite his consuming interest in new wonderweapons, Hitler didn't fully appreciate this qualitative shift and refused to learn from his generals. At OKW Keitel and Jodl had long before become rubber stamps in any case. And the OKH chief reported his Führer's attitude:

Since he continued to believe that he was the only real front-line soldier at Supreme Headquarters—and indeed so far as the majority of his military advisors were concerned he did know far more about active service than they—and since the grotesque flattery of his party comrades, led by Ribbentrop and Göring, had given him the illusion that he was a great military leader, he absolutely refused to learn from others.

Hitler told Guderian:

There's no need for you to try to teach me. I've been commanding the German army in the field for five years and during that time I've had more practical experience than any gentlemen of the General Staff could hope to have. I've studied Clausewitz and Moltke and read all the Schlieffen papers. I'm more in the picture than you are.

So Hitler plunged deeper and deeper into his dream world, and the real world swirled around him, ignored, with the war growing more desperate for the Germans every day.

And day by day matters continued to deteriorate. General Miklos of the Hungarian army drove off one day in his Mercedes and appeared next at the Red Army headquarters on his front. Hitler then overthrew the Hungarian government and installed the Salaszy regime, which was guaranteed to be loyal to the Germans, but had little else to recommend it.

In Slovakia affairs moved from bad to worse. Trains were stopped by the Slovakian partisans, and German officers and men riding them were taken off and shot. The SS and the Gestapo then took vengeance on the civilian population, and the partisans revenged themselves in turn. It was a never-ending struggle.

In the autumn Guderian moved his headquarters to the Maybach camp near Zossen. At the end of December he drove to Hitler's OKW headquarters to plead for more troops for the eastern front. Hitler was still preoccupied with the west; his Ardennes offensive was in progress. But Guderian had bad news for him. He had information that the Soviets were planning an even more extensive offensive than they had staged anytime in the past. He had identified three major attack forces, and he said that the attack would begin on January 12. The force ratios were enough to make any general shudder. The Russians' superiority over the Germans was:

Infantry: 11 to 1

Armored units: 7 to 1

Artillery: 15 to 1

Air force units: 20 to 1

The German troops were excellent soldiers—no matter the early war complaints of the General Staff about lack of training and discipline. Combat was the best teacher, and the German units had been baptized in fire. Guderian would have been content with ratios of 1 German unit to 5 Soviet, but these odds were impossible. Moreover, the German soldiers were tired. They had been fighting for five years, some of them almost steadily. Each year of the previous three they had seen their stocks of supplies diminish and their weapons grow less effective. They had grown accustomed to retreat and unaccustomed to even small victories. Guderian wondered if the German soldier could stand the strain much longer.

To stop the Russians he would have to have more arms and more men on the eastern front. That is why he had gone to see Hitler.

His plan was to build up strong reserves in the Lodz-Hohensalza area. Then, when the Russians broke through the link, as they were expected to do, the Germans would fight a war of movement, the sort of battle at which they still excelled. So when Guderian arrived at OKW headquarters to confront Hitler on December 24, he knew that the first task was to convince the Führer of the desperate need before them.

Present at the meeting were Keitel and Jodl, the ardent Nazis; General Wilhelm Burgdorf, and a number of junior officers who had not heard all these arguments before.

To all of them, General Guderian presented a brand new report from the *Abwehr*'s Foreign Armies East office. The study gave the cold facts and colder prospects. It was absolutely accurate and was so proved by the turn of events.

But Hitler chose not to believe.

The army staff had been gulled by Soviet propaganda, he sneered. A Soviet rifle division had a maximum strength of 7000 men, said Hitler. The Russian tank units had no tanks.

"It's the greatest imposture since Genghis Khan," shouted the Führer. "Who's responsible for producing all this rubbish?"

Hitler was beguiled by his own guile. For months he had been inventing military organizations. He had created artillery corps which had no guns. He had commissioned new panzer brigades which had only the tanks of battalions. His new tank-destroyer brigades consisted of a single battalion each. His methods so confused the German army's planners that they had no way of putting together a meaningful order of battle or reports on real strengths and weaknesses. Now he assumed that because he did this, the enemy must be doing the same thing, and that is the basis on which he operated.

"The Russians," Hitler said on December 24, 1944, "will not launch a serious attack in the near future."

Guderian could not argue. No one was allowed to argue.

At dinner that night at OKW, Guderian was seated next to Heinrich Himmler, commander of the replacement army, commander of Army Group Upper Rhine, minister of the interior, chief of the German police, and national commander of the SS. Himmler had risen far; he now was perhaps the second or third most important man in all Germany.

"You know my dear general," he confided to Guderian, "I don't really believe the Russians will attack at all, ever. It's an enormous bluff....They're far too worried. I'm convinced there is nothing going on in the east."

And then Jodl made things difficult by directing the conversation to the war in the west, where the Ardennes offensive was breaking down. Jodl knew that the Ardennes offensive had not accomplished what he had hoped, but he insisted that it had upset the western Allies' timetable, and that was very valuable. The thing to do, said Jodl, was to continue to launch minimal attacks all along the British and American lines. These attacks would so confuse and cripple the enemy units that ultimately the western Allies would seek a negotiated peace. He had just ordered a new attack in Alsace-Lorraine for that very purpose.

So Jodl bitterly opposed the demands of Guderian for more troops for the east. "We must not lose the initiative that we have gained," he kept saying. Guderian shut his mouth. It was no good saying that the initiative they had gained had already been lost and that what Jodl now proposed was national suicide.

Guderian did point out that the recent military activities in the west had cost the Germans the use of the Ruhr industrial basin. Bombing attacks had paralyzed most of the factories. But in the east the Silesian sector was still working at full blast. Now the center of the German armament industry had moved east. Let them lose Upper Silesia, said Guderian, and the German war effort must collapse within weeks.

But Guderian's argument meant nothing to this crowd.

Hitler dismissed Guderian that night with instructions that the eastern front must take care of itself. Hitler had neither time nor resources to put there. Before the general left, he made some final requests. Let them evacuate Kurland, then, he said. Let the units that had been fighting in Finland before the Finnish capitulation to Russia now be brought back to the eastern front. Let OKH have the troops that were sitting idly in Norway.

No, said Hitler. Those troops were going to the Vosges Mountains to stem the tide of the Allies in the southwest.

And so, on Christmas day 1944, General Guderian took the train back to Zossen. When he got there he discovered that Hitler had again taken one of those arbitrary, senseless actions that could only weaken the whole eastern front. Hitler had ordered General Herbert Gille's SS corps, with two SS divisions, to leave the area north of Warsaw where it was holding a section of the line and to move to intercede in the siege of Budapest and break the Russian ring around that city. What Hitler was saying was that to him the relief of Budapest was more important than the defense of eastern Germany. That way, Guderian knew, lay disaster. He protested. The protest was ignored. Thus, one-sixth of the panzer forces defending the eastern front against the coming Soviet offensives were suddenly pulled out of the line and sent to a secondary theater.

Back at his OKH headquarters, General Guderian conferred with his staff, but they found no solution to the impending Soviet offensive. Only the immediate discontinuance of the German offensive operations in the west and the transfer of many thousands of troops to the east might stop the Russians.

So on New Year's eve, General Guderian once more set off for the OKW headquarters, now at Ziegenberg in Hesse. This time, Guderian hoped to enlist some allies before he spoke with Hitler. He paid a call on Field Marshal von Rundstedt and explained the situation on the eastern front in great detail to the marshal. Von Rundstedt was very sympathetic and gave him the names of three divisions on the western front and one on the Italian front which could be spared and which could be transported swiftly to the east.

Guderian then called on the chief of army transport and told him to have trains ready to take these troops east.

Then he called on Hitler.

But once more Keitel and Jodl were present, and the latter said that he had no available reserve forces. Guderian quoted von Rundstedt in contradiction. Jodl was flustered and then angry, particularly when Guderian named the specific units and their commanders. Even Hitler was impressed. Jodl was stunned into silence, and Guderian got four divisions. But even these were to go to Hungary, by the Führer's orders.

On the morning of New Year's day, Guderian went to see Hitler again. He informed him that Gille's SS corps would launch an attack that very afternoon to relieve Budapest.

Hitler was immediately put into a jolly mood, for he expected much from that attack. Yet he was to be disappointed. The attack was launched, but it failed to break through the Russian lines around the Hungarian capital.

But by that time Guderian was back at his own headquarters on the eastern front. He wondered why the attack had failed. Getting no answer at OKH headquarters, he decided to make a tour of the southeastern fronts to see for himself what might be expected in the future. He headed for the headquarters of Army Group South. From there he would go to Cracow, and then he would check every bit of the 750-mile front. Then he would report to Hitler once again.

31

THE ARDENNES

For months Hitler had been talking about striking the western Allies a blow that would turn the war on that front completely around. After the failed assassination attempt of July 1944, his attention to this goal became an obsession. Something had to be done to relieve the two-front pressure. It could not be done in the east—the front was too long, from 750 to 1000 miles, and the resources were too slender. No matter how much Hitler railed at those who suggested the Russians were now more powerful than Germany, in his heart he knew the truth. In the west, then, he hoped to find the miracle that would save the Third Reich.

The planning began in October. One day Hitler took Albert Speer aside and told his minister of armaments to be prepared with a corps of construction workers who would be able to build bridges and make it possible for an army to move swiftly.

This last offensive in the west was to be the great gamble.

"If it is not successful then I no longer see any possibility for ending the war well," Hitler said. "A single breakthrough on the western front...will lead to a collapse and panic among the Americans."

His forces would drive to Antwerp, take that supply port from the British, and then surround the British army and capture it. He would take hundreds of thousands of prisoners and the western Allies would fold up.

That was Hitler's dream in the fall of 1944, as misty and phosphorescent a dream as that of any addict smoking his opium. The men around Hitler knew that it was a desperate and futile gamble, but no one could stop him. Out of hearing of the Gestapo, those men wondered aloud when it was all going to end.

On October 21, 1944, Aachen (Aix-la-Chapelle) fell. The Americans were now in Germany and could be expected to begin exploiting their successes.

On November 3, at Field Marshal Model's Army Group B headquarters, a vital conference was convened. Present were the three army commanders who held the northwest sector of the western front, Model himself, and General Jodl, chief of staff of OKW.

The importance of the meeting was indicated when, before it properly began, Model passed around a document for each man to sign. It guaranteed his absolute silence on the matters about to be discussed, and it promised that if any officer broke his pledge he would be punished by death. They all signed, and then General Jodl began to talk.

Germany was going to launch a new offensive, Jodl said, one which Hitler expected to turn the war around completely.

The place for the attack was to be the Monschau-Echternach sector—the Ardennes. There, a careful study had indicated, the western Allies' forces were strung out thinly, but their reserves were right behind the front. The Allied troops were tired from their dash across France. Moreover, their supply train had not caught up with the front-line troops, and supply was short in almost every category. And, because of the Germans' continuous retreat to reach their west wall, the Allies were psychologically unprepared for a possible German counteroffensive.

The sort of weather needed was soon to come: cold, heavy precipitation, and heavy cloud cover that would prevent the Allied air forces from exerting their superiority to help the ground troops. Every reserve, particularly of panzer units, had been strained to secure the fighting force to make this attack. Everything depended on lightning speed and quick response. The panzer units would seize the bridgeheads over the Meuse River between Liege and Namur;

they would then drive swiftly for Antwerp, knock out that city, and then have the Americans and the British just about where the British were at the time of Dunkirk. Only this time the advantage would be fully exploited by the Germans before the Allied troops could get away.

Once the German troops passed the Meuse River, they could cut the American First Army's communications lines, which followed the Meuse valley. When the panzers reached the Brussels-Antwerp region, the British Twenty-first Army Group lines would be similarly at risk; with the capture of Antwerp British supplies would be cut off. The Germans could then attack the Americans and British from all sides, seal off some thirty divisions, destroy the enemy's ability to attack, and capture so much matériel that the Germans could continue to prosecute the war for months.

The field generals quickly saw some holes in that plan. Any army that had to depend on capturing enemy supplies to continue its offensive was already in bad shape.

But Jodl went on.

The Führer said that this operation would tie down the Allies for a long time to come, completely disrupting their war plans. The delays would cause them to postpone any decisions about driving against Germany. This would give Germany what it must have, "a pause to draw breath," said Hitler.

So Hitler was preparing just then to make another drastic mistake, and the generals around him knew it, although there was nothing they could do to stop the process. Hitler now would listen to no one at all.

The flaw was that the action was too little and too late. The generals could see that there was the germ of a brilliant plan in Hitler's mind. But in implementing it, he refused to take the risks inherent in the proposition, the risks that could make it succeed. To succeed, he would have had to withdraw troops from the south, from Italy, and from areas of the eastern front. It could have been done; the lines elsewhere could have been shortened to the benefit of the German defenders.

But he would not withdraw from the Luftwaffe, the navy, and the replacement army forces that were marked for future operations in other theaters. As General Hasso von Manteuffel put it: "The dictator, in his decline, could not or would not order the concentration of effort necessary to create a force strong enough to smash the enemy front."

Here is the plan in more detail:

> Colonel General Sepp Dietrich's Sixth SS Panzer Army was to seize the Meuse crossings on both sides of Liege and then to cross the Albert Canal between Maastricht and Antwerp and to advance in the area north of Antwerp.
>
> General von Manteuffel's Fifth Panzer Army was to cross the Meuse near Amey and then cover the rear of the Sixth SS Panzer Army.
>
> The Seventh Army, under General Erich Brandenberger, was to cover the southern and southwestern flanks.

And here is the force they had: twenty-three divisions with a thousand tanks and armored assault guns. Specifically:

> *Sixth SS Panzer Army:* four SS panzer divisions and five infantry divisions
>
> *Fifth Panzer Army:* four panzer divisions and three infantry divisions
>
> *Seventh Army:* six infantry divisions and one panzer division

With the slender reserves available the total number of German divisions to be engaged numbered about thirty. And this, after five years of war, was the total force that Hitler could pull together to commit to a major new operation. Thirty divisions...once he had dreamed of three hundred. That was how far the Thousand-Year Reich had shrunk in eleven years.

The initial attack was to be made by the German infantry in bad weather, against a line of replacement troops that they expected to find. The penetration was to be swift and solid; then the panzer units were to be moved right on through deep into the enemy's rear positions. The German troops were not to stop to take fortified villages or other positions, but simply to bypass them and rush on.

The date for the operation, General Jodl said, was to be November 25, the day of the new moon. The preceding dark period of the moon would provide cover for movement of the forces up to the jumping-off point.

Then the attendees were asked to comment. The result was an agreement among the field generals that the attack had to wait until December and that it must be concerned with limited objectives at the beginning, with regrouping to achieve the next set. In the discussion that followed, one of the central notions of Hitler's new military policy was exposed starkly. Hitler preferred the SS to the army. He wanted the SS panzer divisions to have first place everywhere. Thus he had encouraged the SS panzer leaders to refuse to cooperate fully with the army panzer generals. Because of this General Dietrich, the SS Sixth Panzer Army commander, and General von Manteuffel of the Army's Fifth Panzer Army, found themselves in basic competition.

In Berlin on December 2 the field generals worked out the details of the assault with Hitler. Field Marshal Model, General Dietrich, and General von Manteuffel were there, along with General Siegfried Westphal, chief of staff to the commander in chief, west.

Model did the exposition that day. He had made plans with Armaments Minister Speer for a special supply line for armaments for this particular operation. Special trains would be made available.

But when the conference was over, Hitler returned to his original plan and said no modifications were accepted. Antwerp was the objective. The headlong rush would go forward as stipulated.

The conference lasted seven hours. When it ended, Hitler took von Manteuffel aside. They talked for a further hour and a half. The reason obviously was that Hitler did not trust the army, and von Manteuffel represented the army. So Hitler wanted to discover every objection that might be raised and to meet those objections before the drive began.

Several factors worked in the Germans' favor that December. First, the fighting in the Aachen area made it possible for them to move troops up behind that front without attracting any special attention.

Second, the Germans were quite familiar with the territory of the Ardennes sector. They had fought there in 1940 and won, and they had retreated through that area a few months earlier. They knew all about the narrow roads with their hairpin turns and the herculean measures that had to be used to move heavy equipment through. Even so, the generals expected plenty of problems. The German equipment was not in good shape, so they would have many breakdowns. The standard of training of the German armored troops had fallen so far that the generals were not sure how the men would behave. They had not put on a major Panzer offensive since mid-1943. The breakdown of the German railroad service west of the Rhine also would cause all sorts of transport problems.

But the plans went forward. When the troops were withdrawn from the front for regrouping and some rest before the attack, the greatest security was observed. Panzer officers discarded their distinctive uniforms and dressed as infantry. Charcoal was issued to the troops so that the smoke of their cooking fires would not betray the units. The horse-drawn artillery was moved up behind the front; when it was brought closer, night fighters from the Luftwaffe flew along the roads to cover the noise of the horses' hooves. Vehicles were moved forward with great care. If a vehicle went off the road, its telltale tracks were brushed out of the snow by the following infantry.

The result was that the whole German attack force was brought up to the jump-off point without the Allies suspecting that anything was about to happen.

*   *   *

During the last two weeks of November the fighting around Aachen was especially violent. American troops penetrated the west wall near Walendorf. The Germans managed to drive them out, but it was apparent that the next time it might not be quite so easy. By the end of the month it had become clear that the Allies were prepared to fight a long war of attrition along the west wall and that the Americans and British intended to take the Ruhr. The Germans did not have time on their side. But in this heavy fighting the American Second, Fourth, and Twenty-eighth Infantry Divisions had been badly hurt and had been transferred from the west wall front to the Ardennes sector for rest and rehabilitation.

On December 11 von Manteuffel's Fifth Panzer Army took over the sector of the front from which it would attack. That day all the important commanders who would participate in the attack were summoned to Hitler's headquarters at Eagle's Nest, near Ziegenberg.

Here is von Manteuffel's recollection of that meeting:

The assembly presented a striking contrast. On one side of the room were the commanding generals, responsible and experienced soldiers, many of whom had made great names for themselves on past battlefields, experts at their trade, respected by their troops. Facing them was the Supreme Commander of the Armed Forces, a stooped figure with a pale and puffy face, hunched in his chair, his hands trembling, his left arm subject to a violent twitching, which he did his best to conceal, a sick man apparently borne down by his burden of responsibility. His physical condition had deteriorated noticeably since our last meeting in Berlin only nine days before. When he walked he dragged one leg behind him.

At his side was Jodl, an old man now, overworked and overtired. His expression used to be taut and his bearing rigid, but this was no longer so. He was mentally and physically exhausted. Later in conversation with small groups of assembled officers, he was both touchy and irritable. As for Field Marshal Keitel, his manner showed that he had not been informed.

Hitler spoke for an hour and a half, but he did not make a good impression. He seemed an old, sick man. To those who had been through many previous phases of the war, Hitler's words now were more than a little contradictory. He had previously said that the preliminary condition for launching a successful military operation was the establishment of fresh battleworthy formations for the offensive. But this had not been done for the Ardennes attack, and everyone knew it. Germany did not have the manpower and the equipment to set up the force that Rundstedt needed to make the assault. Still, as von Manteuffel noted, they all knew that they had received everything that the beleaguered German war machine had to give at this point.

When the meeting ended, the officers went away with the feeling that Hitler had higher hopes than he really should have held.

The attack was launched on December 16, and the Allies were completely surprised. They were suffering from too much success. Eisen-

hower and Montgomery had been betting whether the war would
be over by Christmas. Since it did not seem to be, they declared a
respite, and many of the high-ranking Allied officers were in London that Christmas, celebrating. The heads of many of the higher
field commanders were swollen with victory, too, to such a degree
that although captured prisoners in early December indicated a coming German offensive, no one at the higher headquarters believed
the reports.

The main point of attack was on the right, where Dietrich's Sixth
SS Panzer Army had the best equipment that could be found. The SS
troops also had rounded up all the German troops they could find who
spoke American English. These men were dressed in American army
uniforms and equipped with American weapons, maps, and jeeps so
that they could confuse the American troops in the line. They infil-
trated on that first day and began to foul up American communications by switching road signs, breaking down radio sets, and the like.
The move worked beautifully at first, but the Americans caught on
quickly and became very cautious about any soldiers they did not
know personally.

But even on that first day, Field Marshal Model saw something
that presaged defeat: he drove along the rail line of supply and saw
his precious materials on freight cars east of the Rhine—jammed up
there because heavy enemy bombing had stopped them.

And Model knew something else. Back in Berlin the deskbound
soldiers had estimated the requirements a division would need to drive
100 kilometers. But at the front the panzer generals knew that the actual consumption of fuel was twice as high under battle conditions as
the estimates and that to secure that amount, five times as much as
estimated had to be sent from the rear because so much was delayed
or lost in transit. But when the offensive began, only one and a half
times as much as the Berlin estimate had been provided.

General von Manteuffel's Fifth Panzer Army was in the center
and Brandenberger's Seventh Army was on the left.

The attack went very well in the beginning. Von Manteuffel's
army successfully penetrated close to the Meuse. The Germans did
not know it, but one reason for their ease of movement was a total
miscalculation on the part of the Allies. The U.S. 106th Infantry
Division, the newest in the American line in Europe, was woefully
inept and untried. Thus elements of the Second Panzer Division actually reached the banks of the Meuse before the Americans knew

it. But the Americans began to rally, and the Christmas party in London broke up.

Soon the Germans were bogging down. On December 18 the Germans very nearly reached the important road junction of Bastogne. They were almost on schedule, Bastogne was to have been reached on the second day. On December 18 it was bypassed since the Americans had rushed new troops into the town. On December 20, along the Seventh Army's front, the Germans began to lose ground. By December 22 it was plain that the armies could never reach Antwerp. The Fifth Panzer Army kept moving, and it made some progress. But without supporting pressure on its flanks, that purpose made no real difference. As the battle turned against the Germans, they became unusually vicious. In the Ardennes battle came the worst troop massacres of the western front in World War II. American soldiers were shot down by the Germans *after* surrendering at Malmedy forest and elsewhere.

At one point the vanguard of von Manteuffel's force was only 3 miles east of Dinant, but the offensive in the Monschau-Malmedy sector was a failure. The attacking forces were split.

The key to all now was Bastogne, the road junction that separated the German armies. It was surrounded, but only by taking troops from the Fifth Panzer Army's attack force. And this attempt failed because on December 23 the weather cleared and the Allied air forces dropped supplies into the town from the air. So on December 24 the Germans began to go on the defensive.

Now Hitler took a hand, issuing orders to the Twelfth SS Panzer Corps of the Fifteenth Army to attack, and later issuing orders to the unit to attack in a different place. The situation at Bastogne grew worse as the Americans continued to hold out and were resupplied by air, and the Germans detached part of the Sixth SS Panzer Army to try to take the place. But by December 26 General Patton's Third Army troops were coming to the rescue of Bastogne.

Then, as the weather cleared, for the first time the Allies were able to take advantage of their air superiority, and they attacked.

By the end of December German casualties were so heavy that the Germans regarded the battle as having moved into its final defensive phase.

Early in January Bastogne was out of danger. At that point the whole battle became meaningless. There was no way the Germans could drive on to Antwerp or threaten the rear of the Allied line. Von Rundstedt ordered a swift retreat to save forces and equipment. As usual, Hitler gainsaid him. He wanted a slow retreat. He was waiting for the miracle that would never come. The Allied forces now began to inexorably push in the German flanks and squeeze them in the center.

Then, on January 13, the Russians began a new offensive in the east. Something had to be done about that. The great decisive battle of the west had been lost. The only thing to do now was throw those troops, which had been rounded up at such cost, into the battle of the east to try to save what could be salvaged. And so the Ardennes offensive came to a halt, and the Germans turned their attention east. Even Hitler could not think of anything cogent to say to stop it.

32

THE LAST OFFENSIVE

On January 9 the German Ardennes offensive stopped and was reversed in the west; in the east General Guderian worried about the coming Russian offensive. So much did he worry that he made another trip to Ziegenberg to see Hitler and try once more to convince him that the east must be shored up immediately if disaster was to be averted. He took with him his chief of staff, General Gehlen, and his inspector of armored troops, General Thomale. The former made a strong presentation with maps and figures. Hitler did what he had so often done: unable to argue from facts, he shouted Gehlen down.

"Completely idiotic," he said of Gehlen's report, and he demanded that the general be relieved at once.

Guderian lost his temper and told Hitler that if Gehlen were relieved, he, too, would be relieved.

Hitler then quieted down. "The eastern front has never been possessed of such reserves as now. That is your doing," said the Führer.

Guderian was not interested in hollow compliments. Jodl kept telling Guderian that the intelligence they had from the Soviet front could be just a Soviet bluff. Guderian, who knew precisely what he faced, could not budge the OKW chief of staff. So now OKW had moved into a period of what Guderian called "Ostrich strategy." Stick your head in the sand and pretend the Soviet threat does not exist.

All sorts of thoughts buzzed through Guderian's head at this point, even some that were seditious. He wondered, although not publicly, how much Hitler's and Jodl's attitude derived from the fact that they came, respectively, from southern and western Germany, and the part of Germany under threat was East Prussia.

The Soviet assault began on January 12, 1945, at the Baranov bridge-head. The Soviets sent their "punishment units" in first—units composed of men who had been sentenced to death or long prison terms and who now were given an opportunity to become live heroes and salvage their careers or to die like heroes. That was the way it was at the Pulavy bridgehead. The mines had been cleared away from the attack zone by the Soviet engineers. Forty tanks rested in a wooded area 2 miles behind. Then the punishment units came up and began to march across the no-man's-land.

At Baranov fourteen Soviet rifle divisions, two independent tank corps, and elements of still another entire army were committed.

During the first day the Russians did not commit their tank divisions. They wanted to wait and see which way to move them. But the movement that day was not only at Baranov. The bridgeheads over the Vistula at Pulavy and Magnuzev were also showing movement. North of Warsaw the Russians were moving. It was, undoubtedly, the greatest combined offensive of the war. And the Russians had prepared well for it. For as the Soviets began to move, the Germans saw that the Russian engineers had very quietly cleared away their minefields.

Army Group A began to move its reserves forward to counter the Russian thrust that day. But Hitler had insisted that the reserves be not more than 2 miles from the front, so just what Guderian had predicted happened. The German reserves came forward and immediately fell under an intense artillery barrage. The casualties among the reserves were very heavy before they ever got into action.

The Russians then attacked and got behind the reserves and partially surrounded them. Then the reserves had to fight their way out of the trap. They managed to do so under General Nehring. The success was such that it was almost regarded as a victory, when actually it was merely the salvaging of major forces from defeat. And Hitler was personally to blame.

*

On January 13 the Russian forces broke through west of Baranov and advanced northward. The Russian Third and Fourth Guards tank armies appeared for the first time. The Russians had committed thirty-two rifle divisions and eight tank corps to this offensive. The Germans realized that they were facing the greatest concentration of forces in a narrow area that had occurred on either side since the beginning of the war.

Now came indications that another advance would be launched south of the Vistula. The first step by the Russians was always the clearing of pathways through the minefields. This would occur two to three days before the actual attack.

And in East Prussia, German soil, the attack on the Ebenrode-Schlossberg area began. Fifteen rifle divisions supported by tanks began to move forward.

The Soviets intended to move into Upper Silesia to destroy the German industrial complex there; it now was the most important such area in the country, since the Ruhr had been bombed so many times that many factories there were destroyed or severely damaged.

Thus far the Germans had been able to contain the thrusts from the bridgeheads, but how long they could continue would depend on the number of troops the Russians threw in and the number of troops the Germans could put together at any point to resist. It was a huge guessing game—even more vital than usual because the German lines were so thin.

From Magnuzev, a few miles south of Warsaw, forces were moving toward that city. From Baranov the Russians were moving northwest to try to outflank Warsaw on the west. Southeast of Cracow the Russian attack also began. So daily the situation of Army Group Center and the German line became more critical, as the Russians kept piling one troop column on another and then diverging slightly to create an enormous broad front of penetrations.

From East Prussia down south to Romania the Russians were on the move, with the greatest danger to Germany in the East Prussia region.

Hour by hour General Guderian kept Hitler informed of the developments. Almost all the reports were negative. Hitler seemed strangely unconcerned. He was still all bound up in the failed west-

ern offensive, refighting every action on his map table, showing how
his generals had let him down. He would not return to the eastern
area, or to Berlin, but remained in his western command post. Guderian thought this very dangerous; it gave the people around Hitler
all the wrong ideas about where the greatest danger lay. He pleaded
with Hitler to at least return to Berlin so that the Nazis would see
that the Führer was taking the eastern defense problem seriously.
But Hitler gave him no consolation.

"The Eastern front will simply have to do with what it has,"
said Hitler again.

*

Then, suddenly, Hitler began interfering in the daily conduct of operations in the east. On January 15 he issued an order transferring the
Gross-Deutschland Panzer Corps from East Prussia south to Kielce.
Its job would be to stop the Soviet breakthrough toward Posen. When
Guderian heard of the order he knew it could not possibly arrive in
time. What Hitler had ordered was bound to weaken the East Prussia
front dangerously.

The quarrel with Guderian had finally persuaded Hitler to move
back to Berlin to face the problems of the eastern front. On January
16 Guderian had a conference with Hitler at the Chancellery, now
badly bombed. But even so, it was here that Hitler now chose to
establish his supreme headquarters permanently. Here, too, was his
bunker.

Finally, far too late, Hitler had decided that the western front offensive could not be resumed, and that the forces allocated for it could
be taken to the eastern front to try to stem the Russian advance.

But where on the eastern front? This was the question that interested General Guderian. And the answer given to him by General Jodl was most disconcerting: "To the Hungarian front."

Guderian had planned to use the Sixth Panzer Army in the Oder
River area to attack the flank of the Soviet offensive forces, and
perhaps to turn them. He went to see Hitler and pressed this view.
Hitler refused to accept the army chief's proposal. The troops would
go to Hungary, he said, and there they would relieve Budapest and
throw the Russians back across the Danube.

Guderian argued the military issues. Hitler switched to economic
reasons. Since the bombing of the German synthetic oil factories

had been so very effective, and since the Romanian oil fields were lost and the Caucasus oil fields had never produced anything for Germany before they were lost, the Hungarian oil fields were of enormous importance, said Hitler.

"If you don't get any more fuel your tanks won't be able to move and the airplanes won't be able to fly," said Hitler. And he would not be dissuaded from that view, no matter what Guderian said about the impossibility of moving the fuel and the availability of fuel even then from German sources.

Then came the inevitable argument over tactics. Hitler tried to blame his generals for the defeats caused by having the reserves too close to the front line. Guderian produced the stenographic record showing that Hitler had made the decision over his generals' objections.

Hitler then blamed General Harpe, commander of Army Group A, for all that had happened on the central Russian front. Harpe was to be the scapegoat for his Führer's errors, and he was fired. Into the picture stepped Field Marshal Schörner, one of the Nazi generals. He began his campaign on January 17 by firing the most capable field general he had, the commander of the Ninth Army, Freiherr Smilo von Lüttwitz. Three other generals were fired by this Nazi braggart. Guderian was kept busy rushing about, finding new posts for them in the west, for these were the most valuable officers Germany had: von Lüttwitz, von Saucken, Harpe, and Balck.

In the south Tito's partisans were threatening the supply lines of German Army Group E. Not far off the Russian bridgehead across the Gran was growing larger. The Germans of Army Group A were retiring before them. In southern Poland the Russians were turning toward Cracow. Further north they were attacking toward Czestochowa. Soviet troops released from the far north by the collapse of Finland had come down to join in these pushes. In the Army Group Center section, the Russians were attacking steadily through Bialystok and Ostrov, in the Schlossberg area.

In spite of this, Hitler again refused to allow the evacuation of German troops in the Kurland area, a withdrawal Guderian had advocated for weeks.

The disparity of forces was now growing staggering. Against

Army Group A the Russians had fifteen tank corps. Powerful enemy forces were moving on Warsaw. The German Forty-sixth Panzer Corps was withdrawing from that area. The Russians cut off this corps and began pouring toward the German frontier. East and West Prussia were threatened.

Late on the afternoon of January 17 Guderian's staff said they would now have to change the German defense line, on the supposition that Warsaw was either already in Russian hands or would be in a matter of hours.

Guderian went to see Hitler with this bad news. Just as he was leaving his office he had another message from Warsaw. The city was still in German hands, said the defenders, but it would have to be evacuated the following night.

Guderian faced Hitler with this dispatch.

"Warsaw must be defended to the last man," Hitler said. It must be defended at all costs.

The Führer would not acknowledge that he, himself, had predestined the loss of Warsaw by refusing Guderian's request to make it a fortress city. Hitler had insisted on transferring all major units west for his Ardennes offensive. He had left only four battalions of combat troops and some scattered engineer and other units. They did not have the strength to defend the city.

OKW ordered the commander of Warsaw to defend, but the commander knew what was happening and withdrew. Hitler's fury was almost unbounded. For the next few days he spoke of nothing but Warsaw, how he had been betrayed yet again by his generals. He ranted at them and the OKW staff for their failures.

On January 18 the Germans attacked in the mountains west of Budapest. But that same day the Russians entered the Hungarian capital.

All up the line the Soviets were attacking. When German troops were cut off in some area, Hitler refused to allow them to be withdrawn. Let them stand and fight it out, he said. And so they did.

Hitler now spent much of his time trying to find someone to blame for the fall of Warsaw. Despite Guderian's resistance, several colonels were arrested on Hitler's personal orders. His vendetta against the army Officer Corps now extended down to the level of colonels. Several of them were imprisoned. Guderian claimed that this move put an end to some of his best staff work.

But it was not going to make much difference. Events were moving too quickly for that. North of the Carpathian Mountains, the Russians were pushing toward the industrial area of Upper Silesia, and the city of Breslau in particular. Lodz fell. The Soviets were moving forward south of Memel. Army Group North, in Kurland, was completely cut off from defense of the fatherland.

On January 20 the Russians were on German soil. They crossed the border of the Reich very near the home of General Guderian, and his wife was forced to flee from their estate. The Russians kept moving. In Silesia they were moving closer to Breslau. In Posen they crossed the frontier. South of Memel the Russians were moving on Königsberg, the East Prussian capital.

By January 21 several German armies were in danger of being surrounded and cut off. Particularly endangered was the Fourth Army, whose withdrawal Hitler refused to permit. So General Friedrich Hossbach, the commander, simply set out on an attack to the west, through the Russian lines. OKW was not even advised of it, nor was OKH. Then, on January 24, when the fortress of Lötzen was lost without a fight because of this withdrawal, it came as a complete surprise to Hitler. He lost all control, and threatened the lives of all those concerned.

The truth was unavoidable, and the people on the scene knew it: the German defenses of East Prussia were crumbling.

Seeing the handwriting on the wall, General Guderian began thinking of some way to save Germany from the trap that was closing about the nation. He went to see Foreign Minister von Ribbentrop and suggested that they approach Hitler and try to persuade him to seek an armistice with the west. Von Ribbentrop refused. Hitler did not want it, he said.

Then how would the foreign minister like it when he saw Russian tanks at the gates of Berlin in about three weeks?

Von Ribbentrop recoiled; he had never believed it possible.

"Well," said Guderian, "it is a certainty given the current leadership."

Von Ribbentrop did not have the courage. His parting remark was a plea to Guderian to keep their conversation secret.

But by the time Guderian went to Hitler's briefing that same night

(January 25), Hitler accused him of treason for talking to von Ribbentrop. The foreign minister, fearful of his own position, had spoken to Hitler.

January ended. Upper Silesia was now in Russian hands. The industrial base was gone. The war could not be sustained more than a few weeks longer. Speer, the industrial wizard, had warned of this, but Hitler had not listened, so insistent was he on the western offensive that had failed. Speer wrote a memo. "The war is lost," it began. He showed it to Guderian, who could not have agreed more. Then Speer gave it to Hitler, who took one look at the first sentence and locked the memo away in his safe.

Of course the war was lost. Königsberg was being encircled. Stettin was threatened. Hungary was finished. By the end of the month the Soviets had severed East and West Prussia from the rest of Germany.

With Hitler, fantasy had taken over.

At the end of the month Hitler personally ordered the establishment of a new tank-destroyer division. It was to consist of bicycle companies, commanded by lieutenants. They were to be equipped with antitank rocket grenades. With these they were supposed to stop the Russian T-34 tanks. A few months later the Japanese would send men to similar certain death; they would call them kamikazes.

33

THE END NEARS

At the close of January 1945 Hitler summed up his feelings about the army at a situation conference in the Reich Chancellery:

> This whole bureaucratic structure is going to be cleared out now because it has been overstaffed to the point where it compares to the civilian bureaucracy like the dinosaur to the rabbit. That is connected with the fact that at the beginning of the war the Army naturally drafted all people with previous service or any sort of record. They drafted them on the basis of their previous ranks.
>
> Then they were promoted some more. These people have grown old and can serve as leaders only in a very limited way. [Von Rundstedt, for example, was in his seventies.] They are officers from the First World War who hold general's ratings and are not capable of leading a battalion any more. The situation which now arises is that I draft all men out of the whole nation who are even slightly or in part capable of military service, no matter what kind of jobs they might have had in civilian life, while on the other hand I dismiss men who are just sitting in unnecessary positions and send them home. Because I can't use them, I can't give the general a division or a regiment because he couldn't handle it. He has been promoted automatically but he can't even lead a company. That is the problem. That has nothing to do with their pension rights. But at the same time I am calling on the Volkssturm

[People's Army] and drafting God knows what kind of people into the armed forces under the lowered age limit, I go and send home people who are perfectly fit for service, just because they are doing jobs which obviously don't have to be done, which they aren't even filling because those jobs are superfluous, because they are squatting in a bureaucracy which we want to air out. In other words I am sending home people who are fit for military service and drafting others who are not soldiers and who are only partially fit.

This long, rambling talk was typical of Hitler now. It was the sort of thing his OKW chiefs and others had to listen to day after day, sometimes for five or six hours. The whole point of this particular monologue was the manpower shortage. At that time, January 1945, 12- and 13-year-old boys were appearing in uniform. So were 60- and 70-year-old men.

The *Volkssturm* was ordered into action in the east to shore up Guderian's badly belabored divisions. When the first *Volkssturm* units went rushing into action, they were killed by the Russians. Hitler hastily amended his orders: the *Volkssturm* was not to be sent into the field alone, but only in connection with Regular Army divisions. The generals were ordered to form mixed brigades, to make use of the *Volkssturm* troops.

The generals tore their hair. Take these infants and relics and put them together with trained soldiers? What Hitler was doing would destroy every first-class fighting unit left in the German army.

But by this time Hitler did not care. He was sitting in his ruined Chancellery in Berlin, waiting for the end to come. There was no doubt about it now. At the end of January the Russians were only 40 miles from Berlin.

In East Prussia German civilians took ship by the thousands and fled across the Baltic to Denmark to escape the Russians. The refugee trains from the east were jammed to overflowing with people bringing their personal luggage and heading west. The squeeze was on. Only 380 miles separated the Russians from the Americans and British.

In February the Germans dug in along the Oder-Neisse line and held. Although the British and the Americans were now threatening along the Rhine, Hitler had to see the Soviet menace as worse. Thus, at long last, some reinforcements were sent to Guderian in the east, and some units were even pulled away from the western defenses to try to save Berlin.

The situation meetings were regularly attended by Göring, Goebbels, Speer, Keitel, Jodl, Guderian, and Dönitz. Every day they sat for hours and listened to Hitler talk. What he said now was not much more than gossip. There was very little real information; in many areas communications had broken down completely.

The Nazi leadership was desperate. Goebbels and Bormann wanted to destroy every building and every house in the cities and towns that were to be invaded by the Russians and the western Allies. They spoke of scorched earth, and out in the provinces the party *Gauleiters* prepared to do their bidding, to wreck everything they left behind them. As the Nazi party went down in flames, so would all Germany.

The thieves began to fall out. Speer decided that he ought to get rid of Hitler. He proposed to put poison gas in the bunker ventilator system. But somehow Hitler had a presentiment; he changed the system so that no one but his authorized people could get into it, and he doubled the SS guard.

As the military situation worsened, Hitler ranted more and made sense less. He flew into furies. His favorite target was General Guderian, whose armies were being sliced to pieces in the east. Guderian was a coward, Hitler said, otherwise the war would not be lost. He said this a dozen times. Guderian did not even listen. Nor did the others. Hitler's propensity for finding a scapegoat for his every error was now too well known.

Eva Braun, Hitler's mistress, had spent almost all of the previous two years of the war at Berchtesgaden, which was an oasis of quiet amid the tumult. But now, when Hitler said he would not come to Berchtesgaden again until the war was over, Eva Braun came to Berlin.

She came into a Berlin she did not know. The Wilhelmstrasse had been bombed so many times that the buildings were virtually unrecognizable. The whole look of the avenue had changed. The Propaganda Ministry building was a shambles. The Ministry of Foreign Affairs was in similar shape. The old Radziwill Palace was completely destroyed, and the Kaiserhof Hotel was so structurally weak from repeated bombings that its guests feared it might collapse on them at any time.

In the Chancellery bunker Eva Braun had her own apartment.

She had her own hairdresser, and in spite of the bombings he came every day. She walked her dogs in the Tiergarten between air raids. She drank champagne with her friends and the others in the bunker but not, of course, with Hitler, who never drank champagne. Every night she dined with Hitler. Usually now they were alone. He had given up the circle of admirers who had surrounded him in all those years past. He no longer trusted any of them, except Dönitz, the incorruptible Dönitz, the man who could have won the war for him in its first year if he had been allowed to do so.

Life in the bunker was unreal. On the lower levels of the bunker one scarcely heard the bombing outside. But in little ways the war penetrated even there. Food was still served by liveried servants in the dining room, but now there were shortages for the first time. Generals coming back to report to General Guderian brought news of the troops and news of the refugees streaming into western Germany. Hitler talked about going to "the front." Which front? All Germany was now the front.

All his fronts were folding, but even in collapse the German army was impressive. On the Italian front alone half a million German soldiers were fighting. Von Kesselring was prepared to defend northern Italy until the last, as he had been ordered to do. And then, in the waning days, von Kesselring was called by Hitler to take over from von Rundstedt. For the fourth time Hitler had lost confidence in the old field marshal. When the word came to the Chancellery that the western Allies were getting ready to start a new offensive in April, Hitler ordered von Kesselring to stop it.

By mid-March, much of Germany was rubble. Hitler was giving orders from Berlin every day, orders that could not be obeyed because the generals did not have the troops he thought they had.

One day, Hitler ordered Field Marshal Model to stage a counterattack on the enemy at Remagen. He stipulated the divisions that should be thrown into the attack, neglecting the fact that these divisions had lost nearly all their weapons and were mere skeletons of their former selves. The unit name was the same, and Hitler would believe the facts were the same. So Model and the others knew that the Führer was now living in a dream world and no help could come from him.

At the Chancellery the only person who would tell Hitler the facts was Guderian, but Hitler would not listen to much Guderian had to say, so the general stopped trying.

Besides, Hitler's paranoia was now so serious that those around him were afraid to speak. The People's Courts were busy, trying offenders rounded up by the Gestapo. At any moment Hitler might mention the name of some person who had offended him in some obscure way and order him arrested. The Gestapo was always there to oblige. The most common offense was defeatism. If a man talked defeat, he was a traitor; he was tried, convicted, and shot. His family was arrested, and his goods and wealth confiscated.

By March Heinrich Himmler, as head of the *Volkssturm* and just about every other military ground organization except the remnants of the Regular Army, had taken personal charge of the eastern front. But Himmler knew virtually nothing about military affairs. The Regular Army units, too, were made subject to his whims, and he was making impossible demands on the generals. If a position was hopeless and its commander said so, he risked immediate court martial and execution.

Speer traveled about, taking stock of what was left of Germany's industrial plant. He took photographs, and brought them back to the Reich Chancellery, where Hitler refused to look at them.

Hitler began talking about releasing convicts from prison to put them into the line to fight. He bragged about Heinrich Himmler as a general. Himmler, he said, did not waste time or material. He brought up tanks and dug them into the ground. Then the gunners stuck with the tanks until they were blasted out. This, said Hitler, was the way to fight a war. As for his Regular Army generals, they had brought Germany to this terrible pass. "They just don't have any vision," he said.

What he did not say about the Himmler solution was that the German tanks always *were* blasted out.

By February 1945 the navy and the Luftwaffe had almost completely abandoned combat operations so that all war material could go to the beleaguered armies on east and west, north and south. By February Hitler had two pockets of resistance that never should have been allowed to become such. One was Army Group Kurland, which

was surrounded and could be supplied only from the air or by sea.
That meant twenty infantry divisions and two panzer divisions. They
were absolutely useless for the defense of Germany. The other surrounded group was Army Group North (until January 25 known as
Army Group Center), which had been forced into a pocket around
Königsberg. It, too, could be supplied only by air or sea. Its nineteen infantry divisions and five panzer divisions were also worthless to Germany.

One day in February Guderian again approached Hitler to suggest that the army in Kurland be evacuated. Hitler flew into such a
rage that an aide grabbed Guderian by his coattails and hustled him
out of the room, fearful lest the general be physically assaulted by
his Führer.

February 13 was the date of a crucial conference at the Reich Chancellery. In attendance were Himmler, General Sepp Dietrich of the
Sixth SS Panzer Army, Guderian, and his aide, General Walther
Wenck. Himmler had been talking about a German assault in the
Arnwald area, to strengthen the position of West Prussia. But Guderian knew it had to come fast if at all, because the Russians were
strengthening their own positions in the area at the rate of four divisions a day.

On February 15 the attack began and made good progress. But
on February 17 General Wenck, relieving his exhausted driver at
the wheel, drove into a bridge abutment and was severely injured.
He went to the hospital and was replaced by another general. The
attack then bogged down and ultimately failed. Wenck was replaced
as Guderian's assistant by General Karl von Krebs, a bright and
ambitious, but not very wise, officer.

Guderian was now having a dreadful time trying to keep the armies
going. The Allies had all but destroyed the German synthetic-fuel industry. The only supplies now came from Hungary and from Austria.
This situation explained Hitler's sometime preoccupation with the
south.

Finland switched sides and declared war on Germany on March 3.
The Hungarians in Budapest signed a separate peace with the Soviets.
The Russians attacked in the Baltic area on March 4, and all Pomerania
was lost to Germany. On March 6 the western Allies penetrated deep
into Cologne on the Rhine. In the east the Russians were pressing on
Stettin. A day or two later the western Allies pushed toward Koblenz,
and on March 8 they captured the bridge at Remagen intact. Hitler

began ranting in his situation conference and demanded victims. He selected five officers. They were summarily executed that very day.

On March 9 the Russians reached the eastern bank of the Oder River. The Germans attacked in Hungary and achieved an initial success, but the battle became a standoff. On March 12 there was street fighting in Breslau. Berlin was bombed for the twentieth night in succession.

Now Hitler's favorite troops, the SS, began to collapse. Whole infantry units retreated without orders, and against orders. Hitler was almost out of his mind with rage when he heard the news, and he demanded that the SS troops be deprived of their special armbands. These troops included his own special bodyguard units, which had been involved. He wanted Guderian to strip them of the honor, but Guderian declined.

Now up came Dr. Willi Ley, the *Reichsorganisationsleiter* of the Nazi party. He proposed to form a new army of 40,000 Nazi officials in western Germany who no longer had any employment because their territories had been occupied by the Allies. The "*Freikorps* Adolf Hitler," it would be called. It would hold the Black Forest and the upper Rhine until hell froze over. Guderian must supply him with 80,000 submachine guns.

Guderian listened to this suggestion without much interest. He knew his Nazis. When Dr. Ley had a table of organization and the names of the volunteers, he, Guderian, would see that they were all armed, he said. He never heard any more of that suggestion. Hitler did not ask any questions, either.

But Hitler kept interfering with the conduct of the war. He brought generals in to discuss the situation of their armies; he interrupted them constantly with questions, and then, when they did not answer the way he thought they ought to, he fired them.

By mid-March Hitler knew that it was only a matter of days before the enemy triumphed. He proposed to blow up all factories, public utilities, railroads, and bridges before they could fall into enemy hands. Said Hitler:

> If the war should be lost, then the nation, too will be lost. That would be the nation's unalterable fate. There is no need to consider the basic requirements that a people needs in order to con-

tinue to live a primitive life. On the contrary, it is better ourselves to destroy such things, for this nation will have proved itself the weaker, and the future will belong exclusively to the stronger Eastern nation. Those who remain alive after the battles are over are in any case only inferior persons since the best have fallen.

He gave the order for demolition of all industries and utilities. Martin Bormann followed that up with specific instructions to the *Gauleiters*. Now the military authorities stepped in to try to stop the insane plan. Speer visited many areas and explained the horrible consequences for postwar Germany if the Führer's orders were carried out, and the munitions industry management refused to issue the explosives to the *Gauleiters*. So most of the destruction was prevented, although not all.

At least Hitler had proved consistent in one way. He had once said that his real war was with Communist Russia. Now he saw that Communist Russia had proved more powerful than Nazi Germany, and he was prepared for the end. But of course, when the end came, he wanted to take all Germany with him.

34

THE LAST ACT

In March 1945 the military actions directed by Adolf Hitler became virtually pointless. He made a big issue of the relief of the fortress of Küstrin, near Frankfurt-on-Oder. But Hitler interfered with Guderian's management of the campaign, and the relief failed.

At the situation meeting on March 18 Hitler heard a story that came up via Field Marshal von Kesselring's command. The people of one western German village had come to the nearby military camp and asked the commander not to defend their homes. That way, said the mayor, the village would not be destroyed by the Allies or by the fighting.

Hitler was beside himself as he heard this tale. He drew up an order: all villages in the threatened areas of the west would hereafter be evacuated, he proclaimed. His generals listened in dismay. There were no trains. There was no transport of any sort for these people.

On March 23 the western Allies reached the upper and central Rhine along its entire length. North of the mouth of the Ruhr, they crossed the lower Rhine on a broad front. That day the Russians broke through the German line near Oppeln in Upper Silesia.

On March 24 the Americans crossed the upper Rhine and ad-

vanced toward Darmstadt and Frankfurt-on-Main. In the east the
Russians attacked Danzig. They also attacked Küstrin.

On March 26 the Russians launched a new assault in Hungary. The
Germans failed again to break through to the defenders of Küstrin.

On March 27 General Patton's tanks entered Frankfurt-on-Main.
The next day, Hitler had another temper tantrum over the failure of
his troops to break through to Küstrin. His rage was directed at
General Busse, the commander of the Ninth Army. But Busse was
not Hitler's only target that day. An irrational Führer was now once
again fighting World War I.

Busse had erred by not firing a long enough artillery barrage before the attack, Hitler said. It was stupid generalship. In World War
I on the western front it was customary before launching an attack
to fire at least ten times as many shells as Busse had fired.

Busse had not fired more shells, Guderian said, because he did
not have more shells.

"Then you should have arranged for him to have more," Hitler
shouted.

Patiently, as if reasoning with a child, Guderian showed Hitler
the figures of his total artillery ammunition allocation for the week.
All his ammunition had been given to Busse.

"Then the troops let us down!" shouted Hitler. Guderian then
showed Hitler the casualty reports for the battle. They were extremely
high, indicating that the German troops had done their very best.

Hitler turned on his heel and left the meeting.

Guderian knew that Hitler was nursing another grudge over being corrected and that logic or truth would make no difference to
the outcome.

When they met the next day, Hitler demanded a report from
Busse. The general began to talk, and Hitler interrupted him constantly, making the same charges he had made earlier to Guderian.

Guderian grew very angry with Hitler then, and spoke up, asking the Führer formally and pointedly to make no further accusa-
tions against Busse.

Hitler then asked all the others to leave the room, except Field
Marshal Keitel and General Guderian. Then he told Guderian that
he was fired.

"Colonel General Guderian, your physical health requires that
you take an immediate six-week leave of absence."

"I will go," said Guderian, and he started for the door.

"Please remain until the end of the conference," Hitler said.

The others returned to the room. Hitler made no more charges and was very silent. The conference lasted for several hours. Afterward, Hitler appeared very solicitous of Guderian's health. He must come back in six weeks, Hitler said. He would be needing Guderian then. So Guderian left, both men knowing they would not meet again. Guderian returned to his headquarters at Zossen. His wife was there. She had been living with him there since she had been forced to evacuate her East Prussian home several weeks earlier.

Guderian said he was delighted to have been dismissed. He and his wife headed south, into Bavaria and ultimately to the Tyrol, where they waited until the war ended.

By the third week of March 1945 the eastern front stretched from Stettin to Frankfurt-on-Oder. The Russians had encircled Königsberg, Danzig, and Breslau, but all were still holding out. In the southeast the Russians had advanced halfway from Budapest to Vienna. In the west the Allies were moving steadily, and on March 18 General Patton forced the Rhine at Oppenheim, between Mainz and Worms.

Hitler said, at his situation meeting that day, that the Patton threat was the worst.

Goebbels, who had been given the task of defending Berlin, wanted to talk about that. So he did. He wanted to cut down the lampposts on the east-west avenue of Berlin and make an airplane runway out of it. This runway would be used first for fighters and bombers, but later for evacuation of the Nazis and their families.

Hitler assented. He who had planned to make Berlin the most beautiful city in Europe was seeing that city blasted before his eyes.

The situation meetings had assumed an Alice-in-Wonderland atmosphere. Hitler spoke of munitions production, although virtually no munitions were being produced. He spoke of secret weapons, and Bormann, his contact with the party outside Berlin, spoke to the *Gauleiters* of secret weapons. In the countryside they still believed that somehow Hitler was going to produce a miracle.

Speer went off on a trip to the west. He told Hitler he was going on sick leave, but his real purpose was to try to stop the *Gauleiters* from destroying everything. He returned at the end of March. His activities had come to Hitler's notice before he got back.

Hitler called Speer in to chastise him, and for a time Speer's fate was in the balance. Speer had become far too negative, Hitler said. He reminded his minister of that memo of several weeks earlier, the one that began, "The war is lost." Now the Führer made a most remarkable statement.

"I demand that you hope that the war can be won," said Hitler. "I give you twenty-four hours to do so."

And Albert Speer, who had been known for a long time as one of the few men who could speak the truth to Hitler, came back within the twenty-four hours and said he hoped. He really hoped.

By the end of the first week of April Hitler was losing control of the various fronts where German troops were fighting. He did not even know from hour to hour what was going on with the armies in west and east. He recognized this fact officially by authorizing Field Marshal von Kesselring to take control and issue orders when communications were finally broken with Berlin. It would not be long before this happened, he had been told by Keitel and by Guderian.

In Berlin, the situation grew more desperate by the hour.

On April 12 Hitler enjoyed a moment of euphoria. He learned of the death of President Franklin Roosevelt, a principal author of the unconditional surrender doctrine. For some reason Hitler seemed to think this death was a boon to him personally, and he went wandering around the Chancellery babbling to anyone who would listen. The death of Roosevelt was a sure sign that providence was looking after Adolf Hitler and Germany, he said.

Hitler now was talking about leaving the Chancellery and Berlin and moving to the Alps. There, he said, he would build an "Alpine Redoubt." He and a few loyal followers would lead the final struggle. But first he would see the Russians and the western Allies fall out and fight among themselves. They would destroy each other.

On more sober days, Hitler was talking of realities. He would stay in Berlin, he said, and he would die in the bunker by his own hand. He and Goebbels discussed suicide. Goebbels said he would commit suicide too, but only after killing his wife, Magda, and his children. For in the Germany of the future, enslaved by the Allies, anyone named Goebbels would have no chance of a normal life.

*

On April 14 the Americans and the British began a new assault on the German forces in Italy.

The German generals, as usual, asked to be allowed to move from their fixed defense positions to retire to the natural defense line of the Po River. Only a flexible defense could cope with the Allied advance. But Hitler was true to form. No, he said. The Germans would hold every foot of ground and give up nothing.

Thus the Allies were able to descend on the flanks and the front of the Germans, who had the river behind them. Before the end of April the Allies reached Trieste, and the German generals, with nowhere to go, had to surrender their entire army. The war in Italy was over, lost by Hitler's intransigence.

When Hitler learned of the surrender, he was furious again. But what was to be done? The communications had failed, and he did not even know about the surrender until it had happened.

Almost everywhere the story was the same. The Russians took Vienna, and by mid-April they were only 50 miles south of Berlin.

So Hitler issued new orders. Admiral Dönitz, he said, would become commander of the northern areas of Germany when all communications failed. Von Kesselring would take over the south.

Hitler then issued his last order of the day to the German soldiers:

Soldiers of the German Eastern Front

For the last time our deadly enemies the Jewish Bolsheviks have launched their massive forces to the attack. Their aim is to reduce Germany to ruins and to exterminate our people. Many of you soldiers of the East already know this fate which threatens, above all, German women, girls, and children. While the old men and children will be murdered, the women and girls will be reduced to barrack room whores. The remainder will be marched off to Siberia.*

---

* One of the remarkable aspects of Hitler's last message to the troops was its similarity to the messages of the Japanese government to Japanese military men in the last months of the Pacific war. They bear precisely the same propaganda: that the Allies would enslave the whole population, destroy the race, and make playthings of the women. Here, as noted earlier, was one of the unpleasant fruits of the unconditional surrender policy.

We have foreseen this thrust and since last January have done everything possible to construct a strong front. The enemy will be greeted by massive artillery fire. Gaps in our infantry have been made good by countless new units, newly raised units, and by the Volkssturm. This time the Bolshevik will meet the ancient fate of Asia—he must and he shall bleed to death before the capital of the German Reich. Whoever fails in his duty at this moment behaves as a traitor to our people. The regiment or division which abandons its position acts so disgracefully that it must be ashamed before the women and children who are withstanding the terror of bombing in our cities. Above all, be on your guard against the few treacherous officers and soldiers who, in order to preserve their pitiful lives, fight against us in Russian pay, perhaps even wearing German uniforms. Anyone ordering you to retreat will, unless you know him well personally, be immediately arrested and if necessary killed on the spot, no matter what rank he may hold. If every soldier on the Eastern Front does his duty in the days and weeks which lie ahead, the last assault of Asia will crumble, just as the invasion by our enemies in the west will finally fall, in spite of everything.

Berlin remains German, Vienna will be German again, and Europe will never be Russian.

Form yourselves into a sworn brotherhood, to defend, not the empty conception of a Fatherland, but your homes, your wives, your children, and, with them, your future. In these hours, the whole German people looks to you, my fighters in the East, and only hopes that, thanks to your leadership, the Bolshevik assault will be choked in a bath of blood. At this moment, when Fate has removed from the earth the greatest war criminal of all time [Franklin D. Roosevelt] the turning point of the war will be decided.

If rhetoric could have won the war, Hitler's words were worth legions. Even at this late moment there were some who believed him. But Hitler no longer believed. He knew the war was lost.

He talked vaguely about having someone fly to America to meet with President Truman and "arrange things." Now that Roosevelt was dead, perhaps the Americans would not hold out for the unconditional surrender policy.

But Hitler did not really believe that, either. It was just more of the talk that went around the Chancellery those days, endless talk to ward off the fears that assailed them all: What were they going to do when the Russians came?

On April 15 the Russians opened their offensive against Berlin.

By this time Hitler had abandoned the upper levels of the Chancellery, which were heavily damaged anyhow, and had moved down into the deep bunker beneath the building. He lived like a cave dweller there. It was somehow symbolic to all those around him that he should withdraw as he did. The Chancellery was only a shell now. All the rich drapes had been removed. All the paintings and statues had been hidden for safekeeping. All the carpets and furniture had been carted away. The dusty, vacant building looked abandoned as it truly was.

But beneath the facade was the bunker, 16 feet of reinforced concrete below 6 feet of earth. The Allied bombings were so powerful and so frequent that the earth shook a half-dozen times a day as bombs struck nearby, but there was no structural damage to the bunker. Even a direct hit would not break through.

Sometimes Hitler emerged to participate in some ceremony. On his birthday, April 20, he received a delegation of Hitler Youth who had been fighting at the front. They were just boys—but soldiers now—dying in a war that was already lost.

Even late in April Hitler was talking about moving to the Alpine redoubt and carrying on the war. He knew he would never do it. The people around him knew he would never do it. But he talked.

Should he really go to the redoubt? Speer asked one day. There remained now but one road open through the Bavarian forest, just one road left in German hands to take him to Berchtesgaden. It might be cut at any time. Was he ready to go?

Not really. Hitler admitted then that he would not move from Berlin. He would die with the capital of the Thousand-Year Reich.

He was exhausted. His hands quivered constantly. Goebbels said he had aged a dozen years in the past six months.

When Hermann Göring heard that the last road through the Bavarian countryside was threatened, he suddenly remembered important business in the south and prepared to leave. So did dozens of others. Hitler never batted an eye. He shook hands with Göring and Speer and the others and said goodbye.

A few days later Speer came back to Berlin, but this time he came by air; it was the only way. Berlin was cut off. He came in aboard a small plane, which landed near the Brandenburg Gate. One of the really faithful had come to pay his last respects to Hitler.

Hitler asked Speer one question: Should he go to Berchtesgaden or should he remain in Berlin? He had been thinking it over again.

Speer was honest to the last with his Führer. It would be best, he said, if Hitler would remain in Berlin and die with the city. If he went to Berchtesgaden, he would only carry on a hopeless struggle from a summer house, with no dignity about the end. This way, the end would be like one of Richard Wagner's high tragedies that Hitler loved so well.

Hitler nodded. He agreed. And he began to tell Speer what he was going to do in the last days.

He would shoot Blondi, his big German shepherd dog; Blondi would never become a Russian slave.

Eva Braun would die.

And Hitler himself would die, by his own hand.

Their bodies would be cremated, thus denying the Russians the pleasure of displaying them like freaks.

*   *   *

Hitler said that he had considered going out to fight in the streets with the members of the *Volkssturm* but that he was afraid he might only be wounded and the Russians would capture him. He could not bear that thought.

After they had talked thus, Hitler took Speer into the conference room for another of the endless situation report meetings that he continued to have, even though with communications broken he had no real idea of the situation anywhere but around Berlin.

General Krebs, the new army chief of staff, came in to tell Hitler that there was no news at all that day. So they held a situation conference without a situation report. It was all gossip and rumor.

*

April 22, 1945: The end was very near. Goebbels and his family had moved into the bunker at Hitler's invitation. Their home had been badly damaged by American bombers and was now threatened by the Russians.

April 23: Into the bunker came a message from Hermann Göring in Bavaria, asking if Göring should now assume command of the Reich.

Furious, Hitler stripped Göring of all his rights of succession, which had been inherent for years. The Führer directly accused Göring of treason. He demanded that Göring resign all his offices. If Göring did not obey, said Hitler, he would be punished further.

Even at this late date, even hundreds of miles from Bavaria without any way of getting there, Hitler still had the power to force his will on his Nazis. Like a lamb, Hermann Göring allowed himself to be shorn of his honors and his offices.

In Berlin Martin Bormann was making his bid for power, sending messages everywhere in Hitler's name, establishing himself as the real ruler of Germany. But power over what?

The sound of Soviet artillery was loud in the ears of those inside the bunker. The Russians were everywhere. Hitler was skittish, ready at the first word of a Russian breakthrough into the bunker to take his own life rather than be captured.

He discovered that Heinrich Himmler was trying to seize power in what remained of the Reich. The SS chief had gone north and was trying to negotiate in the name of Germany with Count Folke Bernadotte of Sweden. Hitler was furious, and, as with Göring, he expelled Himmler from the party and took away all his honors. Strange as it seems, such actions were meaningful to the party faithful even in the death throes of their dream.

Generals Keitel and Jodl argued that at least Berlin could be saved from the Russians. They wanted to move enough troops from the west to fight on the eastern side. Then the Americans and the British would break through, and they could pick up the fighting with the Russians where the Germans left off. They all believed that it would be only a short time before the ill-assorted Allies would fall out.

Now, with no more situation reports, Hitler *played* at being general.* He moved troops around on a board. But the troops and the tanks and the armies that he moved no longer existed. He did not issue any more orders, but stayed in the bunker and played with his maps as a child plays with tin soldiers. He sent Keitel away, and Jodl, too. He had no further need for military advisers, he told them, because he had just abdicated supreme command of the German military forces to Grand Admiral Dönitz.

On April 29 the Russians were only a few blocks from the Chancellery. Hitler made his will. He and Eva Braun were married. For once he drank champagne with her and they spent the last few hours of April 29 making bequests to their servants and others.

On the morning of April 30 the local SS commander reported to Hitler that the Russians were very close. They could be held off for perhaps half a day, but no longer.

Hitler spent the morning playing with his maps and telling anyone who would listen how he could have won the war. Then he said goodbye to everyone, lastly to the Goebbels family. He and Eva Braun Hitler retired to his study. After a while came the sound of a shot. Goebbels and Bormann went into the study. There on the sofa lay the dead Eva, a vial of cyanide on the floor beside her and the reek of bitter almonds in the air. The odor mingled with that of burned gunpowder. Sitting on the sofa, next to Eva's body, was the body of Adolf Hitler with a neat bullet hole in the front of his head, but not so neat a hole at the back. Blood ran down, staining the freshly pressed uniform he had donned that day.

Hitler's war was over.

---

* Does life imitate art? Hitler's behavior at this point of the war is reminiscent of nothing so much as the scene in the Charlie Chaplin movie *The Great Dictator* wherein Chaplin does his ballet with the globe of the world.

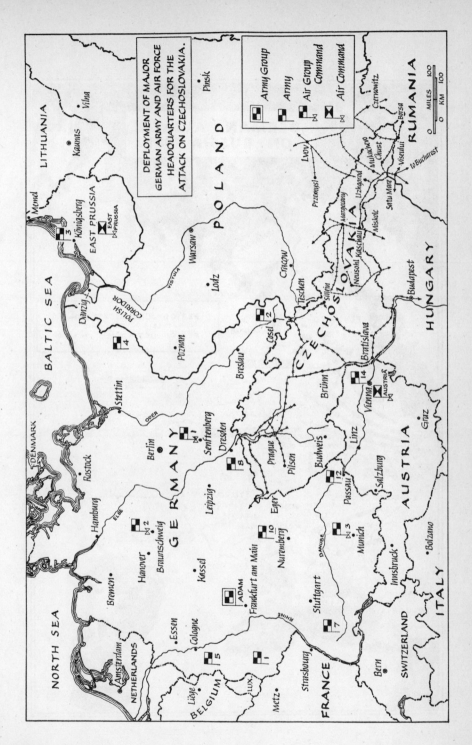

DEPLOYMENT OF MAJOR
GERMAN ARMY AND AIR FORCE
HEADQUARTERS FOR THE
ATTACK ON CZECHOSLOVAKIA.

GERMAN ATTACK ON RUSSIA 1941

PERIOD JUNE – SEPT.
1941
PERIOD OCT – DEC.

0   300
MILES

MURMANSK

ARCHANGEL

FINLAND

L. ONEGA

L. LADOGA

REVAL

LENINGRAD

L. PEIPUS

KALININ

RIGA

MOSCOW

ARMY GROUP "C"

SMOLENSK

WARSAW

MINSK

TULA

ARMY GROUP "B"

BRYANSK

BREST LITOVSK

OREL

LUBLIN

KURSK

LEMBERG

VORONEZH

KIEV

KHARKOV

KREMENCHUG

ARMY GROUP "A"

STALINGRAD

ODESSA

ROSTOV

KERCH STRAITS

BULGARIA

SEBASTOPOL

TUAPSE

BLACK   SEA

CASPIAN SEA

R. VOLGA

BALTIC SEA

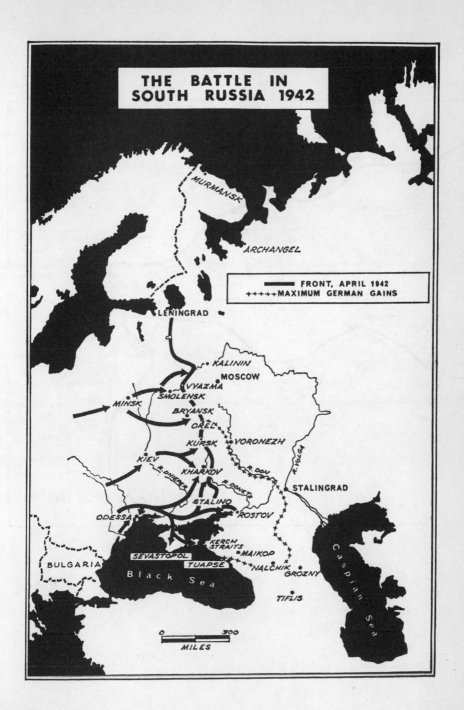

THE BATTLE IN
SOUTH RUSSIA 1942

MURMANSK

ARCHANGEL

—— FRONT, APRIL 1942
+++++ MAXIMUM GERMAN GAINS

LENINGRAD

KALININ
MOSCOW
VYAZMA
SMOLENSK
MINSK
BRYANSK
OREL
KURSK   VORONEZH
KIEV
KHARKOV
R. DNIEPER   R. DON   R. VOLGA
R. DONETS
STALINGRAD
STALINO
ODESSA   ROSTOV
KERCH
STRAITS   MAIKOP
SEVASTOPOL   NALCHIK   GROZNY
BULGARIA   TUAPSE
Black   Sea   TIFLIS

Caspian Sea

0   300
MILES

365

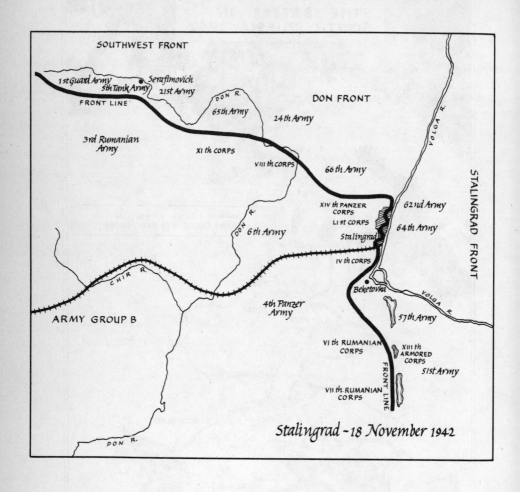

SOUTHWEST FRONT

1st Guard Army
5th Tank Army
Serafimovich
21st Army
FRONT LINE
DON R.
65th Army

DON FRONT

24th Army

3rd Rumanian Army

XI th CORPS

VIII th CORPS

66th Army

DON R.

6th Army

XIV th PANZER CORPS
LI st CORPS
Stalingrad

62nd Army

64th Army

STALINGRAD FRONT

VOLGA R.

IV th CORPS

CHIR R.

ARMY GROUP B

4th Panzer Army

Beketovka

VOLGA R.

57th Army

VI th RUMANIAN CORPS

XIII th ARMORED CORPS

51st Army

FRONT LINE

VII th RUMANIAN CORPS

DON R.

Stalingrad ~ 18 November 1942

NOTES

Introduction

The material for the introduction comes from J. W. Wheeler-Bennett's *The Nemesis of Power* and from Hitler's own *Mein Kampf.* William F. Shirer's *Rise and Fall of the Third Reich* was invaluable in helping set the scene as it existed for the emerging German politician who ultimately became dictator of the Third Reich.

1

Several sources contributed to this chapter: Shirer, Wheeler-Bennett, and Hitler himself. The material itself is derivative, but the conclusions are largely my own, as is the selection of materials. This book, above all, is an attempt to trace—through common materials—Adolf Hitler's manner of thinking and acting and the influences that it seemed to me were most important in the development of his career. The material abounds, and sometimes the search for the important wends its way through mazes of detail. Although the accuracy of some of the detail is debatable, the important point is that in his early years Hitler was a creature of fate, blown this way and that. Had he not felt himself mistreated by the labor union authorities in Vienna, he might never have become anti-Semitic; it is apparent that his prejudices were born there and then. The army "made" Adolf Hitler. Although only a corporal, he felt that in the military he had found a home and a personality. Coming out of the

war he, like so many other German soldiers, found himself utterly shocked at
the "betrayal" of the people by the High Command, and especially by the
government of Germany. When he saw a chance to use the aging General
Ludendorff in an attempt to take over the government, he did not hesitate.
He had already developed a fine contempt for the military leaders who had
let Germany down.

I have gone into some detail in the delineation of *Mein Kampf* because
that book explains so clearly what Hitler was going to do in the future,
particularly in its presentation of his racial and social ideas, which led to
the great bloodbath against the Jews, Poles, and other "inferior" types.
From this beginning it was apparent that one reason Hitler tried so hard to
bring Britain around to an acceptance of his moves was his reluctant admiration for things British. The British were, to him, Anglo-Saxons, the
sort of beautiful people he admired. There were, indeed, at least as many
of the blue-eyed, fair-haired *wunderjugend* in England as there were in Germany. Much as Hitler might revile the leaders of Britain, he did not hate
the British. And that accounts for much of his attitude.

2

Having taken power, Hitler saw the dangers of the party-state and determined
never to yield to them. Thus he emasculated the *Sturmabteilung* in the "night
of the long knives," when Ernst Röhm was eliminated. The SA was sacrificed so that it could not become "the tail that tried to wag the dog," as
Röhm had already indicated it might. The army was very pleased, and the
military caste was temporarily brought under the spell of Hitler's personality. Thus was the groundwork laid for the preparation for war, which
Hitler knew depended on the goodwill of the generals. I have devoted a
great deal of attention to the relationships between Hitler and the army
leaders because they would become the key to his power structure. As of
1934, when he marched into the Rhineland, Hitler's hold on power was
extremely tenuous. The generals did not believe he could pull off his bluff,
for bluff it was. As noted in the text, had the western Allies called the
bluff, the Germans would have had to beat an ignominious retreat. But the
western Allies did not respond with strength. Thus Hitler won two victories: one over the Allies and a more important one over the generals, who
began to doubt their own competence in strategic matters.

This was, of course, the period in which everything in Europe was turned
topsy-turvy. Hitler had grown up admiring Il Duce, the Italian dictator. Now

he realized that he had become far more important and more active than Mussolini. From 1934 until 1938 the two sparred, with Mussolini not quite sure where Italy's interests really lay. But in the end he succumbed to the lure of power and to Hitler's implied promises, and Italy's fate was settled.

3

The von Blomberg affair was important because it marked the real end of Hitler's consideration of the German military class. Had the generals rebelled, Hitler would have been in a terrible quandary. But once more he managed to bluff his opponents; when the quarrel was over, the army had lost. The von Fritsch affair was icing on the cake. It showed, among other things, the growing importance of Heinrich Himmler in the Hitler scheme.

4

The year 1938 marked the consolidation of Hitler's power. Before that time he could not have embarked on so risky an adventure as the annexation of Austria. But by the end of the winter of 1938 he had cowed the army and knew no trouble would come from that quarter. He could also sense that the western Allies did not know what to make of him and his plans, which from his point of view was all to the good. Part of the reason for his outrageous behavior toward the Austrian political leaders was to test the water, to see just how far he could go in making demands. He discovered that in the political climate of the time he could go as far as he liked; no one was ready to stand up to him. And thus was born the concept of bluffing everyone right up to the last. Britain, he was now convinced, had become a nation of cowards who would not fight for anything at all, except their own narrow interests. Thus in the winter of 1938 the way was opened for a whole new series of adventures, each more outrageous than the last, as Hitler gestured and pontificated, leaving a trail of open mouths behind him. Hitler learned the advantages and limitations of the Nazi parties. He was not too well served by the Nazis in Vienna, eager as they were for power. Nor was he well served by the Nazis in Czechoslovakia, who had to be pushed to demand more than even they wanted. But in all this, these parties were merely Hitler's pawns.

Once he had taken Austria, Hitler had no doubt in his mind that he could achieve the triumph of Pan-Germanism that had become a cornerstone of his policy. There was no doubt at all. He would not be restrained.

5

At the time of the Czechoslovak crisis, Hitler spoke and thought often about war. But the war about which he thought was not real war, not a total war on which he would stand or fall. That much was apparent in Hitler's treatment of the German navy. For years Captain Karl Dönitz had held that in a future war against England, Germany's best weapon would be the submarine, which could starve out England. This had very nearly been done in 1917. But as Hitler prepared to complete his pan-German acquisitions, he did not heed Dönitz's pleas for money to build up a mighty U-boat arm that could control the Atlantic Ocean.

In this Hitler showed his major limitation as a strategist. He could not think beyond the initial phases of war. He could plan for land control of Europe, but he could not see that without control of the seas the land control could never end British power. And unless British power were ended, the war in Europe would go on and on. Ultimately Germany must lose. When Hitler did think about naval affairs during this period, he thought like a general, in terms of a battleship or two that did whatever battleships do and emerged triumphant. He was lucky that the British naval leaders tended to think the same way in those days. A handful of advanced planners in England knew that the aircraft carrier would become the dominant naval weapon, but not nearly so many as knew it in Japan. And nobody at that moment knew that the battle for the seas would narrow down to a struggle between submarines and aircraft before it would end. For that is what happened: despite all the heroic deeds of the men in small ships, it was the airplane that decided the fate of the U-boat in the final years of the war. Had Dönitz had his way, the war would have been decided before the airplane and its carriers were that far developed.

6

After the success in Munich over Czechoslovakia, the war with Poland became inevitable. Hitler had convinced himself that the western Allies would never fight. Why should he feel otherwise? The westerners were not so sure of it themselves. Within their own councils, the voices of despair were too often heard.

7

On the eve of the march into Poland, Hitler's intuition told him that he had miscalculated and that Britain would back the Poles. For a time he nearly panicked. But in the end Poland proved to be an easily digestible morsel. The Polish armies were brave but totally outmoded, and the German war machine cut through them swiftly. Also, although Britain did go to war and so did France, they were not prepared to move swiftly in a manner that would have forced Germany to retreat. Once more, a Hitlerian bluff brought victory.

8

For much of this book the memoirs of Field Marshal Keitel were vital in tracing the behavior of Hitler. He left no record of his own, and most of the generals who did leave personal records were not that close to Hitler during the war. Keitel, facing death as a war criminal at the end of the war, decided to try to put together his own record to show how Hitler had behaved. In one sense it must have been self-justification. But in a larger sense it showed the processes by which the dictator Hitler wielded military power during the war. What happened, as can be seen in the record, was a gradual move away from reality as the war took a turn for the worse and never snapped back again. But the roots went far. "I never eat with the troops except standing at a field kitchen," the remark made by Hitler when he turned down the invitation to eat at the victorious banquet in Poland with the high officers, was a non sequitur in a sense, but it showed Hitler as he really was. The truth was that he only ate with "the troops" as a public relations gesture. He felt no kinship with soldier or officer. He was a totally political creature without an iota of warmth in him. And he was bemused by Britain, and remained so all during the war. If only he could bring the British (and later the Americans) around, then his trouble in the east would end oh, so quickly. Until Norway, Hitler really believed that he could talk Britain out of the war. But Norway was the deciding factor.

9

When Hitler saw that the British were serious about invading Norway, he knew that the war was going to be costly and difficult. But he moved with alacrity nonetheless. He accepted the change—not really a change in fact but a change in his perception of the facts.

10, 11, 12

Once Norway was taken into charge, Hitler moved to win the war in the European fields. He and his generals moved swiftly and with great skill, as is outlined in the works of Guderian, Deutsch, and Shirer. The daily news-papers of the period tell the story in their headlines; the blitzkrieg, so swiftly developed in Poland, worked in Europe as well, as German armor sliced through the western defenses. By summer Hitler had won control of Eu-rope. But still he faced war, and that was galling. Britain would not give up, and despite Hermann Göring's promises, the Luftwaffe was not strong enough or well enough employed to destroy Britain's air defenses. And so the campaign to beat Britain in 1940 ended, but the war went on. It was all very well for Hitler to do a little dance as he contemplated his victories at the forest in Compiègne. It was all very well for him to walk on the Champs-Elysées, and to cast an amused glance at the tomb of his hero, Napoleon. But as Hitler knew, the war was fact.

13

Hitler's attitude toward the United States was anything but ambivalent. From the outset he had recognized the communality of interests between the United States and Britain. At no point did he make a serious effort to woo the Americans away from Britain as the kaiser's forces had done in World War I. Part of the cause was his conviction that the United States was controlled by capitalists, that capitalism was controlled by Jews, and thus that the United States was the next thing to a Jewish state. This was the maniacal Hitler in thought. He did have, however, some understand-ing of the potential industrial might of the United States; for that reason in the years 1940 and 1941, when the Americans were giving ever more open help to Britain, Hitler did not fulminate. Admiral Dönitz reported frequently on the violations of the rules of war by the United States in the Atlantic Ocean campaign, but Hitler did not strike out in speech or act. He waited. Ultimately he expected to fight the United States, but he saw no need to hurry. He played a waiting game.

Why not? Hitler had plenty on his plate, as the war dispatches and the records of the period show. He moved into Yugoslavia. He had to bring some order to the Balkan States. He had to give a hand to Mussolini, who had overreached himself in the south. Thus was Hitler drawn into the Med-iterranean to fight, and hopefully to destroy the British there.

14

For this chapter, as for many others, Field Marshal Keitel's memoirs served as a basic outline. After all, he was Hitler's chief military administrator at the time and he knew what was happening every day and where it was happening. What is remarkable about the position of Keitel is how little effect his experience and opinions had on Hitler's judgments.

In his speech to his generals in the middle of June 1941 Hitler outlined his hatred of communism. Keitel was surprised. If he had read *Mein Kampf,* however, Keitel clearly would not have been surprised, for antibolshevism and anti-Semitism were keystones of Hitler's policy from the outset.

Hitler had already made up his mind to destroy Soviet Russia; his rhetoric was merely window dressing. At that moment, conquest seemed relatively easy. Hitler was flushed with victory. The involvement in the Mediterranean seemed to be going all his way, and it was inconceivable that the British could turn the war around. In conjunction with the Italians, the Germans controlled all of continental western Europe. No trouble was expected from Vichy France, but if there was trouble, all Hitler had to do was move in and take total control. Hitler had a mental picture of a Soviet Union that was ready for the picking, a Soviet army that could not fight, a Soviet air force that had no decent planes. On the basis of this misinformation, and a totally faulty understanding of Russian psychology, Hitler had decided that the Russian peoples, the various peoples of the Soviet Union, would flock away from the Soviet banner at the first sign of trouble. Thus he did not share his generals' aversion to the idea of a war on two major fronts. So the war on the eastern front was begun. At first it looked very, very easy.

15

The study of Rommel's activity comes from several biographies of Rommel and from the memoirs of Generals Alexander and Montgomery. Winston Churchill's *The Second World War* (volumes III and IV) was also pertinent. Admiral Dönitz's *Memoirs* was important, as were several of my own books that contain studies of U-boat operations in the Mediterranean: *U-Boats Offshore, The U-Boat War,* and *Death of the U-Boats.*

16

Hitler's decision to declare war on the United States, so unnecessary at the time, played directly into the hands of Winston Churchill and his good friend Franklin D. Roosevelt, who was having considerable difficulty in persuading Congress that American interests and British interests were the same. After the German war declaration, the argument became moot. Had Hitler not declared war, American society would have pressured for the war against Ja-

pan, and Hitler would have had at least two or three years' respite before the
addition of an enormously powerful new enemy to his foes in Europe. But he
did declare war and thus unleashed the power of America, which was very
quickly focused against Germany, not against Japan.

General Guderian's account of fighting in Russia after the winter broke
tells the story of what happened to Hitler just as it had happened to Napoleon in a previous century.

The material about the fighting at sea off the American coast comes from
several of my books on the U-boat war, written over a period of ten years.
Each time I write about the total unpreparedness of the American fleet for
anti-U-boat warfare, I get a sort of chilly feeling. Even today no one in America seems to realize that if Dönitz had been able to throw a dozen more submarines into the fight in the winter months of 1942, he could have completely
paralyzed the American war effort at a time when Britain was desperate. The
reason that Dönitz was not able to use the submarines as he wanted was Adolf
Hitler. The Führer had the mistaken notion that the U-boats would turn the
tide of war for him in the Mediterranean. That they never did.

17

The bogging down of the German war machine in Russia in early December 1942 was a portent of things to come. But Hitler never seemed to realize what had happened to him. Within a matter of hours he had become
involved in a major war with a major new power and had seen his army in
the east stopped cold. It was time for a major reassessment of the war
situation, but Hitler did not stop for a moment to think. His course was
set, and even at that early date it was apparent that the course was going
to lead to ultimate destruction. Heinz Guderian saw it, and his efforts to
save his troops brought him to disgrace and loss of command. Hitler always claimed that he was closer to the common soldier than to the Officer
Corps. That claim was, of course, balderdash. Had there been any truth to
it he would have known that his troops had no gloves, no mittens, no cold
weather clothing and that they were suffering enormously. At that point
Hitler neither knew nor cared about the condition of the front-line soldier.

18

For those who believe that by the spring of 1942 Hitler had gone quite
mad, a modicum of proof is lent by his insistence that the German forces
take Stalingrad, even when it was pointed out to him that the goal was not

worth the effort, that the danger was so enormous that it would threaten the entire German position in the east.

Hitler was still talking (to Keitel and others) about the coming "negotiated peace" to be achieved with Britain. Once that was done, he said, he could turn his full attention to the east and remove the Bolshevik menace from the world, an act for which Britain and the United States ought to thank him. Meanwhile, as indicated by all Germany's field generals in the east, the situation grew more desperate there every day. Several books about German military operations in Russia have been published over the years, and they all indicate the same thing: by the summer of 1942 the possibility of victory in Russia was almost nil. Whatever difficulties the Russians had faced before, after the beginning of 1942 they were receiving mountains of assistance from the United States.

Until Stalingrad, however, Hitler might have achieved a negotiated peace that would have bought him some time. He did not even think of it.

19

The various biographies of Field Marshal Erwin Rommel all indicate his brilliance as a field commander and show how his difficulties with Hitler prevented him from ever achieving what he had hoped to accomplish. He very nearly did it in the summer of 1942, when the Axis was at its height of power in the Mediterranean. But the British Royal Air Force and the Royal Navy held out against great odds and kept the supply line open for the troops fighting in Africa. When the test came, the Axis powers could not keep their logistics in order. That was the real meaning of the campaign against Alexandria.

20

Shirer, Trevor-Roper, and Deutsch were all very important to my study of Stalingrad and its effects on Hitler's psychology. Keitel again provided the framework of time and place. The concept "Where the German soldier sets foot he remains" was one that would control Hitler's mind for the remainder of the war. Time and again whole armies and lesser units could have been saved to fight again had they been allowed to retreat from impossible positions. But Hitler was adamant. Right down to the end, he insisted that German soldiers must hold their positions, no matter what.

Constantly, from the end of 1942, the Germans were being forced backward, but Hitler would never admit this fact. And on that stubbornness rested the fate of the finest men of Germany.

21

Hitler's defeat in the desert is well told by the enemy. Montgomery's memoirs and Bradley's memoirs record it without fanfare. The Germans had technical superiority, but they lost control of the air, they lost control of the pattern of the land fighting, and they had already lost control of the Mediterranean Sea. In north Africa the enormous industrial potential of the Americans began to become apparent. It was true that the British had little regard for the fighting qualities of the Americans in the beginning, and they were more than a little right in their complaints. But the Americans learned fast. And where they had a paucity of equipment—such as inadequate artillery to fight tanks— they soon made virtue of necessity, bringing fighter-bomber planes to attack tanks, which they did with great skill and enormous effect. Also, in north Africa the enormous power of American artillery made itself felt. As Bradley's memoirs and Eisenhower's memoirs show, the artillery saved the day in the Kasserine area after the armor and the infantry had failed.

22

The end of the saga of Stalingrad is well told in Keitel and Kerr. Ronald Lewin deals with it to some extent in his *Hitler's Mistakes*. Jimmy Doolittle told me personally about some of the problems of the Eighth Air Force, as well as of the air forces he had previously led in north Africa. Dönitz was the source of most of the material about the submarine campaign of that period.

23

The attack on Italy by the Allies brought a fierce resistance from Hitler. Some of the detail has been told by General Mark Clark in his memoirs; more information, giving the feeling of the fighting, is presented in Chester Tanaka's *Go For Broke,* one of the books about the Nisei Americans fighting in the 100th Battalion and the 442nd Regimental Combat Team in World War II in Italy and later in France. I also had access to a number of letters and diaries written by GIs at the time.

24

The story of fighting in the west comes largely from the diaries of American soldiers. Keitel's recollection of various conferences and Hitlerian ac-

tivities was also vital. The material about the sea war comes from my own
studies of the U-boat campaigns and from Dönitz.

Keitel tells the story of the German tank, the *Ferdinand*.

25

The story of the cross-Channel attack comes largely from my own research.
Hitler's actions and reactions come from the studies of Keitel, Trevor-
Roper, and Hans Speidel, Rommel's chief of staff.

26

Hitler had allowed himself to be gulled by the British propaganda machine.
The disinformation program was enormously successful, really aimed to convince one man that the cross-Channel attack—the real one—would be made
at the Pas de Calais, where the English Channel narrows, and not at Normandy. There are many good descriptions of this program. General Morgan's
story of his tenure as chief of staff of SHAEF tells much of it. Bradley's story
tells more. Ladislas Farago's *Game of the Foxes* gives some insights; R. V.
Jones's *The Wizard War* gives more. In any event, by the summer of 1944
Hitler was convinced that the Allies would attack near Paris, and that conviction governed his actions. By the time the truth was known, it was too
late: the Allies were racing through Normandy toward Paris, and the
German divisions were trapped or fragmented. Hitler could not be blamed
entirely if he failed to give full attention to the problem. This was the July
in which the German generals made their long-awaited attempt on his life—
and botched the job. Shirer tells this story better than anybody.

27

Guderian is the source for much of this chapter. He became chief of the
army, and his account of his immediate difficulties with Hitler is lucid and
indicative of the real problems that had emerged within the Third Reich.

28

This chapter is largely an account of Guderian's difficulties in dealing with
Hitler. At the same time it reveals the dreadful straits into which the German
military machine had descended, although it was still able to continue the war.

29

Keitel, Shirer, Speer, and Guderian were important here. As for the Allied efforts, much of the material comes from my own studies.

30

Again, Guderian's and Keitel's memoirs carry the story in this chapter.

31

The story of the Ardennes offensive comes from Guderian and from various American sources which I studied. Charles Whiting, the British popular war historian, has devoted an entire book, *The Ardennes,* to the campaign. *Death of a Division,* also a Whiting book, tells of one green American unit that was decimated in the battle. The author used original documents, including the stories of survivors of the American artillery unit who were basically affected at the Malmedy massacre.

32

The rapid collapse of the German armies after the Ardennes offensive in the west is indicated in Guderian's memoirs. Wheeler-Bennett, Deutsch, and Trevor-Roper were also vital.

33

Trevor-Roper's book on the last days of Adolf Hitler was vital to this chapter. Toland was useful; Shirer was more so. The *Goebbels Diaries* and his *Final Diaries* were also used.

34

I used Shirer for this final act in the Hitlerian drama, as well as Trevor-Roper's book on the last days of Hitler. Also, I used Guderian's memoirs and Keitel's memoirs, and various materials I had assembled earlier for a study of Martin Bormann's last days.

BIBLIOGRAPHY

Albert F. Simpson Historical Research Center Air University and Office of Air Force History Headquarters USAF. *The Army Air Forces in World War II. Combat Chronology 1941–1945*. Washington, D.C.: U.S. Government Printing Office, 1973.

Arnold-Forster, Mark. *The World at War*. New York: Stein and Day, 1973.

Bennett, Ralph. *Ultra in the West. The Normandy Campaign of 1944–45*. New York: Charles Scribner's Sons, 1979.

Black, Peter R. *Ernst Kaltenbrunner*. Princeton, N.J.: Princeton University Press, 1984.

Bradley, Omar N. *A Soldier's Story*. New York: Henry Holt and Company, 1951.

Bullock, Alan. *Hitler, a Study in Tyranny*. New York: Harper & Row, 1962.

Churchill, Winston. *The Second World War*, vol. 1: *The Gathering Storm*. Boston: Houghton Mifflin Co., 1948.

———. *The Second World War*, vol. 4: *The Hinge of Fate*. Boston: Houghton Mifflin Co., 1950.

Deutsch, Harold C. *Hitler and His Generals*. Minneapolis: University of Minnesota Press, 1974.

———. *The Conspiracy Against Hitler in the Twilight War*. Minneapolis: University of Minnesota Press, 1968.

Downing, David. *The Devil's Virtuosos*. New York: Playboy Press Paperbacks, 1977.

Gorlitz, Walter (ed.). *The Memoirs of Field-Marshal Keitel*. (Trans. by David Irving.) New York: Stein and Day, 1966.

Guderian, Heinz. *Panzer Leader*. (Trans. by Constantine Fitzgibbon.) New York: Ballantine Books, 1957.

Hitler, Adolf. *My New Order*. New York: Reynal & Hitchcock, 1941.

————. *Mein Kampf.* New York: Reynal & Hitchcock, 1939.

Höhne, Heinz. *The Order of the Death's Head.* (Trans. by Richard Barry.) New York: Coward-McCann, 1970.

Hoyt, Edwin P. *Airborne. The History of American Parachute Forces.* New York: Stein and Day, 1979.

————. *The U-Boat Wars.* New York: Arbor House, 1984.

————. *U-Boats Offshore.* New York: Playboy Press Paperbacks, 1980.

Irving, David. *The War Path.* New York: Viking Press, 1978.

Kerr, Walter. *The Secret of Stalingrad.* Garden City, N.Y.: Doubleday, 1978.

Langer, Walter C. *The Mind of Adolf Hitler.* New York: New American Library, 1973.

Lewin, Ronald. *Hitler's Mistakes.* New York: William Morrow and Co., 1984.

Lochner, Louis P. (ed.). *The Goebbels Diaries.* Garden City, N.Y.: Doubleday Award Books, 1943.

Nee, Victor, and James Peck (eds.). *China's Uninterrupted Revolution from 1840 to the Present.* New York: Pantheon Books, 1973.

Overy, R. J. *The Air War 1939–1945.* New York: Stein and Day, 1981.

Payne, Robert. *The Life and Death of Adolf Hitler.* New York: Praeger Publishers, 1973.

Prittie, Terence. *Germans Against Hitler.* Boston: Little, Brown, 1964.

Shirer, William L. *The Rise and Fall of the Third Reich.* New York: Simon and Schuster, 1960.

————. *End of a Berlin Diary.* New York: Popular Library, 1947.

Speer, Albert. *Inside the Third Reich.* (Trans. by Richard and Clara Winston.) New York: Macmillan Co., 1970.

————. *Infiltration.* (Trans. by Joachim Neugroschel.) New York: Macmillan Co., 1981.

Taylor, Telford. *Munich: The Price of Peace.* Garden City, N.Y.: Doubleday, 1979.

Toland, John. *Adolf Hitler,* vol. 1. Garden City, N.Y.: Doubleday, 1976.

Trevor-Roper, H. R. *The Last Days of Hitler.* New York: Macmillan Co., 1947.

————, (ed.). *Hitler's War Directives 1939–1945.* London: Pan Books, Ltd., 1966.

————, (ed.). *Final Entries 1945. The Diaries of Joseph Goebbels.* (Trans. by Richard Barry.) New York: G. P. Putnam's Sons, 1978.

Wheeler-Bennett, J. W. *The Nemesis of Power. The German Army in Politics 1918–1945.* New York: St. Martin's Press, 1964.

Whiting, Charles. *Kasserine.* New York: Stein and Day, 1984.

————. *Death of a Division.* New York: Stein and Day, 1981.

Young, Desmond. *Rommel, The Desert Fox.* New York: Harper & Brothers, 1950.

INDEX